Other Books by Theodore Draper

The Six Weeks' War
The Roots of American Communism
American Communism and Soviet Russia
Castro's Revolution: Myths and Realities
Castroism, Theory and Practice
Abuse of Power
Israel and World Politics
The Dominican Revolt
The Rediscovery of Black Nationalism

PRESENT HISTORY

Theodore Draper

PRESENT HISTORY

RANDOM HOUSE · New York

These essays had been previously published in *Commentary*, *Dissent*, *Encounter*, *The New Republic*, *The New York Review of Books*, and *The Washington Quarterly*.

Grateful acknowledgment is made to The New York Times Company for permission to reprint a review by Theodore Draper. Copyright © 1982 by The New York Times Company. Reprinted by permission.

Library of Congress Cataloging in Publication Data
Draper, Theodore, 1912–
Present history.
1. Atomic weapons and disarmament—Addresses, essays,
lectures. 2. Security, International—Addresses,
essays, lectures. 3. World politics—1975–1985—
Addresses, essays, lectures. I. Title.
JX1974.7.D82 1983   327.1'74   82–42822
ISBN 0–394–53093–4

Manufactured in the United States of America

24689753

First Edition

For Priscilla

Contents

Introduction:

What Is Present History?

The title of this book needs an explanation. The two words, "present" and "history," are not usually linked so closely. The past, not the present, is supposed to be the stuff of history. Yet I have chosen this title because it suggests better than anything else the sort of thing I have tried to do in these essays, articles and reviews, all written in the last ten years. I may explain the title best by telling something about how I have worked.

I have usually written about subjects of the greatest urgency and controversy while they were still urgent and controversial. Some time had to pass, however, before I could make up my mind about what was going on and gather enough information to permit even a tentative understanding of the issues. The interval was generally more than for journalism and less than for traditional history.

My aim was to analyze present-day events historically. The events themselves were still hot, even boiling. Nevertheless, they had to be in such a state that they could be analyzed coolly with convincing documentation and reasoned judgment. Others might not agree with the judgment, but they could at least judge for themselves the evidence and reasoning on which it was based.

I have written for the reader who was no longer merely interested in the daily or even weekly ration of news; this reader wanted to understand it in some organized form and in some historical perspective. No doubt the organization and perspective would change as time went on and more information or insight became available. Life cannot wait, however, for historians to gather enough evidence to satisfy them or to make up their minds once they get it. Even a preliminary organization and perspective represent an advance, however provisional. We must make do with what we have while it is still possible to do something about the matter. It is usually at this stage that I have been moved to write.

Some, if not most, historians write for other historians. That has not been my aim. I have tried to write for almost anyone who is willing to make some effort. I consider it to be my problem to provide enough information for the reader to follow the argument; since I do not know how much the reader knows, I do not believe in putting that burden on him. The readers of the publications represented in this collection—*The New York Review of Books, Encounter, Commentary, Dissent, The Washington Quarterly, The New Republic* and *The New York Times Book Review*—are the readers I have had in mind.

This kind of enterprise is not wholly unrelated to the more traditional historical work. Some rules hold good for both the shorter and longer historical perspectives.

One is that the evidence should be clearly, accurately and as fully as possible laid out. The sources should be open. Anyone should be able to check on them. For this reason, I have often provided notes for my sources, so that there should be no doubt where the information came from. I have not hesitated to quote at whatever length necessary from those sources. Present History should have as much as possible the concreteness and objectivity of traditional history.

I have also sought to use primary rather than secondary material. When the original was available, I have used it. If something else was used, I have said so. Journalists are accustomed to using unattributed sources; I believe in using them most sparingly, if at all, or when nothing else will do, and then giving the reader ample warning. The evidence should be presented critically rather than as the latest news bulletin. In short, the material should be treated in a way that any historian would recognize and respect.

Though I may be dealing with events no more than months away from the present, there is no cut-off date for what may be useful to understand those events. I have felt free to go back ten or twenty years and as far back as necessary if I thought some useful perspective could be gained. Here, again, Present History uses whatever it can from the past to understand the present. I have also seized on some bit of information that came up just before turning in an article or even during the reading of proofs. In this work, one must have one foot in the past and one in the present.

It cannot be denied, however, that the subject-matter is much closer to the present than traditional historians feel comfortable with or may even approve. It is as a result a much riskier business, though it is not quite so risky as it may appear to be. An amazing amount of information may come out relatively quickly, even from the mouths of statesmen and politicians who do not intend to inform. The reason is that they tend to live in the moment and say what will get them by from day to day or at most from month to month. They have no way of knowing how quickly their words may have revealed far more than they intended. Close reading and assiduous research combined with a reasonably keen critical faculty can turn up a surprising amount of useful and solid information sometimes in a relatively short time. Enough information may, of course, not turn up, in which case there is nothing to do but wait or write about something else.

Rereading these pieces, I realize that I have written mainly about the past that leads up to the events that had originally set me going. The present, in truth, is so evanescent that, in one sense, it is impossible to grasp and write about. One is necessarily dealing with some sort of past, if one is to write at all. Yet we do think and speak of the "present" and "present-day events" in a sense that differs from what we mean by the "past" and "past events." The difference, I suppose, is relative. The present encompasses a past so near and relevant that it seems to be part of a single process that we feel to be still with us.

Perhaps even more significant is the factor of perspective. Some historians believe in reinterpreting the past in terms of the present; their subject is the past, even the distant past, but it must be shaped by some concern or ideology in the present. My view of Present History takes the opposite course. The subject is always the present, but it must be understood in terms of the past or whatever parts of the past seem to have shaped it. Since the entire past is an inexhaustible, chaotic mass, some principle must govern the selectivity of the historian. That principle is, above all, relevance, and it, of course, may differ from historian to historian. The all-important thing, I feel, is to play fair with the reader, so that he may make up his own mind or at least know what made up the historian's mind.

Contemporary history is a more ambiguous and elastic term than Present History. It may, in our time, mean anything that has occurred since the Second World War or whatever is contemporaneous with the present generation. Present History concerns itself more with the here and now at the time of writing—such as the state of the Western alliance when I was writing about it in 1980 or the dispute over nuclear arms in

1981. Or else Present History may be thought of as the cutting edge of contemporary history.

Political commentary is also a different genre. Its modern master, Walter Lippmann, wrote about events that were still appearing on the front page. He depended on his readers to have the details freshly in mind; it was usually enough for him to refer to them. He provided a minimum of new information or source-material. Commentators tend to work in much shorter forms and to use a much thinner factual texture. Yet Present History seeks to do the same thing as commentary—to make sense of what has been going on.

Whether it is called commentary or analysis, the means to achieve understanding cannot be wholly or strictly factual. I have taken fairly strong positions on matters that concern me. In fact, I can rarely write unless I have come to some position that seems to me to emerge from the material. Here again, however, there is a difference between history, including Present History, and opinion or propaganda. The important thing is not so much the position as the reasons for coming to it. If the reasons are clearly and fairly given, the reader can make up his own mind. He may even be able to come to a different position based on the material I have given him.

A friend used to play an amusing but revealing game. He would ask: Which writers need to use what amount of words to express themselves best? He would say that he thought that one writer we knew could not write more than 700 good words; a Congressional Act should be passed to stop him from writing one more. Others were good for a thousand, two thousand, five thousand words. He himself was an addict of ten thousand. He was sure that I was a twenty-thousand-word man. He may have been influenced by the fact that I had just then written a piece of about twenty thousand words, but he had a point. I do seem to need a good many words to get to the end, though I usually start out by intending to write something much shorter. I would like to think that it takes all those words to tell the reader why and how I have come to a position on a pending issue. The verdict may be disputed, but the evidence should stand.

In general, I have devoted myself to one subject for some time. There also comes a time when I do not feel that I have much more to say, and then I turn to something else.

In preparing these essays, articles and reviews for publication, I must confess to a temptation. It was to revise and edit in the light of later knowledge. In the end, I decided that the very essence of Present History would be lost if I tampered with what I had originally written. The present collection, therefore, is presented almost exactly the way it was first published. No substantive changes have been made. The reader should be "present at the creation," as former Secretary of State Dean Acheson entitled his memoirs, for a quite different reason. The temptation to revise was the more easily resisted because I found on rereading that I would change very little of substance as a result of later information. I would still put things in quite the same way about the events that I wrote about. These articles cannot be torn out of their historical context and are themselves part of it.

One problem that resulted from the decision to leave well enough alone was that of repetition. I had written more than once on the same subject, and this recurrence of themes sometimes necessitated a recapitulation of basic information or background. I have permitted the repetition to remain, though it is never exactly in the same form. I hope that the reader will not find it too disturbing or irksome.

Only once was it impossible for me to resist temptation. The exception occurs in the penultimate essay on "Prophets of the 'Cold War,'" where I made some additions, such as the remarkable prophecy by Baron Friedrich Melchior von Grimm, which I had not been able to track down when I wrote the piece. The last two essays are far more "historical" in nature, but they also have a clear bearing on present-day concerns and show in a rather startling fashion how long ago they were foreseen.

It would help for the reader to bear in mind when the several parts of the book were written and published. For this reason, the publication and date have been put at the end of each article or review. Nevertheless, I would consider them failures if they merely reflected their own times. The test of Present History is how well it stands up in the light of future knowledge and further work in the same field. It should not be as ephemeral as most journalism, even if it may not achieve the durability of traditional history written long after the event. No type of history stands still, but the closer to the event, the greater the gamble that the work will soon be "dated." If I did not think that these contributions might have some enduring value, I would be loath to see them resurrected.

T.D.

I

ON NUCLEAR WAR

1

How Not to Think about Nuclear War

Suddenly, "no-first-use" and "the freeze" have become the talismanic slogans of the antinuclear war movement. They have been around for years, but they have recently gained renewed urgency both by having been taken up by outstanding proponents and by increasing popular support. They are not similar, and the freeze may be left for later in another connection.

No-first-use owes its present prominence more than anything else to the plea made in its behalf by four distinguished advocates, McGeorge Bundy, George F. Kennan, Robert S. McNamara, and Gerard Smith, in the Spring 1982 issue of *Foreign Affairs*. As they put it in their admirably measured and tentative approach to the problem, they have aimed "to start a discussion, not to end it." If I am skeptical about their proposal, it is not for lack of respect for the reasonableness of their effort and the authority they bring to it.

The first thing that strikes one about no-first-use is that it belongs to the declaratory school of diplomacy. The authors refer to it variously as a "policy," a "pledge," and a "declaration." In fact, it amounts to little more than the latter. Nothing would or could enforce it. At best, both the United States and the Soviet Union would jointly declare that they intend to renounce the first use of nuclear weapons. They need do nothing more.

The second striking thing about the proposal is that it has one unnecessary or superfluous word. It is really equivalent, if taken seriously, to *no-use* of nuclear weapons. If no nuclear weapons are ever used first, they will never be used at all. Why, then, should the slogan or declaration be no-*first*-use? The answer, I suspect, is that no-use would immediately expose the nature of the proposal as a disembodied exhortation rather than as a practical policy. The use of "first" somehow appears to give a specious operational character to the declaration. No-use would make it too clear that we are dealing with a statement of the problem, not a step toward its solution.

If a declaration of peaceful intentions were enough to prevent any kind of war, the deed would have been done a long time ago. The history of war and peace is littered with such professions of virtue. In 1928, for example, sixty-two nations signed a pact outlawing war. Its enforcement was supposed to rest on the moral strength of world opinion. It was signed, celebrated, and forgotten. With evident understatement, the four authors themselves say that "such declarations may have only limited reliability." The awful truth is that they have no reliability at all.

There has been no first use of nuclear weapons for almost four decades, because it has not been in the interest of any nuclear power to use them; and that condition will—or will not—continue to prevail whether or not declarations of self-denial are made. The reliability of that continuing self-interest, not the reliability of any declaration, is what matters. It is, moreover, hard to take seriously the contention that "to renounce the first use of nuclear weapons is to accept an enormous burden of responsibility for any later violation." Any nuclear power that used such weapons would be moved by such an imperious need or irrational aim that the burden of the responsibility for violating a previous declaration would be trivial, not enormous.

In fact, the main argument for the declaration rests not on its credibility but on its allegedly positive advantages for the United States and the Atlantic Alliance. The first advantage is said to turn on the difference between a first- and second-strike nuclear strategy. The reasoning leaves much to be desired.

By adopting a no-first-use policy, the United States would still—the authors agree—have to maintain nuclear forces strong enough to launch a second or retaliatory counterattack. The main reason they give for depending on a second strike is that it would require a smaller and cheaper nuclear force. That is a most dubious assumption. It would require the United States to possess sufficiently large nuclear forces to absorb a potentially all-out Soviet first strike and still have enough left over to mount a second strike so punishing that it would deter the Soviet Union from contemplating a first strike.

This point cannot be emphasized too strongly—the strategic function of a potential second strike is to deter a first strike, not merely to engage in a mutually suicidal nuclear exchange. When he was still secretary of defense, Mr. McNamara convincingly held that the function of the second strike was fundamentally to deter an enemy's first strike, and that to do so it would be necessary to be able to "utterly destroy them, and I mean completely destroy them." Such a second-strike capacity, after taking all possible punishment from a first strike, would hardly be the "more modest program" that is now offered. In fact, the rationale of the first and second strikes makes little difference between whether a nuclear power uses a first strike and absorbs a second or vice versa.

The second alleged advantage is even more questionable. It is claimed that no-first-use "will also reduce the risk of conventional aggression in Europe." This claim has already been repudiated by various European spokesmen, who believe that a commitment to no-first-use would produce just the opposite effect. If no-first-use really means no-use, the field is left open to conventional warfare in which, for the Europeans, a nearby Soviet bloc is vastly more formidable as an enemy than a far-away United States as an ally. But the reasoning behind the claim of a reduced conventional risk is worth considering.

It is important to note that no-first-use is only half of the new equation proposed by the four authors. The other half "would require" a greater conventional defense force in Europe, including a strengthening of the American conventional forces there. No-first-use, then, does not stand by itself; it depends on what happens to the conventional forces of the alliance. This need to compensate for no-first-use suggests that it is not as useless militarily as the authors otherwise imply. The threat of first-use must serve some practical military function if its withdrawal requires an increase in conventional forces.

Actually, the demand for increased conventional forces has been made for years without the spur of no-first-use. The best minds wrestling with this intractable problem have advocated more and better conventional defense irrespective of where they stood on first-use or no-first-use. What has the trouble been? The four authors assure us that the obstacle has not come from budgetary restraints; it is the fault of "political will." Unfortunately, they do not look deeper into the flaw in Europe's "political will."

After two world wars fought in Europe, a large-scale conventional war is a European nightmare second only in horror to a nuclear war. Americans find it much easier than Europeans to contemplate a conventional war in Europe as the alternative to a nuclear war. The European psyche cannot stand the specter of either one. Such security as Europe has enjoyed has been based on a mixture of conventional and nuclear forces for the purpose of preventing both types of war, not merely nuclear war. The present agitation aimed only at nuclear war has obscured this fundamental purpose.

The proponents of no-first-use approve of the original nuclear guarantee, based on first-use, because only a conventional Soviet threat existed at the time. They want the guarantee changed now, though no-first-use would ensure that any Soviet threat would still be conventional. Above all, they seem to be telling Europeans that, if there has to be a war in Europe, let it be a conventional war or anything but a nuclear war. But the original aim of the alliance is not as obsolete as they make it appear to be. It was designed to deter a conventional war in Europe—and that is still the major threat to the alliance and the primary mission of the nuclear deterrent.

Curiously, the question is never raised about what is to be done in the event that Western Europe continues to resist providing for an adequate conventional defense. The two policies, no-first-use and an adequate conventional defense, are so closely linked in the authors' view that they are logically committed to retaining no-first-use if the conventional defense remains inadequate. The decision in the end must be made by the Europeans themselves; they were the ones who originally urged first-use, and the alliance could hold together only if they took the initiative to give it up. Americans are not the best ones to tell Europeans what is good for them. Their decision will be made not on the basis of preferring a conventional war to a nuclear war but rather on the answer to a different kind of question: Is a purely conventional defense or a conventional defense plus the nuclear deterrent more likely to prevent a conventional *and* a nuclear war in Europe?

If Europeans have to choose between a conventional war and a nuclear war, they would be mad to choose the latter. A conventional defense is really the only kind of defense rationally open to them in the event of an actual war; a nuclear defense can be justified only as a way to prevent all war, conventional and nuclear. Nevertheless, the anti-nuclear-war movements in Europe are not agitating for a greater conventional defense, and the degree to which they favor such a defense is not clear; the decision is not yet in on whether Europe wishes to be defended one way or the other or both—or neither.

What is really at stake comes out most starkly in the authors' view of the German problem. They stipulate that some sort of nuclear guarantee is still necessary for West Germany. But they seek to redefine it to mean an American readiness to reply with nuclear weapons to any nuclear attack on the Federal Republic. In effect, the Germans could no longer count on the threat of a nuclear reply to deter a conventional attack. They would first have to suffer a nuclear attack to bring on a nuclear reply, after all the damage had been done.

Thus the reliability of a declaration of no-first-use is so limited that the four authors must still address themselves to the possible first-use by the Soviets against Germany. Is it conceivable that a second strike by the Americans in these circumstances would be—as the authors themselves demand of their program—responsive to the basic desires of the German people? This scenario is more like an old-fashioned artillery exchange than a foreshadowing of nuclear warfare.

At best, no-first-use offers many fewer and far less obvious benefits than have been claimed for it. At worst, it raises more acute problems than it seeks to solve. It surely merits the discussion which its advocates have sought to arouse, and for that alone we may be grateful to them.

II

Jonathan Schell's new book, *The Fate of the Earth*, also grapples with the problem of the first and second strike. Ironically, his view is directly contrary to that of the no-first-use authors. They insist that the United States must maintain a second-strike capacity in order to adopt a no-first-use policy. He insists that a second strike loses all meaning and rationality in the event of an enemy's first strike. Both cannot be right.

Schell's book has received a rapturously favorable reception. Even partially critical reviews have been unduly respectful. The same sort of reception greeted that classic of puerility, *The Greening of America*, also first published in *The New Yorker*. They belong to the same genre of political fantasy and millennial daydreaming. They are *Zeitgeist* books that tell more about their times than about anything else.

About three-quarters of Schell's book is devoted to a single theme—the horrible destructiveness of nuclear weapons. Those who still need to be taught or reminded of this lesson will undoubtedly find it rewarding. It evidently stirs readers by a type of overkill typical of nuclear weapons—hammering on the same note of doom, as if the reader were so dull that he could not get the message the first time, or the tenth time, or the twentieth time. If the subject were anything other than nuclear destructiveness, the method would quickly pall and exhaust itself as well as the reader. But the subject lends itself to this kind of repetitiveness, and perhaps Schell is right that there are too many people out there who need this incessant, deafening drumbeat to make them pay attention to the threat of nuclear war. The danger is that many of Schell's readers or disciples will go on mindlessly beating the same drum, as if the threat could be exorcised by shouting hysterically that the threat exists. What is no more than a starting point threatens to become an end in itself.

For Schell's purpose, it is first necessary to reject and denounce the policy of nuclear deterrence, which rests on the threat of a retaliatory second strike by the victim of a first strike in order to avert both strikes. In brief, he rules out the possibility of a second strike on the ground that an enemy's first strike would be so totally devastating that it would make a second strike useless or senseless. If a second strike cannot follow a first strike in any circumstances, the reasoning goes, the whole concept of deterrence must be given up.

One thing stands out in this argument—it rests wholly on the assumption of a totally devastating first strike. In Schell's world, it is always all or nothing, total oblivion or total salvation. At this point, he needs total oblivion. If the first strike should be less—especially considerably less—than totally devastating, the possibility of a second strike would reappear and thus serve to deter a first strike from being launched.

Is it wise or prudent to reject deterrence with such finality on the assumption of a totally devastating first strike? Such a strike would have to benefit from total surprise and from the willingness to risk a one-shot, all-out nuclear attack. No one really knows what a nuclear war would be like, since one cannot be sure of anything about a type of war that has never been waged. Nevertheless, among the lesser probabilities is the achievement of such total surprise that it would enable a would-be nuclear attacker to launch an annihilating first strike without provoking its equally capable nuclear enemy to get its own attack in first. The time and effort necessary to prepare and launch an operation of such unimaginable magnitude are themselves conducive to deterrence by alerting the intended victim to the danger. One form of deterrence does not entail a second strike at all: it arises from the danger that, without total surprise, a first strike cannot be mounted without inviting a preemptive first strike by the other side. Schell never even considers this aspect of deterrence. Totally devastating first strikes are more easily written about in theory than carried out in practice.

But even on the assumption that a major nuclear power could get away with launching a first strike, it could never be sure that it would be totally devastating. The US and the USSR are large countries. The efficiency of the new nuclear weapons has never been tested. The nuclear agencies of both countries have been straining for decades to guard against just such a totally devastating first strike. The United States possesses a triad of deterrents, one of which, the submarine, is peculiarly difficult to destroy with one blow.

Schell himself recognizes that something less than total devastation might be the result, and that the survivors might be able to manage an equally or substantially devastating second strike. At this point, his argument changes from the impossibility to the irrationality of a second strike. It would not be rational, he holds, to go through with a second strike merely for the sake of "revenge," because "national security" would no longer be meaningful and "since the retaliatory strike might be the action that would finally break the back of the ecosphere and extinguish the species." He concludes: "In these circumstances, it seems to me, it is really an open question whether the leaders would decide to retaliate or not."

It may or may not be an "open question." But if it is truly an open question, its deterrent value should not be underestimated. The perpetrators of a first strike could not be sure that there would be no retaliation—and retaliation of a sort that would destroy them as well as the ecosphere and the entire species. To rule out the deterrent force of a second strike on what is admittedly an "open question" begs the question. On this reasoning, it is not only the victims of a first strike that would have to be irrational to launch an annihilating second strike. The first strike would be equally irrational if it put at risk the country that launched it with an unresolved and unresolvable "open question."

Thus the argument against a second strike is also an argument against a first strike; the one is, in effect, a deterrent to the other. Deterrence is not based solely on the known and determinable; it also rests on the unknown and imponderable. The latter are not always working against us. Schell almost invariably chooses to construe them so as to make our flesh creep and our minds grow dizzy by holding out the worst possible case imaginable.

.   .   .

This contradiction at the core of Schell's critique of deterrence permeates his entire argument. It is necessary for him to maintain that a devastating first strike is practicable, but that a second strike is not. Yet depending on which part of the book one reads, he makes both equally senseless and irrational. It is not enough for him to demonstrate that the US and USSR could destroy each other. He also undertakes to show that even the "local destruction" following a large-scale nuclear attack would or could or might (one is never sure which one he wants us to believe) destroy all mankind and all living matter on earth through its "direct global effects," such as depletion of the ozone layer protecting the earth's surface. Assuming that his scientific data is valid or even plausible, the attacker would pay for a large-scale first strike as high a price as the victim. It may be senseless to contemplate a retaliatory strike if it is assumed that the first one has been carried out successfully; it is not senseless to contemplate a retaliatory strike if it could successfully deter a first strike by making the latter as devastating to the attacker as to the attacked.

Schell is so fixated on the alleged senselessness of a second strike that his mind seems to be hermetically sealed against the full logic of his own reasoning. For example, he writes:

> The policy of deterrence does not contemplate doing anything in defense of the homeland; it only promises that if the homeland is annihilated the aggressor's homeland will be annihilated, too.

Is that doing nothing? If an aggressor has reason to believe that his own homeland will be annihilated, he is well on his way to being deterred from devastating the homeland of the defender. One cannot one-sidedly argue that the threat of annihilation must inhibit the defense if the same threat of annihilation must inhibit the aggressor. Yet Schell obsessively works only one side of the street, almost always confining himself to what the Soviet Union might do to a mortally wounded United States without the latter being able or willing to do anything comparable in return.

Or take another example of Schell's strange illogic. After devoting most of his book to the threat of nuclear extinction, he tells us that "nuclear weapons, if they were ever used in large numbers, would simply blow war up, just as they would blow up everything else that is human." This leads him to this unexpected thought:

> There is no need to "abolish war" among the nuclear powers; it is already gone. The choices don't include war any longer. They consist now of peace, on the one hand, and annihilation on the other.

If this were true, it would hold for all nuclear powers, for the aggressor as well as for the victim, for the first strike as well as for the second. By writing off nuclear war in this way, Schell implicitly permits the doctrine of deterrence to return through the back door. For if the choice before all nuclear powers is as stark and simple as that between peace and annihilation, we can take some comfort in the probability that they will seek to avoid annihilation. It may not be foolproof, as little in this world is, but it is not nothing.

All that Schell's implicit form of deterrence requires is that we should recognize the futility of using any nuclear weapons. He writes:

> If we did acknowledge the full dimensions of the peril, admitting clearly and without reservation that any use of nuclear arms is likely to touch off a holocaust in which the continuance of all human life would be put at risk, extinction would at that moment become not only "unthinkable" but also undoable.

Now we know. Nuclear war is, in effect, irrational. It is irrational whether it takes the form of aggression or of defense. A first strike is just as irrational as a second strike. The ultimate rationale for deterrence is, in fact, the elementary rationality required for mutual survival. As Schell himself says, "A world that has embarked on a holocaust is in its nature irrational and out of control." At least this tells us this much— that rationality is a safeguard, even though it may be less than infallible and decisive, against a nuclear holocaust.

One of the difficulties in reading Schell's book, however, is that much depends on which page one reads. He is quite capable of asserting that nuclear powers "are ultimately prepared to bring an end to mankind in their attempt to protect their own countries." But he had previously tried to convince us that it made no sense to try to protect one's own country if the result could only be the end of mankind. Are we to infer that the best way to prevent an end to mankind is *not* to attempt to protect one's own country? Yet, after all this, it turns out that Schell himself is willing to give the present Soviet and American leaders some credit for aversion to nuclear weapons:

> I believe that without indulging in wishful thinking we can grant that the present leaders of both the Soviet Union and the United States are considerably deterred from launching a nuclear holocaust by sheer aversion to the unspeakable act itself.

Well, at last Schell tells us that they are deterred by something. But is it merely "sheer aversion to the unspeakable act"? Too many leaders in this century have not been averse to the "unspeakable" to accept this explanation. If the act were not so suicidally dangerous, the aversion to this unspeakable act might not have been any more prohibitive than to any of the other unspeakable acts. Curiously, Schell has to fall back on such a soft psychological term as "aversion" in order to avoid confronting the hard, physical basis of nuclear deterrence.

Schell's zealotry is so intense that he is not above tinkering with evidence to make it serve his purpose. He cites the statement of former President Carter during the Iranian crisis to the effect that any outside attempt to gain control of the Persian Gulf region "will be repelled by any means necessary, including military force." Schell thereupon accuses Carter of having threatened "to unleash a holocaust in which the life of mankind might be lost." Immediately afterward, Schell goes on to wonder "what Carter would have done if the Soviets had ignored his threat and invaded Iran or Saudi Arabia."

A holocaust, in Schell's terms, means that Carter actually threatened to use nuclear weapons. He did not—"any means necessary, including military force" left Carter so much room that it can be construed as specifically threatening to unleash a holocaust of nuclear warfare only by the wildest and most irresponsible exaggeration. And if we are left to wonder what Carter would have done, how can anyone be sure that he actually threatened "to unleash a holocaust"?

Deterrence is admittedly no total, final, absolute answer to the nuclear problem. No one has ever claimed that it was. But why is it necessary for Schell to reject it totally, finally, absolutely?

The answer lies in Schell's own panacea for ridding the world of nuclear war. His is a mind that operates only between extremes. If anything like deterrence offers any protection at all against nuclear war, it must be denied and denounced. Nothing must be permitted to hold out any hope that does not pass the tests of eternal peace and everlasting love.

Schell's solution to the problem of nuclear war calls for an end to "national sovereignty." To get rid of nuclear war it is necessary to get rid of "sovereign states." Schell scorns them because they were "not intentional" in their origin; no one wrote a book proposing them; no parliament voted them into existence. They were "simply there, at the beginning of recorded history"—as if it would be more in their favor if they had come about intentionally, if a book had proposed them, or if a parliament had voted them into existence. One would suppose that an arrangement which goes back to the beginning of recorded history would be far harder to get rid of than the kind of institution that Schell seems to find more acceptable.

Once Schell gets rid of "national sovereignty," he enters a realm of utopian obscurantism. What the world needs is "a political means of making international decisions" and "the invention of political means by which the world can peacefully settle the issues that throughout history it has settled by war." That is hardly a new or original thought. But then we wait breathlessly for Schell to give us a glimmer, an inkling, of the "political means" that would peacefully settle the issues hitherto settled by force.

Instead, Schell first disclaims responsibility for giving us as much as a glimmer or an inkling. He has not, he coyly explains, "sought to define a political solution to the nuclear predicament." This abdication comes only a page away from where he distinctly sought to define it. Then follows the listing of quite a few requirements for his new political order. One of them is for universal disarmament, including conventional as well as nuclear weapons. The reasoning here is that nations could still maintain their sovereignty with conventional weapons; therefore, conventional weapons must also go.

Finally we get to Schell's grand climax: "In sum, the task is nothing less than to reinvent politics: to reinvent the world." How to do it? As a start, Schell recommends that each person should "make known, visibly and unmistakably, his desire that the species survive." Schell then tells us how to go about doing this—by letting "our daily business drop from our hands for a while" and causing a "disruption in our lives." By disruption, Schell means something "as simple as a telephone call to a friend, a meeting in the community." And from this "first, urgent, immediate step" we will get to "global disarmament, both nuclear and conventional, and the invention of political means by which the world can peacefully settle the issues that throughout history it has settled by war."

This is a travesty of thinking about nuclear war. It is also the most depressing and defeatist cure-all that has ever been offered. If we have to "reinvent the world" to control nuclear war, the chances of saving the human race must be somewhere near the vanishing point. Deterrence is child's play compared with what Schell demands of us. His prescription is a disguised counsel of despair. It gives up the struggle against nuclear war in the world as it is in favor of chanting and shouting for a world that does not exist. Utopians are like that: they hold out the vision of a feast to starving people, who are never permitted to eat any of it.

III

Whatever is wrong with no-first-use and reinventing the world is not likely to be set right by official policy.

American nuclear doctrine has always claimed to be based on deterrence. But it has not always been satisfied to stop with that. It has also, of late, been preoccupied with fighting a nuclear war as well as deterring one.

The reasoning goes that it is necessary to prepare to fight a nuclear war if deterrence fails. As a consequence, American officials say they believe it is necessary to be able to fight a nuclear war on all levels, from the most limited and local to the most uncontrollable and widespread. Such a nuclear war is conceived of as if it were an endurance contest, with victory going to the side that lasts the longest. Victory rather than deterrence would dictate preparations for a drawn-out, escalatory nuclear combat. A program of nuclear deterrence could stop at some point deemed necessary to make a nuclear attack mutually impracticable or irrational; a nuclear-fighting program has no such recognizable stopping point, for it requires open-ended preparations in behalf of a war which has no rational boundary and whose nature cannot be foreseen.

The nuclear-fighting doctrine was embedded in Presidential Directive 59, adopted by President Carter in July 1980 and later reaffirmed by President Reagan. This directive was defended by former Secretary of Defense Harold Brown on the ground that it was not incompatible with deterrence and gave the United States more "options" than one of simple retaliation. As Brown put it in a speech the following month, "In our analysis and planning, we are necessarily giving greater attention to how a nuclear war would actually be fought by both sides if deterrence fails." The assumption here is that the failure of deterrence would not be catastrophic; it would rather signal the outbreak of an extended nuclear war.

The word "options" in this context conceals as much as it reveals. The requirements for nuclear fighting are far more extensive than for nuclear deterrence. They may to some extent coincide, but only because part of a nuclear-fighting capacity is the same as that for deterrence. The trouble is that planning to fight an extended nuclear war calls for much more than planning for deterrence. The two objectives are not entirely contradictory, but they are far from the same.

In his speech against no-first-use of April 6 [1982], Secretary of State Haig made an effort to reemphasize the primacy of deterrence.[1] But some of his remarks indicated that nothing had really changed in basic nuclear doctrine since Presidential Directive 59. One of his strangest allusions was historical. Since deterrence presupposes that no nuclear power will deliberately destroy itself in order to destroy others, Haig found it necessary to maintain that societies have always risked self-destruction in pursuit of their aims. He said:

> Throughout history societies have risked their total destruction if the prize of victory was sufficiently great or the consequences of submission sufficiently grave.

Throughout history? Total destruction? There has not been a war of total destruction since the Third Punic War in 146 BC, and that was brought about by the decision of Rome to punish its old rival, Carthage, rather than by Carthage to gain a sufficiently great prize of victory. If wars of total destruction have been prevalent throughout history, it should be possible to cite a few such wars in the past two or three centuries; none comes to mind. Even the Japanese were unwilling to risk total destruction after Hiroshima and Nagasaki.

Why should a Secretary of State in a major pronouncement on the most tormenting problem of our time take refuge in such historical fatuity? The answer manifestly is that he sought to make nuclear wars similar to past wars in order to get across the idea that nuclear wars must be fought, if deterrence fails, as past, prenuclear wars were fought. The concept of nuclear war as an endurance contest, in which the last survivor prevails, came out most clearly in this passage:

> Rather, deterrence depends upon our capability, even after suffering a massive nuclear blow, to prevent an aggressor from securing a military advantage and prevailing in a conflict. Only if we maintain such a capability can we deter such a blow.

Here again, nuclear fighting and nuclear deterrence are hopelessly muddled. The assumption is that an extended nuclear war can be fought to a victorious finish after we receive "a massive nuclear blow." We are not in this scenario dealing with a first and second nuclear strike, in which case the first would presumably be "massive" and the second in retaliation as massive as possible. That is the schema of basic deterrence, which makes the first strike self-destructive through the imminence of the second. No aggressor could prevail in such a conflict, thus making unnecessary and nonsensical the idea of preventing the aggressor from "securing a military advantage and prevailing in a conflict." The idea of "prevailing," even after suffering a massive nuclear blow, opens up the prospect of an endurance contest, in which massive nuclear blows will be exchanged until one or the other side "prevails"—which is a circumlocution for gaining victory.

Oddly, this notion of our fighting a nuclear war after receiving a "massive" nuclear blow comes at a time when Haig's colleague, Secretary of Defense Weinberger, is busy trying to convince the American people that the United States is in no condition to prevail in a nuclear war and will not be for years to come. The Soviet Union, according to Mr. Weinberger, holds "a substantial lead in most of the customary measures of strategic forces—total number of systems, total number of ballistic missiles and total destructive potential." The only US advantage is said to be in total number of "deliverable warheads," and even that is likely to go in the present decade. This Soviet "degree of superiority and strategic edge," Weinberger holds, "will last for some years through the decade even if we pursue all the programs the President has sought" —and which he is not likely to get.[2]

One would imagine that in these circumstances the US government would quietly go about the business of catching up, especially if we even lack "the requisite military capability for adequate nuclear deterrence," as Mr. Weinberger also claims. Instead, we are being subjected to a rolling barrage of unprecedented panic-mongering along with the most grandiose plans for actually fighting a nuclear war. A more rational approach would seem to be to make sure of the requisite military capacity for adequate nuclear deterrence before taking on the far more dubious task of actually preparing to fight an extended nuclear war.

Something is out of joint here. A country that is as far behind as the United States is supposed to be would be expected to behave far more circumspectly and far less blusteringly. Or can it be that the American nuclear arsenal is not in as parlous a state as it is now officially advertised to be? We have been through this before—the propaganda of panic to push through a frighteningly expensive military appropriations bill.

· · ·

On close examination, the immediate problem always seems defined as the theoretical vulnerability of the land-based Minuteman missiles, which are said to be exposed to a Soviet first strike. The alleged solution to the problem—the MX intercontinental missile—has frustrated its backers because they cannot decide where and how to place them. But this is not a quantitative problem; no across-the-board buildup can solve it. It is a qualitative problem, requiring a sufficiently hardened or other type of resistant placement to make these weapons safe from attack. The need here is less for throwing incredible sums of money at the problem than for a new, practical idea.

Even this view of the land-based missile's vulnerability must be qualified. Two little words always creep into the allegations of vulnerability —"in theory." For much of the claim that land-based Soviet missiles could knock out land-based American missiles is not based on tests or experience with those Soviet missiles; the exercise is largely theoretical —and the theory is largely derived from American tests and experience transposed to the larger Soviet missiles. To make matters even more confusing, Mr. Weinberger has testified that American missiles could also take out Soviet missile sites in a hypothetical first strike.

The whole subject has been mercilessly confused by deceptive, one-sided propaganda. This campaign emanating mainly from the Department of Defense and the Arms Control and Disarmament Agency concentrates wholly on the alleged vulnerability of American land-based missiles. It almost completely ignores the other two-thirds of the American "triad"—the submarine and airborne nuclear arms—which were designed to survive a first strike independently and back up the land-based deterrent if it failed. We now have two redundant systems as an insurance policy; they are hardly mentioned, as if all the effort and expense put into them had been wasted. Yet the submarine system is acknowledged to be the most invulnerable and stabilizing. The dooms-day horror stories implicitly presupppose the simultaneous, total destruction of all three American nuclear systems, preventing any of them from playing the deterrent role assigned to each of them.

A different type of deception is being practiced by pretending to equate fighting a nuclear war with deterring a nuclear war. This ambiguity permeated Secretary Haig's reply to the advocates of a "nuclear freeze." We are now getting close to the nub of the matter, so that it is worth paying the closest attention to what he said about deterring and "prevailing in" a nuclear war.

IV

Secretary Haig raised the truly critical question in the following way:

> Much of the argumentation for a nuclear freeze revolves around the ques-
> tion of how much is enough. Each side possesses thousands of deliverable
> nuclear weapons. Does it then really make any difference who is ahead?
> The question itself is misleading, as it assumes that deterrence is simply a
> matter of numbers of weapons or numbers of casualties which could be
> inflicted. It is not.

Why not? The answer given by Mr. Haig turns on the contention that
"the Soviet leaders do not believe in the concept of 'sufficiency' " and
were not likely to be "deterred by a force based upon it." What do the
Soviet leaders believe in? They are arming, he said, to "prevail" in a
nuclear conflict. By implication, we must arm in the same way so that, if
anyone prevails, it will be us. Thus, slippery step by slippery step, Mr.
Haig came to the conclusion that the United States should build up its
nuclear arsenal so extensively that, "even after suffering a massive nuclear blow," it would be able to prevent the Soviet Union from "prevailing" and, inferentially, make sure that the United States would prevail.

This line of reasoning came toward the end of Secretary Haig's speech.
Listeners were evidently not expected to remember that he had earlier
denied that "nuclear war can be controlled." If it cannot be controlled,
what sense does it make to prepare for a nuclear endurance contest in
which both sides possess so many thousands of deliverable nuclear warheads that they are bound to annihilate each other and perhaps everything in between? What meaning could "prevailing in" a nuclear conflict
have? Why, in any case, should we fatuously imitate the Soviet leaders
in an effort to "prevail in" a nuclear conflict, if it cannot be controlled
and must ultimately result in mutual nuclear destruction?

The core of Haig's argument is, in fact, that we must do what the Soviets
do. If they do not believe in the concept of "sufficiency," then we must
not believe in it. If they are arming to "prevail" in a nuclear conflict, we
must also arm for the same purpose. One might almost think that American policy is being made in Moscow.

More significant than anything else was the Secretary's answer to the
question that he himself raised: "How much is enough?" He never said
that anything is enough. In language that defies clear comprehension,
he would have us believe that nothing is ever enough. He made deter-

rence rest "upon a military balance measured not in warhead numbers but in a complex interaction of capabilities and vulnerabilities." By this time, the Secretary of State must have known that the President in early May was going to propose a plan for the reduction of warhead numbers, just what he said the military balance should not be measured in. In any case, Haig's version of deterrence is so vague and open-ended that it could be set forth only in such obscure terms as "a complex interaction of capabilities and vulnerabilities." This jumble of words could have been intended only to evade the real issue.

Speeches and statements by Secretaries Weinberger and Haig, together with a speech by Assistant for National Security Affairs William P. Clark on May 21, prepared the public for the Pentagon's new strategy for nuclear war, revealed by Richard Halloran in *The New York Times* of May 30. This strategy, officially endorsed by Secretary Weinberger last March without any public announcement or discussion, made explicit what had formerly been implicit—planning for an extended nuclear war. This strategy calls for a nuclear arms buildup in behalf of a "protracted" nuclear conflict. The American nuclear forces, according to this program, "must prevail and be able to force the Soviet Union to seek earliest termination of hostilities on terms favorable to the United States."

The line of this document represents a monstrous perversion of the doctrine of deterrence. The new policy accepts the need to prepare for waging a nuclear war for an indefinite period, as if it could be limited and controlled by both sides—a condition previously denied by Secretary Haig. It also envisages that the United States could impose favorable terms—a euphemism for victory—on the Soviet Union, after both sides had inflicted horrible punishment on each other.

This program is as futile as it is forbidding. It presupposes that a nuclear war could go on "over a protracted period" without unacceptable and uncontrollable destruction of the countries waging it. It assumes that "favorable terms" would have some human meaning after such a nuclear conflict. Preparations for it would be so astronomically costly that it would make the entire American economy hostage to the Pentagon's insatiable appetite for the development and production of more, and more advanced, nuclear and conventional weapons—as well as, it may be suspected, a vast and wasteful program of "civil defense." Anything resembling this plan would amount to the long-term militarization of the American economy. In addition, the Atlantic Alliance could not survive this strategy; no European ally could even contemplate taking part in a "protracted" nuclear war. If anything were guaranteed to drive Western Europe into neutralism, it would be this program. The only conceivable war of this kind would be fought directly by the United States and the Soviet Union, in which case the most devastating long-range intercontinental missiles would be employed, probably from the start.

President Reagan's Memorial Day address merely served to emphasize the duality or duplicity of the administration's policy. The President talked amiably about "the quest for peace" through negotiations with the Soviet Union beginning on June 29, while the Secretary of Defense made known that he was preparing for a protracted nuclear conflict. If the negotiations which the President announced on May 31 could be taken seriously, we would hardly have been reading about Weinberger's new program on May 30 and about the confirmation of it on June 3. One can only infer that the President has told his scriptwriters to cast him in the role of the soft-spoken hero, while the Secretary plays at being the hard-bitten villain.

In his address of June 3 at the Army War College, Weinberger pretended that preparations for a nuclear fighting strategy were the same as those for a basic nuclear-deterrent strategy, and that the former was not meant to imply "that nuclear war is winnable." This sort of double talk has become routine in the propaganda to sell the new program. To judge from Weinberger's speech, it cannot be reiterated too often that deterrence requires only as much as is needed to prevent a nuclear attack by making it self-destructive, whereas a nuclear-fighting ability requires far more because it presupposes that deterrence has failed. As for the disclaimer that the new strategy aims at victory, words have lost their meaning, if as the still classified document states, the American nuclear forces "must prevail" and be able to force "terms favorable to the United States" on the Soviet Union after the termination of such nuclear hostilities. Victory in past wars has meant nothing more or less than prevailing over and dictating favorable terms to the enemy. A program that requires such verbal flimflam must on the face of it be a snare and a delusion.

The report on June 1 of the Independent Commission on Disarmament and Security Issues, headed by former Swedish prime minister Olof Palme, also contributed to confusion about the role of deterrence.[3] It tended to play down nuclear deterrence on the ground that it could be "but a temporary expedient" and provide "no permanent solution to international security." Instead, the Commission urged "sharp reductions and qualitative limitations resulting in essential parity at substantially lower and more stable levels of forces." It also held out hope of future agreements for "the elimination of international nuclear arms through interim steps"—a consummation devoutly to be wished, but hardly a foreseeable prospect.

Reductions and limitations, even if they were substantial enough to matter, would scarcely be a substitute for or improvement on deterrence. Whatever level of forces is likely to be reached in the present circumstances, it would still be high enough to result in, as the report puts it, "devastation and suffering of a magnitude which would render meaningless any notion of victory." In this case, the threat of such devastation and suffering would still have to hold back the nuclear powers from engaging in a mutually destructive conflict. It is pointless and confusing to disparage deterrence if that is all we would be left with, even if the Commission's recommendations were substantially realized. The report is otherwise useful and sobering.

v

Yet the question, "How much is enough?" will not go away so easily. If it is not answered, there can be no real stopping point in potential nuclear rearmament. And a stopping point is the very least that any control of nuclear arms requires.

The Reagan administration has entangled itself in a self-made web of palpable contradictions. It has no credible starting point for nuclear disarmament any more than it has a stopping point for nuclear rearmament.

The trouble stems largely from the insistence of the administration that the Soviet Union now has "a definite margin of superiority" over the United States in strategic arms. This supposition has cut the ground from beneath the premise underlying all previous nuclear-arms negotiations. SALT I and II were based on the assumption that both sides were roughly equal. It followed that they could remain in some sort of approximate parity by putting comparable ceilings on different types of nuclear weapons.

This method left both sides with such excessive nuclear power that it hardly touched the problem of reducing their ability to annihilate each other. SALT II also opened itself to the charge that it enabled the

Soviet Union to concentrate on precisely those weapons most threatening to the United States—the largest intercontinental land-based missiles with multiple warheads. By setting the quantity of weapons at an unconscionably high level, the SALT-type negotiations made the limit virtually meaningless and, in addition, encouraged a concentration on improving the quality or destructiveness of all the permissible weapons.

The best that could be said for the SALT method was that it was "symbolic," or that it pointed in the right direction. The real symbolism was SALT's tacit acceptance of an appallingly high level of nuclear weapons on both sides, and the direction pointed right to the present concern with the Soviets' current advantage in weapons of the greatest possible destructiveness.

START's goal of reducing nuclear weapons certainly holds more promise than SALT's far more timid aim to limit their increase. But START has given up the premise of "rough equality" as a starting point. If the sides are as unequal as Secretary Weinberger says they are, START negotiations can only achieve equality by subtracting from one side or adding to the other. In this case, the subtraction must come from the Soviet side or the addition to the American side. Yet both START and SALT have in common that they can only seek to put both sides in a state of some sort of equality; nothing else could possibly be the object of nuclear negotiations.

President Reagan's original program called for building up to obtain equality. Only after perhaps a decade of hectic nuclear rearmament was negotiation contemplated, and then only because some putative status of equality had been reached. The new program, sketched by the President on May 9, 1982, seeks to achieve the same goal by the reverse means. In its simplest terms, it wants to get there by means of Soviet reductions, especially in the case of long-range missiles and their warheads most threatening to the United States. The exact figures—at last count 5,500 Soviet against 2,152 American warheads on these missiles—need not concern us here; the Soviet number is no more than an "estimate," and both numbers are subject to change without notice for technical and other reasons. The important point is that the Soviets are expected to negotiate themselves out of an alleged advantage.

Anyone who has any knowledge of or experience with Soviet policy and its makers can have no illusions about the fate of the Reagan administration's new proposal. The Soviet leaders do not have a disturbed, defiant public opinion to worry about, no "marches for peace," no "demonstrations against war," no retribution at the ballot box. They do not have allies that must be soothed and convinced. If they really believe that they possess "a definite margin of superiority," as President Reagan has assured them, it would be the last thing they would give away.

Politically and psychologically they have been guaranteed "for some years through the decade" an allegedly priceless advantage, which the United States may or may not be able to whittle away. At worst they can force the United States to spend itself into a military-induced budget deficit of ruinous proportions. The nuclear panic-mongering of the Reagan administration has been a free gift to the Soviets, and the wonder is that it has not done more damage to Western self-confidence and Allied unity. Some people might be convinced by what has been coming out of Washington that the Soviets would have us at their mercy if it really came to a nuclear showdown.

If everyone believed the terrifying news that has been bursting forth from the Department of Defense, there should be unconfined joy in Moscow and unrestrained consternation in Washington. But everyone behaves as if no one believes it. It is as if no one really knows what to do with a margin of nuclear superiority, even if it is assumed to exist. The United States did not know what to do with it when it had it, and the Soviet Union does not show the slightest indication of knowing what to do with the superior status which President Reagan and Secretary Weinberger have awarded to it. If actions speak louder than words, we are getting the wrong message from them.

VI

SALT, START, and a "nuclear freeze" have one thing in common— they require negotiations with the Soviet Union. There's the rub.

These negotiations cannot take place in a political vacuum. Nuclear negotiations are not only about weapons; they are also about the balance of power. Neither side trusts the other and seeks to guard itself against bad faith and unexpected loopholes. Experience shows that negotiators find ways to give up what they do not want and hold on to what they consider essential. There is even a "fog of negotiation," as Gerard Smith, one of the no-first-use four and head of the American delegation in the SALT I negotiations, put it in his aptly named book *Doubletalk*; he was referring to an elementary confusion in the Moscow negotiations about missile volume and silo dimensions. Smith's authoritative account of those negotiations, the only fully successful one to date, should be required reading for anyone who thinks that they are anything but a battle of wits and a game of perseverance to see which side can get the better of the other.

The very subject of nuclear negotiations is enigmatic and tantalizing. The goal is always parity, but the Soviet and American systems are so different that a mythical parity can be achieved only by a process of ill-defined "trade-offs." Each side must consider the needs and pressures of its own vested interests before meeting the needs and pressures of the other side. Two sets of negotiations are always going on, the internal and the external, with the former often more difficult and dreary than the latter. Once the trading starts, it can go on for months and even years, until a deal has been reached, if at all, so full of compromises and conditions that no side is finally prevented from doing what it really wants to do or made to give away what it really wishes to keep.

Negotiations with the Soviets must always hinge on what they call the "balance of forces," of which nuclear weapons are an integral part. On the very day, May 9, that President Reagan made known his negotiating position to reduce the Soviet advantage in intercontinental land-based missiles, Soviet Defense Minister Dmitri F. Ustinov wrote in *Pravda*: "The Soviet Union will not allow the existing balance of forces to be disrupted." As long as they are satisfied with that balance, it is naïve to imagine that they will voluntarily give it up. It took them almost two decades to achieve it, at vast cost and immense effort. They are not the only ones who do not like to give up advantages voluntarily.

The "nuclear freeze" proposal presents the same problem with the Soviets. Its proponents do not advocate a unilateral American freeze; such a one-sided gesture would be vulnerable to the charge that it is tantamount to unilateral American disarmament. Thus the recent appeal of the Union of Concerned Scientists—which fatuously featured in the largest type a quotation from Jonathan Schell's book, as if it needed any free advertising—came out for "an immediate bilateral freeze on the build-up of strategic nuclear weapons, and on the flight testing of new strategic missiles."

If a nuclear freeze is ever brought about in the United States, it will be caused by popular pressure against official political and military resistance. No such pressure—not even the possibility of such pressure—exists in the Soviet Union. A freeze in the United States will come, if at all, from the bottom; in the Soviet Union it must come from the top. This is a strange asymmetry for a bilateral agreement. It is equally strange to see how it has been dealt with.

Barbara W. Tuchman tackled the problem in *The New York Times Magazine* of April 18. Here are her suggestions:

> One would be a more massive, more purposeful effort than may now be conducted to promote anti-nuclear sentiment and fear of their own policies among the people of the Soviet Union and satellite countries. We are always blaming the Russians for agitating the peace movement in Western Europe. Why should we not do the same behind the Iron Curtain? We could also try what might be called the stuffed-goose option—that is, providing them with all the grain and consumer goods they need in such quantities that they become dependent on us and could not risk the domestic turbulence that would follow if they cut off the source of supply by war.

If the name of a distinguished historian, twice winner of the Pulitzer Prize, were not signed to these words, they would not be worth noticing. As it is, one does not know whether, as the saying goes, to laugh or to cry. The idea that the United States could successfully wage all-out political warfare *within* the Soviet Union and its satellites or that the United States should make itself responsible for feeding, clothing, and otherwise caring for the comforts of almost 400 million people in the Soviet Union and its satellites—this makes one despair of intellectuals in politics. If anything could make the Soviet leadership impervious to any antinuclear proposals, it would be a correlated threat to its political and economic control.

If public opinion is the controlling factor in both countries, as Barbara Tuchman suggests, the future of bilateral nuclear agreements, including a freeze, is dark to the point of invisibility. For her conclusion is: "A start might be made if leaders came to power in Washington and Moscow at the same time who both really *wanted* accommodation. Only both publics can make that happen." If the Soviet public must make it happen in Moscow as more of the American public is trying to make it happen in Washington, that is virtually a guarantee that it will never happen.

Jonathan Schell tries to get around the Soviet obstacle in still another way. Schell shares the view that a nuclear freeze cannot be unilateral; it "should be concerted, as it eventually must be, in a common political endeavor, reaching across national boundaries." But how is it going to reach across national boundaries, especially the Soviet boundary? Here is Schell's answer:

> We do not know what the peoples of the totalitarian states, including the people of the Soviet Union, may want. They are locked in silence by their government. In these circumstances, public opinion in the free countries would have to represent public opinion in all countries, and would have to bring its pressure to bear, as best it could, on all governments.

This is another and similarly absurd cop-out. How in the world could public opinion in the free countries "represent" public opinion in all countries? By what conceivable means could free public opinion bring pressure to bear on totalitarian governments? Well, at least this political daydream is somewhat less demanding than reinventing the world.

Depressing as the news may be, negotiations are not the best way—or even any way—to deal with the intransigent nuclear problem. Negotiations tend to register the progress of the arms race rather than to put an end to it. Any *numerical* change that leaves intact the ability of each nuclear superpower to destroy the other cannot change the fundamental strategic balance between them; the excess of nuclear weapons is so great that a ceiling or reduction which does not get below the level of redundancy cannot significantly change the basic character of the problem. In the world of political rivalry within which nuclear negotiations take place, the question "Who's ahead?" almost always takes precedence over that of "What's enough?" Anyone who expects a great power to give up an advantage in negotiations or not to get the best trade possible for it is already living in Jonathan Schell's reinvented world. Unfortunately, we have only one real world, and it is not hospitable to illusions or fantasies. This way of thinking about nuclear war is a trap for the innocent and a boon to the nuclear warriors.

VII

Is there no other way?

There is. It is not a new way, but it has been peculiarly neglected, especially in the United States. It has most recently been advocated by Lord Zuckerman, the former chief scientific adviser to the British Ministry of Defence, in *Nuclear Illusion and Reality*, a short book that contains more useful knowledge and wisdom about nuclear warfare than a small library on the subject. I happened to arrive at the same basic position independently in an article published in the Winter 1981 issue of *The Washington Quarterly*. Since then, I have become increasingly convinced that it is the best way to cope with the problem of nuclear weapons in the present-day world.

The only cure-all for nuclear war is the complete and absolute abolition of nuclear weapons everywhere and for all time. This said, there is not much more to be said for it; no one believes that it is likely to happen or even that there is the faintest chance that any of us will live to see it. Anything short of this is bound to contain risks and problems. The realistic question is: What policy may contain the least risk and fewest problems? Or to put it more concretely: What policy is most likely to make unnecessary a nuclear arms race and still provide an adequate margin of security?

Parity cannot be the answer. No one knows what it means in terms of different nuclear weapons and systems. The search for parity can go up as well as down, with nuclear rearmament just as feasible as disarmament. Parity is inherently unstable, because there is no agreed-on standard of equality and no numerical basis for arriving at any such standard. The quest for parity guarantees a nuclear seesaw, not a state of assured stability. The mirage of parity cannot possibly lead to the promised land of stable deterrence.

Negotiations are not the answer. They invariably hinge on establishing some form of parity. In this world, no one is going to negotiate himself into inferiority or out of superiority. Once different weapons and even different weapons systems must be evaluated and balanced off against each other, negotiations inevitably degenerate into endlessly futile haggling sessions, brought to a close only by agreement on a crazy-quilt of trade-offs and loopholes. Negotiations of this sort become more important for the mere consolation that the deadly antagonists are negotiating than for anything the negotiations may bring forth.

The last thing the world needs is deterrence interpreted as the ability to withstand "a massive nuclear blow" in order to "prevail in" an extended nuclear endurance contest. The crucial problem of deterrence is how to prevent such a first blow, not how to withstand it, and least of all, how to exchange blow for blow, as if prevailing in such a contest could have any human meaning. The Soviets could not prevail in such a contest any more than the United States could prevail in it, and there is no point in attributing such an intention to them in order to beat them at the same game. This is a game no one can win; that should determine our policy, not whether the Soviets do or do not believe that they can win.

Indeed, Secretary Haig attributed the doctrine of "prevailing in" a nuclear conflict to the Soviet leaders in a most peculiar way. He said:

> Deterrence faces its true test at the time of maximum tension, even in the midst of actual conflict. In such extreme circumstances, when the stakes on the table may already be immense, when Soviet leaders may feel the very existence of their regime is threatened, who can say whether or not they would run massive risks if they believed that in the end the Soviet state would prevail?

On these extraordinary grounds rested the case against nuclear "sufficiency." It would be difficult to get more confusion and sophistry into two sentences on this subject. The entire object of deterrence is to prevent actual conflict. How can it be said to face a "true test" after actual conflict has broken out? Actual conflict means that it has already failed that test. In such extreme circumstances, the problem before Soviet leaders would not merely be "the very existence of their regime"; it would be the very existence of life in their country. Above all, Haig's conclusion is put in the form of a question, not a statement of fact. "Who can say?" "If they believed." This way of putting the question commits him to nothing definite, but is intended to leave the definite impression that the Soviet leaders may be irrational enough to risk "total destruction" in the quest for nuclear "victory," even though there is no such thing as nuclear "victory."

A painstaking study of Soviet policy on this question was made not so long ago in the journal *International Security* (Summer 1978) by Raymond L. Garthoff, a foremost scholar in this field and former US ambassador to Bulgaria. He showed that some Soviet generals used to put forward the same argument as that of American officials to justify a nuclear "war-fighting" and "war-winning" capability as providing the most credible deterrent. "It is of interest," Garthoff observed, "that the political leaders in their programmatic statements endorse the idea that *deterrence* requires strong and ready combat capability, but do not go on to discuss meeting requirements for waging and winning a war." In any case, the basic work on Soviet military doctrine, *Military Strategy*, edited by a commission headed by Marshal Sokolovsky, stressed "the colossal and unacceptable consequences of a world nuclear war," not only to the United States but to "the socialist countries."

Since 1971, Soviet military and political leaders have ceased calling for strategic superiority; the line turned in favor of mutual deterrence, balance, parity, and equal security. Garthoff, no innocent in these matters, disputes the idea that "Soviet statements on such propositions as mutual deterrence and the unacceptability of general nuclear war are 'for export.' " He believes that "the Soviet political and military leadership accepts a strategic nuclear balance between the Soviet Union and the United States as a fact, and as the probable and desirable prospect for the foreseeable future." Finally, he traces the chief problem not to Soviet disagreement with the fundamental principle of deterrence but rather to "differing perceptions, to suspicions, and to the difficulties of gearing very different military forces and programs into balances and mutually acceptable strategic arms limitations."

This last point keeps coming up as a major stumbling block in all nuclear negotiations. It is the source of the most tortuous trade-offs and the trickiest loopholes. It makes parity a guessing game. It is the bane of obtaining stable deterrence by anything resembling numerical equality.

And yet, everything that is being done or recommended, from no-first-use to preparing for a nuclear endurance contest, is supposedly in the interest of deterrence. It may yet equal liberty for the number of crimes committed in its name.

Still, short of abolishing all nuclear weapons forever and everywhere, deterrence is all we have. Like many such terms that are abused and misused, it is best to get back to its original meaning. Deterrence is another way of saying that nuclear weapons will not be abolished and will not be used. If they were abolished, there would be no need to deter their use. But they will not be used because they could annihilate both sides using them. It would concentrate the mind wonderfully to hold on firmly to what pure and simple deterrence means.

The crucial point is that any level of nuclear weapons over and above what is necessary to have a devastating effect on the other side is no more than an exercise in redundancy. There may be a dispute about what that level is or how it can be maintained; there should be no dispute about the principle. Yet it is the very principle that is being insidiously undermined and nullified—in the name of deterrence. The most sinister and dangerous perversion is the doctrine, which has its advocates on both sides, that deterrence requires the ability actually to fight a nuclear war and prevail in it.

This doctrine inevitably legitimatizes a nuclear arms race. Its advocates invariably protest that they never expect such a nuclear war to be fought, but that the nation must arm for it to prevent the other side from possibly being willing to risk it. This alibi is so untenable that it can only provoke the suspicion that it is a mask for something else. It is untenable because the level of nuclear weapons for pure and simple deterrence is already so devastating that the much higher level for nuclear-war fighting is unnecessary as a deterrent. If the former will not deter, the latter will not deter. All the latter can signify is that there are some people in high places who are interested in fighting as well as—or even more than—deterring a nuclear war.

Even if we agree on the principle of pure and simple deterrence, the much harder question is how to put it into practice. Two things may be said about the practical problem: it is not as hard as it may appear, and it is much easier than that of knowing where to stop in order to fight a nuclear war.

This is what Spurgeon M. Keeny, Jr., and Wolfgang K. H. Panofsky, two eminent authorities with much official experience in this field, wrote in the Winter 1981/82 issue of *Foreign Affairs*:

> A devastating attack on the urban societies of the United States and Soviet Union would in fact require only *a very small fraction* of the more than 50,000 nuclear weapons currently in the arsenals of the two super-powers. The United States is commonly credited with having some 30,000 nuclear warheads of which well over 10,000 are carried by strategic systems capable of hitting the Soviet Union. It is estimated that the Soviet Union will soon have some 10,000 warheads in its strategic forces capable of hitting the United States. An exchange of a few thousand of these weapons could kill most of the urban population and destroy most of the industry of both sides. [Italics added.]

McGeorge Bundy, the former Assistant for National Security Affairs, who has been devoting himself to a study of nuclear policy, has been convinced that "our numbers of warheads, and their yields, in fact exceed what we really need." In the Winter 1978/79 issue of *International Security*, he pointed out that each of the two out of three elements in the American deterrent force, the submarine and the airborne, "independently, has much more than enough explosive strength, just in its alert elements, to constitute a deterrent, and indeed a deterrent in depth."

In fact, no one has ever disputed what President Carter said in 1979 about "just one of our relatively invulnerable Poseidon submarines," that made up less than 2 percent of our total nuclear force. One of them "carries enough warheads to destroy every large and medium-size city in the Soviet Union." Yet the United States has that much nuclear power multiplied fifty times over.

Lord Zuckerman states that mutual deterrence was clearly working as long ago as the end of the 1950s. By 1962 and the Cuban missile crisis, he asserts, "the build-up of the American nuclear forces and, correspondingly, those of the Soviet Union, had already gone well beyond the rational requirements of any mutual deterrent threat." Since then, nuclear weapons have piled up, more and more destructively, with no essential change in the operation of mutual deterrence; the same result could have been achieved had we stopped all production and testing of nuclear weapons two decades ago.

What is new and original in Zuckerman's account is the blame that he apportions to the scientific and technical weapons experts who work in the governmental defense departments. He holds them mainly responsible for the arms race and the opposition to a comprehensive test ban treaty. He has a chapter on "The Advice of Scientists," which shows how they have been pushing the politicians and the military around; the arms race, he warns, can be brought to an end only if the politicians "take charge of the technical men." This alleged reversal of the commonly understood roles may come as a surprise to most readers.

The nuclear buildup seems to live a life of its own. As nuclear warheads are turned out, Zuckerman notes, they are given specific targets as their assignments, whether they are needed or not. Nuclear targeting, as described by Admiral G.E. Miller, a former deputy director of the US Joint Strategic Planning Staff, at a Pugwash Symposium held in Toronto in 1978, is a curious process. New nuclear warheads, according to Miller, "are not produced in answer to military demand; they are turned out and then have to be assigned targets, whether or not there is a requirement for additional destructive capacity." This system is dependent on the R and D fraternity within the weapons establishment, and the deadly cycle of research and development thrives on testing new weapons. To reduce the nuclear threat, Zuckerman holds, "the goal should be a halt to all R and D designed to elaborate new nuclear warheads and new means of delivery." He should know. Unlike the limited test ban treaty, a comprehensive test ban, which he advocates, can be achieved without the trade-offs and loopholes of other nuclear negotiations; it is therefore in a class by itself as a desirable step that should be taken by mutual agreement.

Zuckerman prefers the term "minimal deterrent" for the level of nuclear arms necessary to make nuclear war irrational and self-destructive. It may not be the best term for the principle, because it implies that there is also a "maximal deterrent," though Zuckerman himself recognizes that anything above the necessary minimum is actually redundant, unnecessary, and dangerously provocative because it presupposes something beyond deterrence as such.

This is what President Eisenhower meant back in 1955 when he spoke of hydrogen bombs: "There comes a time, possibly, when a lead is not significant in the defensive arrangements of a country. If you get enough of a particular type of weapon, I doubt that it is particularly important to have a lot more of it." A related view, given the changed circumstances, was put forward by General Maxwell D. Taylor, the former army chief of staff and chairman of the Joint Chiefs of Staff, in the *AEI Defense Review* as recently as late 1978. He could no longer see any merit in "the need for rough parity with comparable elements of the Soviet establishment" or "the fixation on weapon numbers," which encouraged "a senseless arms race for numerical parity or superiority." A more rational and effective strategic policy could be based on "the destructive potential of our forces"—a potential determined by the level necessary for mutual deterrence, not by "seeking decisive superiority in all categories of military strength, nuclear and conventional."

Taylor argued against the dependence on intercontinental ballistic missiles and recommended progressive reliance on submarine-launched and cruise missiles. This is not the place to go into details of this sort; the principle of deterrence is what concerns us; and Taylor at that time recognized that the principle was being challenged and ignored.

As Eisenhower had implied almost a quarter of a century earlier, whatever is enough for deterrence is, in effect, a sufficient defense against a nuclear enemy; a "lead" is not significant or particularly important; by the same token, a numerical inferiority in one category or another need not be significant or particularly important. Nikita Khrushchev once said that though the United States "may be able to destroy us two times over, we're still capable of wiping out the United States, even if it's only once." The same holds if the Soviet Union were able to destroy the United States two times over and the United States could wipe out the Soviet Union only once. In fact, only "once" has any meaning; there would be nothing much to destroy the second time.

If only this plain, sober, fairly simple fact of nuclear life could be dinned into the heads of policy makers or, failing that, shouted from the housetops, we might be saved from all the terrifying twaddle that assails us periodically, especially whenever negotiations appear to be imminent. Eisenhower's principle of "enough" is not that difficult to establish, if we have already gone far beyond any conceivable capability of mutual destruction. The principle has already been put into practice many times over, and when we are told that we still need more, there is more than that principle at stake.

There is no need to establish illusory conditions of numerical parity. There is no point in bartering trade-offs and haggling over loopholes. No negotiations are necessary to establish alleged equalities or equivalences. The nuclear numbers game should mislead no more. Deterrence should not be the cat's-paw for the type of bargaining called for by SALT and START. At the very least, the arsenal of nuclear arms should be fixed at some rational level by a calculation of the needs of deterrence rather than by competition and rivalry. American policy should not be hostage to Soviet preferences, which, paradoxically, now dictate American requirements.

The best that can be hoped for, in the present circumstances, is a policy of plain, simple, and sufficient deterrence which any nuclear power can determine for itself. Such a course might be contagious, because it is saner, safer, and cheaper. It could also lead to reductions in the present scale of nuclear arms if both sides calmed down and rationally decided what was best for them. But the main thing is that it does not depend on what others do. It puts the responsibility where it belongs —on each nuclear power, without alibis, scapegoats, trade-offs, loopholes, declarations of good intentions, bilateral freezes, double talk, or reinventing the world.

New York Review of Books, July 15, 1982

2

Dear Mr. Weinberger: An Open Reply to an Open Letter

The following letter was sent by Secretary of Defense Caspar W. Weinberger on August 23, 1982, to thirty US and forty foreign publications.

I am increasingly concerned with news accounts that portray this Administration as planning to wage protracted nuclear war, or seeking to acquire a nuclear "war-fighting" capability. This is completely inaccurate, and these stories misrepresent the Administration's policies to the American public and to our allies and adversaries abroad.

It is the first and foremost goal of this Administration to take every step to ensure that nuclear weapons are never used again, for we do not believe there could be any "winners" in a nuclear war. Our entire strategy aims to deter war of all kinds, but most particularly to deter nuclear war. To accomplish this objective, our forces must be able to respond in a measured and prudent manner to the threat posed by the Soviet Union. That will require the improvements in our strategic forces that the President has proposed. But it does *not* mean that we endorse the concept of protracted nuclear war, or nuclear "war-fighting." It is the Soviet Union that appears to be building forces for a "protracted" conflict.

The policy of deterrence is difficult for some to grasp because it is based on a paradox. But this is quite simple: to make the cost of nuclear war much higher than any possible benefit. If the Soviets know in advance that a nuclear attack on the United States would bring swift nuclear retaliation, they would never attack in the first place. They would be "deterred" from ever beginning a nuclear war.

There is nothing new about our policy. Since the awful age of nuclear weapons began, the United States has sought to prevent nuclear war through a policy of deterrence. This policy has been approved, through the political processes of the democratic nations it protects, since at least 1950. More important, it works. It has worked in the face of major international tensions involving the great powers, and it has worked in the face of war itself.

But, for deterrence to continue to be successful in the future, we must take steps to offset the Soviet military buildup. If we do not modernize our arsenal now, as the Soviets have been doing for more than 20 years, we will, within a few years, no longer have the ability to retaliate. The

Soviet Union would then be in a position to threaten or actually to attack us with the knowledge that we would be incapable of responding. We have seen in Poland, in Afghanistan, in Eastern Europe and elsewhere that the Soviet Union does not hesitate to take advantage of a weaker adversary. We cannot allow the Soviet Union to think it could begin a nuclear war with us and win.

This is not just idle speculation. The Soviet Union has engaged in a frenzied military buildup, in spite of their economic difficulties. They have continued to build greater numbers of nuclear weapons far beyond those necessary for deterrence. They now have over 5,000 nuclear warheads on ICBMs, compared to about 2,000 only five years ago. They have modified the design of these weapons and their launchers so that many of their land-based missiles are now more accurate, more survivable and more powerful than our own. They have also developed a refiring capability that will allow them to reload their delivery systems several times. They have elaborate plans for civil defense and air defense against any retaliation we might attempt. And, finally, their writings and military doctrine emphasize a nuclear war-fighting scenario. Whatever they claim their intentions to be, the fact remains that they are designing their weapons in such a way and in sufficient numbers to indicate to us that they think they could begin, and win, a nuclear war.

In the face of all this, it is my responsibility and duty as Secretary of Defense to make every effort to modernize our nuclear forces in such a way that the United States retains the capability to deter the Soviet Union from ever beginning a nuclear war. We must take the steps necessary to match the Soviet Union's greatly improved nuclear capability.

That is exactly why we must have a *capability* for a survivable and enduring response—to demonstrate that our strategic forces *could* survive Soviet strikes over an extended period. Thus we believe we could deter any attack. Otherwise we would be tempting them to employ nuclear weapons or try to blackmail us. In short, we cannot afford to place ourselves in the position where the survivability of our deterrent would force the President to choose between using our strategic forces before they were destroyed or surrendering.

Those who object to a policy that would strengthen our deterrent, then, would force us into a more dangerous, hair-triggered posture. Forces that must be used in the very first instant of an enemy attack are not the tools of a prudent strategy. A posture that encourages Soviet nuclear adventurism is not the basis of an effective deterrent. Our entire strategic program, including the development of a response capability that has been so maligned in the press recently, has been developed with the express intention of assuring that nuclear war will never be fought.

I know that this doctrine of deterrence is a difficult paradox to understand. It is an uncomfortable way to keep the peace. We understand deterrence and accept the fact that we must do much more in order to continue to keep the peace. It is my fervent hope that all can understand and accept this so that we can avoid the sort of sensationalist treatment of every mention of the word "nuclear" that only serves to distort our policy and to frighten people all over the world. Our policy is peace, and we deeply believe that the best and surest road to peace is to secure and maintain an effective and credible deterrent.

> The purpose of US policy remains to prevent aggression through an effective policy of deterrence—the very goal which prompted the formation of the North Atlantic Alliance, an alliance which is as vital today as it was the day it was formed.

It is not every day, every week, or even every year that a Secretary of Defense sends a letter to thirty US newspapers and forty foreign publications. It is even rarer that such a letter is used to defend his administration's policy against alleged inaccuracies and misrepresentations, as if he did not have any other means to put the facts before the public. Yet, on August 23 [1982], just such a letter was sent by you on the subject of this administration's nuclear-war policy.

I realize that you did not send this letter to me personally. But it is an open letter, and, therefore, anyone may answer it publicly. It requires an answer from someone.

One question immediately arises: What provoked your letter?

It was provoked by "leaks" from your top-secret documents. One of them is "National Security Decision Document 13," adopted by the National Security Council in the fall of 1981. This document was reported by Robert Scheer in the *Los Angeles Times* of August 15 of this year to have specifically stated for the first time that it was US policy to prevail in a protracted nuclear war. In the spring of 1982 this policy was then incorporated in a 124-page document entitled "Fiscal Year 1984–1988 Defense Guidance," parts of which were leaked to *The New York Times* and disclosed by Richard Halloran, its defense correspondent, on May 30. This "Defense Guidance" is a five-year plan, beginning October 1, 1984, to provide general strategic direction to all the armed services. It was approved by you and represents the official view of the entire US military establishment. Most of the leaks came from it. This document is said to have been elaborated in even greater detail in a "strategic master plan" developed by the Pentagon and sent to the National Security Council for approval in early August. Scheer reported that, according to one member of the Reagan administration, it contemplates a nuclear war lasting as long as six months.

Just how such secret documents get leaked is an even greater secret. You fret and fume about it but seem incapable of locating the culprit or stopping the practice. The leaks must undoubtedly come from sources high enough to know what is in the documents, because the leaks come with exact quotations of just what you did not wish to be leaked. No one has denied the accuracy of these quotaions.

That there is a division of opinion in the top leadership at the Pentagon seems clear. When he left as chairman of the Joint Chiefs of Staff last June, General David C. Jones of the Air Force repudiated the idea of a "protracted nuclear war." Money spent to prepare for such a war, he said, would be thrown into a "bottomless pit." If such a high-ranking officer thought it necessary to express himself so openly and so forcefully on this issue, there must be others who are also appalled by the adoption of a plan to prepare for and prevail in a "protracted nuclear war." In fact, the possibility cannot be excluded that the leaks have come with more or less official toleration in order to test public opinion before the president gives final approval to the new "master plan." This technique is not unknown in the American political system.

In any case, in your letter we now have the grave charge that "news accounts" have contained "completely inaccurate" stories about the administration's nuclear-war policy. We have a blanket denial from you that the administration is "planning to wage protracted nuclear war, or seeking to acquire a nuclear 'war-fighting' capability." But your letter never denies or even mentions what was actually in those news accounts or the documents reported by them. I can only conclude that your letter is intended to distract attention from those documents; it is a blocking operation meant to make itself the statement of policy instead of the authentic statements that are actually dictating policy to the armed services behind the scenes. This attempted sleight of hand would not be so disturbing if it presented a credible, perhaps simplified, version of what is in those documents. But that is exactly what it does not do. The juggling act is performed so clumsily that your letter itself gives away what it is intended to hide.

The account of the "Defense Guidance" by Halloran on May 30 was a front-page story, accompanied by your picture, filling almost three full columns of print, most if it direct quotations from the document. Halloran had obviously been briefed by someone on the way the plan had been drawn up as well as on its contents. What attracted most attention were the references to prevailing in a protracted nuclear war. One passage called on US forces to maintain themselves through "a protracted conflict period." Another held that US nuclear forces "must prevail and be able to force the Soviet Union to seek earliest termination of hostilities on terms favorable to the United States."

In an interview with you on August 9, Halloran reported that you had "assailed those critics of the Administration's policy who have protested against provisions that call for the United States to 'prevail' in nuclear war by ending the conflict on terms favorable to the United States and with some nuclear weapons intact." Nothing that you said on this occasion seemed to deny that this was actually the policy advocated in your "Defense Guidance"; you merely insisted that it was right to have such a policy. Halloran again quoted verbatim from the original document, including two passages which he had not used in his previous account—which may have annoyed you even more.

The directive also said that, in the event of an attack, "United States nuclear capabilities must prevail even under the condition of a prolonged war." And it instructed the US armed forces to maintain "under all circumstances, nuclear offensive capabilities so that the United States would never emerge from a nuclear war without nuclear weapons while still threatened by enemy nuclear forces."

Then, on August 24, Halloran again reported a protest by you in your office against "continued criticism of his strategy for protracted nuclear war"—of which one example was my own article "How Not to Think about Nuclear War" in *The New York Review of Books* of July 15. You were disturbed because you had been forced to spend "a very large fraction" of your time defending your policy in speeches, press and television interviews, background briefings, private conversations, and letters to the editor. Halloran's handling of the interview must again have displeased you. He let you have your say and then deliberately went on to quote once more from the "Defense Guidance" in such a way that your disclaimers were belied by the document. In any case, this meeting, which took place prior to August 22, came before you sent your letter of August 23 to US and foreign publications complaining about inaccuracies and misrepresentations in the news accounts. Your letter did not specify which inaccuracies and misrepresentations in which news accounts, so it is difficult to know who was guilty of what.

What we now have, in substance, are Halloran's quotations from the "Defense Guidance" in *The New York Times* of May 30 and August 24 on the one hand, and your letter of August 23 together with the comments made by you some days earlier on the other hand. *The New York Times* and *The Washington Post* did not see fit to publish the text of your letter, so that readers who depend on them had no way of comparing what was in your public letter and what was in your classified "Defense Guidance." Comparing them is just what I propose to do.

Your letter of August 23 to the thirty US and forty foreign publications deserves the closest scrutiny, because it is the most carefully worked out public statement of what the new nuclear-war strategy is.

One thing it does not do. It never mentions the official directives, such as the five-year "Defense Guidance," which it is supposed to clarify. If there were no such documents and no leaks from them, your letter would not have been necessary. Yet we are being told what the policy allegedly is without a word from the actual policy statements themselves.

In your letter, there is only one direct mention of a protracted nuclear war:

> But it [American strategic improvement] does *not* mean that we endorse the concept of protracted nuclear war, or nuclear "war-fighting." It is the Soviet Union that appears to be building forces for a "protracted" conflict.

The implication is unmistakably clear—only the Soviet Union "endorses the concept" of a protracted nuclear war; the United States does not. If that were the real point of the letter, we would expect you to go on and tell us what is wrong with the concept and why the United States does not endorse it. What we get is something quite different. It is:

> We must take the steps necessary to match the Soviet Union's greatly improved nuclear capability.

But it makes no sense to take these "steps" if we do not also adopt the alleged Soviet "concept" for which these steps were designed. You insist that the Soviet capability and concept are coordinated; if we match their capability, it can only be, according to your own logic, to carry out the same concept.

Is it true that your "Defense Guidance" document did not "endorse the concept" of a protracted nuclear war? The very phrase "endorse the concept" is equivocal enough to be misleading. It may be used to deny that the United States deliberately wishes to engage in a protracted nuclear war. Or it may be used to mean that the United States is prepared to engage in a protracted nuclear war if necessary. The latter meaning was clearly the one intended in the "Defense Guidance" document, which instructed US forces to be able to maintain "through a protracted conflict period and afterward, the capability to inflict very high levels of damage" on Soviet industry. The same document also maintained that US nuclear forces "must prevail and must be able to force the Soviet Union to seek the earliest termination of hostilities on terms favorable to the US." This could only refer to a nuclear war that was already taking place and was protracted enough for the US forces to prevail.

No one in his right mind would expect you to say that you want such a war. You would be crazy to want one. But that is not the issue. The question is whether it is only the Soviet Union that, as your letter claims, "appears to be building forces for a 'protracted' conflict." In effect, you deny what you are not charged with in order to cover up what you are actually trying to do.

The same stratagem of obfuscation is used to distort the plain meaning of "prevail" in your "Defense Guidance" document. The dictionary makes it clear that in this context prevail means "to gain ascendancy through strength or superiority." Ascendancy through superior strength is just what nations have always meant by winning a war. In fact, the idea of a "protracted" war and that of "prevailing" in it are intimately related; it is necessary for a war to be more or less protracted in order to prevail in it. These terms were not used in a fit of absentmindedness in the "Defense Guidance"; one implied the other.

Nevertheless, you obviously know that most people are appalled by the prospect of prevailing in a protracted nuclear war. We thus get from you another denial of the line taken in your own document. In your letter, you plead innocence in this way:

> It is the first and foremost goal of this Administration to take every step to ensure that nuclear weapons are never used again, for we do not believe there could be any "winners" in a nuclear war.

The first part of this sentence is a protestation of virtue that is not to the point. The critical question is whether you believe that a nuclear war can be won. If we take you at your word, you do not intend to win—but neither do you intend to lose.

You took this slippery line in two interviews. On August 9, Halloran reported:

> Asserting that there was no alternative, Mr. Weinberger declared, "You show me a Secretary of Defense who's planning not to prevail and I'll show you a Secretary of Defense who ought to be impeached."
> Mr. Weinberger reiterated his view that nuclear war was not winnable. But he added that "we certainly are planning not to be defeated."

On August 24, Halloran again reported:

> "We've said many times that we don't think nuclear war is winnable," Mr. Weinberger said in the interview. Asked how that differed from pre-

vailing, Mr. Weinberger replied: "We certainly are planning not to be defeated."

Humpty Dumpty also used words in this peculiar way. If a secretary of defense ought to be impeached if he is planning not to prevail in a nuclear war, then he is planning to prevail. He is planning, in other words, to come out ahead, on top, to gain ascendancy, or some other circumlocution for winning the war.

On the other hand, you cannot bring yourself to say that a nuclear war is "winnable." But when asked how prevailing differs from winning, you were again forced to take refuge in subterfuge. To believe you, nuclear wars are strangely one-sided—they can end in defeat but not in victory, as if defeat could have any meaning if victory does not. Yet in your "Defense Guidance," you are far more positive and definite, for it gives a fairly clear definition of what it means to prevail—"to seek the earliest termination of hostilities on terms favorable to the United States."

The plain truth is that you really "endorse the concept of protracted nuclear war, or nuclear war-fighting" and "appear to be building forces" for just such a war. As a result, you also have trouble with the concept of nuclear deterrence. As in the other cases we have just examined, you again want to have it both ways.

In your letter, you define deterrence quite simply:

> . . . to make the cost of nuclear war much higher than any possible benefit. If the Soviets know in advance that a nuclear attack on the United States would bring swift nuclear retaliation, they would never attack in the first place. They would be "deterred" from ever beginning a nuclear war.

Whatever the level of arming is that is enough to make the cost of nuclear war much higher than any possible benefit, it is enough for deterrence. The technical details may be disputed; the principle is indisputably clear. There is a stopping point in the accumulation and development of nuclear arms necessary for deterrence. Beyond that point, a nation is no longer arming for deterrence; it is arming to fight a nuclear war with the expectation of prevailing in it.

You are luminously clear on this principle of nuclear policy so long as it applies to the Soviet Union. But why does it not apply to the United States? The principle of deterrence does not stop at the Soviet border.

.   .   .

That both the United States and the Soviet Union have a nuclear capacity sufficient for deterrence there can hardly be a doubt. In a recent article, I cited the testimony of two of our most knowledgeable and independent authorities, Spurgeon M. Keeny, Jr., and Wolfgang K.H. Panofsky, writing in the Winter 1981–1982 issue of *Foreign Affairs*: "A devastating attack on the urban societies of the United States and the Soviet Union would in fact require only *a very small fraction* of the more than 50,000 nuclear weapons currently in the arsenals of the two superpowers" [italics added]. There is no shortage of similar evidence that the quotas for nuclear deterrence have long been overfulfilled.

We must take on trust your assurance that the Soviets now have land-based missiles which are "more accurate, more survivable and more powerful than our own." It presumes an exact knowledge of the most secret of weapons of a country where secrecy is a mania. Whatever justification there may be your claim that you know just how accurate the Soviet ICBMs are, there can be no justification for the way you deal with these weapons in your letter. You try to make our flesh creep with an array of figures about the presumed Soviet advantage. You make it appear that the Soviets need only have these weapons in sufficient numbers to think of beginning and winning a nuclear war. They are not so dumb, and the American nuclear planners of the 1950s and 1960s were not so dumb either.

The past US decision to concentrate on smaller but more accurate land-based missiles was accompanied by another decision not to trust American nuclear defense to a single type of weapon. Thus came about the present arrangement whereby only about one fourth of the US nuclear force is composed of land-based missiles. About one half is seaborne and another quarter airborne. The Soviet triad is just about the reverse in its distribution. In addition, the United States has jumped ahead in the development of cruise missiles, which have become the Soviets' current nuclear bête noire.

The reader will look in vain for any mention of the balance of seaborne and airborne nuclear weapons in your letter or interviews. If your purpose had been to clarify instead of to terrify, you would have found room for a few words on the overall balance of nuclear forces. One-sided figures of Soviet nuclear warheads on ICBMs tell only part of the story. They may have increased from about 2,000 to over 5,000 during the past five years. But other increases give a better idea of the overall balance. From 1970 to 1980, according to Hans A. Bethe and Franklin A. Long in *The New York Times* of September 22, the warheads in the

Soviet strategic forces increased from about 1,800 to 6,000 while those in the US strategic forces rose from about 4,000 to 10,000. Instead, you chose to concentrate on the menace of the Soviets' land-based, long-range intercontinental ballistic missiles, or ICBMs, as if all that stood between us and the Soviet willingness to fight and win a nuclear war was the improvement of our nuclear capability in these same weapons.

Your failure to put the problem of the ICBMs in the perspective of the total balance of nuclear forces did not result from another fit of absentmindedness. The one-sidedness of your presentation was required to create a mood of popular panic with which to put over your new program.

Something about real deterrence can be learned from the statement on the Cuban missile crisis of 1962 in a recent issue of *Time* magazine (September 27) by the six key men around President Kennedy. There has been a myth that the crisis was resolved in favor of the United States because of our nuclear superiority at the time. The six high officials state: "American nuclear superiority was not in our view a critical factor, for the fundamental and controlling reason that nuclear war, already in 1962, would have been an unexampled catastrophe for both sides; the balance of terror so eloquently described by Winston Churchill seven years earlier was in full operation." In 1962, the Soviets had fewer than 2,000 or even 1,000 missiles, and the United States had many more, but all the Soviets needed to cancel out American nuclear superiority was enough nuclear power to bring about "an unexampled catastrophe for both sides."

When it comes to exposing the Soviet Union's dereliction from orthodox deterrence, however, you are worth heeding. You do not seem to realize it, but you tell as much about your own program as about the Soviets'.

One of the most important lessons your letter teaches us is that arming for deterrence is not the same as arming for fighting or prevailing in a protracted nuclear war. This lesson comes out clearly in one of your references to Soviet policy:

> The Soviet Union has engaged in a frenzied military buildup, in spite of their economic difficulties. They have continued to build greater numbers of nuclear weapons far beyond those necessary for deterrence.

I take this to be official confirmation of a key point that I tried to make in a recent article. There is a crucial difference between arming for deterrence and arming far beyond the needs of deterrence. This difference obtains whether it is the Soviet Union or the United States that is doing the arming far beyond the needs of deterrence.

You also said in an interview that planning deterrence "is not planning to fight a protracted nuclear war." That is another and even clearer way of distinguishing between a "nuclear capability" for deterrence and a "nuclear capability" for a protracted war. It would be even clearer if we turned your words around and said that planning to fight a protracted nuclear war is not planning deterrence.

What, then, are you planning for? There is only one sentence in your letter that tries to answer this question. It reads:

> That is exactly why we must have a *capability* for a survivable and enduring response—to demonstrate that our strategic forces *could* survive Soviet strikes over an extended period. Thus we believe we could deter any attack.

"Over an extended period" brings us back to the protracted nuclear war. But what are we expected to do in this extended period? You are telling us that the only thing the United States contemplates doing is to "survive" nuclear attacks. You would like us to believe that the only thing needed to deter such attacks is for the United States to be capable of surviving them.

You express your sympathy with readers who may not be able to grasp the full import and subtlety of your words. "I know," you write, "that this doctrine of deterrence is a difficult paradox to understand." You are wrong. Your version is not difficult to understand, and it is not a paradox. It is a hoax.

Do you really expect any sensible person to believe that all the United States expects to do is to have our strategic forces "survive" Soviet nuclear attacks? No retaliation in kind? No nuclear exchanges? The mere mention of replying to nuclear attacks with nuclear counterattacks, of fighting the same way the Soviets are presumed to plan to fight, would have given the game away. It would have been glaringly clear that the plan attributed to the Soviets is a mirror image of the plan in your own "Defense Guidance."

Let us recall what it is that you approved in that document:

> —US forces must be able to maintain "through a protracted conflict period and afterward, the capability to inflict very high levels of damage" on Soviet industry.

—Should a Soviet attack "nevertheless occur, United States nuclear capabilities must prevail even under the condition of a prolonged war."

—If deterrence should fail, the United States must "deny the Soviet Union or any other adversary a military victory at any level of conflict and force earliest termination of hostilities on terms favorable to the United States."

Could anyone reading your letter and your interviews know that this is what you expect the US nuclear forces to achieve in the event of a Soviet attack? Is this what any sensible person would be led to believe by your assurance that our strategic forces need only demonstrate the ability to *survive*?

Your hoax attributes the key principles in your own "Defense Guidance" document to the Soviet Union. The only time a protracted nuclear war is mentioned in your letter is when you accuse the Soviet Union of believing in and preparing for it. A winnable nuclear war is mentioned only to pin the idea on the Soviet Union. Nuclear attacks over an extended period are mentioned only in connection with Soviet attacks, which our strategic forces would merely try to survive and, by surviving, deter. It may well be that you are right about the Soviet Union. The truth, then, would be that both sides are playing the same game, adopting the same nuclear strategy and blaming the other side for it.

In fact, your letter to those seventy publications attempts to get across the idea that we must do certain things because the Soviets are doing them. There would otherwise be no point in filling the letter with far more about what the Soviets are doing than about what we are doing. The Soviet Union may be guilty of a "frenzied military buildup," but your purpose in exposing what they are doing is to get us to do exactly the same thing.

Logically, you should have been defending a US war-fighting and war-winning nuclear policy, because that is what you are secretly advocating; and some of your colleagues are advocating it not so secretly. If you had been candid, you might well have asked: What is wrong with such a policy?

It is wrong because it goes far beyond what is necessary for deterrence. In the case of deterrence, as you yourself professed to believe in your guise as a true believer in deterrence, there is a level of arms which is enough for the purpose; if a nuclear power goes beyond that level, we are justified in suspecting that something else is going on. For a nuclear war-fighting policy there is never enough, because it is impossible to determine what a protracted war requires. The very nature of a protracted war makes inevitable an open-ended nuclear arms race; there can never be an end to the development and deployment of new weapons in the effort to gain some fleeting and illusory advantage in the hope of prevailing.

When you were asked about the control of nuclear weapons in a protracted war, you replied: "I just don't have any idea. I don't know that anybody has any idea." You were, for a change, being candid; you might also have admitted that no one has any idea of what a protracted nuclear war would be like, for which reason it permits no limits or restraints in its preparation.

We are now in the midst of a real arms race and an unreal arms negotiation. That is not what the world in general and the American people in particular have been given to understand. The result can only be a huge loss of confidence in the integrity and honor of the American government. The disparity between what you are doing and what you say you are doing cannot be concealed forever.

Unless the kind of protracted nuclear war that you envision actually comes to pass, you are going to engage in the most wasteful expenditure of public funds in American history, perhaps in all history. All those arms that go beyond the necessity for deterrence must be redundant. They cannot serve for deterrence; they admittedly go beyond it.

What, then, is left of your perfectly valid definition of deterrence as making "the cost of nuclear war much higher than any possible benefit"? Do you suppose that any benefit could be obtained from a nuclear war between powers so heavily overarmed for it as the United States and the Soviet Union?

You yourself have given the answer: "If the Soviets knew in advance that a nuclear attack on the United States would bring swift nuclear retaliation, they would never attack in the first place. They would be 'deterred' from ever beginning a nuclear war."

Thus, what is necessary is the power to bring on swift nuclear retaliation, a power that we abundantly have in our nuclear submarines alone. If "swift nuclear retaliation" is enough, you have it, or if you need to safeguard it in one way or another, you can manage it within the limits of deterrence.

But what the masterminds behind your letter really look for is a final *struggle for power* by means of a protracted nuclear war in which the United States would ultimately prevail or terminate the hostilities "on terms favorable to the United States." That is what is behind the new policy. It is masked by attributing the idea of fighting and winning a nuclear war to the Soviet Union. But those who want to beat the Soviet Union at their own game have exactly the same end in view. For this reason they believe that there is such a thing as "nuclear superiority" and that we could successfully wage a nuclear war if only we could obtain that superiority.

If all it takes to prevent a nuclear attack on the United States by the Soviet Union is "to make the cost much higher than any possible benefit," you must consider the Soviet rulers to be blockheads or madmen to contemplate a nuclear contest which is far more likely to end in mutual devastation. The Soviets, on the contrary, have always tended to go after prizes where the benefits are greatest and the risks the least. Every nation goes to war expecting the benefits to exceed the cost; it may err and pay dearly for the error, but at the outset there is a calculation that benefits would be considerable and costs tolerable. Such calculation is hopeless in nuclear war. If you and your advisers have not understood— as Henry Kissinger, having changed his mind for the second time, recently put it in the Summer 1982 issue of *The Washington Quarterly* —"that nuclear weapons have added a new dimension to warfare and indeed human existence, that they make obsolete traditional concepts of military victory, that they stake civilized life and perhaps humanity itself"—you have understood nothing of fundamental value for your guidance of American defense.

The search for nuclear superiority, the preparation for a protracted nuclear war, and the goal of prevailing in such a war, all fit together in behalf of a master plan that goes far beyond deterrence; it is the vision of an apocalyptic nuclear war to decide once and for all the issue of world power. Only such an outcome could possibly justify the millions of casualties and the frightful physical destruction that would ensue from such a war. It is an aim that makes no sense in any conceivable cost benefit calculus, and yet it is the hidden agenda of those on both sides who are plotting to win a nuclear war.

In the end, your policy threatens to harm US foreign relations more than anything else. The nearest thing to a commitment to peace that a nuclear power can make in the present circumstances is a program for deterrence, plain and simple. Such a commitment would signify that the United States regards nuclear weaponry as unlike any other in military history. It is not an instrument for fighting or winning. It is an instrument of such universal devastation that its only use is to prevent any use of it; this is the true paradox of nuclear weapons. Your policy can only envenom already strained relationships, not merely with the Soviet Union but with our closest friends and allies, now tugging at the leash. The political costs of a war-fighting, war-winning program vastly exceed any conceivable military benefits.

For all these reasons it is now necessary to let the American people know what is in your secret documents, especially in the "Defense Guidance," which has already been leaked in part. Your letter will not do. It is so maladroit that it can only raise suspicions that something is going on behind the scenes that cannot be divulged publicly and must be covered up by confusing and contradictory verbiage. Those leaks to which you object are the very stuff of democratic policy making. The present system of secrecy is designed to put across a new nuclear-war policy as a *fait accompli*. The policy originates in the Pentagon as Secret, goes to the National Security Council as Secret, and is expected to be approved by the President as Secret.

Why all the secrecy? The passages in your "Defense Guidance" about prevailing in a protracted nuclear war are purely political in nature, not technical. It is one thing to classify as Secret a document on how to make a cruise missile; it is another thing to put the same classification on a document that sets forth a broad policy that should be open to the most searching public discussion. You are not, of course, the first to hide behind this system of secrecy, but you have gone further than ever before in the most dangerous of all spheres of national policy. The challenge before you is whether your new policy can stand the light of day. Can you afford to let the people know?

New York Review of Books, November 4, 1982

II

WHERE ARE THE ALLIES?

1

The Western Misalliance

I

"Where Are the Allies?" The question was peremptorily raised at the head of a column by James Reston, the senior political commentator of *The New York Times*, on November 14, 1979. He was referring to the lack of action on the part of America's allies for the release of the American hostages in Iran. President Carter, wrote Reston, "cannot deal with this diplomatic and religious tangle alone"; he needed a diplomatic boycott of Iran by the allies and, if that failed, an economic boycott of Iran.

The question was raised again five months later on April 10, 1980, this time officially. In a major address, President Carter declared that it was "vital that the burden of sacrifice be shared among our allies and among other nations." He was referring to the burden of American retaliatory measures against Iran and the Soviet Union. He claimed not to know as yet what the answer to the question was. "I cannot tell," he said, "what those allies and other friends of ours might actually do."

Almost six weeks later, on May 21, 1980, a leading editorial in *The New York Times* sought to answer Reston's original question. The United States, it charged, "is being routinely defied by its major allies." The defiance was demonstrated by the failure of Western Europe and Japan to impose effective sanctions against Iran, by the encouragement of a Palestinian state on the West Bank of the Jordan, and other such departures from American policy. If this trend continued, the editorial predicted ominously, the result was going to be the erosion of the basic military alliance between Western Europe and the United States, the purpose of which was "to combine European, Japanese and American economic power for the defense of democratic values."

Four months later, in September 1980, an article in *The New Yorker* again revealed some of the popular confusion attending the alliance. It explained that the North Atlantic Treaty relationship, which had started out as a "simple U.S. military guarantee to Europe" and a qualified military association of the North Atlantic nations, was "soon expanded" into "an extremely ambitious political framework." The article counselled that what the United States and Western Europe needed was "not closer alliance, restored alliance, or improved alliance, but less alliance" without the "political ambitions that have become attached to it." The underlying assumption of the article seemed to be that the alliance had long ago become a political instrument and that its outmoded politicization had made it in important respects an "anachronism."[1]

In those months, Americans were constantly reminded of their seemingly unaccountable and inexcusable disappointment in "our allies." Almost imperceptibly, a sea change had come over America's place in the world. When the alliance was formed, America did not need allies; they needed America. There was nothing in the alliance that was supposed to work automatically, even in the event of a military attack on one or more of its parties. The alliance had nothing to do with combining "European, Japanese and American economic power for the defense of democratic values." It had never developed a political framework, ambitious or otherwise; on the contrary, all efforts to give it such a framework had failed. If such myths can find their way into leading editorials and articles, one can imagine how far illusions and misconceptions about the "alliance" have gone in less well-informed quarters.

The crisis of the "alliance" is an old story. What is new about the present crisis is the turnabout in the relationship between the United States and its allies. The crisis in the past was mainly about the reliability of the American commitment to come to the aid of Western Europe. The crisis in the present is about the reliability of an assumed commitment by Western Europe to come to the aid of the United States. This reversal of roles has been gradually approaching, and none of the main factors that have entered into it is actually new. What is new is the crystallization of these factors by events that have an immediate, tangible bearing on policy and power. What is also new is the popular consciousness of a changed relationship among the allies; never before has the United States been so openly on the asking rather than on the giving end. A succession of "new eras" has been regularly proclaimed since

World War II; this one may well be the first that unquestionably deserves the name.

Thirty-one years have passed since the alliance was formed, and even people whose business it presumably is to know such things have but a dim and mistaken notion of what the alliance was and is all about. Thirty-one years is a long time for an alliance to last; this one goes so far back that a new generation can hardly be expected to recall the circumstances that brought it about and that gave it its particular purpose.

Before we ask, "Where Are the Allies?" and why are they not sharing the "burden of sacrifice," it would seem necessary to recall what the alliance was supposed to do. The terms "allies" and "alliance" are being used so loosely that they have come to mean little more than friends and friendships, the implications of which are decided arbitrarily by whoever happens to use the words. The Kennedy administration's "Alliance for Progress" represented an even looser use of the term; it was no real alliance and resulted in little, if any, progress. President Kennedy also anticipated the editorial in *The New York Times* that made the North Atlantic Treaty Organization (NATO) alliance into something it had never been and was not intended to be. In 1961, in one of his more fanciful flourishes, he declared that NATO was "remarkable among the alliances of history in its combination of political, military, economic, and even psychological components."[2] It was nothing of the sort, except for the military component, and Kennedy did nothing to make it so. As a result, the idea of an alliance has been so corrupted that it is well on its way to becoming completely useless. There are diplomatic terms for looser connections—entente, consultation pact, nonaggression pact, community of interest, and the like. An alliance is something else.

For an alliance to be invoked, it is necessary to know in advance just what definite, formal commitments were made, who made them, and in what circumstances.[3] Alliances that are not clearly defined have little chance of being successfully invoked—not that clear definitions guarantee success. The alliance that is now being invoked in the United States is clearly of the traditional kind. It is widely assumed that the United States has a right to count on its allies, as if they had agreed on some clear and specific mutual obligations or had arrived at some general undertaking to come to each other's assistance whatever the place or issue. It may come as a surprise to some that the United States has no alliance with Western Europe or Japan that could conceivably apply to any of the most recent trouble spots—Angola, Ethiopia, Iran, Afghanistan, Pakistan, the Iran-Iraq war, or the Middle East. No ally has defaulted in these areas, because no commitment was ever made to act in concert in any of them. In fact, they were deliberately left out of the treaty on which the alliance is based.

That alliance is based on the North Atlantic Treaty of April 4, 1949, better known as NATO. It is the only diplomatic instrument that has any bearing on our rights and our allies' obligations. It is still in force because, unlike most such agreements, it was intended to last indefinitely unless one or more of the signatories chose to denounce it after a period of twenty years. It was originally entered into by the United States and ten other countries—Canada, Denmark, France, Iceland, Italy, Luxembourg, Netherlands, Norway, Portugal, and Great Britain. Before charges of European default get to be too deafening, it is well to recall just what they entered into.

NATO was designed for one purpose and one purpose only— security. It was not concerned with "the defense of democratic values"; if it had been, Portugal, which was then ruled by the Salazar dictatorship, could not have been one of the members. The heart of the treaty was the commitment in Article 5 that "an armed attack against one or more of them in Europe or North America shall be considered an attack against them all." No provision was made for automatic implementation. Article 4 merely provided for "consultation" whenever one of the parties decided that it faced a threat to its "territorial integrity, political independence or security." Secretary of State Dean Acheson, the chief American architect of the treaty, repeatedly assured congressional committees that the United States would decide in its own good time whether, when, and how to do anything in support of the treaty. He knew that Congress would never have ratified it if it had provided for anything less equivocal.

When the treaty went into effect, as Acheson admitted in secret testimony that was not made public until 1974, by which time it attracted little attention, the United States did not have the military force to defend Europe against a major attack. "There is nothing to meet it at all," he told a senatorial committee at the end of 1950. It would take eighteen months to have "something," two years for "something more," and four years for "something really substantial."[4] The outbreak of the Korean war that year began the remilitarization of the United States and with it the militarization of NATO. At its inception, then, NATO was made up of a defenseless Europe and an unprepared United States. It began life as little more than "a mere political commitment," as Acheson put it in retrospect.[5] The original idea was to encourage Europe to defend itself by giving it an assurance that the United States would immediately be drawn into any new European war. The theory was that Europe could succeed in defending itself if it were united; it needed the American assurance in order to gain time and confidence for unification to proceed. It is difficult, decades later, to recapture the faith and hope that were put in a truly united Europe; without that faith and hope NATO might never have won the support of the Americans, who were among the most devout converts to the cause of European unity.

The alliance was deliberately limited in scope. One limitation was geographical. Article 6 restricted it to Europe and North America but, peculiarly, went on to mention Algeria and islands in the North Atlantic "north of the Tropic of Cancer." The French were so worried that the reference to Europe might be narrowly interpreted that they insisted on explicitly including Algeria, though it was then an official part of France. The Tropic of Cancer was dragged in to establish a definite southern boundary. As a harassed Acheson explained in further secret testimony, Alaska was in but the Panama Canal Zone was out. The Canary Islands were problematic, but Crete was definitely out. An American or French battleship attacked by a Russian submarine in the Indian Ocean was not protected by the treaty. Syria was offered as an example of a Middle Eastern state that was definitely excluded.[6] Later, when Turkey and Greece were admitted to NATO in 1952, the North Atlantic area was defined as extending from the eastern frontier of Turkey to the Bering Straits.[7] In effect, any crisis outside this area did not come within the terms of this alliance, the very name of which was made obsolete by the admission of Turkey and Greece.

The alliance was also limited in function. The Canadians at first wanted it to include cultural, economic, and social cooperation. Acheson found that the senators would have none of it.[8] As a result, Article 2 was watered down to promote "stability and well-being" and to encourage "economic collaboration," without any indication that anything had to be done about them. In practice, NATO has consistently ignored these vague sentiments.[8a] Efforts to use them to enlarge the scope of NATO, especially one by German Chancellor Konrad Adenauer in 1956–1957, have consistently failed. In 1957, a report by a NATO Committee of Three, known as "The Three Wise Men," made up of

Lester Pearson of Canada, Halvard Lange of Norway, and Gaetano Martino of Italy, advocated a much greater degree of political cooperation by enhancing the role of the NATO Council. Nothing came of it.[8b]

The United States may have reason to expect the support of Western Europe for its policies in the Iranian and Afghanistan crises, but not on the basis of this alliance. Indeed, it is even questionable whether the North Atlantic Treaty represented an alliance in any true sense of the term. We habitually refer to "America's allies," and the use of the term in this connection may be unavoidable, but it conceals as much as it reveals.

On the surface, Europe promised to defend America if attacked, and America promised to defend Europe if attacked. But that was not the reality. No one expected Europe to be capable of defending America; the problem was always to ensure the defense of Europe by America. To this extent, the alliance was hopelessly one-sided. The Americans, to be sure, did not enter into it for purely philanthropic reasons. They acted on the assumption that European independence and recovery were essential to American security and well-being; that another war in Europe was sure to drag the United States in anyway; and that the best way to prevent such a war from breaking out was to make sure that everyone knew the United States would be in it from the outset. Nevertheless, the alliance was strictly Europe-centered; the interest of the United States in Europe was fundamentally to keep Europe from being taken over or dominated by the Soviet Union and thus putting its enormous economic, technical, and other resources at the disposal of the Soviet Union. NATO was realistically intended to prevent Europe from being used against the United States, not to ensure Europe's aid to the United States.

In effect, the European members of NATO are allies in their own self-defense; they are allies in no other sense.

The question arises whether such a one-sided arrangement was ever a true alliance. "The distribution of benefits within an alliance," states a classic text by the late Professor Hans J. Morgenthau, "should ideally be one of complete mutuality; here the services performed by the parties for each other are commensurate with the benefits received." The ideal is seldom attained, of course, but the principle of mutuality is still essential in alliances. If "one party receives the lion's share of benefits while the other bears the main bulk of burdens," Morgenthau continues, "such an alliance is indistinguishable from a treaty of guarantee."[9] A decade and a half after the North Atlantic Treaty was signed, Dr. Henry Kissinger thought that it amounted to just that—"a unilateral American guarantee."[10] He was not the only one, and this view persists to this day, at least with respect to the strategic element of NATO's defenses. The alliance was certainly a unilateral American guarantee at its inception, and there is no reason to believe that it has ever changed in essence. The European end of the alliance was long accustomed to think of the alliance unilaterally, not without American encouragement, with the result that coming to the aid of the United States was hardly something that Europeans ever contemplated.

The transition of the North Atlantic Treaty from a mainly political and diplomatic structure to a predominantly military system, which came about after the Korean war of 1950, was originally demanded by the Europeans, who were not satisfied with a mere declaration of intent. Ironically, the French regime of the day, headed by Prime Minister Henri Queuille and Foreign Minister Robert Schuman, was most exigent on this score. Europe was too cold, hungry, fragile, and fearful to trust in a mere piece of paper; it wanted substantial evidence that the Americans would live up to their word and not come in, as Queuille put it, to "liberate a corpse." The Americans, especially the armed forces, were soon glad to oblige, and their own General Dwight D. Eisenhower was appointed NATO's first supreme commander. The French at different times have been the most extreme exponents of two contradictory European tendencies—to give the Americans military responsibility for NATO and to accuse them for that very reason of exercising "American hegemony."[11]

II

NATO has been a peculiar alliance—we will agree to use the term—for a peculiar military reason that Walter Millis, the military historian, once ascribed to a peculiar dilemma—that NATO's planners could not decide "what kind of war they were preparing to fight."[12] This dilemma is as baffling as ever. For the past three decades, it has been expressed by a succession of catchwords and slogans, such a "massive retaliation," "flexible response," "deterrence," and "stability." There is as yet no escape from them, even if the terminology is sometimes changed to escape boredom or feign originality. We need not refight the doctrinal battles that have raged over them, but the past, present, and future dilemma of the alliance is so deeply enmeshed in them that it is necessary to look back to see how the present impasse came about. Our interest is not so much in the military problem as in its bearing on the alliance.

At the outset, the kind of war NATO's planners were preparing themselves to fight could not be a war with conventional weapons, because Soviet Russia's preponderance in conventional warfare was so great that there would have been no point in fighting the Soviets at all. If atomic weapons were usable, however, conventional arms seemed to be superfluous or at best good enough for a holding operation until a decision could be made to employ nuclear weapons. By the 1950s, American military doctrine, somewhat reluctantly adopted by NATO, gave up fighting a conventional war altogether and switched over to the idea of nuclear war or nothing—the now notorious doctrine of "massive retaliation." This position implied that Europe was not going to be defended at all on the ground, or at least was not going to participate in its own defense. The implications of massive retaliation were so disagreeable that then Secretary of State John Foster Dulles, its main public proponent, had to back away from it almost as soon as he had propounded it.[13] By the end of the 1950s, the dilemma was excruciatingly acute—the next war could not be a conventional war and it could not be a nuclear war. What then could it be?

It was opportunely discovered, or at least believed, that the seemingly hopeless choice between conventional and nuclear warfare had an escape hatch. The way out was "deterrence." It apparently offered a solution to the dilemma that conventional warfare was unprofitable and nuclear warfare was unthinkable. The ultimate weapon, it now appeared, was not intended to fight a war; it was intended to deter one. No one then knew—or now knows—how to defend Europe without destroying Europe. No one then knew—or now knows—how to fight a nuclear war without destroying the nuclear powers. But if the purpose was to deter, not to fight, the problem was amenable to a relatively satisfactory resolution, as long as an absolute solution was not available. Deterrence for this reason has played such a large part in the military-political thinking of the past era, down to the present. So far as the alliance was concerned, however, the doctrine of deterrence hinged on American nuclear superiority and hence unhinged any mutuality inherent in the alliance. This more than anything else gave rise to the view that the alliance was really a unilateral American guarantee.

But nuclear deterrence unhinged the alliance in a still more disturbing way. The difficulty with deterrence was that it was soon seen to be mutual. If American atomic or nuclear forces could deter the Russians, Russian atomic or nuclear forces could deter the Americans. But deter the Russians and Americans from what? From a nuclear war or any kind of war? From wars between themselves or wars waged by other means and in other places? These questions hung in the air unresolved. In January 1955, the National Security Council foresaw for the first time the mere possibility of "a condition of mututal deterrence." By 1958, American military circles were familiar with the joint themes of "nuclear parity" and "mutual deterrence."[14] But what effect parity and deterrence would have on the alliance was much less clear and much less clearly confronted.

A new element was introduced in the second half of the 1950s. It was brought about by the development of intermediate nuclear weapons, placed in Europe but long enough in range to reach the Soviet Union. They were developed, built, and effectively controlled by the United States. These theater nuclear weapons or forward-based systems, as they were called, were intended to counteract the Soviets' advantage in conventional warfare without resorting to strategic or intercontinental nuclear weapons. The theater nuclear weapons, together with a NATO buildup of conventional forces, created the need for a new doctrinal move in the effort to escape from the straitjacket of all-out intercontinental nuclear war or nothing.

The new doctrine of "flexible response" posed a different kind of dilemma for the alliance, one no more reassuring than that of "massive retaliation." The new dispensation sought to combine conventional, theater, and intercontinental nuclear weapons in an indeterminate mixture depending on unforeseen circumstances. To have given "flexible response" a chance, it would have been necessary to build up NATO's conventional forces to within range of Soviet strength in this category. No such effort was ever made. It could not be made without knowing just what kind of war NATO's planners were preparing to fight. If it was to be a largely conventional war, it was bound to be fought mainly in Europe a horror which the European allies were determined to avoid at all costs. The addition of theater nuclear weapons to conventional forces promised to make it an even more frightful European war; it could be assumed that the Soviets would seek to take them out at once; and it was hard to believe that a nuclear exchange would stop there. If it turned into a full-fledged nuclear war, without the use of conventional or theater nuclear weapons, it would be fought over the heads of Europeans on Soviet and American soil.

. . .

The kind of war, then, determined whose ox was going to be gored first or last. The allies could not help viewing these options from the viewpoint of national interest and survival. Europeans ultimately preferred to put their trust in the American "nuclear umbrella" to avoid, at least theoretically, a conventional-plus-theater nuclear war in Europe. The United States put more and more stock in the buildup of NATO's conventional arms. In the end, "flexible response" was apt to be more flexible in theory than in practice; it all depended on how long a conventional war could be fought in Europe and whether Europeans really wanted another and more ruinous conventional war fought in Europe at all.

The doctrine of deterrence was so agreeable because it seemed to avoid all of these dreadful options. If the buildup of conventional and nuclear arms was necessary primarily to deter rather than to fight a war, Europeans did not need to care whether it would be fought in Europe and Americans whether it would be fought over Europe. Deterrence, however, had two disagreeable aspects. One was that it might not work, in which case it was still necessary to plan for fighting some kind of war. The other was that it encouraged Europeans to put their real reliance on American strategic nuclear weapons—the ultimate deterrent. The European reluctance to give up nuclear deterrence is another way of saying that Europe would like to be defended outside Europe if the deterrent should fail to deter.

By the 1960s, a new escape hatch—"stability"—was discovered. It implied that it was a good thing for neither the United States nor the Soviet Union to possess a military advantage. If a stable military balance could be achieved, neither side would be tempted to take advantage of the other, on pain of unacceptably destructive retaliation. Stability theorists took the position that Soviet strategic parity with the United States actually benefited the United States by committing the Soviet Union to the mutual-assured-destruction doctrine.[15] The Montague Burton professor of international relations at Oxford has expressed the view that "the old American strategic ascendancy" was "basically at odds with the requirements of international order," and that it was important for the Soviet Union to have undertaken "the task of balancing the power of the United States."[16] Unfortunately, it has come to be recognized that the Soviet Union does not share the touching Western faith in the stability of arms stabilization.[17] Even the Oxford professor had to recognize that the overall balance of power between the Western powers and the Soviet Union had apparently become less stable in 1978, though he could not resist the temptation to have it both ways.[18]

. . .

But what of the alliance? If a stable nuclear balance could be assured, the deterrence of nuclear war would at least in theory become automatic. The stability theory is thus the deterrence doctrine writ large. For the alliance, the dilemma of mutual deterrence would be extended indefinitely, not removed. The European allies could count less than ever on the United States' using the "ultimate deterrent" to save them. Even if it were credible, which is highly doubtful, stabilization is no escape hatch or nuclear panacea. Stabilization, like parity, is a will-o'-the-wisp because it means, in reality, repeated stabilizations at increasingly higher levels. The only way to stabilize once and for all is to put an absolute and permanent end to technological and scientific development, a cure that might be worse than the disease, even if it were feasible. It would also help the cause of stability to do away with the struggle for power.

One reason for bringing up all this is that "deterrence" and "flexible response" are still very much with us. They appear to be the poles of present-day military doctrine from which there is no escape. "Deterrence—The Countervailing Strategy" was the title of Secretary of Defense Harold Brown's most recent annual report [1981]. It affirmed that "assured destruction is the bedrock of nuclear deterrence," and that fully effective deterrence required an ability to respond "at a level appropriate to the type and scale of a Soviet attack."[19] Whatever problems were posed by "massive retaliation" and "flexible response" for the alliance in the past are not likely to go away in the future.

The very nature of the alliance dictated that the issue of nuclear versus any other kind of war should be the heart of the matter. The issue is not as abstruse or esoteric as nuclear-arms experts like to make it. The grand lines of strategy have always been recognized as relatively simple and fundamental, however complicated the tactics or technology may be to carry them out. There is nothing mysterious or incomprehensible about what makes nuclear weapons different strategically from all previous innovations in weaponry. The difference lies in the level of destructiveness. The unimaginable horror of that level is what makes nuclear weapons unique. In all past history, new weapons, such as the machine gun and the tank, were used to wage wars, not to deter them. The doctrine of deterrence applied to nuclear weapons implies that they are so destructive that they cannot be used for any rational political purpose, based on any calculation of more gain than loss. Such a weapon is different in kind, not merely in degree. Yet the temptation to figure out some way to use nuclear arms in actual war never seems to go away.

By now, however, it is clear that nuclear arms can at best deter nuclear war only. They cannot deter any other kind of conflict. The struggle for power goes on, and is obviously going on, below the level of nuclear war. A position of dominance in world affairs may be established by a power or group of powers using force considerably short of the level of nuclear war; and a position of inferiority may be suffered without its going so far as self-destruction. Even as a last resort, suicide is not a rational or inevitable course. The idea that the struggle for power must escalate to nuclear war is a form of political blackmail put forward, especially in the United States, as a means of persuasion to give up the struggle for power altogether. Yet as long as the struggle for power persists, the danger of nuclear war cannot be ruled out.

The paradox of the alliance is that it was founded on the American monopoly of atomic arms. Such weapons have also been its unbearable burden and dilemma.

The contradictions that have beset the European-American alliance from the outset were recently expressed with admirable candor by Sir Hermann Bondi, formerly chief scientific advisor to the Ministry of Defense and at present chief scientist at the Department of Energy of the United Kingdom. "Turning to 1949 and the origins of NATO," he recalled, the American guarantee to protect Western Europe "gave many of us in Europe a slightly uncomfortable feeling. One certainly wants to be protected, but it was at that time a very one-sided relationship." It was one-sided, he explained, because the American guarantee was not given as a matter of necessity; Europe was then too poor and weak to count for much in the balance. But now the industrial resources of Western Europe had grown to such importance that the military balance would probably become impossible to maintain "if those resources were directly or indirectly to fall under Soviet domination." He reasoned that the European-American relationship had thus become two-sided— not because Europe was contributing its share but because Soviet control of Europe's resources would tip the balance against the United States. This new two-sidedness had less to do with Europe's contribution to its own defense than to Europe's potential contribution to Soviet superiority.

Bondi recognized that the Soviets enjoyed a decisive superiority in conventional arms. Indeed, he thought it was a "curious situation" that this disproportion in conventional arms had come about "in view of the fact that the West has twice the population and three times the gross national product of the Soviets." The only possible explanation, he suggested, was that the Soviets were spending "markedly more" on defense than the 12 percent of their gross national product generally ascribed to them. But not to worry, he said—"it is not a cause for worry that the Soviets have more artillery or tanks than we have." His reasoning may take us to the heart of the matter.

A "nightmare" afflicted Europe, he said. It was the nightmare of a "limited liability war." Examples of such a war were Great Britain's Opium War with China and the American war in Vietnam. In both cases, Britain and the United States were able to limit the liability of the war on their side, whereas China and Vietnam could not. It all depended on which side was on the "receiving end." In war with the Soviet Union, Europe was now in the position of the "receiving end," knowing that "the other side can and does hurt you and that you cannot retaliate in a way that really matters; that they can always end the action and you cannot." And so Sir Hermann told his American audience what this logic led to: "Any European sense of security would disappear if we felt that we could be at the receiving end of a limited liability war."

How to escape from this awful logic? Sir Hermann's solution turned out to be an old acquaintance. The possibility of such a limited liability war did not exist, he explained, for one and only one reason—"the deterrent effect of nuclear weapons" and, more specifically, "long-range nuclear weapons." The circle was squared, the contradictions disappeared, the disproportion in numbers of weapons and armed forces made no cause for worry. Deterrence was king again.[20]

This profoundly European view was enunciated in May 1979, thirty years almost to the month after the North Atlantic Treaty was signed. In essence, it meant that there had always been and still was a European understanding that viewed the alliance as having one supreme function —to enable Europe to stay out of a future war because the war itself was too nightmarish and unendurable to contemplate. The one sure means of achieving this end was American long-range nuclear weapons. There was, then, an isolationist side to the alliance from the European point of view—isolationist in the sense that the alliance was designed to isolate Europe from a possible war. The motive is entirely understandable, but it casts a peculiar light on the nature of the alliance. In order for Europe to stay out of war, the alliance had again become one-sided in its dependence on the American nuclear deterrent. No matter how much had changed, we were in 1979 fundamentally back at the beginning.[21]

III

It is richly worth reconsidering what those old warriors, Charles de Gaulle and Konrad Adenauer, thought of the alliance, for we are now in the presence of their successors, who are producing a form of neo-Gaullism.

De Gaulle's original program called for an alliance with the Soviet Union, not with the United States. In December 1944, before the end of the Second World War, de Gaulle had in mind, as he told Stalin in Moscow, a three-stage system. A Franco-Soviet alliance was to be the first stage, followed by Anglo-Soviet and Anglo-French alliances in the second stage. He included the United States in the third stage only within the general framework of the United Nations. De Gaulle's aim was then to form a bloc of European states to act as "the arbiter between the Soviet and Anglo-Saxon camps."[22] Inasmuch as de Gaulle regarded Britain as part of the Anglo-Saxon camp with the United States, his second stage of alliances with Britain lacked the verisimilitude of his first-stage alliance with the Soviet Union. An "arbiter" was hardly in a position to be an ally.

De Gaulle's opening move came to nothing. Stalin had no intention of dealing with de Gaulle as an equal or taking his advice. A ravaged, distraught Western Europe begged for American aid and, with it, American leadership. By the time de Gaulle had retired from office for the first time in 1946, his program had collapsed for lack of support from any quarter, including his own people.

But de Gaulle's second try, after his return to power in 1958, was more fruitful. In a show of nonpartisanship, he denounced the "two hegemonies" of Soviet Russia and the United States. He came to regard NATO as no more than an American appendage, demeaning to France. His goal was now a "European Europe," which partly included Russia, according to his formula of a Europe "from the Atlantic to the Urals," and totally excluded the United States. His "European Europe" was to be led by France in contradistinction to the "Atlantic Europe" led by the United States. To fulfill this vision, de Gaulle no longer took the direct route of a Franco-Soviet alliance. He now set out for the same destination by an indirect route.

The road to Moscow went through the suburbs of détente, which began to take shape in the spring of 1965. In February 1966, de Gaulle announced the French intention to withdraw from the military organization of NATO but not from the North Atlantic Treaty itself, thus keeping a foot in the door. In June of that year, he visited the Soviet Union to make official the new Franco-Soviet détente. At that time, Soviet leader Leonid I. Brezhnev thought the time ripe to come forth with a proposal for a European security conference including the Soviet Union but excluding the United States. De Gaulle himself soon made clear that détente was only a first step, according to his formula "détente, entente, and cooperation." A Franco-Soviet détente was not a substitute for an alliance; it might, depending on circumstances, be the first stage of one. There is thus in Gaullism a tradition of playing the Soviet card against "American hegemony." It is only one strand of that tradition; that this strand has reappeared in a neo-Gaullist guise should not be so surprising or mystifying.

Implicit in this schema of Gaullism were three limiting conditions. De Gaulle's willingness to take the risk of moving closer to the Soviet Union and further from the United States cannot be understood without them.

France, de Gaulle recognized, was no match for the Soviet Union. Before he engaged in the negotiations that led to the Franco-Soviet détente, de Gaulle undertook to arrive at a Franco-German understanding with Chancellor Adenauer. A Franco-German entente was the precondition for a Franco-Soviet détente. De Gaulle's German gambit was initially successful because it appealed to Adenauer's ardent sympathy for what was then known as European Union. The Adenauer–de Gaulle honeymoon did not last long, but it set a precedent for another Franco-German honeymoon in the present circumstances [1981].

The second Gaullist precondition rested on a determination of which of the two "hegemonies" was the weaker. It was a Gaullist principle to support the weaker of the two in order to create a balance of power between them within which a French-led Europe could operate most successfully. In de Gaulle's time, the Soviet Union was considered to be the weaker of the two, thus permitting France to lean over in its favor.

The third precondition of Gaullist policy assumed that the United States, in its own interest, was bound to come to the support or rescue of Western Europe in any serious crisis. For this reason, there was no need for Europe to pay for American protection that it could get for nothing or at least without the necessity of binding itself to the United States in a formal military organization. The presumption of American support, and the assumption that that support had in the last analysis to rest on the threat of nuclear deterrence, made possible the military withdrawal of France from NATO without ostensible sacrifice of anything that was really essential to France in the NATO setup.

De Gaulle, however, became increasingly dubious about the third point. In a notable statement in November 1959, he raised the question whether the atomic "equilibrium" between Soviet Russia and the United States could last. "Who can say," he declared, "what will happen tomorrow?" He speculated that the two superpowers might "divide the world" between them or agree not to wage atomic war against each other. He even speculated that one day the Soviet Union might annihilate Western Europe while the United States did the same thing to Central Europe.[23]

In another famous statement in 1963, de Gaulle went further. He acknowledged that France had to have allies but immediately insisted on France's need to have "the free disposition of itself," because alliances have no "absolute virtues, whatever may be the sentiments on which they are based." In the atomic age, France could be destroyed at any moment unless "the aggressor is deterred from the attempt by the certainty that he too will suffer frightful destruction." An alliance with the United States had once been justified as a means of preventing such an eventuality because the Americans had long been the only ones to possess nuclear arms. The United States could protect France when the former had had a monopoly of those arms and the will to use them as soon as Europe was attacked. Deterrence worked so long as these two conditions were fulfilled. But conditions had changed as soon as the Soviets had come into possession of nuclear weapons powerful enough to threaten the United States with direct destruction on its own territory.

"In these conditions," de Gaulle summed up, "no one in the world, particularly no one in America, can say if, where, when, and to what extent American nuclear weapons would be employed to defend Europe." Yet de Gaulle was not willing to give up the employment of those weapons altogether, for in the very next sentence he turned around and allowed that "this does not at all prevent American nuclear weapons, which are the most powerful of all, from remaining the essential guarantee of world peace." How those weapons could guarantee world peace or even peace in Europe without the certainty that they would be used he did not explain. In other statements that same year, he took the same line of questioning the reliability of the American nuclear deterrent without giving it up.[24]

In effect, de Gaulle reduced the European-American alliance from a unilateral American guarantee to a European insurance policy. The difference was that Europeans had put their trust in the guarantee as their first and only line of defense, not so much to beat back an attack as to prevent one; de Gaulle now wanted to have other options, leaving the American deterrent as a last line of defense if all else failed. His battle cry of "independence" gave France full freedom of action in every contingency except the ultimate one of nuclear attack; for that he reserved the right to call on the "alliance" with the United States for the extreme unction of nuclear deterrence. His juggling act was of the now-you-see-it-now-you-don't kind in which he manipulated three balls at once—one marked "Independence," a second "Alliance," and a third "No Faith in the Alliance." It was a dazzling performance—so long as de Gaulle was speaking to a sympathetic French audience.

As the French experience showed, détente and the alliance have a most uneasy relationship. De Gaulle's policy with respect to the Soviet Union immediately, inevitably, and drastically changed the French position within the North Atlantic alliance. The French détente was not merely a step towards the Soviet Union; it was also a step away from the United States. It is of the nature of détente, whatever else it may do, that it changes the existing balance of forces. The United States could not get closer to Communist China without getting further from Communist Russia. Making friends with someone else's enemy or rival cannot fail to be disturbing and even threatening. Détente is a seemingly innocent word that implies the spread of good will and peaceful intentions where they did not exist before. In the real world, however, its influence is not so innocent. It does not easily do away with the underlying, long-term enmities and rivalries; rather it indicates a shift, however great or little, in the lineup. De Gaulle's methods were open and brutal enough to make unmistakably clear that the lineup had changed. Whenever de Gaulle supported the United States, as during the Cuban missile crisis of 1962, he did so in order to prevent the balance of forces from moving too sharply in favor of the Soviet Union, not because he thought that the alliance required him to come to America's assistance. Détente was for him—and for the Soviets—a weapon, not a token of affection or reward for good behavior.

For all his special pleading, de Gaulle cannot easily be dismissed. He saw some things more clearly than others of his time and dared to speak out about them with vision and eloquence. He was justified to mistrust nuclear deterrence as soon as it had become mutual deterrence. When he wondered aloud whether the United States would use strategic nuclear weapons in the defense of Europe if it were open to similar nuclear destruction, he knew what he was talking about. But Gaullism should not be confused with neutralism. The ideal Gaullist world would permit Europe under French leadership to act independently of the two superpowers, using whatever means necessary to achieve its ends as circumstances dictated. These means might include siding with the Soviet Union or the United States, siding with neither, going off on an independent tack against both, or taking refuge in neutralism—but none of these as a matter of principle. Since all these options would depend on how much power was available to carry them out, the less power Europe or France could actually muster, the more likely it would be to fall back on some form of Swedish-type neutralism or even Finnish-type accommodation. In practice, then, Gaullism may be far more neutralist than it is in theory. A successful Gaullism would take a strong line with both the Soviet Union and/or the United States, as de Gaulle was wont to do from time to time; a failed or illusory Gaullism would run the risk of progressive Swedenization or Finlandization as it came under more Soviet than American pressure.

De Gaulle's view of mutual deterrence was not original with him. Its implications had already occurred to responsible Americans. In 1956, the Army's Chief of Staff, General Maxwell D. Taylor, had written an article, which he was not permitted to publish, in which he had held that, in the condition of mutual deterrence, "the only war worth preparing for is surprise, nuclear attack on the United States."[25] In 1958, the Army, Navy, and Marine Corps combined to advocate that "the United States and the USSR would be increasingly restrained from deliberately initiating a general nuclear war except where national survival was directly at stake." This view, which was at that time resisted by the Air Force, held: "This fact [of increasing restraint] had become so apparent that it was doubtful whether either the Soviets or our allies believed that we would use our retaliatory power for anything other than to preserve our own existence."[26] In 1959, the same year that de Gaulle first brought up the subject, Dulles' successor as Secretary of State, Christian A. Herter, testified at his confirmation hearing: "I can't conceive of the President of the United States involving us in an all-out nuclear war unless the facts showed clearly that we are in danger of devastation ourselves, or that actual moves have been made toward devastating ourselves." Herter also said: "I am sorry that the alliance does not relate to the whole world, but I do not think that is in the cards at the present time."[27] A different line was taken by spokesmen of the following Kennedy administration, especially by Secretary of Defense Robert McNamara. In 1963, he assured Western Europe that its defense was as vital "to us as the defense of our own continent," and that the United States was prepared "to back up our commitments there with our strategic nuclear power no matter what degree of damage might result should the deterrent aspect of this policy fail."[28] But ten years later, David Packard, Deputy Secretary of Defense from 1969 to 1971, was equally sure that "with the present nuclear balance the United States will not use its nuclear force against the Soviet Union short of a dire threat to the survival of the United States."[29]

Whom to believe? That was just the question de Gaulle had asked: "Who can say what will happen tomorrow?" No American President had ever faced such a decision. There was no precedent for nuclear war. The only thing sure about what the United States would do in the event of an attack on Western Europe and on Western Europe alone was that no one could be sure.

What did all of this have to do with the alliance? The answer depended on one's point of view. For the Americans by and large, with the exception of such heretics as Hans Morgenthau and the early Henry Kissinger, the alliance was safe in American hands. From the Gaullist standpoint, nuclear weapons, as General Pierre Gallois argued in 1963, made the alliance obsolete, because no nation would jeopardize its survival for others.[30] It was as if the alliance could hold together only so long as it was not put to the acid test. NATO, in effect, had begun to resemble the Locarno Treaty of 1925, whereby Great Britain and Italy had guaranteed the Franco-German and Belgian-German borders. "The treaty of Locarno," wrote A.J.P. Taylor, "rested on the assumption that the promises given in it would never have to be made good—otherwise the British government would not have given them."[31]

IV

Adenauer apparently began to worry about the alliance almost as soon as it was put together. As early as 1950, he thought it significant enough to record in his memoirs, he had asked an important American political figure whether the United States would use atomic weapons if Eastern forces invaded West Germany. The answer was: No.[32] The German chancellor became increasingly disturbed about the NATO alliance as a purely military structure. By 1956, he thought it necessary to change it into a more political instrument, by which he meant that a common foreign policy was necessary to make a common military policy effective. When he raised the issue with Secretary of State Dulles in 1956, the reply was nominally favorable to the idea, but Dulles offered an objection that then and later precluded any serious effort to do anything about the matter—that the United States, unlike Europe, had worldwide interests that other countries could not be permitted to constrain.[33]

In 1957, after the Russian "Sputnik," Adenauer's conviction that something had to be done to transform the members of NATO into political "partners" deepened. In December of that year, he wrote a memorandum that still seems to have lost little of its force. He criticized the United States for neglecting NATO politically because, he thought, the United States wanted to have a free hand in Asia and the Near East. Like de Gaulle but earlier, he wondered whether a President of the United States could really be counted on to employ nuclear weapons for Europe now that Soviet Russia had missiles with nuclear heads that could directly attack the United States. The lesson for him was ominous: "As soon as the people of Western Europe become more strongly conscious of these facts, the inclination to capitulate to the Soviet Union will presumably become very strong." He concluded that the NATO alliance would continue to have purpose only if it developed into a "political alliance."[34]

What the United States, alarmed by the Iranian and Afghanistan crises, now wants from its allies is just such a common foreign policy, a "political alliance," as Adenauer had suggested, albeit one that follows the American lead. The United States wants this kind of alliance to operate outside Western Europe. When Adenauer prematurely pointed in this direction, the United States held back; when the United States finally wanted to go in the same direction, Western Europe held back.

De Gaulle soon said publicly what Adenauer had written privately. The French had already had some chastening experiences with the Europe-fixation of the North Atlantic Treaty. As soon as they found themselves in serious trouble in Indochina, they wanted help outside Europe. In December 1952, the French cabinet adopted a resolution affirming that the French union "deserved" to receive support "without fail" from their Atlantic allies.[35] Two years later, the French government vainly appealed to the Eisenhower administration for air strikes to save its garrison at Dien Bien Phu. And in 1956, the Eisenhower administration not only failed to give help to the Suez operation of Great Britain and France but implicitly cooperated with the Soviet Union to frustrate it.

Americans, of course, thought that the French did not deserve support at Dien Bien Phu or Suez, but that was not the point for the embattled Europeans. The deeper issue was whether the United States should decide when and if the French or British deserved support, as in the future the French and Germans might decide when and if the United States deserved support. Two or more could play at that game, but the sides were then so unequal that the rules seemed to permit the United States to make all the decisions for the entire team. In any case, the United States refused to aid France and Britain outside the European area in their hours of need; and European memories tend to be much longer than American in these matters.

For this and other reasons, de Gaulle made at least two efforts to broaden the decision-making of the alliance. In September 1958, he proposed the formation of a directorate of the United States, Great Britain, and France to shape the global policies of their alliance. His proposal was generally received as a self-serving bid to increase France's power and was never taken seriously. Eisenhower's reply to de Gaulle's suggestion put him and France in their places in a way that must have deeply rankled. One reason given by Eisenhower was that the United States did not wish to give other allies the impression that "basic decisions affecting their own vital interests are being made without their participation"—as if the United States had not been making such decisions. The second reason had more serious implications for the future. Eisenhower also rejected de Gaulle's proposal on the ground that it was an effort "to amend the North Atlantic Treaty so as to extend its coverage beyond the areas presently covered."[36] The United States, in effect, was perfectly content with an alliance that formally left it with a free hand outside Europe without allied meddling, as if the day would never come when the United States might need allied support outside Europe.

Two years later, just before the Kennedy administration came in, de Gaulle tried again. On September 25, 1960, he made a more far-reaching proposal. He recalled that in 1949, when the North Atlantic Treaty was signed, the immediate question had been the security of Europe. For that reason, the alliance had been limited to Europe within "a very narrow zone of action." But much had changed in ten years. There were now possibilities of conflict and military operations outside Europe extending throughout the world, especially in Africa and the Middle East. Europe, and particularly France, had recovered economically and socially. An alliance narrowly limited to Europe was outmoded, and something more was needed. "We think," he said, "that, at least among the world powers of the West [by which he meant the United States, France and Great Britain], something must be organized, as far as the Alliance is concerned, with regard to the political and occasionally strategic conduct of the Alliance outside Europe, particularly in the Middle East and Africa where these three powers are constantly involved." He made the very preservation of the alliance dependent on its expanded coverage. "If there is no agreement among the principal members of the Atlantic Alliance on matters other than Europe, how can the Alliance be indefinitely maintained in Europe? This must be remedied."[37]

President Kennedy apparently did not know what to make of de Gaulle's proposal.[38] After mulling the question over for almost two years, he appropriated the general idea for a speech on July 4, 1962, in which he offered American readiness "for a Declaration of Interdependence" with a United Europe to form "a concrete Atlantic Partnership" that would also serve "as a nucleus for the eventual union of all free men." Kennedy was obviously taking no chances that anything would come of the idea, by linking it to a United Europe and inflating it rhetorically to the bursting point. The following year, Kennedy also spoke of building an "Atlantic partnership—an entity of interdependent parts, sharing equally both burdens and decisions," though he did nothing to share burdens or decisions.[39]

Others played around with the idea. In 1965, Henry Kissinger was sufficiently inspired by the Gaullist critique to take the position that the Atlantic Alliance needed "a common foreign policy" if it was to retain "any vitality." More concretely than others, he proposed creating "a political body at the highest level for concerting the policies of the nations bordering the North Atlantic." He suggested making this body the Executive Committee of the NATO Council with representatives of the United States, Britain, France, West Germany, Italy, and one rotating member representing the smaller NATO countries. The larger goal was "an Atlantic Commonwealth." In the book, *The Troubled Partnership*, which contained this uncharacteristic flight of wishful thinking, the critique took up all but the last few pages, when the need to say something "positive" and "constructive" apparently took over.[40]

The question, then, that arose back in the 1950s was: More than NATO—or less? It is the same question that haunts the alliance today.

v

The Atlantic alliance is being reduced from the European side by an upsurge of neo-Gaullism of both French and German varieties. As in the past, France has taken the lead, but Germany has followed more closely behind than it had ever dared in the past.

The foreign policy of President Giscard d'Estaing clearly takes its inspiration from the legacy left by de Gaulle. The controlling concept in both cases is that of an "independent" French policy. In an interview on May 23, 1980, Giscard was asked to explain why the French ambassador in Moscow was the only Western diplomat to present himself on the reviewing stand at the May 1 demonstration and why Giscard himself soon afterwards met with Soviet leader Brezhnev in Poland following arrangements so secretive that they betrayed an uneasiness that France's "allies" might have interfered if they had known about the meeting too far in advance. With evident rancor, Giscard replied that France had the right "to have an independent policy without immediately being accused of breaking with Western solidarity." He pledged himself to continue to carry out "an independent policy, in natural solidarity with our partners in Europe and in the world."[41] Independence always came first, with solidarity hitching lamely along.

For Giscard as for de Gaulle, "independence" is not enough. It must be an independence that enables France to fall back on Western solidarity if all else fails. Giscard's foreign minister, Jean François-Poncet, had the month before struck the same keynote of "an independent French foreign policy in its conception and in its practice." At the same time, however, he insisted that France was still faithful to the Atlantic alliance, though he denied that it was of the nature of "a protector and its protégés." He even spoke of the "solidarity which unites us with the United States" in the matter of the American hostages in Iran, while again emphasizing that France alone could decide what measures, if any, to take.[42] In this balancing act between independence and solidarity, independence decides what form solidarity will take or whether there will be any solidarity at all.

De Gaulle also used to reject Atlantic union in favor of European union without going so far as to break all ties with the United States. Yet the break after the French military withdrawal from NATO in 1966 between de Gaulle's regime and the post-Adenauer government headed by Chancellor Ludwig Erhard was, in the Gaullist view, precipitated by the difference of outlook between France and Germany with respect to the United States. De Gaulle's foreign minister, Maurice Couve de Murville, scornfully recalled in his memoirs how the West German government was "flabbergasted and terrified" at the prospect of following

"French dynamism, audacity, and independence," whenever the United States disapproved of French actions.[43]

The real break with the Adenauer tradition came at the end of 1966 with the so-called Grand Coalition headed by the Christian-Democratic Chancellor Kurt Kiesinger and Social-Democratic Foreign Minister Willy Brandt. They began the redirection of German policy that was consummated in the fall of 1969, when the Grand Coalition fell apart and Brandt took over as Chancellor with the Free Democratic party as junior partner. The new leitmotiv was made up of equal parts of *Ostpolitik* and détente. They performed as the ideological accompaniment to the Soviet-German treaty in August 1970 and the Polish-German treaty the following November. On the occasion of the first, Brandt made a notable address from Moscow to his compatriots in which he clearly signified that the treaty had decreased the distance between West Germany and the Soviet Union and had increased the distance between West Germany and the United States. The new balancing act between East and West was explained by Brandt in these words: "Our national interest does not permit us to stand between the East and West. Our country needs cooperation and harmonization with the West and understanding with the East." Brandt defined this "understanding" as a form of partnership: "Russia is inextricably woven into the history of Europe, not only as an adversary and danger but also as a partner—historical, political, cultural and economic."[44] These carefully chosen words unmistakably represented a basic shift in West Germany's foreign policy and foreign relations.

In this way, a German variety of Gaullism or in the beginning a German appendage of Gaullism came into existence after de Gaulle himself had left the scene. Chancellor Helmut Schmidt inherited this German neo-Gaullism, which he has been carrying out with somewhat more adroitness than his predecessor. Schmidt would no doubt like to have the best of all possible worlds—collaboration with Giscard's variety of Gaullism, the closest possible ties with East Germany, détente with the Soviet Union, and the continued presence of American armed forces in West Germany as human guarantors of the ultimate American nuclear deterrent. The trouble with Schmidt's program is that its pieces are not altogether compatible with each other; something may have to give way, as happened in Adenauer's time. Meanwhile, the juggling act goes on.

Schmidt enjoys one advantage that Adenauer lacked. Germany is no longer the weaker of the two in the Franco-German axis. Schmidt himself was recently recognized by the *Economist* of October 11, 1980, as "the most powerful man in Europe west of Mr. Brezhnev." Yet French neo-Gaullism needs weaker, not stronger, partners, and it may still be an open question who is manipulating whom in the Giscard-Schmidt combination.

In a remarkably revealing interview in February 1980, Giscard, like de Gaulle before him, put West Germany in a class by itself in the French scheme of things. France, it seemed, has a veritable *embarras de richesse* for its foreign policy. First, Giscard said: "We have an alliance, we pursue an independent policy, we also have solidarities." He spoke of the United States as an "ally," based on Article 5 of the 1949 treaty (mistakenly dated as 1948). But an alliance in the current French diplomatic lexicon is sharply distinguished from an alignment. "France belongs to an alliance," Giscard explained patiently. "While belonging to an alliance, it is not aligned." In fact, there could be nothing worse than being aligned: "If France aligned its policy with one or another country, its policy would be simple, but it would cease to exist. France would become, from the external point of view, the province of a superpower." In addition to an alliance, independence, and solidarities, France had something else: "But the German Federal Republic stands in the forefront of our partners." Finally, Giscard said, France wanted Europe to play its pre–World War II role.[45]

The manipulation of such words as alliance and alignment is about as subtle as Giscard's policy is capable of becoming. What it means in practice is that, if France again finds itself in desperate need, it reserves the right to call on its allies for help. But if an ally needs to call on France for support, France can always refuse on the ground that it is not "aligned." An alliance that does not align allies has become one of the mysteries of the French language.

No one can object if France wishes Europe to play its pre–World War II role of being the center of world politics. The French and Europeans have the same right as the Americans to be envied and disliked by the rest of the world for having too much power. The United States is hardly in a position to be grudging or sanctimonious. The only question is whether Europe can reproduce the pre–World War II conditions, especially its relations with Soviet Russia and the United States, that enabled it to play a preeminent role. In that case, Europe would not need détente with Russia or alliance with the United States, least of all the ultimate military protection that it craves. It would seem elementary that, if Europe wishes to play a greater role in global politics, it had better get itself greater global power. Instead, the French vision of Europe is filled with a cornucopia of substitutes for power—alliance, independence, solidarities, nonalignment, partners, détente, America's nuclear deterrent, and a dream of pre–World War II global hegemony.

De Gaulle was a premature Gaullist. Europe did not have the economic, political and military resources to back him up. France by itself was helpless. As a result, de Gaulle tried to make up in acts of will what France lacked in instruments of power. Giscard d'Estaing was not a Gaullist in de Gaulle's time; he has rehabilitated Gaullism because the conditions for its reemergence were ripe for him. The resurgence of Gaullism without de Gaulle suggests that Gaullism was not merely the emanation of one man, that it had authentic roots in French and European conditions, and that, as an expression of independence from the United States, Gaullism can also take a German or other European form. The difference is that de Gaulle expounded Gaullism with nobility and passion; Giscard's Gaullism is intellectually dull and mediocre.

There is one other marked similarity. De Gaulle was paid off by the Soviets for his independence from the United States in that he did not have to worry about the threat of the French Communists. They were neutralized by de Gaulle's foreign policy, which they were careful not to denounce. Giscard is benefiting from the same benevolence. So long as his foreign policy sufficiently pleases Soviet Russia, the French Communists will continue to aim their main fire at the French Socialists rather than at the real holders of power.

Gaullism was the solvent that first began to dissolve the Atlantic alliance. French Gaullism by itself could be isolated and ignored. Franco-German Gaullism commanding the heart of Western Europe can neither be isolated nor ignored. It is an incipient alliance which is still too shy to call itself by its right name.

Despite his debt to the prime Gaullist principle of French "independence" in foreign policy, Giscard has never been accepted by the Gaullist Old Guard. They have regarded him as an interloper who came too late with too little to the true faith. Once in power, he succeeded in stealing much of their political thunder without giving due credit to the hallowed source. Yet Giscard has been sufficiently Gaullist to keep them in a state of fuming frustration. They have been reduced to complaining that he has not been firm and daring enough in his foreign policy owing to his evasive and furtive style. They have complained that he has violated the Gaullist principle of siding with the weaker of the two superpowers, meaning that he has been too pro-Soviet despite their judgment that the United States has become the weaker of the two. In this case, Giscard's fault is that he has remained only too faithful to the letter of de Gaulle's legacy, though it is anyone's guess what de Gaulle himself would have done in the present circumstances. De Gaulle's own tactics were flexible and changeable enough to provide plenty of scope for his successors to differ over how to apply the basic Gaullist strategy. To add injury to insubordination, Giscard has thwarted the presidential aspirations of Michel Debré, Jacques Chirac, and other officially anointed Gaullists. Perhaps anything could be forgiven but that.

VI

What role is left for the United States? The answer used to be clear and simple—if the United States, as the saying goes, sneezed, its allies took out their handkerchiefs. But that day has passed. Whatever "American leadership" means today, it does not mean what it once meant.

When did it end? How long did it take for the United States to recognize that its role had changed?

There has been no end of ends of an era. The prize for the earliest end of the American era undoubtedly goes to Professor Andrew Hacker. He had it coming to an end "ever since the closing days of the Second World War." If we take him seriously, it almost never began. By 1970, he had America's "terminal hour" arriving; the United States was not even capable "of being a great power" any more. As if this were not enough, he recorded that "America's history as a nation has reached its end." His book, as one might suspect, is called *The End of the American Era*,[46] though it is not clear why it is not called *The End of America*.

Ronald Steel came a close second. He had the "American Century" lasting "barely a few months," because it could not survive "the collapse of great-power unity." He did not explain why, in that case, it should be called the "American Century" if it did not last a century. Why not the "American Months"? By 1967, he saw America and Russia as the two nuclear giants whose days "seem to be numbered" and who were "in the declining days of their condominium." At the same time, he maintained that the United States was still "currently *the* world power."[47]

Others have been less drastic. Henry Brandon, the veteran British correspondent in Washington, thought that confidence in American leadership "began to sag" during the Eisenhower administration. In 1973, American power was still retreating, "faster than any other in modern history—faster even than the British or the French retreated from their imperial role."[48] The period of American hegemony, according to Henry Kissinger, came to an end in the late 1950s and early 1960s.[49] In perhaps the most acute of end-of-the-era books, the late Alastair Buchan seemed to share the view of Europeans for whom, he noted, "the days of unquestioned respect for American political, intellectual and social leadership were over" some time in the 1960s.[49a] The most optimistic estimate seems to be that of C.J. Bartlett, who ended the American era in the mid-1970s.[50] The only thing on which apparently everyone agrees is that it has come to an end.

Official admissions of this sort go back at least as far as President Kennedy, though he can be quoted on both sides of the issue. In 1961, he told the American people to face the fact that "the United States is neither omnipotent nor omniscient," and "there cannot be an American solution to every world problem."[51] Presumably, the United States had previously considered itself omnipotent and omniscient with an American solution to every world problem and needed to be admonished that that era had come to an end. But this comedown did not mean that Kennedy was willing to give up assuming responsibility for freedom everywhere. In 1963, he called on his generation to recognize that it was "by destiny rather than choice—the watchman on the walls of world freedom."[52]

It took another decade for an American president to give up the status of "dominance" within the Western alliance. Nixon did so in terms that also reflected on American behavior in the past when he acknowledged that "the United States had led without listening, talked *to* our allies instead of *with* them, and informed them of new departures instead of deciding with them." By early 1970, Nixon announced that the time had come to move "from dominance to partnership."[53] None of this newfound enthusiasm for partnership was original. Kennedy had already in the previous decade held out to the European allies such phrases as "partners in aid, trade, defense, diplomacy, and monetary affairs," "a partner with whom we could deal on a basis of full equality," "a full and equal partner," and "partners for peace."[54] Phrases they were, and phrases they remained, until Nixon picked them up again. Nixon's own offer of partnership was soon qualified. In early 1971 he saw fit to assure European allies and friends that "the United States will continue to play a role of leadership, commensurate with our position in the world." He now offered allies "more nearly equal partnership" based on "sharing the responsibilities of leadership."[55] These formulas were slippery enough to mean anything or nothing, mainly nothing. Something had clearly changed in the relations among the allies, but what and how much were not so clear.

The difficulty of moving from dominance to partnership, as Kissinger had once loftily advised President Kennedy, is that "real partnership is possible only between equals."[56] Partnerships with senior and junior partners tend to give juniors the privilege of obeying the seniors. If the partnership were really between equals, it might last just as long as their interests were equal and the same—a condition not often encountered in the real world. Real partnership is not the only thing possible between equals; independence and antagonism are not only possible—they are probable. These contradictions and paradoxes of alliances would be easier to deal with if nations were single-minded in their aims and interests. In fact, nations pursue a variety of aims and interests, not usually compatible with each other. Substituting partnership for dominance in the American diplomatic vocabulary was more a matter of form than of substance.

Subsequently, the Nixon-Kissinger policy toward the alliance differed from that of the past, but not in the way it was advertised. Partnership continued to be just as far away as ever. Instead, the United States bore down less heavily on Europe because the United States ignored Europe now. Embroiled in the Vietnam war, the Nixon administration had little time or mind for anything else. Nixon admitted as much in 1971 when he said that the tendency had for five to six years past been "for us to obscure our vision almost totally of the world because of Vietnam."[57] Kissinger told President Nguyen Van Thieu of South Vietnam in 1972 that the United States had for the past four years "mortgaged our whole foreign policy to the defense of one country."[58] The United States had no claim on Europe to take part in the Vietnam war because it was far outside the limits set by the North Atlantic Treaty, and Europe had no claim on American attention because Vietnam was all-absorbing and all-consuming.

Another reason why the alliance changed very little during the Nixon-Kissinger years was the division of labor allotted to it in American policy. It had long been an axiom of American policy that the United States was the only power in the alliance able and willing to bear global responsibilities, and that its European "partners" were supposed to mind their own business except where Europe itself was directly concerned.[59]

The policy was restated by Kissinger in his "Year of Europe" speech in 1973: "The United States has global interests and responsibilities. Our European allies have regional interests."[60] Kissinger had played variations on this theme ever since 1965.[61] As American foreign policy increasingly turned towards the "underdeveloped," "Third World" areas, Europe was left largely without a role to play outside itself. American policymakers complained that Europe was regional-minded, introspective, and provincial, and then they encouraged Europe to be regional-minded, introspective, and provincial to fit into American policy. When de Gaulle had tried to break out of this European straitjacket, he had been treated as an interloper, a spoiler, or a dreamer. After several presidents had suffered from his bitter protests and unsolicited advice, President Johnson had decided simply to ignore him as the best way to deal with his irritating presence.

Still, the Nixon-Kissinger revision of American policy did make some difference in American policy vis-à-vis the European allies. It told them that they could not expect the United States to carry the entire burden in their defense, that they had to expect less from the United States, which had to divert more of its hard-pressed resources elsewhere. It did not ask the Europeans to do more for the United States outside Europe, for that would have cut the ground from under the principle that the United States had global and Europe only regional interests and responsibilities. Such suggestions as were made about a wider role for Europe were so vague and general that no one took them seriously. Yet American politicians continue to rediscover the virtues of "partnership," as if it were an infallible remedy for what ailed and ails the Western alliance. On July 23, 1980, Representative John B. Anderson, the forlorn presidential aspirant, came back from a trip abroad lasting all of twelve days and immediately called for reshaping the alliance into a "union of equal partners," as if he had thought it up all by himself and no one had thought of it before.[62]

Kissinger himself acutely reflected American ambivalence towards its European allies. Until 1969, when his White House years began, he was one of the most sympathetic academic protagonists of Europe. He had advocated a change "from tutelage to equality," and his visionary "Atlantic commonwealth" went far beyond the terms of the Atlantic alliance. Once in office, however, Kissinger found the Europeans just as frustrating and exasperating as his predecessors had. The global-regional distinction that he made in his "Year of Europe" speech came too late to be received in Europe without resentment and defiance. It did not take long for the Europeans to annoy the United States by stretching out beyond their region to the Middle East and beyond, either by going their own way or by refusing to go along with the United States. Familiarity apparently bred contempt, because Kissinger's memoirs do not deal kindly with the European allies. Of NATO, he wrote that it was "an accidental array of forces in search of a mission." About the prospect of nuclear war, he makes this biting observation:

> They [the European allies] wanted to make the Soviet Union believe that any attack would unleash America's nuclear arsenal. If the bluff failed, however, they were not eager to have us implement the threat on their soil. Their secret hope, which they never dared to articulate, was that the defense of Europe would be conducted as an intercontinental nuclear exchange over their heads; to defend their own countries, America was invited to run the very risk of nuclear devastation from which they were shying away.[63]

America's secret hope, Kissinger might have added, was that the defense of the United States would be conducted in or through Europe —or at least anywhere but in the United States. The two secret hopes did not make for secret confidence between the United States and its allies.

Kissinger's successor as assistant for national security affairs, Dr. Zbigniew Brzezinski, has had still a different view of the place of the alliance in American policy. Brzezinski had for years promoted a theory that sought to replace the Atlantic community with a "larger conception." It envisaged "a future cooperative community, involving eventually four major units, America and Russia as the peripheral participants, and West and East Europe as the two halves of the inner cores (in time perhaps becoming still more closely linked). . . ." He maintained that this cooperative community "would promote a more constructive and politically appealing image of tomorrow than a troubled Western partnership." The Atlantic community could be but one component in this East-West-Soviet-American "partnership," first put forward by him in 1965.[64]

Two years later, Brzezinski again envisaged the ultimate objective as "a world of cooperative communities," including this time Japan as well as the United States, Western Europe, Eastern Europe, and the Soviet Union. Communism, according to Brzezinski, was now "dead" in the sense that "it was no longer capable of mobilizing unified global support," though how it could be said to be "dead" if it was still able to mobilize something less than global support he did not explain. As for the "Atlantic concept," it would have to adapt itself "to the post-cold war era," which he assumed had come into its own. In this period, the Western alliance as such clearly had no signficant or secure place in Brzezinski's scheme of things.[65]

By 1968, Brzezinski cut the ground from under the original and still accepted raison d'être of the alliance—to protect its members against the real or potential threat of the Soviet Union. For the rest of the century, he announced, the United States was less likely to be concerned with "fighting communism." In quasi-utopian fashion, he gave the United States the task of "helping to develop a common response with the rest of mankind to the implications of a truly new era."[66] This new era was Brzezinski's version of the by now familiar postindustrial society, to which he gave a more pretentious title, the "technetronic age," a name which never caught on. In his book on the subject, he considered that the Atlantic world or concept was "now historically and geographically limited" and had to be replaced by "a broader, more ambitious, and more relevant approach." He now wanted "a community of the developed nations" because it was "historically more relevant" than the Atlantic community.[67]

In 1973, the year in which Brzezinski godfathered the Trilateral Commission, to which Jimmy Carter was an early recruit, his two basic premises again directed attention away from the Western alliance. The first held that "the primacy and centrality of American-Soviet conflicts has ended." The second replaced Europe with Asia as potentially the more dangerous to the international order.[68] If Brzezinski was right, the Western alliance was located in the wrong place, without a real opponent to be allied against. In any case, it is clear where President Carter derived the inspiration for the much-quoted statement at Notre Dame on May 22, 1977, that "we are now free of that inordinate fear of communism." Brzezinski had been trying to rid the United States of the inordinate fear of communism, especially as embodied in the Soviet Union, for at least a decade. If the Soviet invasion of Afghanistan in 1979 made Brzezinski as well as his chieftain suddenly and dazzlingly see the light out of the East in its true intensity, the revelation was so sudden and dazzling because it had reversed their whole system of belief about the Soviet Union and its candidature for the world's cooperative community. Those who have written about Brzezinski's inveterate anti-Soviet hawkishness seem never to have read what he had written, often and at length.

Thus, two successive assistants for national security affairs, the chief intellectual conceptualizers in two administrations, had found no real or important place for the alliance. Yet the worst crisis that can befall a nation is the one at home, and the crisis of the alliance was, historically, culturally, politically, and spiritually, a crisis at home. While the United States was neglecting Europe and Europe was pulling away from the United States, the common European-American heritage was falling apart. The primacy and centrality of American-Soviet conflicts are never so acute and critical as when they move into the European arena. Yet for the eight years of the Nixon-Kissinger-Ford regime and the first three years of the Carter-Brzezinski regime, Europe was the aggrieved stepchild of American policy. Worst of all, theories such as Brzezinski's had long tried to persuade American policymakers that the Soviet-American conflict and the European connection were less important than they had long been and were long to be.

VII

European allies who have criticized American foreign policy makers for their ineptitude and instability have had more than enough reason to complain. From a longer perspective, however, the trouble goes much deeper; its roots cannot be found in individuals or individual decisions. More important than anything else are the structural changes that have taken place since the alliance was formed. These can be understood and heeded; they cannot be repealed, no matter who is in the White House or State Department.

One of the most far-reaching structural changes has been economic. At the end of the Second World War, the United States had a virtual monopoly of the world's productive capacity and monetary reserves. One estimate put Great Britain and France at no more than 6 or 7 percent of the "free world's power" in the 1950s and the United States at 70 percent.[69] In the ten-year period 1946–1955, the U.S. trade surplus was so great that the current-account deficit of the world with the United States reached $38 billion, with almost the entire deficit occurring in 1946–1949.[70] Looking back at 1946, a veteran American foreign correspondent recalled in wonder: "The United States was not just a super-power; it was the monopower of the earth."[71] Exaggerations of this kind were common; only the United States emerged from the war immensely strengthened; the rest of the world including Soviet Russia appeared to be hopelessly devastated or at least mutilated.

The first danger signals came early enough to have given plenty of warning. Europe recovered with surprising speed, helped by the Marshall Plan, but too quickly and too fully to be attributed primarily to American aid, no matter how large it may have been ($26 billion for 1946–1955). German production, the hardest hit by the war, almost doubled between 1949 and 1955. Europe as a whole went from a $7 billion deficit on goods and services in 1947 to a small but telling surplus of almost $1 billion in 1952 and $2 billion in 1954. By 1955, Europe's exports of goods and services had risen to more than two and a half times the volume of 1947. The then six Common Market countries more than doubled their reserves between 1958 and 1967; U.S. reserves steadily declined from nearly $23 billion in 1949 to about $16 billion in 1957 to only $7 billion at the end of 1960. The "dollar crisis" was born.[72]

If the alarm bell first rang in any one year, it was in 1958. It was the year of the first American postwar downturn. It was also the year the American balance of payments went into a permanent state of deficit. Arthur F. Burns, the former long-time head of the Federal Reserve Bank, described what happened that year to bring on the alarm:

> During 1958, imports rose sharply, exports fell, and our stocks of gold were cut by two billion dollars. More ominous still, foreign financiers, who hitherto appeared to have unbounded faith in American finances, began to whisper serious doubts whether the integrity of the dollar could be counted on in the future.[73]

The shock effects were felt the following year. The Eisenhower administration, nearing its end, was sufficiently disturbed to send Under Secretary of the Treasury Douglas Dillon to Europe at the end of 1959 to ask the Europeans to reduce their protective tariffs against American goods. As one unkind version preferred to put it, he went "tin cup in hand, to solicit contributions from the Europeans."[74] He asked politely, but the United States was still too proud and self-important to insist or twist arms. The urgency of the problem was hushed up by succeeding administrations in the interest of refraining from drawing back from America's international commitments and commanding presence in the world. By 1963, 95 countries and territories were receiving some form of American assistance. By 1969, the United States had 302 major and 2,000 secondary military bases abroad. Meanwhile, the trade balance had begun to shrink. By 1965, the first year of the massive intervention in Vietnam, the alarm bells should have been earsplitting. The war was ruinous to Vietnam, to the American political and social fabric, and to the American economic system. President Johnson's Council of Economic Advisers recommended in January 1966 that the war should be paid for by increased taxation.[75] Afraid that it would make an unpopular war even more unpopular, Johnson took the easier way out by resorting to "deficit spending." In effect, Johnson financed the Vietnam war with massive inflation. This in turn encouraged a massive rise in imports into the United States and a massive drop in American exports, which were progressively priced out of foreign markets. As the American economic system weakened, American multinational corporations invested more heavily abroad in what one economic historian called a "defensive investment" made "to forestall the relative decline of American economic and political power."[76] What was in part an American invasion of foreign economies was also a flight from the American economy.

One experienced financial expert, wise in the ways of politics as well as of economies, has chosen 1965 as the year in which the United States began to lose its dominant military and economic position in the world. If so, it was the worst possible year for the United States to get mired in Vietnam. The war convulsively accelerated and intensified a downward trend that was already evident but that could have been less costly and more controllable in a more normal period. One major victim of the war was the alliance, which could not remain immune during the next fifteen years when, as Felix Rohatyn put it, "I don't know of another major power that dissipated its leadership as rapidly as we have, across the board, because essentially our system is very wasteful."[77]

The result was a balance-of-payments crisis that finally could not be covered up or contained. The U.S. trade surplus began to decline sharply by 1967 and turned into a trade deficit by 1971. American productivity suffered, dropping in the decade 1960–1970 to the lowest percentage of growth of any non-Communist country (United States, 2.8%; West Germany, 5.5%; Japan, 10.8%). The U.S. Treasury's gold stocks, symptomatic of the exploding balance-of-payments crisis, fell from $24 billion in 1949 to $18 billion by 1960 and to $11 billion by 1970. In 1971, the United States found itself with its first trade deficit in a century. The American monetary system could stand no more pressure. On August 15, 1971, President Nixon ended the convertibility of the dollar into gold, bringing about the long-delayed devaluation of the dollar, which proceeded to fall by about 40 percent. The postwar era of the American economy had officially come to an end—if there is such a thing as the end of an era.

The United States had been asking for the cooperation and forbearance of its European allies in the economic sphere ever since the end of the 1950s. Little had been forthcoming, partly because the Europeans had their own economic grievances against the United States. Foremost among them was the European financial burden caused by the enormous balance-of-payments deficit incurred by the United States. The position of the American dollar as the European reserve currency had forced European countries to accumulate increasing hoards of dollars that were worth less and less as American inflation rose higher and higher. Europe, in effect, was made to finance a part of the American deficit. Europe complained of the dollar glut, and the United States complained of unfair European and Japanese trade practices. The abruptness with which the Nixon administration went off the gold standard in 1971 demonstrated that the United States had lost control of an international financial system based on the stability of the dollar and set up at Bretton Woods in 1944.

This structural change altered beyond recognition America's economic relationship with its allies. In the initial phase, the United States could afford to run up large deficits in its balance of payments while large surpluses were built up in Western Europe. The United States encouraged the creation of a preference area in Western Europe that discriminated against American goods. Japanese expansion was promoted even as Japan hindered American companies from entering the Japanese market. In the later phase, the American economy had hopelessly overextended itself. Its monetary system and key economic sectors could not compete even on equal terms. A decade after Nixon's devaluation, a former chairman of the Council of Economic Advisers was still convinced that "the United States carries on with an economic leadership out of proportion with its economic power."[78] He might have said the same about the political leadership.

Official recognition of the structural change in the American economy was long put off and thus made worse when it came. But coming down was much harder than going up, and the United States still has not come fully to terms with the facts. The conflict inherent in this structural change is, however, not between the United States and the Soviet Union; it is between the United States and its allies. The Soviets have benefited from it without lifting a finger.

VIII

The second structural change was strategic. It was directly related to the Soviet-American balance of power but rebounds against the American relationship with its allies.

The original military problem had been characteristic of the period of decisive American nuclear superiority. Despite this acknowledged superiority, the essential points had been made by former President Eisenhower—in 1953, that the new weapons had almost totally eliminated America's former unique physical security and, in 1955, that it was more important to have "enough" of the new weapons than to have "a lot more."[79] This line of thought, embellished by others, had later brought about the strategic doctrines of "mutual deterrence" and "mutual assured destruction," which implied that both the United States and the Soviet Union were equally endangered by the use of nuclear weapons. Yet the North Atlantic alliance had hinged on the ability and willingness of the United States to use nuclear weapons in defense of Western Europe if the ultimate need arose. The paradox of "mutual deterrence" —that it deterred the United States from deterring the Soviet Union— was recognized without being faced.

Nevertheless, so long as the United States was clearly and generally understood to enjoy decisive nuclear superiority, the paradox of an alliance resting on mutual deterrence was not psychologically or politically demoralizing. If deterrence were mutual, the emphasis could be put on the deterrence of the Soviet Union without enquiring too closely about how such deterrence would work if the United States were also deterred. The alliance struggled with its strategic conundrum, blew hot and cold, from massive retaliation to flexible response, and somehow seemed to survive.

The structural change came about with the recognition that the United States no longer enjoyed strategic superiority. Indeed, it is now debated whether the Soviet Union has gained strategic superiority. At best, the United States and the Soviet Union have sought to place themselves in a position of nuclear parity since the SALT I agreement. The alliance was never meant to function on this basis. Yet it had been coming on for some time, even though it has only lately aroused acute anxiety, mainly in the United States.

The strategic changeover came in the 1960s. The Soviet fallback during the Cuban missile crisis of 1962 apparently determined the Soviet leadership never again to be caught in such an embarrassing position in a state of strategic inferiority. Though President Kennedy continued to emphasize American strategic superiority, it is now said by one of his closest aides that he really agreed with Professor Raymond Aron that the Soviets had achieved strategic parity as early as 1959–1960, before the Cuban missile crisis, when they had begun to possess a significant number of intercontinental missiles.[80] In any event, the Soviet leadership was taking no chances and clearly intended by mid-decade to catch up and even surpass the United States. By late 1964 or early 1965 at the latest, it is believed, the Soviets set out on this course. At about the same time, American policymakers decided that the Soviets would be unwilling to pay the price for nuclear parity.[81] As a result, the Johnson administration decided in 1966 to build no more nuclear weapons and to limit itself to the improvement of existing weapons.[82] Just then, the Soviets were building new nuclear weapons and improving all existing weapons furiously.[83]

During Henry Kissinger's tenure in the Nixon and Ford administrations, the American response to the change in the strategic balance was to aim at nuclear parity through the SALT negotiations. Kissinger—or one part of him—was then convinced that the difficulty of conceiving "a rational objective for general nuclear war" on either side had made such a war most unlikely or at least much less likely than conventional wars, defined as anything below the threshold of nuclear war.[84] By 1976, towards the end of the Ford administration, Kissinger's State Department had made resistance to attack in Western Europe by conventional forces "central to a realistic strategy."[85] The swing away from reliance on nuclear weapons could hardly have gone further.

Out of office, however, Kissinger felt free to speak his mind. In September 1979 at a conference in Brussels, he shocked an audience of professional students of strategy with his brutal candor. He was certain that in the 1980s

> the United States will no longer be in a strategic position to reduce a Soviet counter-blow against the United States to tolerable levels. Indeed, one can argue that the United States will not be in a position in which attacking the Soviet strategic forces makes any military sense, because it may represent a marginal expenditure of our own strategic striking force without helping greatly in ensuring the safety of our forces.

He then stunned his auditors with some advice and a confession. He noted caustically that NATO had always wanted "additional reassurances of an undiminished American military commitment." Whenever the commitment was given, NATO ministers could return home "with a rationale for not increasing defence expenditures." If his analysis was correct, he went on, the words in the American commitment "cannot be true, and if my analysis is correct we must face the fact that it is absurd to base the strategy of the West on the credibility of the threat of mutual suicide."

Then came the confession:

And therefore I would say, which I might not say in office, the European allies should not keep asking us to multiply strategic assurances that we cannot possibly mean, or if we do mean, we should not want to execute because if we execute, we risk the destruction of civilization.

In other words, American leaders, including Kissinger, had been accustomed to giving the Europeans in NATO assurances that the Americans could not possibly have meant and which the Europeans should stop asking for because they merely forced the Americans to dissemble.[86]

A week later, at a conference in Stresa, McGeorge Bundy, Kissinger's predecessor as assistant for national security affairs, took a rather different line. Essentially he held fast to the original dependence of NATO on the American strategic "guarantee" of nuclear protection. It was still true, he maintained, that "the strategic protection of Europe is as strong or as weak as the American strategic guarantee, no matter what American weapons are deployed under NATO." The guarantee was nuclear, but its continuing effectiveness depended on keeping U.S. military forces in Europe and holding out a very evident risk that any large-scale engagement between Soviet and U.S. forces, "would rapidly and uncontrollably become general, nuclear, and disastrous."[87] We were all the way back, in fact if not in name, to "massive retaliation."

Thus Kissinger and Bundy represented in 1979 sharply opposed views in the conceptual contest over nuclear war. Bundy never explained why the American "guarantee" to Europe should unquestionably hold if such a war would inevitably be as general, nuclear, and disastrous to the United States as to the Soviet Union. Only one year later, Kissinger came out—not without some embarrassment—in support of a Republican candidate and a Republican party platform that advocated a return to U.S. "superiority," an objective in the nuclear era that Kissinger had long condemned as meaningless and even absurd.

If leading American thinkers are divided in their approach to the structural change in the military balance, Europeans are even more confused and confusing. They almost never know what they want, but they sometimes know what they do not want, which is usually what the Americans want.

The French, as usual, want the most for the least. The present regime, in the approved Gaullist manner, will have nothing to do officially with the way NATO or the United States handles its nuclear problems with the Soviet Union. But the French also wish to influence the course of events in a direction most favorable to French interests. So they hoot and carp from the sidelines about anything that comes forth without their direct participation. Thus, we are assured by a leading French authority, "the French to tell the truth have never liked the idea of détente between the superpowers and its corollary: arms control."[88] The French of course like détente madly, but only for themselves or other Europeans. When Franco-German relations are firmly controlled in Paris, the French want Washington to leave the Germans alone; but as soon as the Germans become restless about their security, the French want the Americans to demonstrate more determined leadership to reassure the Germans. When the Americans urge the Europeans in NATO to increase their conventional forces, the French see it as a ruse to downplay the American nuclear deterrent, the efficacy of which de Gaulle taught them to doubt. It is almost a French reflex to oppose what the United States wants, as they alone rejected the concept of flexible response in the early 1960s, without feeling it necessary to propose anything different or better.[89]

A most revealing exposition of current French foreign policy was made by Foreign Minister François-Poncet before the National Assembly in April 1980. He defended détente on the ground that it "has not prevented crises but it has avoided their deterioration." When crises deteriorate, as they have an unfortunate tendency to do, détente will no doubt prevent them from deteriorating even more. He then explained that French foreign policy seeks "neither to bow before an accomplished fact nor to participate in the escalation of confrontation." Having made clear what France was not prepared to do, he let France out of doing anything much at all because it "does not dispose of any other arms in the present circumstances than firmness and dialogue." He demonstrated this firmness and dialogue by holding that the Soviet invasion of Afghanistan was "unacceptable." But then what? Answer: "The question is not to know if the departure of the Soviet forces will be easy to attain. It is to know if it is necessary." Having come to this smashing climax, François-Poncet looked up, solemn and satisfied.[90]

. . .

Since entering into their special relationship with the French, the Germans have begun to sound as logical or illogical as the French. Or, to put it another way, the present German government wants to have its own Gaullism but without tears.

Détente has become almost an obsession in German governmental circles. In concrete terms, it means vastly increased trade with the Soviet Union and Eastern Europe, closer relations with East Germany, and a community of interest with France. In order to gain these benefits from détente, though, it is necessary to interpret it primarily in terms of German, or at most European, national interest. Détente holds out short-run gains that may be less promising in the long run. A strictly German-Soviet or European-Soviet détente holds the Soviets' European front quiet and stable while Soviet expansionism has a free hand elsewhere. Moreover, a German-Soviet détente may work at cross-purposes with German-American relations when a Soviet-American détente breaks down. These contradictory and dangerous aspects of détente present Germany with difficult choices that it did not have before when its options were far more limited. The German conceptualizers also have their work cut out for them if they are to make all the pieces of German policy fit together.

Take the case of Theo Sommer, a noted German political commentator and copublisher of the important journal, *Die Zeit*, of Hamburg, Chancellor Schmidt's unofficial organ. In an article invitingly entitled "Europe and the American Connection," he gave a fair account of what Europeans understand by détente:

> Most Europeans—with the possible exception of the British—have long believed that détente along the central front must be insulated against the effects of peripheral turbulence; that linkage was not only impractical but unwise. . . . Europe must not become an area of tension simply because there is tension elsewhere.

If Sommer had stopped there, he might have been ahead. But he knew or suspected that this isolationist or insulationist view of European détente might leave something to be desired by Americans. So on the very next page he offered a somewhat different version:

> A French-German axis of interest is emerging whose leaders are intent not on cancelling détente in Europe but extending it to the outlying areas, on continuing the dialogue with Moscow across the endangered European front while containing Russian transgression and aggression in Asia and Africa.[91]

Détente had now been given three functions—to insulate Europe from tension elsewhere; to be extended to outlying areas of peripheral turbulence; and to contain Russian aggression in faraway Asia and Africa. How could the Franco-German axis extend détente to outlying areas without getting itself drawn into the tension of those areas? And how could that lovely new détente and that horrible old containment—in Asia and Africa no less—be legally joined in political holy wedlock? The mind boggles. Yet this is an authoritative unofficial exegesis of Germany policy offered to the most informed American readers.

Or take the strange case of the neutron bomb. It is supposed to have the virtue of achieving its end without causing as much indiscriminate destruction as its predecessors. Inasmuch as the Europeans had always complained that they were not consulted about American military innovations even when they were intended for Europe, the Carter administration decided to ask its European allies for their opinions. This maneuver proved most embarrassing. As Marion Gräfin Dönhoff, co-editor of *Die Zeit* and long an outstanding figure in German political life, explained: "The Europeans, however, wanted the bomb but did not want to say so publicly." As for Germany, Countess Dönhoff reports: "But the Federal Republic wanted to be pushed into accepting it rather than openly come out in its favor."[92] President Carter decided that the bomb was causing more political trouble in Europe than it was worth, and its production was put off indefinitely.

None of the parties involved in the neutron bomb fiasco had reason to be proud of his performance. The Germans have charged that President Carter double-crossed them by failing to live up to a private agreement to go ahead with the bomb if it could be stationed in Germany and one other European country.[93] Chancellor Schmidt thought that his agreement to station the bomb in Germany was already such a political risk for him that the Americans should have bailed him out by accepting final responsibility for the decision. President Carter went through his usual flip-flop with more than his usual clumsiness. The deeper lesson of the neutron bomb affair was, however, that the Europeans wanted more political influence without accepting responsibility for more power. When the Europeans want something but do not want to say so publicly, they want to benefit if all goes well and blame the United States if all does not. It is a game that has lost its charm for the United States, which has taken about all the blame it can absorb.

The Germans have of late pushed themselves to the forefront of such troublesome problems, as a result of which they are getting more attention and less sympathy. Another contretemps arose over theater nuclear weapons or forward-based systems.

Chancellor Schmidt used the Alastair Buchan Memorial Lecture of the International Institute for Strategic Studies in London in October 1977 to make himself the spokesman for European misgivings about the SALT negotiations. It is little appreciated in the United States how greatly SALT has troubled European officials and observers. The fundamental premise of the SALT negotiations limited them solely to Soviet and American strategic weapons, defined as those that can reach the Soviet Union from the United States and the United States from the Soviet Union. This arrangement deliberately left out the medium-range or theater-nuclear weapons that could reach Europe from the Soviet Union and the Soviet Union from Europe. The Europeans, as usual, wanted a combination of incompatibilities. They insisted that theater weapons should be excluded from SALT. At the same time, they worried that, if such weapons were excluded, the achievement of Soviet-American parity as the aim of SALT would leave the Soviet Union with increasing superiority in theater-nuclear as well as conventional forces. Though both sides had deployed theater weapons ever since the mid-1950s, the Soviet Union had seized the advantage by modernizing and augmenting their theater arsenal first. The presumed balance between Soviet-American intercontinental strategic nuclear weapons and the assumed imbalance between the theater-nuclear and conventional weapons of the two sides set the stage for Chancellor Schmidt's lecture-sermon.

Schmidt bravely took on SALT. By codifying the nuclear strategic balance between the Soviet Union and the United States, he complained, SALT "neutralizes their strategic nuclear capabilities." By so doing, it magnifies "the significance of the disparities between East and West in nuclear-tactical and conventional weapons" in Europe. The principle of parity was "sensible," but it should not be limited to Soviet-American strategic intercontinental nuclear weapons. It "must" apply to all categories of weapons, that is, theater-nuclear and conventional. If it did not, Schmidt charged, SALT would actually endanger Western Europe:

> But strategic arms limitations confined to the United States and the Soviet Union will inevitably impair the security of the West European members of the Alliance vis-à-vis Soviet military superiority in Europe if we do not succeed in removing the disparities of military power in Europe parallel to the SALT negotiations.

This was refreshingly tough talk, aimed primarily at the Americans, who were implicitly accused of impairing the security of their Western

European allies by concentrating on strategic parity with the Soviet Union. Schmidt volunteered that there were only two ways, in theory, to correct the imbalance. Either the Western alliance had to "undertake a massive buildup of forces and weapons systems," or both sides had to reduce their armed forces massively in all categories. Unfortunately, Schmidt observed with regret, the Soviet Union had shown no willingness "to accept the principle of parity for Europe, as she did for SALT." The inevitable conclusion seemed to be that the Western alliance had to build up its theater-nuclear and conventional forces massively to equal those of the Soviet Union. Otherwise SALT was implicitly equivalent to the imperilment and betrayal of America's Western allies.[94]

The Americans, as it turned out, were delighted with Schmidt's recommendation of a massive buildup of European theater-nuclear weapons. In December 1979, NATO agreed to deploy 572 new medium-range missiles in Central Europe by approximately 1983. It would seem that no one should have been happier than Chancellor Schmidt and those Europeans who thought like him.

Ah, but nothing in this nuclear-war world is so simple.

The Soviets soon launched a campaign of intimidation against those Europeans hardy enough to entertain the aim of parity with them in arms. If NATO went through with the planned theater-nuclear buildup, Soviet propaganda warned, SALT itself would be threatened. Since the theater-nuclear weapons were produced and controlled by the United States, not Europeans, the Soviets considered these weapons to be as much a part of the American nuclear arsenal as the strategic intercontinental nuclear arms stationed in the United States or at sea. They had a point—the Soviet theater-nuclear weapons could reach Europe but not the United States, whereas NATO's theater-nuclear weapons could reach the Soviet Union.

The main European apprehension about a buildup of theater-nuclear as well as conventional arms is older and deeper. Such a buildup raises the spectre of "decouplement." This term refers to the European fear that the United States might prefer to wage a war against the Soviet Union, if it ever came to that, from Europe rather than from the United States. In order to use Europe as its main forward base, it would be necessary to build up the medium-range nuclear and conventional arms stationed in Europe. Instead, NATO has planned resistance to attack in Europe for ninety days in order to provide a period of deliberation before any resort to the strategic nuclear forces stationed in the United

States.[95] Any delay worries Europeans that they will be the first targets of Soviet attack and more particularly that it will be necessary at the outset for the Soviet nuclear forces to take out the anti-Soviet theater arms stationed in Europe. The stronger the forward-based systems in Europe become, the more incentive the Soviets have to knock them out at the earliest possible moment, and the more reason the Americans have to rely on them before resorting to presumably suicidal strategic nuclear warfare. The specter of decouplement is that of disjoining a future war in Europe from the American nuclear deterrent, with which Europeans want to prevent an attack on Europe altogether rather than to hold the deterrent in reserve until it could deter nothing but a Soviet nuclear attack on the United States itself.

An American authority has made this sympathetic analysis of the European fear of decouplement:

> Europeans are justifiably concerned about any decoupling of the fate of the United States from the fate of Europe. They are therefore concerned about any decoupling of U.S. "theatre forces" from U.S. "strategic forces" or any sharp distinction between "theatre" and "strategic" war. They may see this as implying an absolute discontinuity between the risks that the United States might undertake in the event of an incursion into Western Europe and the ones it might undertake in the event of a violation of U.S. boundaries. The Europeans would then tend to interpret American strategic policy as implying that the U.S. and S.U. [Soviet Union] homelands would be sanctuaries in the event of an attack on Europe and that the war would be fought out in Europe.[96]

This line of reasoning should be enough to show that the problem is objectively head-cracking; politicians, American or European, good or bad, clever or foolish, cannot be blamed for it. It is of a piece with the European dilemma, which has been described in these terms—"Europe wants a theater-nuclear posture that leaves the Soviet Union with absolutely no doubt that the weapons will be used in defense of NATO—and the NATO members with absolutely no worry that they will ever have to be."[97] The problem of nuclear war is inherently intractable, both how to wage it and how to avoid it. Now that Chancellor Schmidt has partially taken over the responsibility for negotiating with the Russians over it or at least the European portion of it, Americans should have a fine time watching him handle or mishandle its ambiguities, ambivalences, and contradictions as Europeans have for so long enjoyed watching Americans.

All of these variations on the theme of nuclear war testify to the structural change that has taken place in the military relationship between the Soviet Union and the United States and between the United States and its European allies. A French commentator has, as usual, defined the problem most clearly without giving any practical advice about what can be done about it: "Things were clear and simple when the United States took us under their own umbrella of deterrence and any Soviet attack against Western Europe would bring about a strategic response based on American territory. We now know that that time has passed."[98]

The third structural change has significantly altered the relationship between the United States and its European allies. It can, however, hardly fail to influence the relations between the Soviet Union and the United States as well as between the Soviet Union and Western Europe.

As we have already noted, such doubts or questions as there used to be about the U.S.-European relationship turned mainly on what the United States could or would do for Europe. What is new in the present situation is the growing doubt about what Europe can or should do for the United States. The changeover had been coming gradually, but it had reached an acute stage when the senior political commentator of *The New York Times* could ask, "Where Are the Allies?" as if they were supposed to be where we wanted them to be, and the President of the United States could publicly berate the allies for having failed to live up to their supposed obligations.

President Carter's litany of allied woes of April 10, 1980, may well be the classic American statement of the contradictions tearing the alliance apart.

> Nations ask us for leadership. But at the same time, they demand their own independence of action.
>
> They ask us for aid. But they reject any interference.
>
> They ask for understanding. But they often decline to understand us in return.
>
> Some ask for protection, but are wary of the obligation of alliance.
>
> Others ask for firmness and certainty. But at the same time, they demand flexibility required by the pace of change and the subtlety of events.[99]

The European response might go as follows:

If the United States had provided more adequate leadership, we might have demanded less independence of action.

The aid asked for from the United States in the realm of security, which is the only aid provided for in the treaty of alliance, has become more and more problematic. This aid in no way implied interference in European affairs in any other respect.

Past American policy itself restricted the obligation of alliance to European security.

Firmness is not the same as certainty, and flexibility is not the same as unpredictability, vacillation, inconsistency, and even incoherence.

When allies talk to each other in these terms, there is more than misunderstanding at stake. They have begun to understand each other only too well. The contradictions and incompatibilities in their aims and interests have become too flagrant to hide or disguise. An alliance made in response to one set of conditions is coming apart in response to another. The changed conditions have put the giver in the role of the receiver and vice versa.

Oddly, a leading member of President Carter's cabinet soon explained why the United States could not count on its allies to share the burden of defending Persian Gulf oil. "It's going to be very difficult to do that because the alliance, by its own terms, is confined to the territory of its members," said Secretary of Defense Harold Brown. "Moreover, except for the U.S. the forces are ill-suited for operation outside the region of the alliance."[100] The lesson would seem to be that, for purposes outside the region of the present alliance, the United States needed a different kind of alliance. For President Carter to ask for European cooperation so far afield as Iran and Afghanistan was sure to subject the alliance to intolerable strain. The alliance of 1949 was not suited to the crises of 1979–1980. As a result, the European response was in almost every case grudging, ineffectual, or hostile. Just when it was more necessary than ever for the Western powers to act decisively, they had never appeared to be so far apart.

IX

What lies ahead?

As for the United States, it is no longer governed by policy; it is ruled by necessity. Whatever its politicians say or promise, they have less and less control over events. The economic and military fat that used to give the United States a protective layer has all but disappeared. Global power must in any case derive from an adequate base of domestic economic power and depend on political acceptance of its cost.

As for the Europeans, their ideal world would be made up of three parts:

—Economic competition: unconditional and unlimited.
—Global politics: complete and unqualified independence.
—European defense: ultimate dependence on the United States.

There is nothing inherently wrong in these aims, singly or together. Every nation or group of nations has the right to pursue those policies that it considers to be in its interest. The United States has been doing just that throughout its history; its most philanthropic acts have been defended on the ground that they were also good business or in the national interest. The problem for Europe is not whether it ought to adopt this program but whether it can get away with it. How far can independence from the United States be stretched without breaking the ties that have bound them for almost four decades? How close are we to the point of no return?

In economic competition, that point has just about been reached. Europe is not responsible for the American economic decline. The basic reason for that decline is structural—too many years of vast and easy profits; weakening of the competitive fiber; an almost deliberate abdication in the mass-consumption industries, which had been the glories of the American economy; a decade or two of wrongheaded and short-sighted decisions by those who manage the American economy. European nations and Japan cannot be blamed for taking advantage of their opportunities. But in a contest for economic survival, blame is beside the point. A large part of the American economy must either recover its markets or go under; a considerable part has already gone under and must, if possible, be revived.

By 1980, the American business community could no longer hide from itself the acuteness of its crisis and the direction from which the main threats came. This unprecedented self-examination and its implications were reflected in American business organs, as two outstanding examples clearly show.

A full-scale trade war was part of the recipe for American economic recovery in the special issue of *Business Week* (June 30, 1980), entitled

"The Reindustrialization of America," the slogan of the 1980s. This leading American business organ first made a scathing indictment of the American economy and its managers. Some of its main points were:

—*Standard of living*: The United States was still first in 1972; it was fifth in the world in 1980.

—*Competitiveness*: American industry's loss of competitiveness over the past two decades had been "nothing short of an economic disaster."

—*Innovation*: "Frightening evidence" that the ability of U.S. industry to innovate "is slipping."

—*Basic research*: "a dangerous deemphasis."

—*State of mind*: A leading public-opinion expert, Daniel Yankelovich, reported: "The state of mind of the public is worried sick and in a state of panic."

—*Industries in crisis*: Automobile, steel, rubber, textile, machinery, metal-working machinery, consumer electronics, apparel, shoes.

—*Manufacturing exports*: In 1960, the United States had over 25 percent of the manufacturing exports of industrial nations. It lost 16 percent of its share in the 1960s and 23 percent in the 1970s.

—*Who was most to blame?*: The "managers themselves." They have become "business mercenaries who ply their skills for a salary and bonus but rarely for a vision."

After more of this, a program of American economic recovery emerged. Its main emphasis was on a new "social contract." One provision would entail a new trade policy that would require

the U.S. to renegotiate its economic, financial, and perhaps even political ties with Europe and Japan. America's major allies are now its chief competitors in global markets. Just as a new social contract is needed within the country, so, too, is a new international concord needed within the alliance.

The new American trade policy would carry a threat—"that if countries close off trade and investment channels for American goods the U.S. will retaliate by closing off imports and investments from those countries." The Computer Services Corporation was cited as an example. It had been waiting for four years to hear from the French Treasury about setting up a subsidiary in France, permission for which seemed unlikely. A new French plan for the 1980s, however, would put six entire industries, ranging from electronic office equipment to robots, "effectively off limits to new U.S. participation." At the same time, the giant French oil-drilling company, Schlumberger, was "freely buying up a dozen high-technology U.S. companies, such as Fairchild Camera and Instrument Corporation, without any resistance from Washington." The leading American trade competitor was actually Germany, the "world's most formidable exporter."

In the end, the prescription for American economic recovery called on the United States "to join in the scramble for world market shares, a crucial element in the 'export-led' growth strategies of Germany and Japan, as well as 'new Japans' such as Korea, Taiwan, and Singapore." If, as another postmortem put it, "scrambling to export" is what we are in for, it will be hard to distinguish from a trade war.[101]

Another leading business organ, *Forbes* (October 13, 1980), took the chemical industry as a text on American decline and European competition. Once upon a time, E.I. Du Pont was the world's biggest producer of chemicals. No longer; three German chemical giants— BASF (Badischen Anilin & Soda-Fabrik), Hoechst, and Bayer— outrank Du Pont. The German companies have invaded the American market, still the world's biggest, not only in sales but in the acquisition of American affiliates and by the erection of their own plants in the United States. The *Forbes* article poses the "big question": "Can the U.S. chemical industry stand up to the onslaught?" The article also recalls that the U.S. Seventh Army once marched through Hoechst's plant outside Frankfurt, and concludes on this note: "But who's marching through whom today?" The author conveys admiration for, not antagonism to, the German achievement. Yet the American business leaders who read *Forbes* could hardly fail to get the point—that America's most important ally in Western Europe is also its most important economic rival.

Even more irksome has been the American loss of huge foreign contracts to European allies for political reasons. Two outstanding cases have occurred in Brazil and Argentina. The United States had helped both countries to build experimental nuclear reactors in the 1950s. When they wanted to acquire more advanced nuclear technology that might also be used for weapons production, the United States demurred. A West German nuclear consortium stepped in to give Brazil and Argentina what they wanted. When the United States refused to provide a heavy-water plant to Argentina on grounds of human-rights violations, a West German–Swiss group promptly took over its construction. The president of the Brazilian state nuclear company happily explained why the United States had been outmaneuvered. "I don't think," he said, "the United States ever expected that another developed country would go so far in sharing its technology in a full partnership for our nuclear development."[102] In both cases, the West German decisions were as much political as economic. American diplomatic displeasure merely incurred the wrath of the Germans, Brazilians, and Argentinians.

The "scramble" for Soviet contracts has been even more disquieting. In 1980, Armco of the United States lost two large contracts to Creusot-Loire of France when U.S. government action prevented Armco from building steel mills in the Soviet Union. The French again took over a Soviet contract owing to U.S. procrastination about issuing an export license for an American gas-lift system in petroleum technology. After a joint Soviet-American undertaking to drill for oil in the Caspian Sea was held up, a French company replaced two American companies. The Aluminum Company of America was forced to withdraw from an agreement to build an aluminum plant in Siberia; this time the Klöckner-Werke of West Germany stepped in to replace the American company. The French and German companies claimed that their contracts called for different types of plants and products and, therefore, did not substitute for the Americans'. The Americans were not impressed, because the French and German companies were satisfying Soviet needs in their own way and because, in any event, the French and Germans would not have been able to move in if the Americans had not been forced to move out for political reasons.[103]

West Germany, moreover, has become far and away the Soviet's biggest trading partner. German exports to the Soviet Union rose from 2.8 billion marks in 1977 to 3.1 in 1978 to 3.6 in 1979. German imports from the Soviet Union rose from 1.99 billion marks in 1977 to 2.5 in 1978 and to 3.9 in 1979. Immense credits have made such trade possible. The total debt of the Soviet Union and its Eastern European bloc was estimated in 1980 at $65 billion, up from no more than $6 billion in 1971. At the end of 1979, Poland owed $20 billion, the Soviet Union $10.2 billion, East Germany $8.4 billion, Hungary $7.3 billion, and Rumania $6.7 billion. Poland, by far the largest debtor, owed so much that it needed loans to pay interest and principal on previous loans, a burden that took over $7 billion of Poland's exports in 1979 to carry. West German banks have risked most to finance the booming West German–Eastern European trade in the 1970s.[104]

There is such interweaving of the political and economic in all these transactions that decisions are made on the highest government level, sometimes against what the banks and other economic agencies consider to be in their best interests. The United States plays the same sort of game and complains when other countries follow its example but on their own terms. Political independence and economic advantage are, however, hard to bear from an ally supposedly dependent on American military protection. The life blood of every power, and especially every great power, is economic, and that life blood has been draining away from the United States. It cannot, at any rate, sustain the kind of sovereign style to which Americans became accustomed after the Second World War. It tells much about the seriousness of the American economic decline that so many American industries should now think of themselves as fighting for survival, not style. No economic war, with enemies or allies, can fail to have incalculable political consequences.

Western Europe's increasing independence in global politics, outside the NATO area, is another question about which there is no right or wrong. There is no law, certainly no NATO law, that says that Western Europe should not be as independent as it pleases in the Middle East or elsewhere. There is no international morality that requires Europeans to obey the political dictates of the United States, to which they deferred for so long. There is only the question of what such European independence is likely to do to its relations with the United States, assuming that Europe does not wish those relations to change too much or in ways that might damage Europe's other interests.

European independence almost always takes the form of independence from the United States. The trouble is that there is no shortage of other nations in the world that are habitually independent from and, indeed, hostile to the United States. Vote after vote in the United Nations in recent years testifies to that. When Europeans join the independence-from-the-United-States bloc, they make it almost unanimous. In a world of conflicts, there is no such thing as *Ding-an-Sich* independence. Every independence from one side leans over towards independence in favor of another side, sometimes by strengthening one side, sometimes by weakening the other.

European independence is increasingly isolating the United States. How far European nations have gone to isolate the United States was shown in two recent votes in the United Nations.

The first came on July 29, 1980, in the General Assembly on a resolution sponsored by Arab nations calling for the formation of a

Palestinian state. In November 1979, six of the West European allies had voted with the United States against a similar resolution. Only eight months later, all nine members of the European Common Market, almost the entire corps of nominal European allies, broke with the United States by collectively abstaining. The United States was left with only six other countries, including Israel, to vote against the resolution, which was passed with 112 yes votes and 24 abstentions. The issue itself had not changed all that much in eight months; what had changed was the relationship between the United States and Western Europe.

The second vote came a month later, on August 30, 1980, in the Security Council on a resolution calling on all nations with embassies in Jerusalem to withdraw them. This time the vote was 14 to 0 with one abstention—that of the United States. The Western allies on the Security Council, including France and Great Britain, had chosen to isolate the United States even more demonstratively than in the previous vote in the General Assembly. If the new Secretary of State, Edmund S. Muskie, was right, the allies had voted for an "unbalanced and unrealistic" resolution and had joined in attempts "not to advance the cause of peace but to restrain it." Secretary Muskie may have been wrong and the allies may have been right in their view of the resolution. But UN votes are rarely based on abstract rights and wrongs. They almost always represent national or regional interests. The United Nations hardly ever makes history, but it can register history that is made in the world outside. These votes were such registrations. Never before had European states so strikingly demonstrated that, in anything except their own self-defense, they had a political alliance among themselves, not with the United States. If UN votes are mainly symbolic, this was the symbolism of the vote on August 30, 1980. European statesmen could not have chosen a more sensitive area than the Arab-Israeli conflict in a presidential year to make clear that they wanted to stand by themselves in global politics.

If any crisis was made to order for allied action outside the NATO territory, it was brought about by the Iraqi-Iranian war, which broke out on September 22, 1980. All the Western allies had a pressing national interest in keeping the oil flowing from the Persian Gulf area. Indeed, the European nations had a stake much greater than that of the United States. France and Germany get half their oil from the Gulf, the United States only one-eighth. Yet when President Carter suggested a few days after the outbreak that the allied and interested powers should hold a conference to discuss the conflict, the immediate response from Chancellor Schmidt was enough to spike the proposal. The "most powerful man in Europe west of Mr. Brezhnev" chose to interpret the West German constitution in such a way that it forbade him to contemplate possible allied action in the Persian Gulf area. No more was heard of the proposed conference. No doubt more will be heard of the demand that the United States should consult its allies.

The North Altantic Treaty had not called for anything else, but neither had it foreseen any such eventuality. The founding fathers of the alliance had devoutly believed in European unity, recovery, and eventual independence. They had assumed that such a Europe would be able to defend itself and be better able to stand with the United States as a strong and loyal ally. What they did not anticipate was that after more than thirty years Europe would still not be able to defend itself but would use its increasing unity and recovery to make itself more independent of the United States at the expense of American influence and prestige throughout the world. European independence from the United States is only one side of the coin; the other side is American independence from Europe. American isolationism can make a comeback via American isolation.

Yet American isolationism is still the terror of Europe. It was abandoned so completely with the Second World War that even the disillusionment of the Vietnam war could not bring it back. It can, however, reappear in another guise—that of de facto isolation within a de jure alliance.

The most critical and painful aspect of the present reality is the problematic defense of Western Europe. It has already been noted that Western Europe was supposed to be protected by American atomic power in order to compensate for the Soviet advantage in conventional arms and until Western Europe could defend itself. The population and resources of Western Europe were theoretically equal to the task. The missing link was believed to be the political and economic unity of Western Europe, the necessary condition for its ability to use its manpower and resources to the fullest.

The original balance of Soviet conventional power against American atomic power was then unbalanced by the acquisition of nuclear arms by both the United States and the Soviet Union. As the hope for European unity faded and as it was replaced by the reality of a West European trading bloc, each member bargaining in its own interest and combining against everyone else's interest, Europe's relationship to the United States changed drastically. Thus developed the paradox that Raymond Aron has characterized with his accustomed lucidity: "The United States appears as a rival and protector, a rival in the economic field, and a protector from the military standpoint."[105] This duality was fixed by the mid-1950s, and it might have brought about a mortal crisis for the alliance if the United States had not then felt so confident that it could afford the rivalry and so pleased that it could play the role of military protector.

The facts of life are now that the American commitment can no longer rest on a treaty made in 1949 under quite different political and economic circumstances. The validity of the American commitment was always based on the American perception that it was a matter of unimpeachable national interest to keep Western Europe friendly to the United States or at least out of Soviet control and exploitation. This perception is still widely held in the United States, but no treaty can make it automatically operative. The question is how favorable or unfavorable the circumstances will be when it is put to the test.

Nuclear parity or superiority is no panacea because it is inherently unstable. Neither the United States nor the Soviet Union is ever likely to accept outright inferiority passively. The very search for parity or superiority implies a recognition of temporary inferiority or superiority that must be corrected by moving upwards or downwards. The quest for parity or superiority guarantees a nuclear seesaw, not a state of blissful nuclear equality. The mirage of parity is a standing invitation to escalation since no one can be sure what parity is or when it has been achieved. McGeorge Bundy has argued that parity has prevailed between the United States and the Soviet Union for the past twenty years and has proven itself to be an effective guarantee.[106] If he is right, the United States did not possess the superiority that it claimed to have had in all those years. Yet the figures emanating from Washington in most of those years were said to show clear American superiority. It apparently did not matter very much.

Parity—whether anyone really knows what it means for two such different military systems as the Soviet or American, and how it could be maintained whatever it means—cannot be the answer because it is illusory. The key to the puzzle of nuclear peace or stalemate may well be President Eisenhower's dictum—enough is enough. The point is worth repeating in his own words:

> There comes a time, possibly, when a lead is not significant in the defensive arrangements of a country. If you get enough of a particular type of weapon, I doubt that it is particularly important to have a lot more of it.

Eisenhower at that time was thinking of what was enough to deprive the United States of its formerly unique physical security. The long-range bomber and "the destructive power of a single bomb" were then enough in his opinion to produce a fundamental structural change in American defense. Curiously, President Carter made almost the same kind of observation a quarter of a century later about the destructive power of another weapon—but aimed at the Soviet Union. In his State of the Union message in January 1979, he declared:

> Just one of our relatively invulnerable Poseidon submarines, comprising less than 2 per cent of our total nuclear force, carries enough warheads to destroy every large and medium-size city in the Soviet Union.

That much power, multiplied fifty times, would seem to be enough of any particular weapon and make it doubtful that "it is particularly important to have a lot more of it."

The Eisenhower principle of "enough" may be defined in a general sense as whatever level of destructive power would make more such destructive power wasteful and unnecessary. Another test of "enough" would be the level of destruction necessary to deprive nuclear war of "a rational objective," as Kissinger put it in his less politically intoxicated days. Unless one assumes that the United States or the Soviet Union would have to have a rational objective to wage a mutually suicidal nuclear war, all calculation is vain, all bets are off. The concept of "enough" does not mean that the nuclear guard can be let down; one inviolate condition is that the ability to deliver must be ensured. But that is not the same as the competitive conditions of nominal parity. "Enough" needs no negotiations to establish alleged equalities or equivalences; it is not a numbers game; it is not determined by SALT-type bargaining. It has at least an upper limit determined by rationality rather than by competition. That limit may from time to time move up or down as technological requirements dictate; it would not change merely to keep pace numerically with the Soviet Union, which, in that case, would paradoxically possess the power to dictate American requirements.

McGeorge Bundy was right about the effectiveness of parity over the past twenty years—but the parity he had in mind was not that of numbers or correlations of different kinds of weapons. By "underlying parity" he specified that he meant "mutual destructive power." That kind of destructive power can exist whether the numbers favor the United States, as they did in the Kennedy years, or the Soviet Union, if that should ever be the case, or neither side. Any *numerical* change that leaves untouched the capacity of each nuclear superpower to destroy the other cannot change the fundamental strategic balance between them; a numerical change may save them money; it will not save lives. SALT-type negotiations will never bring about stable parity acceptable to both sides; they will merely register the progress of an arms race and periodically change the essential question from "What's enough?" to "Who's ahead?"

Yet Europeans shudder at the prospect of the failure of the negotiations; they shudder at a parity that inexorably implies mutual destruction; they shudder that SALT leaves them out; they would shudder even more if they had to take part in the negotiations and make up their own minds about just what they wanted. As Chancellor Schmidt once had the hardihood to suggest, SALT has been a divisive force in the alliance because parity between the United States and the Soviet Union leaves out Western Europe. The inclusion of Western Europe will not make the already formidable task of parity-mongering any easier.

x

What does the Soviet Union want of Western Europe? At this stage, the Soviet Union clearly does not seek to add Western Europe to its political and military empire. The Soviets have enough to cope with for quite a while. What the Soviet Union wants for the time being is to make Western Europe serve Soviet purposes in the struggle for power against the United States. Western Europe can serve the Soviet Union in essentially two ways.

One, *by making Western Europe's economic and technological resources available to the Soviet Union.* Europeans are not unaware of this Soviet aim. An astute American foreign correspondent reported from Europe in mid-1980:

> There is a fairly general assumption that Moscow's objective is not conquest or direct dominion, but the acquisition of a docile, if independent, productive backyard sufficiently detached from the United States influence to provide reliable compensation for Communist bloc economic failures. This European view further suggests that the Soviet Union seeks to use its

frightening military shadow to control vital avenues of supply, as the means of forcing that role on Western Europe.[107]

The fulfillment of this Soviet objective cannot any longer be dismissed as fantasy. In 1976, total Soviet imports from all sources amounted to $38.5 billion, of which approximately $2.3 billion came from the United States (including large grain imports) and $9.3 billion from the other Western industrialized countries. Of Soviet imports of machinery, $605 million came from the United States and $3.5 billion from the other Western countries. Virtually anything that the Soviet Union cannot get from the United States it can get from Western Europe. Huge factories have been put up in the Soviet Union and Eastern Europe by Italian, German, French, and combined enterprises. The chief limit on this transfer of Western resources and technology seems to be the credits that Western countries are willing to hand out. There has been no such phenomenon since the early years of the Soviet regime. Western help was then needed for the Soviet regime to survive; it is now needed for the Soviet regime to gain ascendancy. The more the Western economies come to the rescue of Soviet nonmilitary production, the more the Soviets can pour into their military economy, which operates on a separate and higher level.

It pleases Western European leaders for the present to pretend that economic collaboration with the Soviet Union and economic rivalry with the United States do not have political consequences. They know better, of course, but the pretense or illusion is necessary to insulate the military alliance with the United States from the economic association with the Soviet Union. The intimate relationship between politics and economics is such a commonplace in European thought, from which it spread to the rest of the world, that it would seem to be insulting to bring it to the attention of Europeans. Still, official European policy prefers to put economic relations with the Soviet Union and political relations with the United States into separate compartments. Marxists and even Social-Democrats ought to be the first to protest that the politics of economics does not stop at the border of the Soviet Union or Eastern Europe.

Two, *by a more docile and independent Western Europe.* Docility and independence do not usually go together, but they are able to cohabit in this case. Docility is for the Soviet Union, independence for the United States. For there is a peculiar thing about European independence—it is invariably independence from the United States. The stronger the American line towards the Soviet Union is, the more independent Europe becomes. European independence never seems to work the other way. If the United States takes a weak line with the Soviet Union, as it has done occasionally, Europe never seems to pull independently for a strong line. The preference for anything but a strong line was angrily and perhaps inadvertently expressed by Chancellor Schmidt: "We can't afford gestures of strength, we are fed up to the teeth with them."[108] Since Europe is not strong enough to stand midway between American and Soviet power, holding off both equally, independence from the United States and abhorrence of a strong line with the Soviet Union make for greater docility. Or if docility offends European sensibilities, let us say that more distant relations with the United States and closer relations with the Soviet Union are symbiotic.

In an interview with a Cologne newspaper in August 1980, Chancellor Schmidt for the first time laid claim publicly to a "leadership role" for West Germany in certain international situations, as a result of its increased political and economic importance. West Germany was no longer, he asserted, a "dependent client" of the United States; it had become "a weighty partner of the United States in very many fields." About all that Schmidt abjured was his country's ambition at present to become a nuclear or world power. He evidently placed West Germany in the hierarchy of power below the United States and the Soviet Union and above the other European nations. How German-American partnership could rest on economic rivalry on the one hand and German dependence on American military force on the other was not altogether clear. If the West Germans could not afford "gestures of strength" and were fed up to the teeth with them, the Western alliance would have to get along without gestures of strength altogether or get them from the United States alone. Schmidt's intellectual self-confidence suggested that he was willing to provide the political brains, which he thought the United States lacked, while the United States contributed the military brawn, which West Germany lacked. Schmidt's problem would seem to have been that he was in charge of the wrong country.

The Soviet Union does not and need not demand in this phase of its expanding power that Western Europe should align itself with the Soviet bloc. Such a precondition for Soviet favor would be politically unrealistic, frightening too many antagonistic or fence-sitting Europeans into the anti-Soviet or even pro-American camp. The next best thing, and almost as rewarding, is the encouragement of European independence, with the consequent further isolation of the United States. The removal of an American ally is itself a gain for the Soviet Union by changing the balance of forces against the United States; the attachment of that ally to the Soviet Union may be left open and and need not even be murmured about at this historical juncture. The Soviet Union has everything to gain and nothing to lose by playing the anti-American rather than the pro-Soviet side of the street in Western Europe, though of course nothing prevents it from doing one or the other whenever the opportunity offers.

Détente can also take a negative form. At minimum, it requires that Western Europe should do nothing to disturb relations with the Soviet Union, though half-hearted and make-believe gestures may be tolerated. In practice, this negative détente takes the form of European criticism of, or even holy horror at, any American policy that may disturb the Soviet Union. Détente thereby gives the Soviet Union an effective, if under-the-table, veto over European policy. Whenever Western Europe does or says anything that may ruffle Russian sensibilities, détente is immediately said to be threatened, and the specter of nuclear war—which détente is supposed to be holding off—is brought forward. The junction of détente and independence leads Europe into a one-way street that takes it further and further away from the United States.

The immediate reward to Europe for such a policy should not be underestimated. It provides the political underpinning for ever-growing trade with the Soviet Union and Eastern Europe. It enables Europe to deluge the Soviet bloc with credits with which to finance the trade, the same credits that can threaten the stability of the European financial system if they should be defaulted in case the trade breaks down. Local European communist parties, especially of the unreconstructed variety, fine-tune their domestic opposition to take account of European foreign policies of which the Soviet Union approves or at least does not strenuously disapprove. West Germany is most vulnerable to this political and economic blackmail. Soviet Russia has it in its power to determine the state of East and West German relations, which are played like an accordion. For West Europeans, the compensations for not unduly disturbing the Soviet Union are concrete, lucrative, and immediate; the compensation for maintaining a friendly alliance with the United States in the event of war is hypothetical, uncertain, and abhorrent to contemplate. It is all understandable and even in the nature of things. The one thing not easily forgivable is the pretense that such a state of affairs does not exist, that it does not strengthen the Soviet Union, and that

Soviet demands on Western Europe will not rise with the changing "balance of forces."

For years after the Second World War, the deafening anti-Americanism of European intellectuals seemed to be a luxury the United States could afford. Not that there was lacking more than enough in the United States to criticize. But this type of European anti-Americanism struck even a self-critical American as obsessive and repetitive to the point of psycho-pathology, especially when countries and systems deserving of far more strident criticism were let off with threadbare alibis and tattered apologies. There were notable European exceptions, but they were scorned, shunted off to a kind of intellectual ghetto, and sometimes more severely penalized. As much as intellectual pro-Americanism was in short supply in Europe, political parties and leaders were still loath to give up the American connection. Even that has changed. "Unlike the fifties, and to some extent the sixties," a prominent German international-affairs expert reports, "there is today almost an absence of distinctly pro-American political parties in Western Europe" and "a positive stand on preferential cooperation with the United States is not currently seen to pay political dividends." Yet the same writer considers ties with the United States "the single most important element in the foreign relations of any Western European member state."[109] How the two manifestations can continue to coexist remains a mystery.

The former British ambassador in Washington, Peter Jay, was moved to warn against "this sytematic European ambivalence, willing to wound but afraid to strike, tempted by the glamour of status and gestures but shy of the responsibilities and burdens of real power." Of the European attitude toward the United States he has written: "But it boosted and boosts European morale to spotlight American errors, to savour its failures, to exploit its market, to resent its overseas investments, to have a critic's ringside seat at its global tribulations, to mock its culture, to deride its leaders and to bewail the 'weakness' of its currency."[110]

Americans have been slow or reluctant to draw the full implications of Europe's increasingly demonstrative independence. It was formerly the policy of American administrations to indulge Europe psychologically as if to make up for its physical weakness. This indulgence mixed with indifference encouraged further alienation by spreading the illusion that a price would never have to be paid for it. As always, the longer the illusion continued, the higher the price was sure to be.

Hans Morgenthau foresaw more than a decade ago that the Western alliance had three ways to go. It could maintain the status quo, which he considered "unviable"; it could go forward to "a much more intimate cooperation among members of the Alliance," which he viewed as unlikely; or it could go backwards toward "a narrower and more specific definition" of its scope. He believed that it was necessary to narrow the gap between "our comprehensive legal commitments and the limited sphere within which our interests and policies coincide with those of our allies."[111]

The alliance has certainly not remained the same. It has certainly not gone forward. It has gone backwards, almost far enough to defy recognition. The gap between legal commitment and coincidence of interest has widened dangerously. But it has not been widened by common understanding or deliberate agreement. It has been widened by the force of events that have relentlessly undermined the original purpose of the alliance. Americans and Europeans have drifted from alliance to misalliance by staking out their own territories of independent action. A series of accomplished facts has reduced the credibility of the 1949 treaty to the vanishing point. It is typical of such unorchestrated changes that recriminations should fly in all directions. As matters stand, the only thing that Europe really wants of the alliance is that the United States should defend it, if necessary, by nuclear arms; and the one thing the United States needs most from the alliance is that Europe should support American global policies outside the area of the treaty on which the alliance rests. A house divided by such an alliance cannot stand.

It is easy enough to say that if the alliance cannot remain the same and should not go backward, it must go forward. When these things are easy to say they are said, without anything being done about them. In this case, nothing will be done without facing the reality that the alliance of 1949 cannot provide a basis for forward movement. It is fixed in its own time and circumstances, based on a different Europe, a different United States, and a different world. It was, even in its heyday, a unilateral military guarantee more than a true alliance. Its fatal flaw, as Adenauer and de Gaulle tried vainly to get across, was that it lacked an adequate political dimension. A unilateral military guarantee may have been enough in a period of seemingly unchallengeable American nuclear superiority, when Europe was obsessively interested in the threat of attack and was far from seeing itself as America's main economic rival or as a protagonist of its very own independent global politics. Today,

Europe prefers détente with the Soviet Union to American nuclear protection to exorcise the threat of attack, and it sets no bounds on its economic rivalry and independent global politics, even if they are sure to cause embarrassment and anger in Washington.

The alliance is mortally ill because it cannot much longer pretend that a unilateral American military guarantee or nuclear insurance policy is enough. It was long ago recognized that an alliance resting on a purely military foundation was dangerously fragile. In 1962, McGeorge Bundy, then speaking for the Kennedy administration, said: "The problem of defense in the nuclear age is as much psychological as military."[112] In 1963, Dean Acheson wrote: "In short, a successful military policy is possible when, and only when, it is one of at least three strands of the policies of the allied countries. The other two are the political and the economic."[113] And yet, in 1979, Professor Michael Howard thought it necessary to protest against the tendency to ignore "the social dimension of strategy" and the "societal implications" for any defense of the West.[114] If the problem of defense is psychological, political, economic, and social as well as military and technological, then the Western alliance must be psychological, political, economic, and social as well as military and technological. It is much easier to count troops, tanks, and missiles than to assess the fortitude necessary to use them.

The obsolescence of the alliance does not mean that the Western powers and Japan cannot take common action in case of need. If they do so, however, it will be because they have been driven to it, not because the alliance has called for it. They will act together, if at all, on an ad hoc, intermittent, circumscribed, concrete basis. They will be guided by immediate self-interest, not by the ties and trust that make alliances work. Yet, if these occasions of common danger and common action should recur often enough, a new compact may well emerge. Alliances arise out of just such compelling experiences, not out of well-meaning but futile preachments. For the time being, however, we are most likely heading into a period when the new West European alignment will have to run its course, without or against the United States.

Meanwhile, a first step towards a new compact would be to face the present reality and see the old alliance in all its nakedness. If we are engaged in any kind of war, it is a war of attrition with many twists and turns, ups and downs. The decisive weapons in such a war are political, economic, social, and cultural, not the missiles of the apocalypse. A new Western front will be restored only when the isolation of the United

States is seen as the greatest danger to Europe, and the estrangement from Europe is seen as the greatest danger to the United States. An isolated America and an insulated Europe could threaten to bring about a condition of the greatest ultimate peril to both.

The Washington Quarterly, Winter 1981

2

The Dilemma
of the West

One way to understand what has been happening to the Western alliance is to go back to the beginning. It is usual to treat a patient by enquiring into his history, but in this case there is an additional, more pressing reason for going back into the past. It is that both the United States and the Europan members of NATO are in their own ways trying to restore the original basis of the alliance—not so much in words, though there is some of that, as in their behavior.

In its origins, the North Altantic Treaty was not an alliance at all. It was, in effect, a unilateral American guarantee of European security. It no doubt assumed the outward form of an alliance; each member promised to come to the defense of the others. But its inner content was something else; only the United States was able to defend itself and any of the members. In the circumstances of 1949, that sort of arrangement seemed reasonable and necessary. Europe, shattered after the War, could not be expected to stand up to the Soviet Union's overwhelming superiority in conventional arms. The only counter-force appeared to be the American monopoly of atomic weapons. The implicit promise of NATO was that the United States could and would deter the Soviet Union by threatening to use its atomic and later nuclear weapons against the Soviets' conventional and later nuclear arms.

There is no need to go into the history of NATO in greater detail. What is important now is to keep in mind the essential conditions of the original US-European relationship. It was totally one-sided. Its raison d'être was European security. It was explicitly limited geographically to the defense of Europe. The geographical limitation was then most agreeable to the United States, which was enabled to do as it pleased outside Europe, sometimes against the interests and wishes of its European allies. The commitment was at the outset only political, with nothing to back it up. The Americans gave the commitment with the idea that Europe in order to defend itself needed the American assurance. Eventual European unity and European self-defense were corollaries of the North Atlantic Treaty. It is doubtful whether the US Senate would have approved of the treaty if it had not been for these two presuppositions. History then played one of its famous pranks—the corollaries faded, the treaty persisted.

Nevertheless, neither the Europeans nor the Americans had in 1950 any trouble making the transition from a wide-open political commitment to a full-fledged integrated military organization. The Europeans wanted the change most of all because they—especially the French— had little confidence in mere words. The appointment of General Eisenhower as NATO's first supreme commander and the stationing of American troops in Europe symbolically assured the Europeans that they had an American trip-wire to set the bombs flying over their heads if massive Soviet armies started to move west. The presumption then prevailed that the United States was sure to be drawn into another European war anyway and that the best way to prevent it was to announce the American intention in advance.

Part of the problem of the alliance is linguistic. The terms "alliance" and "allies" appear to be open-ended and generalized. In fact, this alliance was narrowly circumscribed. The European members of NATO are allies in their own defense and in nothing else. That is how they understand the original compact, and they wish to keep it that way. It was satisfactory to the United States as long as the United States felt strong enough to carry the burden largely by itself. The change came with the relative decline of American power and increasing recognition during the past decade that the United States needed help from its European allies (and Japan) to cope with crises and collapses outside the NATO area. The United States began to call on its European allies for types of allied activity that would have required a new and different compact and division of labor. But attempts to smuggle the new into the old repeatedly failed. Tactical, organizational, and other changes have been made in the military arrangements of NATO, but the basic understanding reached in 1949 has never been altered. As matters stand, there is no longer any real understanding. Each ally does as it pleases on an ad hoc basis and not because the alliance calls for it.

· · ·

In retrospect, this set-up represented the original sin of the Western alliance, from which it has never been able to free itself. Like the original original sin, it apparently gave pleasure and hurt no one; unfortunately, its consequences also could not be foreseen. The strategic deterrent, on which the alliance was based, was an American monopoly. It was a substitute for building up enough conventional forces in Europe to match the Eastern bloc. The Europeans benefited from the strategic deterrent without paying for it or controlling it. Europe could devote itself wholeheartedly to economic recovery while the United States took care of its security.

It all made sense, until the Soviets developed their own nuclear weapons. That might have been the time to reconsider the entire arrangement. One man thought so.

II

A specter is haunting Europe—the specter of Charles de Gaulle.

French policy has veered wildly. At the outset, the government of Prime Minister Henri Queuille and Foreign Minister Robert Schuman was the most zealous advocate of direct American intervention in Europe. In a famous phrase, Queuille protested that a political commitment was not enough, because it might be nothing more than a promise "to liberate a corpse."

Towards the end of the 1950s, however, President Charles de Gaulle sent French policy spinning in the opposite direction. By 1959, de Gaulle was questioning whether the atomic "equilibrium" between Soviet Russia and the United States could last; he speculated upon whether the two superpowers might not "divide the world" between them or agree not to wage atomic war against each other. Seven years later, de Gaulle brought about the French withdrawal from NATO, by which time the alliance had become little more than a military organization.

De Gaulle's critique of NATO was devastating. It is still, with left-wing and right-wing variations, the heart of the matter.

De Gaulle aimed his most deadly blows at the unilateral American guarantee. Once the Soviet Union had broken the American atomic monopoly, de Gaulle argued, Europe could not count on the United States to risk its own devastation in order to defend Europe. He built up France's own nuclear armament to give France an independent, if lesser, deterrent. He ridiculed NATO as a mere appendage of the United States. He sought to draw West Germany away from the United States into the French orbit. He was the architect in 1965 of France's détente with the Soviet Union, the first in the West. He adopted a nuclear-arms policy of *"tous azimuts"* or targeting in all directions, East and West, to show that he played no favorites between the USSR and the United States.

Yet, even as de Gaulle withdrew France from the military organization of NATO, he claimed to adhere to the North Altantic Treaty. On the surface, it looked as if de Gaulle had gone back to the conception of the treaty as a political commitment shorn of its military obligations. In practical terms this dual policy made little sense, inasmuch as the political commitment was military in nature, and de Gaulle had done more than anyone else to make Europeans disbelieve in its military efficacy. But there was a different kind of logic to de Gaulle's double bookkeeping.

In effect, de Gaulle traded in the unilateral American guarantee for a European insurance policy. The guarantee had started out as Europe's first and only line of defense; the American deterrent was now demoted to the last line of defense if all else failed. The essence of Gaullism was the complete freedom of France or a French-dominated Europe to do as it pleased, independently of the United States, in diplomatic, economic and military affairs. As a last resort, however, de Gaulle was unwilling to give up the possible benefits of the North Atlantic Treaty, which he did not rate very highly, for whatever they might be worth. There was not much risk in retaining this last, tenuous link to the United States, since France was bound to make all decisions unilaterally and in its own good time.

We have now had four versions of Gaullism in France—de Gaulle's, Pompidou's, Giscard d'Estaing's, and Mitterrand's. The last three are variations on the theme of Gaullism, depending on circumstances and personalities, and may therefore be called neo-Gaullist. The last is the newest and, therefore, the least well known and understood.

III

The best introduction to Mitterrand's neo-Gaullism is his most recent book, *Ici et maintenant*, completed in October 1980, only seven months before the recent French presidential elections.

One chapter is entitled *"La drôle d'alliance,"* which may be translated as "the funny alliance," or "the phoney alliance" (as in the case of the "phoney war" of 1939-1940).

Here are some of the things said by Mitterrand on the Atlantic alliance in the book:

> . . . there is no Atlantic alliance, or more exactly that it no longer has any meaning (p. 230, paperback edition).

> The Atlantic alliance provides for consultation between the partners in case of danger—that is all. The treaty of Brussels says a little more, but in truth no one in the West knows where the Alliance stands, its scope, what reciprocal relations it calls for, and how automatic it is. . . . What is known for the time being is that the Alliance rests on a fiction—American intervention in Europe in the event of Soviet aggression (p. 232).

> I am no more attached to the Atlantic alliance than a Rumanian or a Pole to the Warsaw Pact (pp. 241–42).

> France left NATO, that is, the integrated command which had placed her, indirectly, in a position of dependence on the Pentagon, without suffering any other punishment than bad temper. We have gone out of it, and we won't go back to it (p. 242).

> Nothing leads me to postulate the necessity of the Atlantic alliance, and I would be satisfied with a situation which would make it defunct (pp. 242–43).

> I have a desire to cry out: enough hypocrisies, enough of the American hypocrisy which reduces its allies to the status of satellites in exchange for a hypothetical protection . . . (p. 244).

> The Soviet machine bungles, and America is no longer a reliable partner for anyone (p. 246).

> I have not chosen either Russia or America. I am trying to confront the double danger (p. 253).

These excerpts are enough to give the substance and style of Mitterrand's thought on the alliance not so long ago. They are essentially Gaullist, though more extreme than anything de Gaulle permitted himself to say. After his election, however, Mitterrand stopped saying these unpleasant things about the United States and instead began to make cooling sounds in the direction of Washington. The shift in tone seems to have come about because Mitterrand was converted to the view that new Soviet nuclear arms had upset the balance in Europe and made necessary a Western rearmament effort.

The key term here is "balance." French policy ever since de Gaulle has been based on the premise that France needs a balance of power between the United States–Atlantic Alliance and the Soviet Union–

Warsaw Pact in order to pursue French interests most successfully. The difference is that the East was considered to be the weaker in de Gaulle's time, the West now. France wants a change in the Atlantic Alliance to make it stronger, but that does not mean that France wants a change in its own relationship to the alliance.

When the French Foreign Minister, Claude Cheysson, was in Washington last June [1981], he told reporters that he emphatically supported the emplacement of the 572 new American medium-range missiles in Europe "to counter what is regarded as a Soviet advantage in that field." But when asked what France would do to emplace those missiles, he replied that "there are no plans to station them in France." The other Europeans must enjoy getting advice from France which the French are not willing to take for themselves.

The German weekly *Der Spiegel* published a paraphrase of the record of a meeting between Mitterrand and the former German Chancellor Willy Brandt last July. Mitterrand told Brandt that France "needs equilibrium between the blocs," has no intention of assuming any responsibility for the defense of its German neighbor, and prefers to concentrate totally "on the nuclear deterrent for its own territory." Brandt apparently complained that the Germans "were fed up with being treated as a colony by the Americans." Mitterrand gave him no sympathy.

In effect, post-Gaullist France has been in the position of manipulating much stronger forces than itself, and it needs an "equilibrium" between them in order to play off one side against the other. For the time being, France feels the need to help create a better balance by tilting over to the American side in the East-West arms equation. It is the alleged arms imbalance on the continent of Europe that has brought about seemingly better Franco-American relations; elsewhere in the world, as in the Middle East and El Salvador, French policy is as ruggedly independent of and obtrusively annoying to the United States as before. No one need complain that the French are self-seeking; everyone else is.

The defection of France was, in truth, a deadly blow to the alliance in its original form. Without France, Western Europe is a political and geographical amputee. France set the example, now being followed by others in varying degrees, of doing or not doing whatever it pleased, while holding in reserve "a hypothetical protection" and "a fiction of American intervention in Europe"—in Mitterrand's words. That de

Gaulle's arguments and actions were not taken more seriously and debated more openly at the time has now to be paid for. Anyone reading Mitterrand's book still has to face essentially the same arguments and the same actions.

De Gaulle's withdrawal from NATO, however, presupposed that the military structure would remain substantially intact, for only in that way could he safely perform his balancing act. One of the peculiar aspects of Gaullism is that it pays off the most when the French are the only ones to practice it. Too many Gaullist-type nations in Europe would produce a confusion of weak, free-wheeling nationalisms in the West, leaving France with no backstop in case of need. As a result, French officials have taken the lead in warning against a European neutralist epidemic. It was Foreign Minister Cheysson who not so long ago saw fit to denounce the neutralist trend as a "danger," which he attributed to "immense weariness" and which made him "despair."

The French example is, therefore, not easily transferable. The Papandreou government in Greece may imitate French Gaullism by removing all nuclear weapons from Greek soil and withdrawing from NATO's military establishment. But these moves were only *half* of de Gaulle's strategy. The other half was building up France's own nuclear and conventional forces to a respectable level of defense and deterrence. Papandreou's Greece is only half Gaullist—the negative half.

West Germany is in a somewhat similar position, even though it is much richer and far more industrialized than Greece. The Germans can get rid of NATO's American nuclear weapons, but they are most unlikely to substitute their own. For a while, it seemed as if West Germany and France might form a new European axis, half in and half out of NATO. This eventuality now appears to be remote because Germany is being tempted by a pacifist-neutralist option that estranges it from France as well as from the United States. The French option turns out to be peculiarly French.

Yet the French case is most instructive because only France seems relatively immune today to the anti-nuclear and anti-American mood in much of Europe. The French do not need to demonstrate against nuclear weapons, because they do not have foreign nuclear weapons to demonstrate against; they have their own, and the French are *not* demonstrating against them. They are not demonstrating against NATO, because they do not have NATO in their midst. The clue to a critical aspect of the European anti-nuclear and anti-American campaign may well be in France.

IV

The clue is, fundamentally, simple and obvious. It helps to explain why a weapon that in its atomic form gave birth to the Western Alliance has now in its nuclear form become the favorite argument against it.

The short answer is the same in both cases: They are American weapons. Europeans first wanted them because they were American weapons, and now many do not want them for the same reason. The trouble is not so much in the weapons, as the French experience shows; the trouble is in the changed relationship between Western Europe and the United States.

The changes since 1949 are too familiar to be belabored—"rough parity" between the Soviet Union and the United States; nuclear weapons stationed in and targeted on Europe; the recovery of Europe as an economic and political rival of the United States; the authority squandered by the United States in Vietnam, Watergate, Iran, and elsewhere. Changes of such magnitude could not leave the alliance—or even illusions about it—unshaken.

A singular shift has taken place in the focus of the alliance. The main conflict is now within the alliance rather than between it and potential enemies. The campaign to get nuclear weapons out of Europe is at the same time a campaign to get the United States out of Europe. The anti-nuclear campaign is shot through with anti-Americanism. It is particularly virulent in West Germany, which was once "the most solid ally of the United States" and "has become the allied country in which anti-Americanism is sharpest," as Professor Alfred Grosser, the distinguished French historian who follows German events with particular care, recently put it. To make matters worse, the German manifestation of anti-Americanism is most extensive and vitriolic in the governing Social-Democratic Party.

Egon Bahr is not a run-of-the-mill German Social-Democrat. He has long been one of former Chancellor Willy Brandt's closest associates; he was a State Secretary during Brandt's chancellorship, and was entrusted with the negotiation of the détente agreements with the Soviet Union and Poland in 1970. He is now head of the Social-Democratic Party's disarmament work and will undoubtedly play a leading role in the separate Soviet-German arms negotiations arranged during the recent Brezhnev-Schmidt talks in Bonn. A few months ago, Bahr accused the United States of "using NATO to run Western Europe as their protectorate," as if the Egon Bahrs would be in a position to make such an accusation if the United States were actually running Western Europe as a protectorate. What was most notable about Bahr's line of attack was its Gaullist overtones. Bahr, however, did not follow de Gaulle to urge West Germany to substitute its own nuclear weapons for NATO's. The nationalist side of Gaullism lends itself to disarmament as well as re-armament, as long as both exclude American weapons.

At about the same time, another leading German Social-Democrat, Günter Gaus, came forward with similar views. Until recently, Gaus was the chief West German diplomatic representative to the Communist régime in East Berlin. He is now adviser on German and international affairs to the Social-Democratic Party's top leadership of which Brandt is the titular head. Gaus charged that the deployment of the new Ameri-can medium-range missiles in Germany would make it the equivalent of a Roman-style American "province"—as if Roman rulers would have asked permission of their provincial officials to put certain weapons in their territories! Gaus also imputed to the United States a virtual con-spiracy to use those missiles in Europe as a means of keeping nuclear conflict away from the United States and restricting it to Europe. Here again, a Gaullist element—that the United States would never open itself up to devastation through an intercontinental nuclear exchange—was employed without fitting into the entire Gaullist program. Brandt and de Gaulle are also not without some intellectual affinity; Brandt's recent memoir, *People and Politics*, has a chapter on his conversations with de Gaulle that reads like the lectures of a teacher to a pupil.

On November 8, 1981, Gaus produced a full program of his own in a speech at a Social-Democratic conference in Berlin. Startlingly, he called for a return to the old policy of "massive retaliation" and for repudia-tion of its successor policy, "flexible response." He demanded the re-vival of NATO's original strategy of 1949, by which he understood that any attack on Western Europe, nuclear or conventional, should be an-swered immediately by the most devastating *American* intercontinental missiles. Such a guarantee of American reprisal, he explained (as re-ported in the *Frankfurter Allegemeine Zeitung* the following day), could give Europe the possibility of reaching "a new stage of détente through the removal of atomic weapons from Central Europe." Europe, as Gaus sees it, should aim at an expansion of détente with the Soviet Union, a nuclear-free Europe, and the old American unilateral guarantee of *"totale Vergeltung."*

. . .

On the face of it, this arrangement would seem to be somewhat one-sided. The United States would commit itself to the risk of devastation on behalf of European security, while Europe would go on establishing closer ties with the Soviet Union under cover of American protection. Whatever one may think of this type of reciprocity, it has the virtue of making some things clear. A nuclear-free Europe in this scheme is intended to save Europe from a nuclear war by limiting it to the United States and the Soviet Union—just the opposite of the "American conspiracy" that Gaus had earlier imputed to the United States. We have here a yearning to return to the original basis of the Atlantic alliance in circumstances altogether different from those that originally prevailed. If Gaus had not fallen back on the unilateral American guarantee, he would have left a nuclear-free Europe in a state of nuclear pacifism. Here we have a kind of prestidigitator's trick of pulling out of the bag at the last possible moment the American "ultimate deterrent" to enable Europe to take out a pseudo-Gaullist insurance policy as it goes on with détente and nuclear disarmament.

Anti-nuclear West Germans are not the only ones who are struggling with the problem of backing up neutralism with some residual force. Professor E. P. Thompson, the British campaigner for a nuclear-free Europe, has rested his hopes on a different kind of force. The European peace movement, he has written, can be called "neutral" in the sense that it refuses to take sides at all. But he wants the term to embrace a "peaceful European opinion acting as a Third Negotiator, between both superpowers, with the ultimate objective of reunifying European societies and cultures." His force, then, is that of "peaceful European opinion." One is tempted to tell him what the Duke of Wellington in full regalia is said to have told someone who greeted him on the street as Mr. Jones: "If you can believe that, Sir, you can believe anything."

Another hint of how Europe might make itself nuclear-free without worrying too much was given by Tony Benn, the left-wing Labour MP to whom the new British Social Democratic Party owes much of its success. Benn gave a speech in which he held out the cheerful prospect that the experiences of Afghanistan, Vietnam, and Algeria "may prove" that "a determined people is the best guarantee against permanent domination from outside." A nuclear-free Europe might become another Afghanistan, Vietnam, or Algeria, but no need to fret—the domination from the outside world would not be "permanent."

It is much easier, then, to get rid of American weapons than to put something equivalent in their place. Unfortunately, the United States has not made the problem any easier for the Europeans.

V

The United States in its present incarnation has also been straining to throw off the constraints and contradictions of the alliance.

The original program of Candidate Reagan and the Republican Party to restore the country to the once blessed state of "superiority" betrayed a wish to re-establish the old relationships with both opponents and allies. This outburst of nostalgia evoked a time when American atomic or nuclear superiority appeared to be so decisive that opponents were apparently daunted and allies reassured. The goal of superiority never made military or economic sense; when Ronald Reagan implied that he relished the prospect of an arms race because "they can't win," he should have added—"and neither can we, even if we could afford it." The level of destructiveness from no more than a small part of the existing stock of nuclear weapons is so appallingly high that a race for superiority can only be a competition in redundancy. Nevertheless, even fantasies have their meanings—in this case, a return to a paradise lost of American prepotency.

The way the Reagan administration handled the affair of "the neutron bomb" was also evidence that it sought to break through the confines of alliance politics. The military aspect of the neutron bomb is not the point here. More significant was the official explanation for the administration's abrupt decision to go ahead with its production. The bomb's limited range makes it totally useless in the United States. In the face of European resistance, it was made known in Washington that the United States could not permit the Europeans to exercise a "veto power" over an American weapon. It was left unsaid that the United States could not prevent the Europeans from exercising a veto power over the use of that weapon. If the neutron bomb is not an "alliance weapon," it is utterly irrelevant and immaterial. The West German government, caught in the middle, played along with the sham by calling the Reagan decision an "exclusively American affair." If this was an exclusively American affair, it is hard to see why any short-range or intermediate nuclear weapon is also a European affair.

What this byplay meant in effect was the potential transfer of American nuclear weapons back to the United States. If the successful European opponents of the neutron bomb have their way, the same fate awaits the other nuclear weapons stationed in Europe. In principle, all of them raise the same problem. The real issue is not whether Europe wishes to be defended by neutron bombs or Pershing IIs but whether Europe wishes to be defended by American nuclear weapons at all.

The handling of the neutron bomb enabled the United States to take unilateral action to get out of an impasse in the alliance. American unilateralism seeks to do for the United States what neutralism seeks to do for Europe—to regain freedom of action or inaction. The Americans are mainly interested in freedom of action, the Europeans in freedom of inaction. The case of the neutron bomb illustrated both freedoms—the Americans insisted on freedom of action to produce the bomb, the Europeans maintained freedom of inaction to refuse the bomb.

The United States has increasingly taken unilateral action in order to take any action at all. Unilateralism has, in fact, become an alternative to isolationism. The United States is not isolationist today; it is isolated. Isolationism is a policy—being isolated is a condition. If the United States were isolationist, it would not take *any* action, unilateral or otherwise, where its immediate interests were not at stake. The chances are that the United States will continue to be more unilateralist than isolationist, if only to safeguard its far-flung interests throughout the world. Nevertheless, some semblance of isolationism may make a come-back. If the condition became a habit, it could easily turn into a reasonable facsimile of the policy. Then there would be no need to make such halfway, unilateral decisions as the production and stockpiling of neutron bombs in the United States for a Europe which did not, at least for the moment, want them.

The neutron bomb and Pershing II missiles are not new types of nuclear weapons; they are "modernized" versions of existing weapons. Much of the pressure for such modernization came from Europe, and especially from Chancellor Schmidt. In a famous public lecture (at the International Institute for Strategic Studies in London, in October 1977), he demanded that something should be done to close "the disparities between East and West" in nuclear and conventional weaponry in Europe. The neutron bomb and Pershing IIs were answers to his prayers.

Yet NATO Secretary-General Joseph Luns recently found it necessary to call attention to a popular European myth:

> I am frankly appalled at the way people who know better have allowed the myth to spread that nuclear force modernization is an initiative being

foisted by the United States on its European allies. The truth is that it was
a European initiative. . . .

The "myth" did not merely spread; it was "allowed" to spread. This
kind of negligence must be attributed to something other than absentmindedness.

Yet absentmindedness is about the kindest thing that can be attributed
to the recent indiscretions by President Reagan and Secretary of State
Haig. If they were blunders, they were the kinds of blunders that tell
more than the most carefully thought-out pronouncements.

A political storm broke in Europe over President Reagan's bumbling
remark about the possibility of a limited tactical nuclear battlefield exchange that would not necessarily bring on a full-scale Soviet-American
nuclear war. As even *Le Monde* (October 21, 1981) recognized, the
idea was neither new nor surprising, "a truth no specialist will dispute,
which is that a limited nuclear war in Europe or elsewhere will not
necessarily lead to either of the two superpowers having recourse to its
chief strategic arsenal. . . ." Yet this "truth" struck a raw nerve. Why
was there such a furious European reaction?

The reason is embedded in the logic of a limited nuclear war, which is
in turn implanted in the doctrine of "flexible response." According to
the doctrine, a future war should be held at the lowest possible level,
nuclear or conventional. A limited nuclear war is obviously a lower level
than a full-scale nuclear war. The principle seems reasonable enough—
so long as no one asks where the level is going to be located or where
that limited war is going to take place.

What is the name of the battlefield on which a nuclear tactical exchange could occur or a limited war break out? The name is obviously
some place in Europe, or anywhere but in the United States. That was
the battlefield President Reagan was actually talking about, however
oblivious he may have been to it. A library of books has been written on
"flexible response" and "limited nuclear war" without making that clear
either. Yet there has long been a European tradition of preferring to be
protected by strategic American nuclear weapons that Europeans have
always believed to be the best ultimate deterrent to any nuclear or even
conventional war in Europe. It may seem reasonable and even obvious to
Americans that it is best to have a variety of options and flexibility of
responses. The trouble is that options and flexibility unerringly point to
a conventional or nuclear war in Europe as against a nuclear war between the Soviet Union and the United States.

Secretary Haig's equally fumbling recollection of a NATO proposal for a "demonstration" firing of a nuclear weapon also came as a shocking revelation in Europe. It should not have come as such a surprise to some highly placed Europeans. For the idea was originally theirs.

What we know about it at present comes almost exclusively from Henry Kissinger's memoirs, *The White House Years*. In addition to its inherent interest, Kissinger's story gets us close to the innermost Western dilemma.

The idea was, according to Kissinger, the brainchild of Denis Healey, then British Minister of Defence in the Labour government headed by Prime Minister Harold Wilson, and today deputy leader of the Labour Party. Since NATO's conventional forces could hold out for only a few days, Healey thought it was essential to use nuclear weapons at an early stage.

> Healey stressed [Kissinger tells us] the crucial importance of making the Soviets understand that the West would prefer to escalate to a strategic exchange rather than surrender. (p. 219)

On the other hand, he wanted to hold nuclear devastation down to a minimum. The upshot was "the use of a very small number of tactical weapons as a warning that matters were getting out of hand."

Britain was supported by West Germany in this proposal for a "demonstrative use" of nuclear weapons. The plan called for setting off a nuclear weapon in a remote location, such as in the air over the Mediterranean, as a signal that something more "drastic" might follow. Kissinger himself never thought much of the scheme. He was persuaded that the Europeans wanted nuclear protection, but not on their territories—"what seemed 'limited' to us could be catastrophic for them." If it came to an ultimate crisis, Europe desired the early use of strategic or intercontinental nuclear weapons from the United States, in effect, "a US-Soviet nuclear war fought over their heads." The Americans sought to develop other options, starting with tactical battlefield nuclear weapons and ending with strategic intercontinental nuclear weapons only as the ultimate recourse.

The result in 1969 was a "temporary compromise" that merely "papered over the dispute." The NATO Nuclear Planning Group, to which the US, Great Britain, West Germany, and Italy belonged, decided to come down in favor of both "demonstrative" and "operational" uses of tactical nuclear weapons. But the American representatives, headed by Melvin Laird, then Secretary of Defense, had no illusions about the gap that was widening between European and American attitudes towards the use of nuclear weapons. Laird reported to President Nixon:

> The longer-term problem of divergence between American and European views on strategy remains.

Kissinger himself recognized that "the real goal of our allies"—to commit the United States to early use of strategic nuclear weapons—underlined "the dilemma of tactical nuclear weapons."

For once, Dr. Kissinger is right. Nuclear war presents a genuine dilemma. The present administration may have exacerbated it, but the dilemma was there long before Reagan, Haig, and Weinberger. The hard core of the matter is one of substance, not style.

The dilemma arises from the very nature of NATO's nuclear arsenal. It is NATO's in form but American in fact. This brutal reality means that the ultimate fate of Europe, if it comes to that, must be decided by Americans or even by a single American, the President, not by Europeans. There would be no dilemma if the interests of Europeans and Americans were the same. Unfortunately, they both are and are not. They *are* the same to the extent of deterring nuclear war altogether. But they are not the same if it comes to nuclear war. It is in the interest of Europe to keep such a war away from Europe, and it is in the interest of the United States to keep it away from the United States. Away, for Europe, means in the United States; away, for the United States, means in Europe.

Nuclear weapons in Europe are inexorably linked with the United States because they are American weapons under American control. Anti-Americanism is, therefore, an inevitable concomitant of anti-nuclear weaponry. Where the weapons are not American, as in France, anti-Americanism of that type has no nuclear base to rest on.

How would the British feel, Chancellor Schmidt recently asked a British correspondent, if neither the British government nor the British nation had jurisdiction over "some 90 to 100 American missiles on British soil"? In an interview in *Time* magazine (October 19, 1981), President Mitterrand expressed sympathy for the difficult "contradiction" that had been created for West Germany by virtue of being "loaded with nuclear explosives that are not under its control." That is where the raw nerve is. West Germany might still have quite a few difficult contradictions even if it controlled its own nuclear explosives, but at least it would feel that it was taking its fate into its own hands.

Is there a way out of the dilemma?

In such a dilemma, there is only one thing to do—to grasp one horn or the other, for one cannot have it both ways.

France grasped one of the horns by leaving NATO's military organization and building its own nuclear and conventional forces. It is a course which Defense Minister Charles Hernu inferentially recommended to other European nations and to the United States. France, he has maintained, became a stronger and better American ally by getting out of NATO. "If France were fully inside NATO," he argued, "Frenchmen might go to sleep, saying to themselves, 'Oh, well, the Americans are there with their nuclear umbrella. There is no point in our making a strong effort.' It is this sense of independence that gives the French the feeling that they are not neutral."

If this prescription has done so much good for France, it presumably should do just as well for the other members of NATO. West Germany or Italy, for example, might get out of NATO and thereby prevent themselves from going to sleep, cease depending on the American nuclear umbrella, make their own strong effort, and wake up feeling independent and unneutral.

NATO itself would in this event be emptied of meaning and membership. The French formula is based on a paradox—get out of the alliance in order to be a better ally. The French, of course, do not literally mean that. Their logic is supposed to hold good only for France. France is in the peculiar position of needing the alliance in order to benefit from staying out of it.

Yet the French are not the only ones to be impressed with themselves. General Bernard Rogers, the present US supreme commander of NATO, made the remarkable statement in Brussels last March that "France is an example for NATO." If that example were followed by other NATO members, General Rogers would not have much to command. The same strange thought has even come directly out of Washington. "From a military point of view," said Assistant Secretary of Defense Richard Perle, "we might wish we had a few more Mitterrand governments." If the United States wanted to inspire an exodus from NATO, it could do no better than to encourage more Mitterrand-type governments in Western Europe, as the Papandreou government in Greece has already demonstrated.

Still, whatever the implications for NATO, the French case cannot be dismissed. The French decision to get out of NATO was linked with a French resolution to have their own nuclear umbrella, make a stronger effort of their own, and develop a respectable sense of independence. If, according to French rationality, the American nuclear umbrella has made other European nations weak-willed and dependent-minded, the clear lesson is that they need to be shaken up and forced to take their fates in their own hands. The French even offer the United States a bonus—a decline in anti-Americanism.

Unfortunately, all this is easier said than done. In de Gaulle's time, independence from American nuclear weapons meant French nuclear weapons. Today, elsewhere, independence from American nuclear weapons is more likely to mean *no* nuclear weapons. The French option is, nevertheless, a theoretical possibility. Those who wish to take it need only build up their own armed forces, nuclear or conventional, individually or within a European framework. That framework is already there in the European Economic Community, which has increasingly taken on political assignments.

An alternative version would be for Western Europe to concentrate on conventional forces without nuclear weapons. Some of the best European minds have been advocating such a course. One school of thought professes to believe that there is little or no danger of a Soviet nuclear attack on Europe, because it would destroy the very assets that the Soviets could hope to gain. Others insist that the Soviets and their satellites are so strained internally that they could not risk launching an attack on Western Europe. If "nuclear blackmail" to extort political concessions is the real European problem, the decisive factor in any such crisis would be Europe's will and resolve to resist. If Europeans really believed that there was no need to worry about a Soviet aggression or nuclear war, they could rest secure in the knowledge that all they need are strong nerves.

The third European option is some form of nuclear pacifism, such as unilateral nuclear disarmament. The Americans and French clearly believe that nuclear force is necessary for an effective defense in modern warfare. On this assumption, nuclear disarmament really masks a more general type of pacifism. The anti-nuclear campaign is, in effect, essentially pacifist unless it advocates some other way to resist. The emphasis of the anti-nuclear movement is in fact almost wholly on what should be banned, not on what should be manned. If Professor Thompson's "peaceful European opinion" can do the trick of acting as a third force, negotiating between the superpowers and ultimately reunifying Europe, it has no need for either nuclear or conventional forces.

For good reason, then, Chancellor Bruno Kreisky of Austria, no admirer of US policy, spoke critically some months ago of "a wave of pacifism sweeping Europe." At a French Socialist conference last year (Valence, October 25, 1981), Prime Minister Pierre Mauroy said that "the upsurge of neutralism in Western Europe, which hides behind pacifist speeches, must alarm us. . . ." If two such statesmen could make such flat and apprehensive statements about the state of Europe in 1981, the pacifist-neutralist tide cannot be easily dismissed as a figment of inflamed American imaginations.

An internecine struggle is being waged passively and actively, in the streets, in governing or opposition parties, and from country to country. The "Dutch disease" is not an American invention. Josef Joffe, an editor of *Die Zeit* (Hamburg), wrote in *Foreign Affairs* of Spring 1981 that "countries like Belgium, Holland and Denmark can no longer be regarded as full-fledged members of the Alliance. . . ." They have begun to play a waiting game, their active membership no more than a historical hangover or convenient fiction. The two countries that count the most, Great Britain and West Germany, are most divided. In Britain, the Labour Party and the Trades Union Congress have officially adopted the policy of unilateral nuclear disarmament; in decline though they may be, they still possess a mass following and show how extreme the opposition, which is not limited to them, has become. A poll published in the London *Observer* reported that 53 percent of the country want an end to US bases. In West Germany, the governing Social-Democratic Party is split from top to bottom, with Chancellor Schmidt fighting a rearguard battle in his party's own executive *Vorstand*.

The final returns are, of course, not yet in, but the forces sapping the alliance have cut deeply into its foundations and show no signs of losing the initiative. These forces do not have to take over countries; it is enough for them to reach a certain critical mass to produce enough turmoil and division to make governments tremble and alliances totter.

Nuclear shadow-boxing between President Reagan and President Brezhnev is not likely to change the nature of the European dilemma.

That dilemma arises from the European dependence on American weapons, not on whether there should be a few less or a few more. The horror of our condition is that there is such a redundancy of entire nuclear systems as well as of individual weapons on both sides that they can make token offers of reductions without essentially changing the devastating power of what is left. The Soviets are in the especially favorable position of being able to threaten Europe with a nuclear catastrophe even if they do away with all their *SS-4s*, *SS-5s*, and *SS-20s*, as demanded by President Reagan. As McGeorge Bundy has pointed out in the *Washington Post* of October 20, 1981, any long-range missile that can reach the United States can also reach Europe.

> There are so many of these missiles—some 2,500—and they have so many large warheads—some 7,000—that less than 10% of the force could produce all the results in Europe that could ever be feared from the *SS-20*. . . . [As a result] when you have vastly more than "enough" for inter-continental strategic deterrence, as both sides do today, you have more than enough for smaller assignments too.

It is one of the wonders of the American political system that President Reagan can make a presumably earth-shaking proposal which high Washington officials immediately tell the press they do not expect the Soviets to accept. A proposal which requires the Soviets to get rid of hundreds of missiles they already have in place in order to save the United States the trouble of producing other hundreds of missiles which might never get placed in Europe is obviously designed to show what good prophets those officials are. By the time this nuclear badminton game is over, the spectators are apt to be more groggy than the players.

In this Soviet-American game, West Germany is the main prize. It has just the right combination of strengths and weaknesses to make it gyrate wildly around and between the two superpowers. Its technology makes it the best Western partner for the Soviet Union. Its exposed military position makes it hesitate to give up the American connection. In effect, it profits from its strong point in the East and trades on its weakness in the West. Like Gaullist France, it can carry on this ambidextrous and ambiguous policy only by manipulating forces much greater than its own. It moves uneasily from being paid off by both sides to being caught in a crush between them. Even more than France, it now requires an "equilibrium" between the US and the USSR to get the most out of its central position and exploitation of détente-cum-deterrence. But in international life, equilibrium is one of the hardest conditions to maintain. The result is that the present German policy of getting into the middle produces both the greatest benefits and the greatest risks.

In this mix-up within and between the blocs, American pressure on Europe will do no good. It has backfired so regularly in the past few years that alliance politics has become an exercise in American masochism. The United States has repeatedly made the mistake of telling its European associates what they should do. No good can come from such American tactics. It would be best for all concerned if Europeans were left to decide their own fate freely, bearing full responsibility for whatever they decide. The shibboleth of "American leadership" has taken on a false and hollow ring that merely serves to point up the lack of it. Every intrusion of American demands and pressures only makes the United States the issue, not the substance of the proposal.

On these matters there is no abstract right and wrong that Americans can decide for Europeans or anyone else. There is a coincidence or clash of national and regional interests, which have a disconcerting way of showing a different face in Washington, Paris, Bonn, London and . . . Moscow. The worst possible outcome is for Europeans to be presented with the choice of deciding for or against the United States. Whatever the future relationship to the United States may prove to be, it should be decided by Europeans for the sake of Europe, without making the United States an alibi, a scapegoat, or a savior.

But dilemmas of this sort cannot last forever. The original conception of the North Atlantic treaty was that it would give Western Europe time and means to defend itself. In strange and unforeseen circumstances, Western Europe is forcing itself to face this old challenge by struggling against being defended by the United States. If the best way out of the dilemma (as Professor Michael Howard and others believe) lies in "the field of conventional armaments," Western Europe is well able to take care of its defense if only it has the will and fortitude to do so. What it cannot have is a defense based on an alliance without allies and a leader without followers. It will be all too easy for Western Europe to get rid of "dependence on the United States." That is not a solution; it is the beginning of the problem.

Encounter, March 1982

3

Western Insecurity

What is to become of NATO? This was really the critical question that confronted the four distinguished authors of *Western Security*, the latest report on the state of the Western alliance. No ordinary quartet, they are the directors of the four leading councils and institutes on foreign relations in Germany, France, Great Britain, and the United States: Karl Kaiser, Thierry de Montbrial, David Watt, and Winston Lord. They were advised by a group of equally distinguished experts from the four countries. Such a collaborative effort had never been made before; it must testify to the acuteness of the problem in the minds of the participants and their organizations. They have produced a report that deserves to be on the desk of every government leader who might do something about it, though not for the reason that the authors themselves might give.

The problem of NATO is not an outgrowth of present or recent circumstances. It is embedded in NATO's entire history. In question is its very raison d'être.

When NATO was formed in 1949, it was a unilateral American guarantee of European security masquerading as an alliance. It was, to be sure, an alliance in form—the United States and the European members pledged to come to one another's defense. In fact, only the United States had the means to defend anyone. On the assumption that overwhelming Soviet superiority in conventional arms could not be overcome conventionally, reliance was put on American strategic superiority—on atomic and later on nuclear weapons. The "ultimate deterrent" more than ever made the alliance a unilateral American guarantee. Another aspect of the North Atlantic Treaty contributed to an American defense monopoly. Geographically, the treaty was explicitly limited; it applied only to the defense of Europe. The United States thus was left to assume full responsibility in the rest of the world. The treaty was also severely limited functionally. It paid lip service to economic collaboration that was never implemented. Later efforts to enlarge the political scope of NATO proved to be equally futile.

In the immediate post-World War II world, all sides wanted to have it this way. Europe—shattered, hungry, fearful—yearned for American protection. The Americans assumed that they would be drawn into a European war in any case. It would be better to get in at the outset than to wait two or three years, as in the past. It would be still better to prevent such a war by removing the temptation of American isolationism. Outside Europe, the United States positively demanded a free hand. Americans justified it on the ground that Europe could have only regional interests; only America had global interests. Secretary of State Henry Kissinger taunted the Europeans with this formula as late as 1973.

The original compact has not remained unchanged. The European members now contribute a large share of the men and materiel for their own defense. In the most important respects, however, little has changed. Because NATO forces are not expected to hold out for more than ninety days in a conventional conflict, ultimate reliance still is put on the "ultimate deterrent" provided by American strategic weapons. Nor have the geographic or functional limits of NATO changed. The security of Europe is still NATO's sole mission. The European members of NATO are, in effect, allies of the United States in their own defense and in no other sense.

The paradox of NATO is that it has contributed to European isolationism, or, of late, to timidly selective isolationism with no risk of real embroilment. What Europe wanted in 1949 was protection against Soviet aggression. What Europe wants in 1981 is exactly the same thing, no more and no less. The more Europe feels protected, the less it wants to be dragged into crises and conflicts elsewhere. Or as Theo Sommer, a leading German commentator and co-publisher of *Die Zeit*, Chancellor Helmut Schmidt's unofficial organ, put it not long ago: "Europe must not become an area of tension because there is tension elsewhere." That is as good a definition of European isolationism as any.

Such European isolationism always was implicit in the Western alliance. It did not matter so long as the United States was able and willing to act unilaterally and did not ask its European allies for help. But toward the end of the Nixon administration and throughout the Carter years this state of affairs changed drastically. The United States increasingly found itself on the asking rather than on the giving end. The Europeans were placed in the novel position of having to decide whether they wanted to give the kind of support, economic, political, and military, that the United States asked for. More often than not, as in the cases of Iran, Afghanistan, and the Middle East, the European response was half-hearted or hostile.

The United States, in effect, called on the alliance to do what it was never intended to do. Yet the United States was never willing to admit that it was demanding a fundamental change in the nature of the alliance. By trying to smuggle in such a change, and failing, the United States missed—or deliberately rejected—the opportunity to call for a basic reassessment of NATO. President Carter himself spoke bitterly of the Europeans as if they had let down the United States. The Europeans reacted sullenly by questioning American motives, stability of policy, and plain good sense. Neither side was willing to bring out into the open what the deeper trouble was—that the covenant of 1949 was based on conditions that no longer existed.

In 1957, an effort was made to enlarge the scope of NATO by appointing a Committee of Three, made up of Lester Pearson of Canada, Halvard Lange of Norway, and Gaetano Martino of Italy, known as the "Three Wise Men." They brought in a report advocating a much greater degree of political collaboration within the alliance. It never had a chance and died aborning.

What have the "Four Wise Men" brought forth in the new report, *Western Security*? Their analysis of the problem is largely familiar by now, but is not any less disturbing for that reason. The present transatlantic crisis, they say, is not merely one more short-term commotion; it is more far-reaching, because it has deeper historical and structural roots. The political and economic balance of power between the United States and Europe has changed, as has the military balance between the United States and the Soviet Union. The European Community has become as rich as the United States and often outsells the United States in the world market. Yet the "protégé" acts as if nothing has changed: "Europe as a whole remains dependent on the nuclear guarantee provided by the United States since the end of World War II" and "does not assume the political and military responsibilities which come with its newly acquired economic might." Militarily, in fact, Europe's dependence on the United States may be greater than ever: "As the increased

Soviet conventional superiority is no longer compensated by US nuclear superiority at higher rungs of the escalation ladder, the Europeans may have in fact become even more dependent on US first use of nuclear weapons." The last five words could not be more ominous.

In this analysis, which I have necessarily compressed, one point stands out most starkly. It is that "neither the United States nor Europe can be expected to face the challenges of the 1980s on its own." To tell the truth, neither the United States nor Europe was able to face the challenges before the 1980s on its own. The difference is that now the United States officially admits that it cannot. In an address in Munich on February 21 of this year [1981], Deputy Secretary of Defense Frank C. Carlucci stated that the United States cannot "unaided bear the burden of promoting Western interests beyond Europe." Since the United States cannot bear the burden alone in Europe either, and Europe can or will do even less by itself, there is general agreement that the challenges in Europe and beyond Europe must be borne by both or by neither.

The only instrumentality the United States and Europe have with which to face this issue is still NATO. One would imagine that the authors of *Western Security* would have NATO in mind as the means to achieve equal and joint challenge-facing and burden-bearing. Unfortunately, NATO has become something of a sacred cow which cannot be given up even if it turns out that NATO cannot be trusted to do the job.

This report skirts the issue instead of attacking it frontally. At first we are told that "NATO must for the first time become a real alliance, not just one characterized by US dominance and European passivity." This is refreshing realism: NATO was never a real alliance and, by implication, should start life afresh as a real alliance and face up to the challenges of the 1980s. But before they get through, the authors have second thoughts about NATO's ability to meet those challenges. In the end, they decide *not* to propose that NATO should change any of its major institutional arrangements with respect to the Third World, that is to say, outside Europe. To make any such innovations would require fundamental amendment of the North Atlantic Treaty by fifteen parliaments, evidently a hopeless prospect. With no real change in sight, the report settles for a reaffirmation of NATO's prime purpose to defend the territories of its member states.

If this report had stopped there, its interest would have been limited. Happily, it does not stop until it puts forward a genuinely new proposal, or rather a new version of an old one. In 1958, President Charles de

Gaulle made a proposal for a directorate comprising the United States, Great Britain, and France to shape the global policies of the Western alliance. It was airily rejected by President Eisenhower, because the United States at that time had no intention of sharing global power. Now the authors of *Western Security* have superficially resurrected the basic Gaullist idea, added two other members to the directorate, Germany and Japan, and renamed it "principal nation groups." The report is likely to be remembered, if at all, for this idea.

The new set-up, however, is not what de Gaulle had in mind. His directorate was global in conception. The "principal nation groups" are to be regional and are to be brought into existence to deal with the Third World. Some groups might be temporary, some quasi-permanent. Some might vary in membership, depending on the area, but the Big Five usually would make up the "core group" in all of them. Only one is recommended for immediate formation—to deal with the Persian Gulf and Southwest Asia regions. Only the Big Five are mentioned as eligible for this one. Other groups might deal with a crisis in the Mediterranean and bring in Italy, or one in the Pacific and bring in Canada and Australia. The functions allotted to them are "crisis management and joint assessments," entailing exchange of information and contingency planning on a regular basis.

In all, this report envisages a three-tiered arrangement. Two of the tiers are already in existence. One is NATO, which would continue to be preoccupied with East-West relations. The second is the seven-nation summits of the advanced industrialized nations, begun in 1975, which deal mainly with economic matters, and of which the authors evidently do not have a high opinion. The new set-up would be put on top of these in order to deal specifically with "political and security developments in the Third World." The authors carefully stipulate that the new groups should be kept separate from NATO and should merely keep NATO and the European Community "closely informed." In the end, the authors of the report have nothing less in mind than "a new transatlantic bargain" and a "restructuring" of the Western alliance.

Can this scheme be taken seriously? I doubt it. It is bureaucratically overloaded and top-heavy. Some top officials might have little time left over from going to and from meetings of NATO, the seven-nation summits, and the new "principal nation groups." If the Western alliance needs to strike a new bargain and to be restructured, the reason is political rather than organizational. If the European members had the will to act in concert with the United States outside the NATO area in the principal nation groups, they would find a way to do so within a renegotiated and restructured NATO. Instead, the new set-up asks the Europeans to do outside NATO what they refuse to do inside. Changing the venue of this problem does not solve it or make it easier to solve.

What is the likelihood that, say, France and Germany would agree to act in concert with the US outside the NATO area if they could do so in principal nation groups? The likelihood is just as slim as it is now. NATO today suits what they conceive to be their national and continental interest. It was set up in their defense, and they want it to stay that way. European isolationism has far deeper roots than this scheme is willing to face. Europe did not become isolationist in a fit of absentmindedness or by a mental aberration. European isolationism may be dangerous and shortsighted, but it is deliberate and deep-seated.

The proposed set-up suffers from another flaw. It implicitly assumes that East-West relations can be separated from Third World relations. The scheme is speciously based on a division of labor between NATO and the principal nation groups. But what if a Persian Gulf/Southwest Asia crisis impinges on Soviet-American interests, as it almost certainly will, in the manner of the Arab-Israeli war of 1973? One must imagine that the European members would do their utmost to stay out of that area of tension in NATO and get into it in a principal nation group. The suggestion that there might be a principal nation group for a crisis in the Mediterranean is an even more far-fetched version of the division of labor. Has the Mediterranean been moved to the Third World so that it may come within the area of a principal nation group? Is it realistic to imagine that Japan would participate in a principal nation group for the Mediterranean or Germany in one for the Pacific?

I refuse to believe that our Four Wise Men and their advisers were not wise enough to see the incongruities and contradictions in their plan. What, then, impelled them to put it forward? I suspect that the answer is practical, not theoretical. NATO, it is clear, has become an obstacle to clear thinking and rational policy. Yet we can neither get rid of it nor reform it. The next best thing is to make an end run around it. The principal nation groups exactly serve this purpose. If ever they were to materialize, it would soon be evident that they were taking over responsibility for whatever and wherever the real action was. In practice, it hardly would matter anymore whether NATO survived or not. What would matter is what the Big Five chose to do in their principal nation groups.

The trouble with this strategy is that it belongs in the too-smart-by-half department of foreign policy. The authors of this report never confront the hard questions their plan evokes. They expect West European nations to make a large contribution to the defense of Western interests outside NATO, but they do not tell the reader why the same nations refuse to do so inside NATO. One is never made to understand why the West European nations are so inhibited about moving out of the NATO area, as if all they needed to get themselves moving was an organizational gimmick that would bypass NATO. The report is brave enough to say flatly that "present institutions are inadequate and at times lack relevance for 1980s" without being bold enough to ask why inadequate and sometimes irrelevant institutions must be maintained or cannot be drastically revised.

Nevertheless, *Western Security* is an important and significant effort, even where it is weakest. It reflects a concern for Western insecurity far more than it contributes to Western security. It suggests that even this high-powered foursome has just about given up on NATO, cannot figure out how to make it adequate and relevant for the 1980s, and thinks we must take refuge in "new mechanisms for truly collective decision-making." Its proposal for new mechanisms may be just what the patient needs, but the patient is unlikely to be receptive so long as he holds on to the nostrum of the old mechanisms. This report brings out the real problem most eloquently by trying to evade it.

The issue is whether Western Europe and the United States can act together wherever their collective interests are threatened, in Europe or elsewhere. Now that the United States admittedly cannot take care of "elsewhere" alone, except in the most local, one-sided circumstances, NATO is not enough. The great merit of this report is that it recognizes this state of affairs and tries to do something about it. However, it refuses to say outright that NATO—or at least the peculiar type of European isolationism typified by NATO—blocks the way. It tells us where we want to go, but until we openly face why we have been unable to go there, we are not likely to make any progress.

The New Republic, March 28, 1981

4

Rolling Communism Backward

The Soviet invasion of Afghanistan and the threatened Soviet military intervention in Poland raise a most disturbing and little discussed question. These actions are usually justified on the ground that both countries were already part of the Soviet political or security system and, therefore, the Soviets have some kind of "right" to keep them there. The question is: should the United States or any other non-communist country accept this justification?

The Soviet policy of military intervention in communist countries was codified in the so-called Brezhnev Doctrine. It was promulgated in 1968 to serve as an ideological shield for the brutal invasion of Czechoslovakia. Soviet leader Leonid I. Brezhnev took special pains to associate the doctrine with his name. In the speech in which he expounded it most fully, he explained that it was applicable whenever "external and internal forces hostile to socialism try to turn the development of a given socialist country in the direction of the capitalist system." Such a threat, he asserted, was "no longer merely a problem for that country's people, but a common problem, the concern of all socialist countries." According to this reasoning, the Soviet Union, backed by all or some members of its bloc, was entitled to send in its army in the guise of "military assistance" to put down the threat.

This speech was delivered on November 12, 1968, in Warsaw at the Fifth Congress of the Polish Communist party. Brezhnev effusively congratulated the Polish party for "its fine example of a principled Marxist-Leninist policy and of fidelity to the principles of socialist internationalism." If the Soviets should decide to apply the Brezhnev doctrine to Poland in the near future, Brezhnev no doubt will have reason to congratulate the now housebroken Czechoslovak party for its "fine example" against the Poles.

The Brezhnev doctrine rests on another article of faith that is more far-reaching in its larger implications and ultimate importance. It is the tenet of communist "irreversibility." This rule holds that a communist state must never be permitted to free itself from communism—in practice the kind of communism that the Soviet Union tolerates—or to break out of the Soviet orbit. Once a communist state, always a communist state—that is the principle. Just what deviations from Soviet theory and practice can be tolerated is no longer as clear as it used to be. But it is safe to say that two things cannot be tolerated: loss of control of its people by a national party, and loss of control of the national party by the Soviet Union. In Poland today, the national party is well on its way to losing control of the Polish people; in Czechoslovakia in 1968, the Soviet Union lost control of the national party.

The Soviet intervention in Afghanistan conforms more to the second criterion than to the first. On the face of it, there would not seem to be much of anything in Afghanistan to warrant a full-scale military invasion. Economically, Afghanistan produces nothing that the Soviet Union does not have or that it needs. Strategically, the Soviet Union does not need to go through Afghanistan to get to Iran and the Persian Gulf. The Soviets have a long border with Iran; they practiced going directly into Iran during their takeover of Azerbaijan in 1942–46. A Soviet takeover of Pakistan would be an economic, social, and logistical nightmare; it would send tremors of insecurity into the domain of the Soviets' good friend Indira Gandhi, who would have no buffer against new neighbors.

There remains only the political reason—the doctrine of irreversibility. That it should have been applied to Afghanistan suggests to what absurd lengths the Brezhnev leadership is willing to go on its behalf.

The dates are eloquent. Mohammed Noor Taraki seized power by a coup in April 1978. Backed by the Soviet Union, he signed a Treaty of Friendship, Good-Neighborliness and Cooperation with the Soviets in December 1978. Taraki was overthrown and murdered by Hafizullah Amin in September 1979. Amin was also backed by the Soviets at first; the Soviet press hailed him as a great leader and worthy ally. Then something went wrong. The assumption is that Amin was guilty of a "nationalist deviation"—that is, he proved to be more independent than the Soviets had bargained for. Amin allegedly called in the Soviets in late December 1979, whereupon he was immediately murdered and replaced by the present puppet, Babrak Karmal. The operation was so clumsy that the world was expected to believe that Amin had asked for help from his own executioners. Karmal made the original story even more grotesque by accusing Amin of having been "an agent of the CIA and American imperialism." No effort was ever made to explain how the Soviets could have been stupid enough to have backed an agent of the CIA and American imperialism, and how such an agent could have been so imbecilic as to have called in the Soviet army to save him.

Unfortunately for the Soviet leadership, the Brezhnev Doctrine could not be applied to Afghanistan in all its primordial purity. The restoration of capitalism could be charged against the Dubček regime in Czechoslovakia in 1968 with at least a semblance of economic rationality; the Czechoslovak social and economic order conceivably could be made to work under some form of capitalism. But Afghanistan could hardly be accused of the same crime, because it would have had to have capitalism before it could be said to restore it. The idea of a dominant capitalism in Afghanistan would have brought tears of laughter rolling down Karl Marx's cheeks. Instead of restoring capitalism, Amin had to be charged with taking Afghanistan out of the "socialist camp" and serving "American imperialism."

Now let us go back to the dates. The doctrine of irreversibility had to be applied in a country where the original Soviet figurehead, Taraki, had been put into power less than two years before the Soviet intervention, and his successor, Amin, had been in power for only about three months. Each of them had hardly had time to do more than murder as many as possible of the other's faction. Yet, as Robert G. Kaiser reports in the current issue of *Foreign Affairs*, a Soviet official, who was himself allegedly unhappy about the Soviet invasion of Afghanistan, explained it in these terms: "The armies of socialism march only in one direction." Unhappy as he may have been, this official apparently thought it was a sufficient explanation from a Soviet point of view. If it must be maintained in Afghanistan, it seems we have reached the point where the doctrine of irreversibility must be upheld at all costs.

The Polish case presents a more orthodox version of irreversibility. Poland has been ruled by the Communist party since the end of World War II. The Polish party's loss of control unquestionably presents the greatest threat to Soviet rule in Eastern Europe in almost forty years. What attitude should we adopt to the doctrine in general and to its application to Poland in particular?

One attitude was expressed by Ronald Steel in *The New Republic* ("After the Binge," February 14, 1981):

> Would we come to the aid of the Poles if the Russians invaded? Of course not. The matter is not even open to question. Poland is an integral part of the Soviet bloc and the Soviet security system. This was tacitly acknowledged in the postwar settlement of 1945 and never seriously challenged since. If we resist telling the Poles to give it a try, it is because we know what will be the likely consequences for them—and for us. And we have to resist giving them any false hopes of armed support that we have not the slightest intention of honoring.

This is bad history and worse politics. There never was any postwar settlement in 1945 that acknowledged, tacitly or otherwise, that Poland was an integral part of the Soviet bloc. Serious efforts were made by the United States to arrive at a compromise on the status of Poland and to resist the total Sovietization of Poland for at least two more years. Those efforts failed because the United States did not have or was unwilling to use the power necessary to make them succeed. The Soviet determination of Poland's fate was a *fait accompli*—that and nothing more. It was so little acknowledged politically by the United States that John Foster Dulles was willing to raise the issue again in the form of "liberation" and "rollback" in the early 1950s. Dulles's catchwords were empty rhetoric; he had nothing with which to back them up. He betrayed his own professions in 1956 when he turned on Britain and France during their Suez operation and turned away from the risings in Hungary and Poland that very year. Actually, Dulles himself never gave Eastern Europe any false hopes of armed support; his fault was that he encouraged them to break away with the understanding that "separation from Moscow" could be achieved peacefully. But whatever Dulles's faults were, they hardly can be said to suggest US acknowledgment of a Polish postwar settlement of 1945.

A "settlement" implies an agreement in which differences have been composed by both sides. In this sense, there was no settlement; there was only an American failure to dissuade the Soviet Union from setting up a Soviet-style regime in Poland. That failure was due to the adverse circumstances of almost four decades ago. Among those adverse circumstances were the catastrophic state of postwar Poland as well as the inability of the United States to influence the Soviet Union by diplomatic means alone. A movement such as Solidarity was unthinkable in

1945–47. That it exists today shows that the internal circumstances have fundamentally changed. The decisive factor is no longer armed support by the United States.

What purpose is served today by sagely advising the Polish workers and farmers that they should not count on any false hopes of armed support by the United States? Is anyone in the United States even hinting at such armed support? What purpose is served by telling the Polish popular leaders that the United States has tacitly acknowledged a settlement of 1945 making Poland an integral part of the Soviet bloc and the Soviet security system? Is this message supposed to mean that Solidarity and its sympathizers are guilty of breaking a settlement tacitly entered into by the United States and, therefore, unacceptable to both the Soviet Union and the United States? Why should we resist telling the Poles "to give it a try" as if we are in a position to tell them what they should try or as if it makes any difference what we resist telling the Poles?

The whole attitude is condescending to the United States and patronizing to the Poles. It is condescending to the United States because it solemnly warns against something that no American of any importance has shown the slightest sign of proposing. It is patronizing to the Poles because it assumes that they are not smart enough to know from their own experience that we could not have the slightest intention of honoring false hopes of armed support.

Steel finds it necessary to threaten the Poles with "the likely consequences for them—and for us" if they try to refuse to play their assigned role as an integral part of the Soviet bloc and the Soviet security system. The not-so-subtle hint is that Soviet-communist rule in Poland is irreversible and that the Polish people need to be forewarned of the likely consequences if they are counting on American armed support to make it reversible. Yet, having gotten rid of this red herring, Steel recognizes that "the Soviet decision will be based primarily on what happens within Poland, and to a much lesser degree on a reluctance to endanger relatively good relations with Eastern Europe." We may ignore those relatively good relations with Eastern Europe, but he is undoubtably right about the primacy of "what happens within Poland." Such irruptions have occurred in Eastern Europe about every dozen years. The system of Soviet bondage and tutelage ultimately cannot survive such regular, increasingly cataclysmic upheavals within the "socialist camp." There is no need in these circumstances to lecture those who have to take all the risks about a fictitious postwar settlement in 1945 or about the likely consequences of trying to challenge it. If we cannot give them armed support, at least we do not have to treat them as if we have to tell them the facts of life in mournful tones.

The doctrine of communist irreversibility is only one side of the coin. The other side is non-communist reversibility. The latter is the unspoken, implicit part of the combination.

In 1960, for example, then Soviet first deputy premier Anastas I. Mikoyan traveled to Havana and made a first commercial deal with Fidel Castro. Since then, Castro has turned Cuba into one of the more oppressive communist states, with a self-styled communist party, vast subsidies from the Soviet Union, and an army at the disposal of the Soviet Union for military adventures in distant continents. Non-communist Cuba was reversed into communist Cuba ninety miles from the United States.

The present case of El Salvador is equally instructive. The political and social virtues and vices of both sides in El Salvador have no bearing on this aspect of Soviet-American relations. We now have confirmation, from the Soviet embassy in Washington, of what was previously known —that Soviet arms shipments to Cuba are transshipped elsewhere without any Soviet restrictions on the destinations of the arms. The Cubans, in effect, act as Soviet agents or intermediaries in supplying Soviet arms to the Salvadoran rebels and others. The difference between direct Soviet intervention in El Salvador and this gimmick of indirect intervention would impress only a political moron.

Is communism in Cuba irreversible? Is non-communism in El Salvador reversible? The answers remain to be seen. Meanwhile, we cannot evade the questions in principle.

Of course the question is not one of principle only. What the United States should do in any given case is conditioned by what the United States can do. Dulles was culpable for pretending that the United States had a policy of "liberation" and "rollback" without any practical means to bring them about. Nevertheless, does it mean that the liberation of Eastern Europe and the rollback of Soviet power to its own borders was wrong in principle? Tilting against John Foster Dulles's windmills in 1981 does not begin to answer this question.

The Soviets constantly invite us to join them in political double-bookkeeping. The whole communist world is irreversible, but the whole non-communist world is reversible. It is astonishing how successfully they manage to play this double game far outside their own ranks. This asymmetry is rarely brought into the open. It is taken for granted, without thought of its implications.

Those implications would foreclose the future. If communism is irreversible and non-communism of whatever variety is reversible; if the armies of "socialism" march only in one direction (forward), and the armies of capitalism, democracy, or anything else also march in one direction (backward), the end of the road has been clearly marked out. The end must be the universal conquest of communism.

This is where the doctrine of communist irreversibility irresistibly leads. It leads there in principle. Whether it can or will ever be achieved in practice may well be doubted. But a victory of such dimensions even in principle is no small gain. If there is to be any reciprocity in Soviet-American relations, there is no reason to concede irreversibility to Soviet political and security interests any more than reversibility to American political and security interests. There is no more reason to acknowledge irreversibility in Afghanistan or Poland than there is in Cuba or El Salvador. Poland may be an integral part of the Soviet bloc and Soviet security system, and the United States may be unable or unwilling to come to the aid of the Poles if the Russians invade. But the Soviet bloc and Soviet security system are not immune—any more than the American bloc and American security system are immune—from being reversed from within as well as from without. Nothing in this world is irreversible forever. If the only thing that can save Soviet communism in Poland from being reversed is the brute force of military invasion, the Soviet system has already been reversed in every respect that humanly counts and ultimately matters.

The New Republic, March 7, 1981

III

GHOSTS OF VIETNAM

1

Ghosts of Vietnam

I

The Vietnam war was beyond doubt the most demanding test of American foreign policy and its makers since the Second World War. The war in Vietnam was not just another crisis in thirty years of successive crises; it was by far the most costly and most stultifying. It lasted longer than any other war and ended in the most humiliating failure in American history. It resulted in over 210,000 American casualties, including almost 57,000 dead and over 150,000 wounded. The monetary cost has been officially estimated at from $180 billion to $210 billion. This bill for the war ignores all the indirect costs, such as the corrosive economic inflation it stimulated and the feverish social turmoil it provoked. As for the havoc inflicted on North and South Vietnam, it belongs to a different order of magnitude. No wonder that the memory of Vietnam is so oppressive that Americans seem to want to stuff it away in their collective unconscious.

One might well assume that the present custodians of American foreign policy had been chosen because they were proven right in their judgment of the war. It could come as a surprise that, in order to rise to the top of the post-Vietnam American political system, it was almost necessary to be wrong, hopelessly and certifiably wrong. Yet, in some odd way, this is what happened. The false counsellors were rewarded with more power than they had had before they made their ghastly mistakes about the war.

President Jimmy Carter consistently supported the war and was saved from making his support too conspicuous only by his relative obscurity in national politics. Secretary of State Cyrus Vance was another proponent of the war, also sheltered from too much public notice by his inability or unwillingness to speak out very forcefully about anything. Both of them seem to think that it was enough for them to say, "Sorry, folks, we were wrong about the war," to gain political absolution. They were more fortunate than Professor Zbigniew Brzezinski and his predecessor as national security adviser, Dr. Henry Kissinger. Kissinger managed to find bad reasons to support what he knew was a bad war; Brzezinski hit on essentially the same reasons for what he thought was a good war. And now, as the most influential member of his staff and his closest confidant, Brzezinski has with him Professor Samuel P. Huntington, one of the hardest of prowar hardliners and the least repentant.

In one respect, the problem of the Vietnam war resembled that of the Korean war. Since American interests in both Korea and Vietnam were minimal, other reasons had to justify American intervention. In the case of Korea, American policy-makers considered North Korea to be nothing but a Soviet puppet ordered by Moscow to attack South Korea as the opening move in a larger strategy to "probe for the weakness in our armor," as former President Truman put it, in order to start a process of disintegration in the entire American structure of allies and dependents throughout Europe and Asia.

Fighting Russia in Korea was what made the war seem necessary and worthwhile. According to this reasoning, the Soviets should have taken advantage of their success in bogging down the bulk of American armed forces in Korea for three years, particularly at the time of the crushing defeat of General MacArthur's forces by Chinese armies across the Yalu River at the end of 1950, which was presumably what the wire-pullers in the Kremlin had been waiting for. Instead, the Korean war increasingly lived a life of its own. The original rationale for getting into it became dimmer and dimmer, and all that remained was to get out of it as gracefully and cheaply as possible. The Korean war turned out essentially to be a *Korean* war, which ultimately made it tangential to America's larger interests and preposterously expensive for what we could get out of it. Whatever the Russian role might have been, and we still know little for sure about it, the Korean war was far more a feint than the real thing.

The Vietnam war followed the same general course. In the beginning, the Truman administration injected itself into the French imbroglio in Indochina with vast amounts of financial assistance and military equipment, ostensibly to bolster French pride and stability and to gain French support for American defense plans in Europe. After the outbreak of the

Korean war, the struggle in Indochina took on a wider connotation as part of a worldwide Communist "conspiracy." With the defeat of France in 1954, the Eisenhower administration took over responsibility for South Vietnam, now split off from North Vietnam by the Geneva accords, on the ground that loss of all of Vietnam would inevitably bring about the loss of all the other "dominoes" in Southeast Asia, including Thailand, Malaya, Burma, and Indonesia. In the stage of massive, direct American intervention during the Johnson administration, the real enemy in Vietnam became China, a point of view put forward most extravagantly by then former Vice-President Richard M. Nixon in 1965 and with monumental obtuseness by Secretary of State Dean Rusk in 1966 and afterward. Without superimposing a larger framework on the Korean and Vietnam wars, American policy-makers would have been forced to acknowledge that essentially they were civil wars—civil wars with outside backing but still primarily localized civil wars—and not the opening shot of the Final Conflict. We might still have been drawn into them, but at least we would have known what we were doing and what they were worth to us.

II

How difficult it was to justify American intervention in Vietnam intellectually is strikingly shown by the travail of two outstanding foreign-affairs intellectuals—Henry Kissinger and Zbigniew Brzezinski. If they could not think up better reasons for supporting the war, no one could.

Kissinger's position on the war made its first public appearance in *Look* magazine of August 9, 1966, in the second year of massive American intervention. In an article written after he had made two trips to Vietnam at the invitation of then Ambassador Henry Cabot Lodge, Kissinger set forth two principal propositions. One was that the war could not be won by military means. The other was that it had to be settled by negotiation. In effect, he succeeded in establishing some distance between himself and both the extreme hawks and extreme doves. Kissinger had clearly learned enough during his two tours of Vietnam and from his Pentagon sources to make him extremely cautious about committing himself to anything that might be called "victory."

After outlining this equivocal approach, Kissinger fell silent on the issue of Vietnam for almost two years, an uncharacteristic reticence that his friendly memorialists have had great difficulty explaining.[1]

Kissinger broke his silence on Vietnam in the summer of 1968, by which time even the inner circles of the Johnson administration had given up the war as a lost cause. At a conference on Vietnam in Chicago in June of that year, sponsored by the Adlai Stevenson Institute of International Affairs, Kissinger savagely criticized American policy, especially its "concepts"—military concepts, traditional liberal concepts, balance-of-power concepts, indeed the entire "American philosophy of international relations." If American policy was that bankrupt, one might imagine that the best thing to do would be to get out of the war as soon as possible at the least possible cost. But Kissinger did not offer any new concepts or policies himself; he merely called for a "prayerful assessment" of the procedures and concepts that had landed us in such a mess.[2]

Kissinger saved his own conceptual prescription for the speeches that he composed for Governor Nelson Rockefeller in the presidential campaign that summer and for an article in *Foreign Affairs* written in his own name in the same period. The basic idea—or, to use Kissinger's favorite term, "concept"—was that of a negotiated settlement, hardly a novel one at the time. More important were the conditions that Kissinger attached to such a settlement. It had to be arrived at in such a way that it did not shake "confidence in American promises" or compromise American "credibility," "prestige," or "steadiness." The key word was "honorably"—the war had to be ended "honorably." He conceived of doing so by means of a U.S.-Soviet-China "subtle triangle," whereby the United States would improve its relations with the two leading communist powers and thereby achieve or at least advance an honorable settlement in Vietnam through them.[3]

By this time, the United States in essence had no other stake in Vietnam than its "honor." Here again, the hard questions were evaded. What if the United States could not end the war "honorably" without paying an exorbitant price for the attempt, and then not succeed anyway? What if the road to peace in Vietnam did not run through Russia and China? What if Russia and China themselves were to work at cross purposes in Vietnam and elsewhere? Kissinger's honorable settlement in Vietnam was fitted into his rickety new "global, conceptual approach," which presupposed that Russia and China could restrain North Vietnam and that the Thieu regime in South Vietnam could be made capable of defending itself without American armed forces. Without these presuppositions, it would have made no sense for the Nixon-Kissinger policy to drag the American people through four more years of a war emptied of all meaning but that of getting out of a trap into which the United States should never have fallen.

When did Kissinger awake to the realities of the war? His friend Professor John G. Stoessinger tells us that it took Kissinger until the fall of 1971, all of three long, bloodstained Nixonian years, to realize that "Hanoi would not compromise." In 1972, Kissinger thought that he could get a Soviet "linkage" to a Vietnam settlement through the grain deal, which gave hundreds of millions of dollars worth of American wheat to Russia at bargain prices at the expense of the American consumer, a price that, Kissinger argued, "was well worth a Vietnam settlement." Again he was disappointed. Finally, on the day that Saigon fell in the spring of 1975, Kissinger told Stoessinger: "Vietnam is a Greek tragedy. We should never have been there at all. But now it's history."[4] As an epitaph on this war, "We should never have been there at all" may never be excelled.

Unlike Kissinger, Brzezinski was at first much less circumspect. He was one of the first of the most militant defenders of the prowar faith; he supported the war aggressively in a notable television debate in which his opposite intellectual number was Professor Hans Morgenthau, who was never taken in by the war. Brzezinski's service in behalf of the war helped to get him an appointment in 1966 to the State Department's Policy Planning Council. *Newsweek* hailed him as "one of the fastest-rising stars in the Johnson Administration" and "one of the architects of U.S. foreign policy" after only four months on the job. As for "his hawkish position on Vietnam," the magazine's piece entitled "Diplomacy: The Thinker," went on, "he is apt to act as though he had a monopoly of the truth." The cheering was premature; Brzezinski returned to Columbia University after two years in Washington, apparently sorely disillusioned with the exercise of planning without power.

In this period, Brzezinski had little sympathy with antiwar demonstrators. In an article in *Foreign Affairs* of July 1966, he put them down as "a manifestation of a psychological crisis inherent in modern society." Vietnam, he wrote scornfully, was merely "an outlet for basic cravings and fears, and if that issue did not exist, some other one would provide an excuse for the expression of personal and political alienation." This was one way of exonerating the Vietnam war of blame for the widespread popular unrest and widespread opposition to the war.

By 1968, Brzezinski's attitude toward the war showed signs of unbearable strain. On the one hand, he gave up a clear-cut victory in Vietnam; he was now satisfied with denying victory to the enemy, though he never explained how the no-victory-no-defeat for either side was going to be calibrated. On the other hand, he told the *U.S. News & World Report* of February 26, 1968, that he wanted the United States to make it clear that it was willing to continue to fight in Vietnam for thirty years in order to prove to the enemy that "we have the staying power" and "happen to be richer and more powerful." He gave as his reason for such a long-range projection that the United States could not "commit itself to the extent it has, and 'chicken out.' "

By now, there was little or nothing in Vietnam that made thirty years of war advisable or necessary, even to a hitherto fervent supporter of the war; it was the American "commitment" itself that condemned us to an almost unimaginably interminable bloodletting. Thirty years of war was so breathtakingly long that Brzezinski might as well have said "forever." And all this for not even victory. Rereading this interview, one cannot take it seriously. What it suggests is that even as sharp and knowledgeable a specialist in foreign affairs as Brzezinski had completely lost his way and no longer made sense when he talked about the Vietnam war.

By 1969, Brzezinski himself must have realized that he had to find his way back to some kind of sanity about the war. Richard Nixon was now president and vast demonstrations all over the country for a Vietnam "moratorium" had just taken place. In these circumstances, Brzezinski advised Nixon to pledge the removal of American forces from Vietnam "by a particular date (say, two years)." In this statement to the *New York Times* of October 17, 1969, Brzezinski forgot about the thirty-years war and neglected to make clear why it was better to "chicken out" in two years rather than immediately.

After this, Brzezinski apparently decided that it was the better part of valor to leave the Vietnam war alone. While the country was in an uproar over it during the first Nixon administration, he turned his attention to other matters—the "technetronic era," Japan and Africa. This intellectual flying-trapeze act took him out of the line of fire and broadened his horizon in preparation for bigger things to come. It was also an admission that the war had become too much for even its most ardent and hardened supporters. It had become intellectually insupportable and even unmentionable.

Brzezinski's advice against "chickening out" and Kissinger's emphasis on ending the war "honorably" were essentially similar in motivation. We were supposed to go on fighting to prove something to ourselves or to the world at large, not to achieve anything of material or political interest in Vietnam. Brzezinski's temporary aberration of fighting on for thirty years was the logical outcome of this line of reasoning. If we could not end the war "honorably" and could not "chicken out," it had to go on and on indefinitely. Brzezinski's bravado was thus the *reductio ad absurdum* of the Vietnam war. Even he seems to have realized it in time.

In the end, Kissinger blamed Watergate and a failure of nerve for the debacle in Vietnam. The American people, Congress, South Vietnam, North Vietnam and the Soviet Union had all conspired to let down Henry Kissinger. The implication that his own people had failed him suggests that Kissinger's understanding of warfare left something to be desired. A good general—and even a good lieutenant—assesses his own strength as objectively as that of the enemy; he does not go into battle without taking into account what his own forces are capable of accomplishing and, in the particular case of the American people, what they are willing to fight for and at what cost. It was violation of this cardinal rule of warfare, not failure of nerve, that brought about the dishonorable end of the Vietnam war. It was the very nature of the war—a hopeless war in a land where we should never have been at all—that made its continuation so intolerable and its end so ignominious. There was no good way of getting out of the Vietnam war but the worst way was to pay the price of getting out later rather than sooner.*

In effect, Kissinger and Brzezinski, two celebrated intellectuals who lent their considerable talents to a prolongation of the war, gave up the job of justification when they fell back on ending it "honorably" and not "chickening out." If they could do no better than that, the job was hopeless. Or so it seemed until now.

III

For we have just been offered a book that promises to relieve the American people of a sense of guilt for the Vietnam war and to absolve the United States of "*officially condoned* illegal and immoral conduct." The book is *America in Vietnam,* by Professor Guenter Lewy of the University of Massachusetts at Amherst. The work comes recommended by

---

* Lest the reader think that this is hindsight on my part, I may be permitted to recall that I also attended the Chicago conference on Vietnam of the Adlai Stevenson Institute of Foreign Affairs in June 1968. In view of the coming presidential election, I said: "Do we have a presidential candidate in sight who can say to the American people, 'We have suffered a failure in Vietnam; it is costly to get out; it is more costly to persist.' I fear that unless this is said now and clearly, we will not get out of this morass" (*No More Vietnams?* Richard M. Pffefer, ed. [New York: Harper & Row, 1968], pp. 97–98).

Charles B. MacDonald, a military historian, as "a sober, objective answer to polemicists on all sides" that "should enable the Vietnam veteran at last to hold his head high." Has Lewy succeeded where Kissinger and Brzezinski failed?

It should be said at once that those who read this book in order to assuage their guilt over the war are doomed to disappointment. The idea that it will enable a Vietnam veteran to hold his head high is utter rubbish. It does not attempt to answer "polemicists on all sides"; it polemicizes almost exclusively against the antiwar "polemicists." The author, his admirers, and his publishers may have made a mistake in presenting the book as if it were a wholesale apology for the war. This presentation may be enough to arouse curiosity but it does an injustice to the book as a whole.

It is a schizophrenic book. In large part, it made me writhe all over again at the willful stupidity and obdurate delusions with which the war was prosecuted. An almost unrelieved recital of mistakes and misdeeds fills pages and pages of the book. There are two Lewys in this work— one makes an admirable effort to get the facts straight; the other wants to give the United States a clean bill of health or at least the benefit of the doubt. Thus the book lends itself to different conclusions or interpretations depending on what chapter and even what paragraph one chooses to cite. The scholar and the advocate struggle for supremacy; sometimes one wins, sometimes the other.

It would be a mistake, therefore, for critics of the Vietnam war to reject Lewy's work *in toto* because he betrays a special animus against them, sometimes unfairly, or for hard-core supporters of the war to accept it with glee because he seems to favor them from time to time. Much of the book is the result of serious and painstaking research. If I had to draw up a list of a half dozen books worth reading on the war, I would put this one among them, despite its flaws.

But does the author make good his claim that "the sense of guilt created by the Vietnam war in the minds of many Americans is not warranted"? That is what the argument over this book is likely to be about.

The answer partly depends on the answer to another question—guilt about what? There may be justifiable guilt about some things and not about others. Lewy never makes the distinction clear. He himself contributes the most damaging evidence that American officialdom was disastrously guilty of misconceiving and mishandling the war; he also attempts to clear it of some specific varieties of guilt on a most selective basis. Yet his generalizations would make it appear that the United States has no need to feel guilty at all about anything. Here and elsewhere, Lewy undermines his own book by overreaching and overstating.

For example, the American forces in Vietnam deliberately pursued a policy of "the encouragement and creation of refugees." This meant that combat operations, crop destruction, and "specified strike zones" were utilized to drive Vietnamese peasants from their homes in the hundreds of thousands. The most cruel and senseless practice for "generating" refugees or as it was also called euphemistically, "relocating populations," took the form of "free-fire zones." An American commander would simply decide to designate an area, often a huge one, as such a zone so that anyone who remained in it was arbitrarily considered an enemy and thereby subject to annihilating artillery or air bombardment. This policy was pursued on a large scale for at least five years. Only in 1968, after over two years of this practice, were commanders in the field advised that they should not generate refugees "needlessly and heedlessly," with little effect on the actual tactics employed; and only in February 1969 were commanders officially instructed to give at least seventy-two hours notice to civilians in the areas, as if Vietnamese peasants in far-flung areas were likely to receive and understand such notices or do more than save their disrupted lives if they did.

Lewy knows what was wrong with this horror. He lists seven "inherent weaknesses," including the fact that it was militarily useless and even played into the hands of the enemy. The vast majority of those driven from their homes were old people, women and children; few refugees were males of military age. Even so, the battlefield was not cleared, because refugees persisted in returning to their hamlets. The political madness of the policy comes out in his words: "Not surprisingly, attitude surveys showed a high degree of correlation between forcible evacuation and pro-Communist attitudes." He acknowledges that the crop-destruction program made the local people, not the Vietcong, suffer. He reveals that the American crop-destruction missions were disguised as South Vietnamese activity because the damage obviously could not be limited to the enemy forces to conform with the Army's own manual of land warfare.

Lewy documents more of the same. The fatuous policy of "body counts" encouraged the indiscriminate lumping of combatants and noncombatants, with the result that the killing of villagers could give as much credit as the killing of enemy soldiers, and the only ones really deceived were the Americans themselves. The strategy of attrition was an abject failure. The villagers turned against the United States because American military doctrine called for methods that were insensitive to political and human costs; the South Vietnamese and Korean allies trained in that doctrine behaved even more abominably. American commanders often gave only "token compliance" to orders from above to restrain their excessive use of fire power, so that "the worst features of the traditional mode of operation persisted." Corruption in the South Vietnamese army was so great that it enabled the enemy to purchase supplies in South Vietnamese cities, obtain war materiel and food from South Vietnamese officials and officers, and buy positions as hamlet and village chiefs. The once highly touted South Vietnamese land reform was no more than an "empty gesture." American brigade and division commanders falsified reports to hide their persistent utilization of an unauthorized herbicide agent. Lewy also retells the story of the secret bombing of North Vietnam, based on fictitious enemy-action reports, which brought about the demotion and retirement of General John D. Lavelle, commanding officer of the Seventh Air Force. He has an entire chapter on American "atrocities" in Vietnam, one of which was the My Lai "massacre," using these very terms—"atrocity" and "massacre." He also describes the leniency of court-martials that dealt with these "war crimes"—again in this context his term.

The single American who comes off worst in Lewy's book is no ordinary officer or soldier. He is General William C. Westmoreland, chief of U.S. forces in Vietnam from 1964 to 1968, when he was recalled to become Army Chief of Staff. Lewy seems to hold Westmoreland most responsible for keeping to the disastrous strategy of "the big-unit war of attrition" long after it had been proven futile and self-defeating. In his most scathing indictment of Westmoreland, Lewy goes so far as to doubt that the general could defend himself against the charge that he was guilty of "dereliction of duty," because he should have known that American "violations of the law of war" were bound to take place in the circumstances of Vietnam and should have taken the necessary measures to prevent them.

If one sought to make a devastating condemnation of the Vietnam war, one could do so out of Lewy's book, as I have just done. But such an exercise would reflect only one side of the work. In another, the author seeks almost desperately to muffle his blows on the war and even to lead the unwary reader into believing that he is rushing to its defense.

IV

One way Lewy tries to make a bad war look better is the soft reproach.

For example, President Johnson told reporters after the decision was made to use American troops in Vietnam that he knew of "no far-reaching strategy that is being suggested or promulgated." Lewy's comment is: "Needless to say, Johnson here was being less than candid." Needless to say, Lewy is being less than candid; Johnson knew that a far-reaching strategic change had been initiated and had deliberately misled the reporters and the American people. Or Lewy demonstrates that the so-called Rules of Engagement, ostensibly designed to minimize the destruction of civilian life and property, were extensively and sometimes wantonly disregarded in practice. Lewy's comment is that "this level of familiarity was obviously less than satisfactory." He might have said more satisfactorily that the level of familiarity was grossly unsatisfactory and even culpably negligent.

Sometimes Lewy likes to have it both ways. He raises the question whether South Vietnam could have survived if U.S. aid had not been cut off in 1975. His first answer tends to be highly pessimistic—"there is reason to believe that, everything else being equal, internal weaknesses on the part of the South Vietnamese armed forces alone might have been sufficient to cause defeat in 1975." A few pages later, however, he seems to backtrack. The odds were still against the South Vietnamese but their defeat was not a "foregone conclusion." If President Nixon had been able to dissociate himself from the Watergate burglars and had been able to reintroduce American military power in Vietnam as he had promised; if Congress had been persuaded to provide South Vietnam with adequate military supplies; if the OPEC nations had suffered an early breakup and oil had continued to be cheap; if the North Vietnamese had made a few major mistakes; if South Vietnamese nationalists and anti-Communist sects had been able to overthrow the Thieu regime. . . . After this long string of "ifs," Lewy concludes: "None of these events was impossible, and if their occurrence in combination was unlikely, this was no more so than the combination of opposite events which did in fact take place." In this way, Lewy cuts the ground from under his own work. He has spent most of his book making quite credible the combination of events that in fact took place, with particular emphasis on the internal weaknesses of the South Vietnamese armed forces. Then he turns around, belies his own work, and makes the historical record no more likely to have happened than the conveniently early breakup of OPEC. This is not the only instance where he seems to flinch from the implications of his own findings.

What, above all, gives Lewy the air of being a defender of the prowar faith is his criticism of the Vietnam war's critics. He always refers to them with a particularly wrathful peevishness. Sometimes, his tantrum gets in the way of elementary fairness.

I will offer myself as a case in point.

My book *Abuse of Power* was published in 1967. It was based on work done in the previous year and a half or so. Since Lewy's book came out in 1978, eleven years later, it would be odd if he had not consulted material not available to me or to other critics a decade ago. In any case, Lewy decided to teach me a lesson about a major turning point in the war—President Johnson's decision in February 1965 to initiate large-scale bombing of North Vietnam.

To justify this momentous step, the State Department issued later that month a White Paper entitled *Aggression from the North: The Record of North Viet-Nam's Campaign to Conquer South Viet-Nam*. The thesis of the White Paper was—North Vietnamese forces had invaded South Vietnam in such numbers that the previously officially regarded civil war had turned into a foreign "aggression." The question naturally arose whether the incursion of North Vietnamese forces was large enough to justify the massive intervention of American ground forces. The White Paper was a propaganda flop because it failed to sustain the claim of a large-scale invasion from the North. Lewy admits the "weakness" of the White Paper. But then he goes on:

> Theodore Draper alleges that at the time the bombing of North Vietnam started, Hanoi had only 400 regular soldiers in the South. The U.S. converted this into an "invasion" in order to have a justification for its own escalation.

The footnote Lewy appends to this discussion goes even further and changes the "allegation" into a "canard." An allegation implies a statement without supporting evidence; a canard means an unfounded and especially a false report. Could my treatment of the issue fairly be described as either a mere allegation or an outright canard?

I devoted almost eight pages to the question of the North Vietnamese infiltration southward. I related that Secretary of State Rusk had claimed that the entire 325th Division had been moved into South Vietnam by January 1965. But I noted that the White Paper the following month had not even mentioned the 325th, as it might have been expected to do. I also pointed out that Secretary of Defense McNamara, who should have known best, had in April 1965 confirmed the presence of only one battalion, estimated by him at 400 to 500 men, of the 325th in the south. Over a year later, in June 1966, Senator Mike Mansfield, the Democratic majority leader, had publicly repeated the number of "only about 400 North Vietnamese soldiers" in the South at the time of "the sharp increase in the American military effort" in early 1965. An enquiring reporter had subsequently learned that Senator Mansfield had obtained his figure from the Pentagon. Other evidence pointed in the same direction.

After laying out all the available information, I commented:

> Clearly we cannot be sure whether a battalion or a regiment or all of the 325th Division crossed into South Vietnam by January 1965 or at any other time. We could not be sure even if Secretaries Rusk and McNamara agreed, and their disagreement adds a dash of farce to what was otherwise one of the most grievous moments of the war. The most we can conclude from the available evidence is that it was extraordinarily necessary for the Secretary of State to have an "invasion" of South Vietnam by a North Vietnamese organized unit at least as large as a division before the United States began its systematic bombing of the North in February 1965.

Thus I did not even foreclose the question of the number of North Vietnamese regular soldiers in the South in February 1965. I rather emphasized the official disparities, which at that time would have led any fair-minded observer not to know what to believe. My final word was: "We may still not know much about the elusive 325th, but we can know a great deal about how it was bandied to and fro by high American officials who could not even convince each other." Nor did I say that the United States had converted the smaller number of North Vietnamese regulars into an "invasion"; I said that Secretary Rusk, the only one who then vouched for the presence of an entire North Vietnamese division in the South, had shown an extraordinary need for at least a division to justify the U.S. bombing campaign in the North. My very point was that leading officials of the United States were divided in their pronouncements on the subject.

Can my treatment be fairly described as an "allegation," as if I had picked out a number without reason, or as a "canard," as if I had spread a demonstrably false, unfounded rumor? The real authors of the report about the 400 North Vietnamese regular soldiers in the South were Secretary McNamara and Senator Mansfield, no inconsequential authorities on such a matter, and their information had clearly come from the Pentagon. The most that could be said at the time was that Secretary Rusk and the State Department claimed to know better.

Lewy, however, has triumphantly brought forth a new source of intelligence on what I called "the elusive 325th." It comes from a "Working Paper of the U.S. State Department on the North Vietnamese Role in the War in South Vietnam," issued in May 1968. According to this "working paper," which did not appear in print in the United States until 1969, 4,000 North Vietnamese regulars went south by February 1965 and another 1,800 by March 1965.[5] If the ultimate source was South Vietnamese, Lewy himself, in other connections, tells us how unreliable this source was; and if the data was provided two or three years after the event, it would be even more suspect.

Lewy's use of this "working paper" is so uncritical that it betrays his anxiety to defend the U.S. bombing at all costs.

First, it appeared in 1968, almost three and a half years after the event and a year after I had shown what unholy confusion had attended the whole matter. Obviously, I could not have known of a 1968 "working paper" in 1967. Neither could Secretary Rusk have based himself on it in 1965.

Second, the 1968 paper originated in the Department of State, not in the Department of Defense. There was nothing new about the State Department claims. I had already made known similar claims by Secretary of State Rusk in 1965. The problem arose because Secretary Rusk was controverted by Secretary of Defense McNamara and Senator Mansfield. A fair treatment would not have taken something put out by the State Department years later and subsequently generally ignored as if it were the last word on the subject; the discrepancy between the State Department and the Pentagon was the real question worth looking into, but Lewy chooses to ignore it.

Third, the reason I was struck by the remarkably dissimilar versions of North Vietnamese infiltration by February 1965 was the inordinate importance attached to it as the justification for America's massive intervention. Whatever was the number of North Vietnamese regular troops in the South in 1965, the U.S. combat force in South Vietnam was already far greater. The U.S. force increased from 23,000 at the end of 1964 to about 125,000 in the summer of 1965. Even if the 1968 "working paper" is taken at face value, the number of North Vietnamese troops in the South increased from 2,000 at the end of 1964 to

7,000 by September 1965. The "working paper" itself alluded to the "relatively slow pace of the [North Vietnamese] buildup" in all of 1965. It was already clear to me in 1967 that the American decision to intervene on a large scale was based "on South Vietnamese weakness rather than North Vietnamese strength." After all his pious protests against my "allegation" and "canard," Lewy ends by agreeing with me on this point. Somehow, a mere "allegation" and an outright "canard" had enabled me to reach the right conclusion.

I have gone into this example of Lewy's polemics against the "polemicists" because it shows how lacking in sobriety and objectivity he can be. It was necessary to go into it in some detail because the present reader could not be expected to have Lewy's book and mine at hand to refresh his memory regarding the background and significance of the question at issue. In effect, Lewy's book sometimes suffers from an excess of zeal, especially in his frequently intemperate dismissal of premature critics of the Vietnam war.

v

The heart of the matter is the peculiar strategy that Lewy employs to relieve Americans of a sense of guilt created by the Vietnam war and to dismiss from their consciences "charges of *officially condoned* illegal and grossly immoral conduct." He convinced me that this form of apologia is as doomed as the American war effort in Vietnam.

It is important to be clear about what Lewy defends. He does not defend the American way of war in Vietnam. He condemns its "obtuseness and mistakes in judgment." All that he affirms is that these were not the result of "culpable negligence." If the negligence was not "culpable," no war crimes were committed. He is operating here on a very narrow defensive front. The only sense of guilt he seeks to relieve is that for very legally circumscribed, intentional "war crimes."

The word "intentionally" plays a crucial role in his brief for the defense. He is willing to admit that "the rather free use of napalm and attacks upon fortified hamlets with artillery and air strikes can be criticized on humanitarian grounds"—to put it mildly in view of his own account of the ruthless, senseless devastation wrought by the "free-fire zones." Yet he can still find it "morally significant" that the tactics employed "did not intentionally aim at inflicting casualties upon the civilian population." Nevertheless, he had previously shown that, year after year, almost all the casualties brought about by these tactics were inflicted on the civilian population. He had previously shown that these casualties had been remorselessly inflicted on the civilian population because Vietnamese civilians and enemy soldiers or agents had been stupidly, arbitrarily, and indiscriminately lumped together. What in these circumstances is the meaning of "not intentionally"? What makes it so remarkably different for our sense of guilt from "intentionally"?

On one page, Lewy's apologia reveals its essential hollowness and heartlessness. His conclusion to a chapter on "American Military Tactics and the Law of War" begins with a general absolution:

> The American record in Vietnam with regard to observance of the law of war is not a succession of war crimes and does not support charges of a systematic and willful violation of existing agreements for standards of human decency in time of war, as many critics of the American involvement have alleged.

But the first sentence of the very next paragraph goes this way:

> If the American record is not one of gross illegality, neither has it been a model of observance of the law of war.

Here we have Lewy trying to have it both ways again. The second time around he merely absolves us of "gross illegality." How gross is "gross"? We can now see why Lewy italicized two words in his formulation of unwarranted charges of "*officially condoned* illegal and grossly immoral conduct." The conduct may be illegal but it is not all that bad unless it is *officially condoned*; it may be immoral but not anything to feel guilty about unless it is *grossly* immoral. How far up in the military hierarchy did illegal conduct have to go in order to be officially condoned? The "free-fire zone" horror was not merely officially condoned; it was officially conceived and carried out at the very top. It was persisted in by the American military command despite what Lewy calls its lamentable "cost-benefit equation." Lewy's tricky formulas do not whitewash illegal or immoral conduct; they defend it only from the most extreme accusations of such conduct.

In fact, Lewy betrays a guilty conscience of his own. In the very last paragraph of the same chapter, he draws back from making his entire case depend on the "law of war":

> In the final analysis, of course, law alone, no matter how comprehensive and carefully phrased, cannot assure protection of basic human values.

Back in the seventeenth century, Hugo Grotius, the father of modern international law, quoted with approval the advice which Euripides in *The Trojan Women* put into the mouth of Agamemnon addressing Pyrrhus: "What the law does not forbid, then let shame forbid." This counsel retains its moral worth. While the law of war is an extremely important means of mitigating the ravages of war, it cannot be considered an adequate and sufficient measure of human decency.

The implication is clear: Americans who read *Americans in Vietnam* should not feel guilty; they should feel ashamed. This substitution of terms is really the core of Lewy's case; it may make some readers feel better. It is a continuing shame, however, that the shamefulness of this war should be incidentally mentioned in a book designed to cover up the shame by taking refuge in narrow and dubious legalisms. I said at the outset that this was a schizophrenic book; it is never more schizophrenic than in a chapter that starts by seeking to acquit us of violating the "law of war" and ends by implicitly condemning us to shame.

I have thought it necessary to deal at some length with *America in Vietnam* because it is the most ambitious effort to decontaminate the American role in Vietnam. It is a vain, self-defeating effort. It will serve a useful purpose only if it makes us more acutely aware how stupid, miserable, and costly that war was.

VI

The main reason for the predicament of Kissinger and Brzezinski in the past and Lewy in the present is that they had difficulty fitting the Vietnam war into a larger framework. The war was never worth fighting for Vietnam alone; it always had to be made subsidiary to a larger purpose. The trouble was that it did not quite fit any of those imposed on it.

Kissinger's reason for going on with the war made the entire American position in world affairs and even world peace depend on an "honorable" ending. "What is involved now is confidence in American promises," he wrote in 1968, and "ending the war honorably is essential for the peace of the world." In the end, an "honorable" settlement came to mean the preservation of the South Vietnam regime or the frustration of a North Vietnamese victory, which amounted to the same thing. Thus the survival of a regime that almost all Americans in positions of authority regarded as hopelessly corrupt and hopelessly weak was endowed with a value and importance out of all proportion to what it could bear. The tangibles of national strength and stability were sacri-

ficed to intangibles such as American "prestige" and "honor." Estimable
as the latter may be, they were not worth the price that had to
be paid for them in real assets. Even worse, honor went when power
failed.

Kissinger's rationale for continuing the war betrayed a basic misunderstanding of both the world and the American people. It was darkly
said that America's allies in Europe would lose all faith in American
commitments if the United States let down South Vietnam. In fact,
America's allies were increasingly alarmed at the frittering away of
American resources in Vietnam and the social turmoil in the United
States that threatened to escalate out of control. Ominous fears were
also expressed as to what the American people might do if and when
they woke up to the reality of a lost war, as if Nixonian America were
Weimar Germany. When the war ended as badly as a war could possibly
end, at least for the South Vietnamese, the popular American reaction
was one of relief and fatigue. If it had been otherwise, former President
Nixon would have been driven out for the sins of Vietnam instead of for
the crimes of Watergate. The American people were not interested in an
"honorable" end, whatever that might have been; they were interested in
the end.

In his fighting-on-for-30-years period, Brzezinski made a similar miscalculation. He thought it was necessary to prove to the enemy "that we
have the staying power" and "happen to be richer and more powerful."
It was wrong for the United States to "chicken out," he said, because
"the consequences of getting out would be far more costly than the
expense of staying in." By 1968, when this rationalization was made, it
was already abundantly clear that the riches and power that we had
were not the right kind for a war in Vietnam and that we would be much
less rich and far less powerful the longer we stayed. It was ludicrously
wrong to have made the consequences of getting out far worse than the
expense of staying in. These terrible consequences were supposed to
have beset the United States in the world at large, not in Vietnam, and
all the world did when we got out was to heave a sigh of relief.

Ten years later, Lewy knows better than to bewail our loss of "honor"
or "prestige." His problem is to explain the American failure in Vietnam, not to prevent it. He hints at an explanation without reflecting on
what its implications might be.

Lewy twice uses the same phrase—that the United States and its
allies in Vietnam failed "to understand the real stakes in a revolutionary
war." He never explains what he understands by an American "revolu-

tionary war" in Vietnam or how we could possibly have waged it. But the suggestion is dropped, and it is worth considering.

To have waged a revolutionary war in Vietnam, we would have needed a revolutionary South Vietnamese regime. Lewy has no illusions about the corruption and unpopularity of the Thieu regime. He even quotes a statement, with which he says many agreed, that "if Thieu wants to eliminate corruption in the army he must fire himself." Lewy also recognizes: "The war not only had to be won in South Vietnam, but it had to be won by the South Vietnamese." In effect, the United States could not have made it a revolutionary war even if it had wanted to do so. The politics of this war, which was decisive, was essentially decided by the Vietnamese themselves. The dilemma that this situation presented was: the war could not be won if it was not revolutionary, and it could not be revolutionary if it was up to the South Vietnamese.

Lewy also makes clear why the American armed forces were incapable of fighting a revolutionary war in Vietnam. He reports "the growing disdain for the Vietnamese people among U.S. military personnel in Vietnam." So many American soldiers were killed or wounded by mines and booby traps in or near hamlets that "it became the prudent thing to doubt the loyalty of every villager." The result was: "Some soldiers began to adopt the so-called mere-gook rule, the attitude that the killing of Vietnamese, regardless of sex, age, or combatant status, was of little importance for they were, after all, only gooks." Elsewhere, Lewy changes "some" to "many" soldiers who lived by this "rule," which helps to explain the high civilian casualties, civilian inclusion in the inflated body counts, and the deliberate "generation" of a vast horde of refugees. A survey of marines in 1966 in one province revealed that 40 percent disliked the Vietnamese; small-unit leaders ranked highest in their "negative attitudes." Fewer than 20 percent of noncommissioned officers had "a positive attitude" toward the South Vietnamese armed forces.

A "revolutionary war," then, was and is a political pipe dream. The Vietnam war could not be put into a revolutionary any more than it could comfortably be put into a larger international framework. When Kissinger at long last saw the light and told his friend Professor Stoessinger that "we should never have been there at all," he was saying only part of the depressing truth. The rest that needed to be said was that we should have decided to get out of the war as soon as possible, to cut our losses as soon as possible, to stop killing Vietnamese and Americans and wasting our national substance as soon as possible.

Of course, if the Carters and Vances and Kissingers and Brzezinskis had said all this prematurely, that is, when it needed to be said, they might not be where they are today. All they might have is the dismal satisfaction of knowing that they were right.

Dissent, Winter 1979

IV

THE DIPLOMACY OF HENRY KISSINGER

1

Détente

I

Not since World War II had there been such an era of ill feeling between Western Europe and the United States as there was in 1973. No sooner had the then Presidential Assistant Henry A. Kissinger issued his call in April 1973 for a new Atlantic Charter to reinvigorate "shared ideals and common purposes with our friends" than it appeared that our friends had begun to change places with our enemies. Six months later, in October, Dr. Kissinger, now Secretary of State, was overheard saying, no doubt in pique, that he didn't care what happened to NATO because he was so disgusted with it. Two months after that, in December, he privately described the behavior of the Europeans during the Arab-Israeli conflict as "craven," "contemptible," "pernicious," and "jackal-like." In March of this year, he unguardedly expressed his disgruntlement by publicly complaining that getting our friends to realize our "common interests" was a bigger problem than "regulating competition" with our enemies.[1] Others have observed this extraordinary topsy-turvydom of friends and enemies. According to so experienced and respected a student of international affairs as George F. Kennan, the United States "now has relations with the Soviet Union fully as cordial as those with most of the European NATO members"—which is another way of saying that we are no more cordial with the latter than with the former.[2]

This is a peculiarly disturbing state of affairs for a country whose leaders, including Dr. Kissinger, have never tired of protesting that NATO, the Atlantic Alliance, or Western Europe, is the very "cornerstone" of U.S. foreign policy. A profound change has obviously taken place, going far beyond the problems and provocations that have presented themselves in the past year. If it continues much longer, the 1970s are unlikely to produce the "structure for peace" pursued by President Nixon; they are more likely to resemble the 1930s in the breakdown of a fragile international order.

"Concepts" and "conceptual" have long been among Dr. Kissinger's favorite terms. Almost ten years ago, he drew up an indictment of U.S. policy which, in part, sounds strangely familiar today: "In recent years this promise [of a partnership between a united Europe and the United States] has been flawed by increasingly sharp disputes among the allies. The absence of agreement on major policies is striking. On the Continent, the fear of a bilateral United States–Soviet arrangement is pervasive." And what was the basic trouble? It was, he wrote, the existence of an open challenge "not just to the technical implementation of American plans but to the validity of American conceptions." In June 1968, after a long silence, Dr. Kissinger finally pronounced on what had gone wrong in Vietnam. He traced many of our difficulties in Vietnam to "conceptual failures" and decided that "almost all of our concepts, the military ones as well as some of the traditional ones, have really failed." A few months later, he flatly asserted that "the basic problem [in Vietnam] has been conceptual." More recently, in connection with his visit to Moscow in March 1974, Dr. Kissinger let it be known that he was looking for a "conceptual breakthrough."[3]

It is all the more surprising, then, that concepts may well be the most vulnerable aspect of Dr. Kissinger's tenure as Presidential Assistant and Secretary of State. He has lived such a charmed life since he went to Washington in 1969 that far more attention has been paid to his personal tactics than to his conceptual strategy, although he used to warn against the danger of "being mired by the prudent, the tactical, or the expedient" and was wont to inveigh against the lamentable disposition of American leaders to act, during periods of détente, "as if a settlement could be reached by good personal relations with their Communist counterparts."[4] Indeed, one of the most intriguing aspects of the Kissinger phenomenon is the curious difference between Professor Kissinger and Presidential Assistant-Secretary of State Kissinger.

II

Professor Kissinger had devoted himself almost wholly to Europe and to European-American relations. In book after book and article after article he had taught that the fate of the United States was bound to be decided in or with Europe. In this view he had not differed from official American policy, at least until the Johnson administration, which had departed from it in deeds if not in words. Yet Presidential Assistant Kissinger went to work for a President who, not long before taking office, had downgraded Europe as secondary in future American policy. This position had been taken by Mr. Nixon in a well-known article in *Foreign Affairs* of October 1967, which has been so distorted in the retelling that one suspects more people have referred to it than have actually read it. The article has been recalled mainly for its alleged foreshadowing of President Nixon's later China policy, because in it he had urged that "our long-range aim is to pull China back into the family of nations" and "into the world community" on condition that it give up the role of being "the epicenter of world revolution." These phrases were subsequently taken to mean that Mr. Nixon had served notice of his intention to establish friendly relations with the People's Republic of China. But there was both more and less to it than that.

The leading Nixonian concept at that time had to do with a question of fundamental importance: What area of the world would be most dangerous to the United States in the final third of the twentieth century? Mr. Nixon's answer in this very article was: "Asia, not Europe or Latin America." He saw the United States as "the greatest Pacific power," propelled westward, as "partners," to be sure, not as "conquerors." Asia was where "the greatest explosive potential is lodged." The rhythm of history, as he put it, had dictated that "the focus of both crisis and change is shifting" from Europe to Asia. Europe having been rebuilt and the Soviets "contained," he urged that we should reserve our main energies for Asia "to reach out westward to the East, and to fashion the sinews of a Pacific community."

It was in this context that Mr. Nixon discussed what to do about China. There was no indication in this article that he thought of using China as a counterweight against Soviet Russia. Rather, he saw China as the "clear, present, and repeatedly and insistently expressed" threat in Asia. In order to meet that threat more effectively, he advocated coming "urgently to grips with the reality of China" by pulling China "back into the family of nations" and into "the world community." At this stage in his rethinking of U.S. foreign policy, Mr. Nixon seemed oblivious to the contradiction inherent in his desire to concentrate American energies in Asia, which could only threaten or disturb China, and his inclination to make some sort of friendly overture to China, which could come to fruition only if America showed signs of leaving Asia alone. Nixon's formula was still so vague that it did not attract much notice at the time. When Dr. Kissinger later said that it "really foreshadowed the Peking initiative"[5] he was hardly justified by anything in the 1967 article itself, since it contained little more than the germ of the idea of establishing some sort of new relationship with Communist China.

Mr. Nixon has had it both ways on the Vietnam war. During the period of the main U.S. build-up in 1965–67, he protected President Johnson's Republican flank and, if anything, out-Johnsoned Johnson in his pro-war fervor. Mr. Nixon would have had U.S. troops in Vietnam as early as 1954 when the French were facing defeat at Dien Bien Phu. On the eve of the massive U.S. intervention in 1965, he went all out for President Johnson's policy. He was one of those who thought the war was being fought primarily between the United States and Communist China. An extreme exponent of the "domino theory," he foresaw Chinese Communist aggression as far as Australia in four or five years if South Vietnam fell. No one in the Johnson administration was more convinced than Mr. Nixon that the only way to end the war was "by winning it in South Vietnam." Nevertheless, by the end of 1967, in his *Foreign Affairs* article, Mr. Nixon drew back somewhat from his previous bellicosity. He now recognized that "the role of the United States as world policeman is likely to be limited in the future," that there was no more "room for heavy-handed American pressures," and that "the central pattern of the future in U.S.-Asian relations must be American support for Asian initiatives." Asia had by far the highest priority in his scheme of things. After he was elected, President Nixon repeated and repeated and repeated that he was not the one who had sent more than 500,000 American boys to fight in Vietnam. That was true; it also was true that he was the one who had done everything a Republican leader could do to make it possible for a Democratic President to send them.[6]

It is more difficult to know what Professor Kissinger thought about Asia and the Vietnam war. His 1965 book, *The Troubled Partnership*, was devoted to the European-American relationship, but in connection with it he made some interesting references to Southeast Asia. He was mainly concerned with getting across the thought—which figured prominently in his "new Atlantic Charter" speech eight years later—that our European allies had "ceased to think of themselves as world powers." For this reason, he warned that the United States could not expect "meaningful support for such United States policies as the defense of Southeast Asia." At the same time, however, he ventured the opinion that "over the next decades the United States is likely to find itself increasingly engaged in the Far East, in Southeast Asia, and in Latin America," in none of which our European allies were likely to see any vital interest of their own.[7] The book was written before President Johnson decided on large-scale U.S. intervention in Vietnam, but judging from Dr. Kissinger's expectation the decision could not have come as a surprise. In 1965–66, Dr. Kissinger made two trips to South Vietnam at the invitation of Ambassador Henry Cabot Lodge. In 1967, he acted as the American go-between in conjunction with two Frenchmen in an abortive "peace feeler." Nevertheless, he published nothing about the war during these three years. His biographer, a close friend for many years, tries to explain this puzzling silence on the ground that Dr. Kissinger "had nothing to say" because he "did not know enough about the issues."[8] Since he knew more and was privy to more than all but a relatively few in the highest official circles, there would have been little protest against the war if his modesty or reticence had been more contagious.

In the spring and summer of 1968, Dr. Kissinger finally found his voice on the entire range of American foreign-policy questions, including the Vietnam war—the voice of former Governor Nelson Rockefeller, who was running for President and who, we are assured, spoke what Dr. Kissinger wrote.[9] Fortunately, however, we do not have to depend wholly on such indirect evidence. In June of that year at a conference in Chicago sponsored by the Adlai Stevenson Institute of International Affairs, Dr. Kissinger spoke for the first time in his own name on the Vietnam war and its lessons. His main contribution, as previously noted, was the concept of our "conceptual failures." Ironically, in view of the later insistence on his alleged infatuation with "balance of power," he then lamented that the epidemic of rebellions in the world "cannot be encompassed at all by traditional theories of balances of power." His comments did little more than to communicate his disenchantment with the war, with U.S. policy, and even with "the American philosophy of international relations."[10]

By chance, Dr. Kissinger's last published article dealt with "The Vietnam Negotiations." Written before President Nixon asked him to serve, it appeared in January 1969, just as he was going into the White House. His criticism of U.S. policy was again "conceptual," though it clearly showed that he had a great deal of inside knowledge about what had gone on militarily and politically in Vietnam. For an inveterate conceptualizer, however, he seemed to give inordinate importance to what he called the "choreography" of negotiations—the way they were carried on. A fascination with tactics, maneuvers, and symbols appeared to preoccupy him as much as grand concepts and large historical movements. After pages on the proper tactics to pursue vis-à-vis North Vietnam, he bethought himself to caution: "The overconcern with tactics suppresses a feeling for nuance and for intangibles." This advice seemed to make the statesman or diplomat a conjurer of the ineffable and the impalpable. One would have expected that an overconcern with tactics would suppress a sense of essence and substance. Concepts and nuances, the philosopher and the fixer, were already struggling for the mind and soul of Henry Kissinger.

The Vietnam war produced another more tangible and immediate conflict. On the one hand, Dr. Kissinger had clearly come to the reluctant conclusion that the war was a bad job and needed to be ended as soon as possible. On the other hand, he held on to the conviction that it had to be ended "honorably" at all costs.[11] The key concept here was "honorable"—although he never made clear how a dishonorable war could be ended honorably. The closest he came to condemning or repudiating the war was a comment that it was open to "the charge of bad judgment." He hastened to add that such a "charge" could not be removed by "a demonstration of incompetence" in ending the war. Another concept mobilized in favor of ending the war "honorably" or not at all—for it came down to this in the end—was a variant of the "domino theory." What was now at stake in Vietnam, Dr. Kissinger argued, was "confidence in American promises," on which the stability of much of the world—the Middle East, Europe, Latin America, even Japan—allegedly depended. He apparently could not envisage anything worse than "unilateral withdrawal," though the settlement which he eventually arrived at was admittedly a bilateral withdrawal only on paper. We have heard ever since that the North Vietnamese have never withdrawn. Judging by President Nixon's own criteria—"honor, a peace fair to all, and a peace that will last," and "with no misunderstandings which could lead to a breakdown of the settlement and a resumption of the war"[12]—this "peace" has already failed the test, at least so far as the Vietnamese themselves are concerned. Long before the end of the Asia-first century once envisaged by Mr. Nixon, it is safe to say, it won't make a particle of difference how the United States got out of Vietnam; all that will matter is that the United States was forced to pull out and that the war between the Vietnamese went on.

There was also at this stage a curious historical disparity in the thinking of Mr. Nixon and Dr. Kissinger. The former went into office with the concept that American destiny would for the rest of the century move westward to Asia; his view of the Vietnam war and relations with China was governed by this grand, if highly dubious, proposition. Dr. Kissinger did not go anywhere as far afield in his outlook; he seemed to worry most about the more immediate consequences, mainly outside Asia, of how the Vietnam war would come to an end. Though their reasons were somewhat different, both were prepared to fight as long to end the war without victory as President Johnson had been prepared to fight for victory. Yet they were luckier than he was. Enough people seemed to think that the war had gone on for so long that it might never end; anyone who could bring it to a close at all, no matter how long it took and at what frightful cost, was entitled to eternal gratitude.

What concerns us here is not so much the Vietnam settlement as the decision which led to four more years of war until the settlement was reached. That decision was made by President Nixon, with Dr. Kissinger's concurrence, early in 1969, in the first weeks of the administration, and it may well be the most critical one that they made. Once they decided on a course which put American interests all over the world at the mercy of such an intangible nuance as "honor" in Vietnam, their freedom of action and even their field of vision were hopelessly restricted elsewhere. That this is exactly what happened as a result of the Vietnam war is not open to question. We have it on the authority of President Nixon himself: "Now, in terms of our world situation, the tendency is, and this has been the case for the last five to six years, for us to obscure our vision almost totally of the world because of Vietnam."[13] In January 1973, he remarked that "it just happens as we complete the long and difficult war in Vietnam, we must now turn to the problems of Europe."[14] The price of the Vietnam war was paid not only in Vietnam; it was paid all over the world. It is with the other price that we must now reckon.

III

Another major related decision was made at the outset of the Nixon administration.

Apart from the Vietnam war, the great question before U.S. policy was whether the problem of our friends was more important and deserved priority over the problem of our foes. Was it better or safer to let Western Europe go its own way and further weaken its ties with the

United States, or to concentrate on working out a détente with Soviet Russia and a rapprochement with the People's Republic of China? The decision went in favor of the latter course. Western Europe was put on the waiting list after China, Russia, and Vietnam. 1971 was the year of China; 1972 was the year of Russia; the Vietnamese agreement came at the end of 1972; and Europe was scheduled for 1973. The stage was thus carefully prepared for a crisis in European-American relations.

This order of priorities was based on several considerations. China and Russia could do far more than Europe to help end the Vietnam war. Russia was North Vietnam's main supplier, and China was supposed to be the chief inspiration of North Vietnam's hardliners. If outside pressure was to be brought on North Vietnam, it clearly had to be brought through them. Thus the Vietnam war was itself partially responsible for the choice of priorities.

Other factors undoubtedly entered into the calculation. By 1969, it was apparent that the Russians were heading for nuclear parity with the United States. For some reason, U.S. officialdom has been prone to underestimate Soviet military intentions and capabilities. It was surprised by the rapidity with which the Soviets achieved the A-bomb, the H-bomb, advanced jet engines, long-range turbo-prop bombers, airborne intercept radars, and large-scale fissile material production.[15] In the mid-1960s, the Americans did not expect the Soviets to be willing to pay the exorbitant price necessary to achieve numerical equality in missiles. In 1966, the United States decided to build no more nuclear weapons and to limit itself to improvement of existing weapons.[16] By late 1964 or early 1965 at the latest, however, the Soviets set out not only to equal but to surpass the United States, at least numerically, in intercontinental missiles.[17] The publicly announced Soviet military budget rose from 12.8 billion rubles in 1965 to 13.4 in 1966, to 14.5 in 1967, 16.7 in 1968, 17.7 in 1969, and 17.9 in 1970—an increase of 40 percent. The real resources devoted to the Soviet military, including secret and hidden allocations, amounted of course to much more.[18] The point here is not whether the world has changed for better or worse because the Soviet Union decided to catch up with the United States in nuclear power. The Soviet decision and achievement faced the incoming Nixon administration with the unpleasant choice of accepting Soviet-American strategic parity or of engaging in another, probably futile arms race. From a strictly military point of view, Europe was out of this contest, and the Soviet Union preempted the fullest attention.

If China and Russia were the pressure-points on North Vietnam,

China was obviously the pressure-point on Russia. By 1969, it was commonly believed that the Russians were more worried about the Chinese menace than about the American threat. Despite the protestations of President Nixon and his officials that nothing was further from their minds than the idea of trying to play off China against Russia, no one else could be prevented from seeing a Chinese-American rapprochement in this light. Again, Europe as well as Japan was out of the contest; they watched from afar, with pleasure, consternation, or indifference, the Soviet-American strategic-arms-limitation talks and the Chinese-American tête-à-tête as both proceeded in 1971.

In his incredible interview with the Italian journalist, Oriana Fallaci, Dr. Kissinger volunteered the information that, from 1969 on, he had wanted to achieve three things: peace in Vietnam, rapprochement with China, and a new relationship with the Soviet Union.[19] The "troubled partnership" between the United States and Europe was significantly missing from the list.

But there was a consolation prize for Europe. The catchword was "partnership." In one of his first Presidential speeches in April 1969, President Nixon pledged the United States to "deep and genuine consultation with its allies" whom he referred to as "partners."[20] In his report to Congress of February 1970, a key document of administration policy, Mr. Nixon said that the nations of Western Europe and North America made up "our partnership"; he also called for both a "genuine partnership" and "a new and mature partnership." To make the Europeans acutely conscious of what a good deal they were getting from him, Mr. Nixon took to telling them how badly treated they had been by his predecessors. Anyone who wanted to demonstrate that the United States had run NATO and the Atlantic alliance as if they were plantations with a master and slaves had only to cite the President of the United States, who now confessed: "For too long in the past, the United States had led without listening, talked *to* our allies instead of *with* them, and informed them of new departures instead of deciding with them." All this was going to change as the United States moved "from dominance to partnership."[21] A year later, in February 1971, Mr. Nixon announced that the move had successfully been made: "In Western Europe, we have shifted from predominance to partnership with our allies."[22]

By 1971, the main concepts of the Nixon-Kissinger foreign policy seemed to have crystallized—rapprochement with China, détente with Russia, partnership with Western Europe. Perhaps because he would not leave well enough alone or because his adviser on national-security affairs was an inveterate conceptualizer, Mr. Nixon could not resist the temptation to bring forth his own grand conceptual structure. In the summer of 1971, he took a group of news-media executives meeting in Kansas City, Missouri, into his confidence and gave them a glimpse of the world in the next five to fifteen years. He characterized the United States, Western Europe, Soviet Russia, mainland China, and Japan as the "five great economic superpowers." The emphasis was clearly on "great" rather than on "economic." These five, he said, "will determine the economic future and, because economic power will be the key to other kinds of power, the future of the world in other ways in the last third of this century."[23] Six months later, in January 1972, Mr. Nixon elaborated on this theme. He fitted the new era of the big five into the traditional theory of "balance and power," which he extolled as having been the only basis for an extended period of peace in the history of the world. "It is when one nation becomes infinitely more powerful in relation to its potential competitor that the danger of war arises," he explained. "So I believe in a world in which the United States is powerful. I think it will be a safer world and a better world if we have a strong, healthy United States, Europe, Soviet Union, China, Japan, each balancing the other, not playing one against the other, an even balance."[24]

Until he became President, Mr. Nixon had belonged to the school of thought which believed in making the United States incomparably stronger than its enemies. If that policy had been good before, however, the decline of the United States in relative strength was apparently even better. And was it really true that the danger of war arises if one nation becomes *infinitely* more powerful than others? One had imagined that the danger increased as the gap closed. In any event, this Presidential analysis of the world in 1972 seemed to make the "balance of power" official doctrine, with each of the five so strong in relation to the others that they could play independent roles and constitute "an even balance."

Other officials, especially in the State Department, made exegetical discourses on the new dispensation. One of their favorite commentaries concerned the displacement of bipolarity by multipolarity. The President had at least qualified the five superpowers as "economic," though he had implied that all other kinds of power flowed from economic power. This distinction somehow dropped out of the exegeses. One official simply spoke of "multiple power centers" emerging in the final quarter of this century.[25] Another expounded on the "new power centers"—Western Europe, Japan, and China—which "by definition relates to the decline in the bipolar structure of the world."[26] A third went into more detail: "First, we are entering a world in which the bipolar pattern dominant in the last quarter century has given way to multiple centers of power and influence. Power, defined in political and economic as well as in military terms, no longer is the near-exclusive province of ourselves and the Soviets. The dominant relationships in this decade will not be between two centers of influence, but among five. Western Europe, Japan, and China have moved to the front of the world stage."[27]

How much Dr. Kissinger had to do with all this higher theorizing was not at first clear. Some seemed to think that if President Nixon had an idea, let alone an entire theory, it must have come from Dr. Kissinger. The mere mention of balance of power set off an epidemic of amateurish historical analogies between Kissinger and Metternich, about whose diplomacy he had written his doctoral thesis fifteen years earlier. A minor annoyance connected with the Kissinger phenomenon has been the excruciatingly bad books that it has inspired. One of them claimed to know that he was already plotting a "conceptual blueprint" for U.S. policy in his doctoral thesis.[28] Dr. Kissinger himself was evidently not amused. He saw fit to tell Oriana Fallaci that "There can be nothing in common between me and Metternich" and that it was "childish" to associate the two of them.[29] He did not say who benefited more from this offer of disengagement.

The licensed experts pounced joyfully on President Nixon's pastiche of ideas about balance of power and the five superpowers. As one heartlessly put it: "Of the so-called major powers, one (Europe) does not yet exist, one (Japan) has not found a role, and one (China) happens to be neither a superpower yet nor a very likely practitioner of the balance of power should it become one."[30] For a while, the foreign-affairs journals were filled with the higher criticism on such urgent matters as the balance of power in the nineteenth as compared with the twentieth century.

By the end of 1972, the theory had been put out of its misery. President Nixon himself distinguished between the Soviet Union, which "is a superpower," and China, which "has the potential in the future."[31] A potential superpower was obviously not yet ready for the role which he had assigned to it. Early in 1973, Dr. Kissinger pleaded innocent. He made known that he had been on his way to China when Mr. Nixon had given birth in Kansas City in 1971 to the five-superpowers-balance-of-power theory and that he had not read the speech or known what was to be in it before it was delivered. He assured his listeners that "what this administration has attempted to do is not so much to play a complicated nineteenth-century game of balance of power" as to do something else, evidently less complicated, which was "to try to eliminate those hostilities that were vestiges of a particular perception at the end of the war."[32] Once the word went out that the line had changed, Deputy Secretary of State Kenneth Rush carefully explained why the original theory could not have been right: "For one thing, the principal participants have different capabilities. Bipolarity still persists in the strategic relationship between the United States and the Soviet Union. Europe is still in the process of developing the voice and organization to fully reflect its international economic position. Japan is still exploring the meaning of its phenomenal economic growth in terms of its international role. China's international position primarily reflects her potential, her great size, and her potential military strength."[33]

Such was the short, unhappy life of the most ambitious concept put forward by the Nixon administration. It was far less important as an intellectual exercise than as a sign of the times. The year of the Kansas City speech, 1971, was also the low point in the fortunes of the dollar that brought about the collapse of the international monetary system. The overall U.S. balance-of-payments deficit had reached the astronomical figure of $9.8 billion, the seemingly inviolate U.S. trade surplus had disappeared, and the convertibility of the dollar into gold, a basic principle of the post-World War II monetary order, was abandoned. The same year seemed to be the high point of European economic and financial strength. It was the turn of Europeans to tell the United States to "put its economic house in order." When former Secretary of the Treasury John B. Connally tried to bully the Europeans, he told them it was now their duty to be philanthropic and their task to correct the imbalances that had developed. If they could have done what he wanted them to do, the implication was inescapable that Europe was more than able to hold its own against the United States. The trade and monetary shocks of 1971 undoubtedly contributed to the elevation of Europe and Japan to the august status of "economic superpowers."

It is also fair to add that the idea of putting Europe on more or less the same plane as the United States was not altogether original. The thought was already in the air, particularly in neo-isolationist circles. One such confident pronouncement in 1970 went: "The Europeans are our best friends in the world; they are also our equals."[34] One year later, the "best friends" quarreled fiercely because the Europeans seemed to be more than equal, and three years later, they quarreled even more ferociously because the Europeans realized that they were much less than equal.

Precisely in this period détente became an active issue in policy.

IV

If anyone should have been prepared for the pitfalls of détente, it was Dr. Kissinger. For about a dozen years before he went to Washington to serve President Nixon, he had been a stern and unsparing critic of anything that smacked to him of "illusions" about détente.[35]

In the first book, published in 1957, with which he attracted widespread attention, Professor Kissinger expressed a certain distaste for, or anxiety about, "peaceful coexistence," the term then in vogue. He twice found it necessary to instruct the reader that "peaceful coexistence" meant for Soviet leaders nothing more than "the most effective offensive tactic" and "the best means to subvert the existing structure by means other than all-out war." It was good Leninist doctrine, he patiently explained, that the Soviets, so long as the relationship of forces was not in their favor, should keep "provocation below the level which might produce a final showdown."[36]

Four years later, in 1961, Professor Kissinger was worried most about the Western tendency to see a Soviet turn from belligerency to détente as evidence of far more than a change of tactics. "But," he cautioned, "one of the principal Communist justifications for a détente can hardly prove very reassuring to the free world; peace is advocated not for its own sake but because the West is said to have grown so weak that it will go to perdition without a last convulsive upheaval." As for the Western attitude, he observed disapprovingly that "all the instincts of a status quo power tempt it to gear its policy to the expectation of a fundamental change of heart of its opponent" and to the imminence of "a basic change in Communist society and aims." Americans, he thought, were especially susceptible to the belief that all problems were soluble and that "there must be some way to achieve peace if only the correct method is utilized." In this work he was especially censorious of President Eisenhower's "ambulatory" personal diplomacy, which inspired him to lay down the general rule that "whenever the Communist leaders have pressed for a relaxation of tensions they have tied the success of it to personalities."[37]

After four more years, in 1965, Professor Kissinger had some more pungent things to say about the American tendency to think of détente in terms of personal relations. It was "futile," he repeatedly stressed, to engage in "personal diplomacy" with the Soviets "even at the highest level," for one reason because their leaders were committed to a belief in the predominance of "objective" factors. Whenever Soviet leaders "have had to make a choice between Western goodwill and a territorial or political gain," he maintained, they "have unhesitatingly chosen the latter." If the Soviets seem to make "concessions," they make them "to reality, not to individuals." He noted that there had been five Soviet periods of "relaxation" since 1917, all of which had come to an end for the same reason—"when an opportunity for expanding Communism presented itself."[38]

As late as 1968, the year before he went to Washington, Professor Kissinger was still of much the same mind about past détentes. "During periods of détente," he observed sharply, "each [Western] ally makes its own approach to Eastern Europe or the USSR without attempting to further a coherent Western enterprise." He summed up the entire process in a way that is still instructive: "Each [détente] was hailed in the West as ushering in a new era of reconciliation and as signifying the long-awaited final change in Soviet purposes. Each ended abruptly with a new period of intransigence, which was generally ascribed to a victory of Soviet hardliners rather than to the dynamics of the system. There were undoubtedly many reasons for this. But the tendency of many in the West to be content with changes of Soviet tone and to confuse atmosphere with substance surely did not help matters."[39]

Judging from his books and articles for over a decade, Professor Kissinger should have been repelled by a Soviet-American détente that was accompanied by unprecedented tension between Western Europe and the United States. His entire *oeuvre* was distinguished by an acute distrust of détente and a moving belief in the need for Western Europe and the United States to be linked by the closest possible ties, going far beyond even the existing Atlantic alliance. In *The Necessity for Choice* of 1961, he appealed for "structural changes" within the Western alliance to make it a federalized "North Atlantic community" or a "confederation of states." Otherwise, as he ominously foresaw: "Without a truly common position Western rivalries will either paralyze negotiations or enable the Soviet Union to use them to demoralize the West."[40] In *The Troubled Partnership* of 1965, he went further prophetically and summoned the West to form an "Atlantic Commonwealth" of all the peoples bordering the North Atlantic. The ability of the West to move from the nation-state to a larger community would, he avowed, "largely determine whether the West can remain relevant to the rest of the world."[41] If one had read what Professor Kissinger had written before going to Washington, one could not have imagined he would put the years of détente first and the year of Europe last.

In fact, he was not the only one in the Nixon administration who had had premonitions of what was going to happen in the name of détente. In 1969, the then Under Secretary of State Elliot L. Richardson had given this assurance:

> We shall not bargain away our security for vague improvements in the "international atmosphere." Progress in East-West relations can only come out of hard bargaining on real issues. A détente that exists only in "atmosphere" without being related to substantive improvements in the relationship between the powers is worse than no improvement at all. It tempts us to lower our readiness, while providing no really concrete basis for a reduction in tensions.[42]

In 1970, Robert Ellsworth, the U.S. representative to the NATO Council, came even closer to one of the real issues that later arose to bedevil the Soviet-American détente. He recognized that the Soviet's and Warsaw Pact's "hunger for access to the science and technology of the West" was a key element in their diplomacy and in their push for "expansion of trade, economic, scientific and technical relations" between East and West. Others have since come to the same conclusion.[43] Ellsworth went on to explain that the principal difficulty confronting the Soviets was their inability to pay. It was still possible for an American official to be brutally candid about what the proposed deal entailed:

> They [the Soviets] would be able to pay if they could balance their imports by increasing exports of raw materials, and oil and gas, but they are unable to achieve this balance. Thus, they must ask for credits—credits which would have to be guaranteed, or possibly even subsidized, by governments. *In essence such an agreement is not trade, but aid.* Decisions about extending such aid, as well as decisions about transferring advanced technology from West to East, are not simply economic or technical decisions. They involve the highest political considerations [emphasis added].

Finally, Ellsworth told the tragic story of the Duke of Urbino who had committed a "classic blunder" four hundred years ago:

> He possessed by far the most advanced artillery of the sixteenth century, which he foolishly loaned to Cesare Borgia for the alleged purpose of a

Borgia attack upon Naples. Instead, Borgia promptly turned the artillery upon Urbino as he had planned all along. That was the end of Urbino.[44]

Who would have guessed that so many American capitalists would become twentieth-century Dukes of Urbino?

V

These premonitions, forebodings, and reflections on détente were not produced in a vacuum. There had been, as Professor Kissinger noted, several periods of détente between the Soviet Union and the West since the Bolshevik revolution, as well as three main Soviet détentes with individual Western countries since 1965. In fact, the Soviet Union has had a waiting-list for détentes, with the United States third in line.

The first to join the elect was France. Its détente had its roots in Gaullist doctrine and went as far back as the end of World War II.

De Gaulle made his first bid to the Soviet Union as early as December 1944, before the end of the war, when France was barely free of German troops. During his first visit to Moscow, he tried to convert Stalin to a three-stage system of alliances: the first Franco-Soviet, the second Anglo-Soviet and Anglo-French, and the third a catch-all in which for the first time the United States was generously included within the forthcoming United Nations, for which de Gaulle otherwise had little use. Since de Gaulle held on tenaciously to his long-term plans, even if he was flexible in his tactics, this scheme cannot be dismissed lightly. It was, in effect, his ultimate view of how to restore France to the position she had held before both world wars, when alliances with Russia had been the cornerstone of her foreign policy. Indeed, de Gaulle explicitly invoked the Franco-Russian alliances of 1892 and 1935 and told Stalin that he wanted another for the same reasons that had inspired them. De Gaulle's final aim, then, required more than a mere détente; it demanded an actual Franco-Soviet alliance based on a mutual recognition of each other's interests. Even in 1944, de Gaulle tried to tell Stalin how far to go—or rather not to go—in Poland.[45]

Toward the end of his life, de Gaulle looked back at this period and revealed more fully and clearly what he had had in mind. He had intended, he explained, to cooperate and contract alliances with both East and West, and to form with neighboring states a bloc that would become one of the three world powers, capable of acting as "the arbiter between the Soviet and Anglo-Saxon camps."[46] As time passed, de

Gaulle and his successors found it more tactful and expedient to put their program negatively—the breaking down of the two "hegemonies" of the Soviet Union and the United States. But there was a positive side to this design—the building up of a third hegemony, that of France in Europe, and through Europe, in the world. De Gaulle's ends, if not his means, were remarkably consistent over the years. In one of his last writings, he still called on France to play "an international role of the first rank" and to take on "world responsibility," not restricting herself merely to Europe. In Europe as well as in the world, he insisted, it was incumbent on France to be free to act by herself.[47]

De Gaulle's first overture to Stalin was, of course, premature. Stalin had no intention of letting de Gaulle get in his way in Eastern Europe, particularly in Poland. At the Yalta conference less than two months later, Stalin did not even wish to give France an occupation zone in Germany, and only Churchill's fight for it made him relent. When de Gaulle left office the first time in 1946, his Russian policy was in shambles.

De Gaulle's second effort was more successful. The latest Franco-Soviet détente, according to Maurice Couve de Murville, de Gaulle's Foreign Minister, began to take concrete shape in the spring of 1965 with a visit to Paris by the Soviet Foreign Minister Andrei Gromyko. When Couve de Murville returned the visit in the fall of 1965, Soviet Premier Alexei Kosygin told him how worried the Soviets were about the United States, already deeply engaged in Vietnam. The United States and Russia were, in Kosygin's view, actually at war, if only because Russia was supplying arms to the other side.[48] Whatever the merits of the Vietnam war may be, the fact remains that Gaullist France chose to inaugurate its détente with a Soviet Russia which considered itself to be, in effect, at war with the United States.

In February 1966, three months later, de Gaulle publicly announced France's intention to leave NATO, a step which had been on the way the year before and was consummated a month later. In June of that year, de Gaulle "consecrated" the Franco-Soviet détente with a triumphal visit to Soviet Russia, during which Party Secretary-General Leonid I. Brezhnev for the first time broached the Soviet proposal of a European security conference excluding the United States.[49]

These moves were highly orchestrated. The French military abandonment of NATO was implicitly an integral part—or price—of the Franco-Soviet détente. In fact, France was not strong enough to offer very much more to the Soviet Union in return for Soviet favor. Ostensibly, the Gaullist position was based on opposition to all blocs, East and West. But France could do very little about breaking up the Eastern bloc; she, however, could do much about breaking up the Western bloc. The Franco-Soviet détente was made between very unequal powers; as a result, its terms were most unequal. If it had been arranged on an equal basis, the Soviets should have withdrawn from the Warsaw Pact as France withdrew from NATO. But of course such a Soviet contribution to détente was unthinkable, and no one in his right mind thought of demanding it. At the very moment that France was mortally weakening NATO, the Soviets were massively strengthening the Warsaw Pact. De Gaulle could not negotiate from strength; his negotiating card, in fact if not in name, was the weakening of the system to which France had belonged—a service for which the Soviets were willing to pay a modest price.

For de Gaulle, détente was only the hors d'oeuvre; the main course, still to come, was a Franco-Soviet entente reminiscent of the pre-war alliances. De Gaulle's formula was "détente, entente, and cooperation." In the end, he disdained the Atlantic alliance as no more than "the military and political subordination of Western Europe to the United States."[50] Russia was at least partly in his Europe "from the Atlantic to the Urals"; the United States was definitely out of it.

This was the Gaullist vision. De Gaulle knew, of course, that the road was bound to be hard and long, necessitating many detours, maneuvers, and ruses. At various times and in different circumstances, Gaullism seemed to be pro- and anti-German, pro- and anti-American, pro- and anti-Russian, pro- and anti-European. It was ready to use almost any means for its own ends, thereby leading others to think that they could use it for their ends. Yet, in the last analysis, there is a Gaullist hard core that comes as a shock to France's European partners and American well-wishers, no matter how much they have been forewarned. The French behavior after October 1973 in the face of the energy crisis would have given them less of a jolt if the Gaullist heritage had been kept in mind and taken more seriously. It is part of that heritage that France should be the rogue elephant of the West, taking advantage of every opportunity to advance its own interests, feeling more immediately threatened by the American embrace than by the Russian hug, savoring situations which force the other European nations to choose between France and the United States.

In a world in which power so often decides the issue, there was no reason why de Gaulle should not have wanted as much power as possible for France. What is more questionable is the admiration that so many non-French Westerners have had for Gaullism without unflinchingly facing up to what they were admiring. President Nixon was a notorious admirer, and French Gaullists have seen his unprecedented aggrandizement of the American Presidency as the sincerest form of flattery. Dr. Kissinger's case a decade ago was more typical of Western intellectuals. His esteem for de Gaulle was not uncritical, but he invariably found more to blame in American policies than in the French. However naughty the French might be, he tended to scold the Americans for provoking or encouraging them. He expected history to demonstrate "that de Gaulle's conceptions—as distinct from his style— were greater than those of most of his critics." He estimated de Gaulle's conceptions to be "greater than his strength," while America's power was "greater than its conceptions." For most of his career, de Gaulle had been an "illusionist," Dr. Kissinger conceded.[51] But, he might have added, Frenchmen were not the only ones bemused by Gaullist illusions.

Thus the Gaullist détente with the Soviet Union in 1965–66 had its own distinctive raison d'être. It cannot be understood merely as an effort on both sides "to relax tensions." Each side was trying to use the other for particular, far-reaching ends. Whatever tensions de Gaulle may have relaxed with the Soviet Union, he enormously increased other tensions with the United States. He was far less interested in relaxing tensions than in utilizing them for his own larger purposes. For de Gaulle as for the Soviet leaders, détente was not an end in itself; it was a means to get whatever they wanted to get with or without détente.

VI

The Federal Republic of Germany was the second country admitted to membership in the Soviet Union's exclusive "Détente Club." Since the position and problems of West Germany were vastly different from those of France, the meaning and consequences of its détente were equally different.

The German détente also did not come cheaply. For almost two decades, German policy had rested on three interlocking premises. In essence, they were: German reunification, European Union, and the Atlantic alliance. The first was fundamental; everything else flowed from it. In the Adenauer era, which lasted until 1963, it was assumed that a united Germany had to be incorporated or submerged in a larger European Union in order to contain Germany's potentially unruly nationalism and thus make German reunification acceptable to Germany's neighbors. But since a European Union would not be strong enough in the foreseeable future to force or to induce the Soviet Union to disgorge East Germany, it was considered necessary to link Western Europe most closely to the United States through the Atlantic alliance to get the desired result. If West Germany was not yet able to do much about achieving reunification, the minimum demanded by this policy was to do nothing against it. By implication, Germany could not recognize the territorial status quo, such as the Oder-Neisse line, or even formally renounce the pre-war Munich agreement, until a final disposition of Germany's status had been made. Until then, everything had to be conditional and provisional, even the status of West Germany itself.

Ironically, in the early years of the Adenauer regime, the German Social-Democrats took an even harder line than the Christian-Democrats on the quest for German reunification; the Social-Democrats bitterly criticized their rivals for not being inflexible enough and exigent enough on the issue. How legitimate and necessary the Adenauerian *Weltanschauung* once seemed to be can also be seen in the past writings of Dr. Kissinger. "Any West German government must advocate reunification, however moderate it may be in the means it chooses to pursue this objective and however patient it may be in bringing it about," he wrote in the heyday of the Adenauer regime. He admonished: "The Federal Republic would suffer a perhaps irreparable blow if its allies accepted its present frontiers as final—even to the extent of not pressing for unification." He cautioned: "If the Federal Republic is persuaded that it cannot achieve reunification through ties with the West, it is likely to seek its aims through separate dealings with the East."[52]

These words were written fifteen years ago. In that period, Dr. Kissinger was a full-fledged Adenauerian and a part-time Gaullist. His views are worth recalling not because of what they may tell about him today but because they so faithfully reflected the Adenauerian credo that they help to recall how seriously it was taken and how much was involved in giving it up. As long as Adenauer's basic policies prevailed, a German-Soviet détente was out of the question. Or, to put it another way, Adenauerism made German reunification a precondition of détente rather than détente a prerequisite of reunification. The Soviets would, of course, have none of this. They were bent on keeping Germany divided; on gaining recognition for the German Democratic Republic as an independent East German Communist state; on separating West Berlin from West Germany; on obtaining formal recognition of the status quo, especially the Oder-Neisse line; on frustrating an effective European Union; and, almost more than anything else, on divorcing the United States from Europe and breaking up the Atlantic alliance. Adenauer was not only allergic to a German-Soviet détente; any suggestion of a Soviet-American détente made him excessively nervous. Toward the end of his reign, he became so despondent over what the United States was doing for him that he turned for support to Charles de Gaulle—who was heading toward a Franco-Soviet détente. The Adenauer–de Gaulle honeymoon was short-lived because the French were far from dissatisfied with German disunity, were not at all satisfied with Adenauer's "supra-national" view of European unity, and were utterly contemptuous of his attachment to the Atlantic alliance, which they interpreted as little more than slavish dependence on the United States.

All this is hardly ancient history. It occurred only a decade ago, and the issues that caused so much trouble then are no less troublesome now. Couve de Murville recalls with relish and scorn in his memoirs how the West German government was "flabbergasted and terrified" at the prospect of following French "dynamism, audacity, and independence," whenever the United States disapproved of French actions. Not, he adds for good measure, that the French ever expected anything else of the Germans.[53]

The Franco-Soviet détente of 1965, accompanied by France's withdrawal from NATO, stunned the Germans. From this point on, West German policy irretrievably shaken from its moorings. The Franco-German rapprochement, the Atlantic alliance, the United States with its increasing entanglement in Vietnam—all seemed to have betrayed the hopes that had been placed in them. During the so-called Grand Coalition of 1966–69, headed by the Christian-Democratic Chancellor Kurt Kiesinger and Social-Democratic Foreign Minister Willy Brandt, more and more was heard of *Ostpolitik* and détente. But, as always, they came with price tags. This was how the tag read to an experienced observer in 1967: "The price held out to the Germans of détente with the Soviet Union is the continued division of Germany and detachment from the United States."[54] It was still possible then to contemplate the price of détente—at least someone else's détente—with blunt candor and realistic concreteness. Just how much the Soviets would get was not clear until the Grand Coalition fell apart and Brandt took over as Chancellor, with the Free Democratic party as junior partner, in the fall of 1969.

Brandt's *Ostpolitik* went into high gear almost immediately; it resulted in a Soviet-German treaty in August and a Polish-German treaty in November 1970. In effect, both documents formally recognized what all West German governments had previously shied away from—the status quo, including the Oder-Neisse line and the border between East and West Germany. To take this step, Brandt's regime had to give West German policy a degree of independence or autonomy that it had never previously had. The German-Soviet détente was before anything else an act of German statesmanship based on a particular interpretation of German "national interest," whatever its effects might be on the so-called European Community and the Atlantic alliance. De Gaulle did not ask the Germans whether to make his détente with the Soviets in 1965, and Brandt did not ask the French—or the Americans—whether to make his détente in 1970.

This form of *Ostpolitik* could not fail to impinge on Germany's *Westpolitik*. Adenauer's *Westpolitik* had been his *Ostpolitik*—that is, he had staked all on the power and determination of the West to force concessions from the East. Brandt's *Ostpolitik* was not in the same sense his *Westpolitik*, but the former now set limits on the latter. The delicate balancing act between East and West was plainly implied by Brandt himself in a notable address from Moscow to his compatriots in August 1970: "Our national interest does not permit us to stand between the East and West. Our country needs cooperation and harmonization with the West and understanding with the East." Virtually paraphrasing de Gaulle, Brandt went on: "Russia is inextricably woven into the history of Europe, not only as an adversary and danger but also as a partner—historical, political, cultural, and economic." He defended the Soviet-German treaty on the ground that "nothing is lost that had not been gambled away long ago. We have the courage to open a new page in history."[55]

This rationale was not altogether disingenuous. It was true that what had been lost had been lost long ago; it also was true that Germany was now giving up all claim to regaining what had been lost. If nothing had really changed, it was hard to see why a new page in history had been opened. Something had surely been changed by the treaty or it would have been inconsequential; the only question was whether it had changed more on the West German side than on the Soviet–East German side.

Compared to the West German détente, the French détente had been comparatively simple. The French could take a most cavalier attitude toward European Union and the Atlantic alliance; the West Germans could not. The latter had to juggle several balls in the air: détente with the East, European Union, the Atlantic alliance, and, above all, relations with East Germany. After the Soviet-German treaty was signed, Chancellor Brandt made known that its effectiveness depended upon a satisfactory settlement of the ever-disturbing fate of Berlin, which, in turn, hinged on an agreement between East and West Germany. This step required an even more far-reaching historic decision on the part of West Germany—whether to give up German unification for the indefinite future, something that Professor Kissinger and others had not long ago regarded as virtually unthinkable.[56] The formula which finally enabled West Germany to give up the substance, while saving the shadow, of reunification was "two German states in one nation." The "two German states" satisfied the inexorable demand of East Germany; the "one nation" held out the consolation for West Germany that both Germanies had something deeper than statehood in common. In any case, the precondition for an East-West German settlement was satisfied by the Allied agreement on Berlin in September 1971, and the full East-West German settlement took the form of a Basic Treaty signed on December 22, 1972. In essence, East Germany got full and unconditional recognition as a sovereign state, and West Germany got freer travel and communication arrangements between the two Germanies.

We do not have to decide here whether Chancellor Brandt's *Ostpolitik* has been good or bad, right or wrong. It would be difficult in any case to make any definitive judgment of Brandt's policy; the deal between East and West was too unequal. What West Germany contributed to the détente were fundamental concessions on great historic issues. It may not be possible to tell for another generation or more what the full price of the formal recognition of German partition is going to be. In holding that the Federal Republic could not safely abandon reunification or accept the present frontiers as final, Dr. Kissinger and others may still prove to be farsighted. In return, all that East Germany promised to give was relatively limited and ephemeral. The German Communists have sought to protect themselves from closer relations with the West by adopting a policy of *Abgrenzung* (separation). Thus far the fruits of détente in intra-German relations have proven to be most disappointing to West Germany. Some gains have resulted from the Basic Treaty of December 1972, but they have been far more restricted than the West Germans had hoped. Observers have also noted that détente has encouraged a growing mood of "inwardness" in West Germany, accompanied by a growing estrangement from foreign affairs.[57] If the German détente needed a symbol, it was provided by the resignation of Chancellor Brandt because his East German confreres had planted a spy in his midst as a token of mutual trust.

As in the German case, détentes may help to stabilize one area and destabilize another. While public-opinion polls showed that 80 to 90 percent of West Germans favored reconciliation with the Soviet Union, they also revealed a disquieting trend away from the Western alliance system. From 1969 to 1971, the percentage in favor of German neutrality rose from 39 to 50. In the same period, the percentage in favor of a firm military alliance with the United States dropped from 48 to 39.[58] In the fall of 1970, a poll presented twenty different political objectives; consolidation of the Western alliance ranked fifteenth, well toward the bottom. In 1972, a majority for the first time favored a neutrally oriented German foreign policy.[59]

One détente may also work at cross purposes with another. The Franco-Soviet détente of 1965 acutely disturbed the Germans, and the German-Soviet détente of 1969–70 intensely disconcerted the French. The German policy of de Gaulle's successor, Georges Pompidou, was essentially one of taking out an insurance policy against Germany. In 1969, Pompidou remarked: "Germany and its economic weight disturbs me." He used this argument to induce the Italians to get closer to the French.[60] In 1971, when Pompidou permitted Great Britain to enter the Common Market, his purpose was not merely to enlarge the European economic community; it was primarily to use Britain against Germany. As soon as France withdrew its veto, former Prime Minister Edward Heath began to talk with an Anglo-Gaullist accent, as Dr. Kissinger had long ago predicted.[61] Most recently, the French anxiety about Germany was discussed by the arch-Gaullist, Michel Debré, former Premier, Foreign Minister, and Defense Minister, with Marc Ullmann, editor-in-chief of the Paris weekly, *L'Express*. Debré explained, according to Ullmann, that France's nuclear deterrent was "intended to enable France to adopt a position of Swedish-style armed neutrality in the event of West Germany being tempted to participate in the creation of a Finland-style Mittel-Europa." Indeed, the latest French *cauchemar* has been the risk that the American-Soviet détente would open the way to the neutralization of Central Europe, including Germany. Pompidou, according to M. Ullmann, was "obsessed, even more than his predecessor was, with the fear that Germany will one day allow herself to be carried away by the wind from the East" and was "convinced that Germany is bound to seek her reunification in one way or another," despite the terms of the German-Soviet détente. It was all right for French nationalism to set the pace of détente with the Soviet Union, but now "French policy appears to be once again dominated by the fear that Germany may start to play a purely nationalist game." For these reasons, M. Ullmann reported, every conversation with former President Pompidou about foreign policy, no matter how it began, always ended up by "invoking the 'German problem.' "[62]

It might be thought that two détentes would be better than one, but that is not necessarily the case. The French détente was a Gaullist expression of French national interest, and the German détente was a Brandtian expression of German national interest. The two détentes did not mesh because the national interests did not mesh. The Germans interpreted the Franco-Soviet détente as essentially inimical to German interests, and the French interpreted the German-Soviet détente as essentially inimical to French interests. It should come as no surprise, then, that the Soviet-American détente was not universally greeted with joy and applause in Europe.

VII

The roots of the current Soviet-American détente go back at least a decade. It originated with John F. Kennedy, not Richard M. Nixon.

In a notable speech at the American University in June 1963, President Kennedy put out a feeler for "relaxation of tensions" based on a common "abhorrence of war." We are told by Arthur M. Schlesinger, Jr., that one of Kennedy's motives was to get a Soviet-American front against Communist China, which the President considered to be "the long-time danger to the peace." Both the French and, of course, the Chinese were then interested in *preventing* a Soviet-American détente.[63]

The mini-détente of 1963 was made up of the same kinds of deals that turned up in the more ambitious détente of 1972. The main consequences of Kennedy's initiative were the Test Ban Treaty of July 1963 on the military side and the first sale of U.S. grain to Soviet Russia on the commercial side. France and China refused to sign the limited Test Ban Treaty. The grain deal of $250 million of surplus wheat was a bagatelle compared with the gargantuan 1972 deal, but it set a precedent and helped the Soviets to get over a serious agricultural shortage. In Kennedy's entourage, détente was very much in the air, if only in an early phase. "The breathing spell had become a pause, the pause was becoming a détente and no one could foresee what further changes lay ahead," Theodore Sorensen writes of the period.[64] Arthur Schlesinger is somewhat more restrained, cautioning that the accomplishment of these and other measures would have stopped short of "a true détente," which would have required a closing of the "philosophical gap" between the two societies.[65] Whatever it was and however far it went, the Kennedy-Khrushchev détente was cut short by the assassination of the President in November 1963.

Among those most disturbed by this first experiment in détente was Richard Nixon.

The wheat deal particularly perturbed Mr. Nixon. The United States, he said, would be "harming the cause of freedom if it sold wheat to the Soviet Union." He wanted to know: "Why should we pull them out of their trouble and make Communism look better?" He suggested selling the wheat to the Soviet satellites "as a business deal, provided that the government involved gives some degree of freedom, more degree of freedom [*sic*] to the people in these countries"—exactly what he thought need not be done nine years later. Mr. Nixon did not like anything about Kennedy's tentative détente because as he put it: "The bear is always most dangerous when he stands with his arms open in friendship."[66]

Yet the rationale for Kennedy's détente was not very different from that adopted by President Nixon for his détente. By 1963, U.S. authorities believed that the United States and the Soviet Union were about evenly matched in antiballistic missiles; the Soviet Union had apparently gained an advantage in very-large-yield nuclear weapons whereas the United States held a lead in medium- and low-yield weapons.[67] Kennedy in 1963 as much as Nixon in 1972 professed to be mainly concerned with stopping or slowing down the nuclear arms race. The times were different but not so different that détente might not have been defended in 1963 on the same grounds that it was defended a decade later. Though Dr. Kissinger does not seem to have commented directly on the Kennedy test-ban treaty or wheat deal, he could not have been overly impressed by them if we may judge from his overall distrust of détente at this time. He certainly did not have a good word to say for them.

In October 1966, even President Johnson made a stab at what he called "reconciliation with the East," but he never got far enough to talk of a more general détente.[68] By the end of 1966, however, the Johnson administration was able to push ahead with the nuclear Nonproliferation Treaty, which was ratified in 1970, and to reach initial agreement on

holding strategic-arms-limitation talks (SALT), which were also consummated by the Nixon administration. President Johnson would have
liked nothing better than to have taken credit for a Soviet-American
détente but the times were not propitious. The Vietnam war on the
American side and the invasion of Czechoslovakia in August 1968 on
the Soviet side were too much to overcome.

The Nixon détente took about two years to set in motion. The final
phase seems to have started with the Allied agreement on Berlin in
September 1971, which apparently convinced the Nixon administration
that a summit meeting in Moscow was feasible.[69] On October 12,
President Nixon was confident enough of the outcome to make a public
announcement of the meeting to be held the following May. In November 1971, then Secretary of Commerce Maurice Stans handed the Soviet
Minister of Foreign Trade Nikolai S. Patolichev a letter of understanding listing conditions for increased trade relations, after which eleven
months of negotiations followed.[70] These three actions indicate that the
turning point came in the last four months of 1971.

The *pièce de résistance* of the summit meeting in Moscow in May
1972 was the antiballistic-missile treaty. The technical details need not
detain us; what is important for us here is the principle of *quantitative
parity* embodied in the agreement. The quantitative aspect made the
agreement possible because both sides had reached a point of diminish-
ing returns which made mere increase in numbers exorbitantly wasteful.
Since the agreement was reached, it has become unmistakable that the
nuclear arms race has turned *qualitative* with emphasis on accuracy and
"payload." As a result, both sides are spending more than ever and
accusing each other of evading the spirit of the May 1972 treaty by
developing new and more sophisticated weaponry. The parity aspect of
SALT I is, therefore, inherently temporary and unstable, even if it
should be possible to determine, which is doubtful, what parity means in
this context. Since the SALT I agreement, whatever its virtues and
drawbacks may be, has a five-year time limit, it must be reinforced by a
more far-reaching, permanent limitation of strategic arms, which is the
task of SALT II, so far deadlocked. If SALT II fails, Dr. Kissinger has
admitted that "a spiraling of the arms race is inevitable" and that the
Soviet Union "could wind up with both more warheads and more destructive warheads than we will possess" by the end of the present
decade.[71] Without a successful SALT II, the United States is apt to rue
SALT I. The final returns, then, are far from in.

John Newhouse, whose study of SALT I, *Cold Dawn*, has been called "outstanding" and "distinguished" by none other than Dr. Kissinger,[72] concluded that "SALT is an obscure, certainly an elusive enterprise," at the heart of which lies "politics."[73] If that was implicitly true of the SALT I agreement, it was explicitly true of another major document that came out of the May 1972 summit in Moscow—the "Basic Principles of Relations Between the United States of America and the Union of Soviet Socialist Republics." In this document there was nothing but politics—the politics of détente.

According to Dr. Kissinger, the idea of setting forth these "basic principles" was initially a Soviet proposal, which the United States "shelved" for some time in order to assure itself that the statement could be "really meaningful." The idea that there should be an expression of general principles was discussed for "some months." The idea that the principles should come out at the end of the summit meeting was "a joint one."[74] We may assume, therefore, that this document was intended to be "really meaningful" and that failure to live up to it would be regarded as equally "meaningful."

It is fortunate that this charter of détente was issued. For if we want to know what détente is or implies, we have it here. It is no longer a vague, amorphous "relaxation of tension." It is a concrete, specific code of behavior. Since the Soviet Union proposed the idea in the first place, and several months were spent working it out to the satisfaction of both sides, the Soviet Union as well as the United States can hardly object if they are judged on the basis of the code.

Of the twelve "basic principles," a few were soon put to the test. Both sides committed themselves, among other things, to the following:

> Prevent the development of situations capable of causing a dangerous exacerbation of their relations.
>
> Do their utmost to avoid military confrontations.
>
> Recognize that efforts to obtain unilateral advantage at the expense of the other, directly or indirectly, are inconsistent with these objectives.
>
> Have a special responsibility . . . to do everything in their power so that conflicts or situations will not arise which would serve to increase international tensions.
>
> Make no claim for themselves and would not recognize the claims of anyone else to any special rights or advantages in world affairs. They recognize the sovereign equality of all states.[75]

There was much more, of course, but these five points will do. The last, which appeared as the eleventh principle, was interpreted by Dr.

Kissinger as specifically renouncing "any claim to special spheres of influence."[76] In addition, according to a high U.S. official, these self-denying ordinances were specifically applicable to the Middle East and were understood to mean that it "should not be an area over which there should be confrontation between us."[77]

From these basic principles we know what détente was supposed to mean operationally. Cynics might suppose that no one in his right mind could have taken these vows of international virtue seriously, least of all the statesmen and diplomats who put their names to them. Was it really edifying to sign a piece of paper which fostered the illusion that the Soviet Union was renouncing its sphere of influence in Eastern Europe? The fact remains that the May 1972 charter of détente was taken quite seriously, at least on the U.S. and Israeli side. It entered into their calculations on the chances of another Arab-Israeli conflict and significantly tipped the balance in favor of an optimistic assessment of the pre-war situation. If the May 1972 summit meeting was the euphoric expression of détente, the Arab attack on Israel in October 1973 was the acid test of its genuineness.

For the fact is that if the "basic principles" of détente had been respected, the Egyptian-Syrian attack should not have taken place. It was clearly dependent on massive, extravagant Soviet support; it could not have failed to cause a dangerous exacerbation of U.S.-USSR relations; it had to have as its objective a unilateral advantage for the Soviet Union at the expense of the United States; and it clearly increased international tensions. After all, the United States and the Soviet Union had been, as Secretary Kissinger himself put it, "essentially allied to one of the contenders in the area,"[78] making a Soviet-American crisis an inevitable result of an Arab-Israeli conflict. If the Soviet Union had made any effort to live up to the May 1972 agreement, it should have done its utmost to avoid the Arab-Israeli military confrontation, let alone to make it possible or to urge other Arab nations to get into it. By believing that these were precisely the Middle Eastern implications of détente, the Americans and Israelis opened themselves to being substantially surprised by the Arab attack. One of the determining elements in the intelligence estimate was the answer to the question: Would the Soviet Union consider it more important *not* to disturb its détente with the United States than to help the Arab states to attack Israel? If the first thesis was adopted, the intelligence estimate was inevitably weighted in favor of discounting the possibility of an Arab attack or even of assuming that any confrontation would be initiated by Israel. If the Israelis, as has been revealed, had sufficient information but interpreted it wrongly, the misleading character of détente was partially responsible for the incorrect evaluation.

The result of this and other illusions was some of the most serious miscalculations in recent U.S. history. When the Soviet planes began to evacuate Soviet families from Egypt and Syria on October 4, two days before the attack, some U.S. intelligence officials interpreted the flights as indicative of an Arab-Soviet break, such as the one that had occurred in July 1972, just after the Moscow summit meeting. On the morning of October 6, the day the war broke out, the highest-level U.S. intelligence report, written the previous day, took the view that hostilities were not imminent and even suggested a crisis in Arab-Soviet relations. After news of the war was received in Washington, high-level U.S. policymakers and intelligence experts at first believed that the Israelis had attacked the Arabs. Not since the Bay of Pigs had there been such a consummate politico-intelligence fiasco.

Détentes may be maximal or minimal or anything in between. The "basic principles" of May 1972 represented détente at its maximum. They proved to be an unmitigated snare and delusion. The official American response was curious. President Nixon had put his name to the "basic principles" and had recommended them to Congress as "a solid framework for the future development of better American-Soviet relations."[79] Not since Franklin D. Roosevelt has an American President had more cause to regret a public expression of confidence in the good faith of the Soviet leadership. Yet so great was the political investment in détente that both President Nixon and Dr. Kissinger publicly reacted to the Soviet role in the conflict as if the "solid framework" had never existed. An official conspiracy of silence protected the once-acclaimed "basic principles" from public scrutiny.

The new party line fell back on the minimal version of détente. In effect, it reduced the concept of détente to little more than the avoidance of nuclear war between the superpowers. Whereas the original "basic principles" of détente were specific and concrete, Secretary Kissinger now described détente as "inherently ambiguous" and "somewhat ambivalent."[80] The best and almost the only thing he could say in favor of détente was that it limited "the risks of nuclear conflict."[81] Senator J. William Fulbright expounded: "Détente, in its essence, is an agreement not to let these differences [between the two superpowers] explode into nuclear war."[82] A distinguished academic exponent of the new line blamed liberals for "reacting to the collapse of their too-high expectations for friendly relations with a liberalized Soviet regime." He did not say whether he classified President Nixon and Secretary Kissinger among those disenchanted liberals. Détente, we were told, is a process with one, two, three stages and beyond, lasting decades; we are now in stage one, or limited détente, the main business of which is "to reduce the danger of nuclear war."[83] Presumably, the "basic principles" of May 1972 had been a much later stage, and we have been going backward ever since—in order to go forward.

This view of détente distinguishes it from hot war, but it comes perilously close to obliterating the distinction between détente and cold war. The cold war was also considered preferable to hot war in that the conflicts and competition between the so-called superpowers were held within bounds short of actual nuclear warfare. The cold war was in any case never a very satisfactory term; John Lukacs was right to observe that "cold peace" would have been a much better metaphor.[84] Both cold war and détente are accordion-like terms; they can be pushed and pulled in and out so that they may mean almost anything. During the cold war, the United States and the Soviet Union could collaborate in 1956 as if they were partners against Britain, France, and Israel; during the détente, the United States and the Soviet Union could threaten each other in 1973 with preliminary mobilizations or precautionary nuclear alerts. If détente means little more than, as Secretary Kissinger put it, that "confrontations are kept within bounds that do not threaten civilized life,"[85] it is not doing much more than the cold war did. It is small comfort to learn that all other confrontations, short of threatening civilized life, are still compatible with détente. It is time to stop using cold war as a scare term and détente as a sedative term; in their relationship to nuclear war, they are not all that different.

A witty French journalist may have said the last word on these terms. Paraphrasing Clausewitz, he remarked that "détente is the cold war pursued by other means—and sometimes by the same."[86]

VIII

It is easy, as most of us have found to our sorrow, to be bewitched by the day-to-day flow of events. As Secretary Kissinger said at his confirmation hearings, the great challenge before the United States is "to distinguish the fundamental from the ephemeral" and for someone like himself in public life, "to leave something behind that would be valid and permanent."[87] With this one can hardly disagree.

What has been fundamental and permanent in this period of "détente"? Everyone seems agreed that a great transition has been going on, but no one is quite sure what it is or where it is going. No doubt we are too close to events to see them in a long enough perspective. Yet, for better or worse, we must try as best we can to take stock and look ahead. We have hardly begun to face the implications and consequences of the Arab-Israeli war of October 1973. But it is not too soon to raise a few questions about some of the deeper premises which have gone into U.S. policy in the past few years. The effort is worth making if only to bring together some strands of the problems that I have been pursuing.

Nuclear and other wars: Long before détente became a household word, it was evident that nuclear weapons were a rare, special breed, in a different category from the kind of weapons on which the accretion of power had traditionally been based. French strategists have long believed that no country would ever use nuclear weapons because they were self-destructive. These strategists have had the advantage that no one wishes to prove them wrong. A policy which is primarily aimed at preventing nuclear war is still going to leave us with the risk of all the wars that mankind used to have before nuclear war was invented. Experience has shown that the United States and the Soviet Union are quite capable of going up to the brink of nuclear war without going over. They did more or less just that during the missile crisis of October 1962 and again during the Arab-Israeli conflict of October 1973. Secretary Kissinger has given détente the special function of preventing a general nuclear war from arising out of "the rivalries of client states."[88] This was, indeed, the rationale of the "basic principles" of May 1972, but their fate is not reassuring. The United States in Vietnam and the Soviet Union in the Middle East have shown that they can take vast risks on behalf of client states without setting off a nuclear war. The possibility of nuclear war is always there, of course, but something else may be more probable. A policy which faces the possible but not the probable leaves something to be desired.

Secretary Kissinger himself suggested where to look for the trouble. "But assuming the present balance holds," he stated at his confirmation hearings, "and granting the strategic significance of what we had both agreed upon, the increasing difficulty of conceiving a rational objective for general nuclear war makes it, therefore, less risky to engage in local adventures."[89] A month later, the Soviet Union engaged in just such a "local adventure." To be sure, it set off a Soviet-American contretemps, the nature of which is not yet entirely clear. But neither side was anxious to push it to a showdown, and the Soviet Union was not penalized for having taken the risk. What operated was not détente; it was exactly the same thing that had operated during the cold war, namely, the inhibition of the two superpowers against hot nuclear war. The Arab-Israeli conflict of 1973 hardly disproved Secretary Kissinger's rule that the increasing unlikelihood of nuclear war makes local adventure less risky—and, one might add, more likely.

Now a new element has injected itself into this equation. The Americans toward the end of the Vietnam war and the Soviets especially during the Arab-Israeli conflict of 1973 introduced what have been called "precision-guided non-nuclear munitions" or "smart weapons." Among them are the new Soviet hand-held antitank guns and surface-to-air missiles, such as the SAM-6 and SAM-7, which enabled the Egyptian ground troops to surprise and at first take a heavy toll of Israeli tanks and planes. The new technology, it is claimed, permits a hitherto unattainable degree of control and precision which makes possible the use of "non-nuclear weapons in many circumstances where a desperate hope had formerly been pinned to using small nuclear weapons." Bigger and bigger weapons having reached a destructive force beyond rational utilization, it would seem that the only way to gain an advantage was to reverse the trend and develop more discriminating and more accurate smaller weapons against the tank-and-fighter-bomber team that had dominated the battlefield since World War II. Professor Albert Wohlstetter, an acute and well-informed authority in this field, who has made the most penetrating analysis of these developments, has persuasively argued that they have signficantly raised the threshold of nuclear war and have substantially increased the likelihood of conventional or non-nuclear warfare.[90]

If so, détente needs some reconsideration from this point of view. The post-October 1973 doctrine of détente has almost exclusively correlated it with the prevention of nuclear war. If conventional war has become less risky as nuclear war has become, in Dr. Kissinger's words, "less and less plausible and a less and less rational method,"[91] and if conventional warfare is making a technological comeback so that it becomes a more plausible and more rational exercise of power, this shift in the credibility of nuclear versus non-nuclear war should be reflected in the function of détente. Primarily it must concern itself with precisely the kind of war which it failed to hold back—and which, as I have tried to show, it may even have encouraged—in October 1973. Too much or one-sided emphasis on preventing nuclear war may be the easy way out; the more difficult and more pressing problem may well be the prevention of conventional or non-nuclear wars.

Marginal advantages: Dr. Kissinger has also put forward another concept in connection with the "nuclear era" that may be open to question. According to him, this era had changed the balance of power in such a way that neither the Soviet Union nor the United States had anything to fear from each other in the competition for "marginal advantages." This theory was another reason why the Arab-Israeli conflict of October 1973 should not have taken place, theoretically.

In June 1972, soon after the summit meeting in Moscow which was the source of so many of these comforting concepts, Dr. Kissinger maintained that "to the extent that balance of power means constant jockeying for marginal advantages over an opponent, it no longer applies." He explained at some length:

> The reason is that the determination of national power has changed fundamentally in the nuclear age. Throughout history, the primary concern of most national leaders has been to accumulate geopolitical and military power. It would have seemed inconceivable even a generation ago that such power once gained could not be translated directly into advantage over one's opponent. But now both we and the Soviet Union have begun to find that each increment of power does not necessarily represent an increment of usable political strength.[92]

Almost a year later, this consoling notion was written into the President's foreign-policy report to the Congress of May 3, 1973. It contended that, although a certain balance of power was still inherent in any international system, the balance was no longer "the overriding concept," because continual maneuvering for marginal advantages in the nuclear era had become "both unrealistic and dangerous." It went on:

> It is unrealistic because both sides possess such enormous power, small additional increments cannot be translated into tangible advantages or even usable political strength. And it is dangerous because attempts to seek tactical gains might lead to confrontations which could be catastrophic.[93]

Five months later, the Arab-Israeli conflict broke out. Evidently the Soviet leaders had not been apt students of Dr. Kissinger's lessons. What did they hope to achieve? No more "geopolitical and military power"? No "increment of power" translatable into "an increment of usable political strength"? No "tactical gains"? Dangerous this continual maneuvering may well be, but "unrealistic"?

This Kissingerian theory was an extrapolation of the "basic principles" of May 1972. He made it seem as if he and the Soviet leaders had seen eye to eye on the practical implications of the principles. Yet whatever the Soviet leaders may have professed to believe, their actions belied their words. They were not deterred by détente in the nuclear era from seeking "marginal advantages" or "increments of power" or "tangible advantages" or "tactical gains."

The true test of a concept is not how persuasive it may appear in the abstract but how close it comes to defining and explaining reality. Dr. Kissinger's theorem on the obsolescence of marginal advantages cannot begin to cope with the reality of the Arab-Israeli war or the competition that has obviously not ceased elsewhere. After that war, Dr. Kissinger somewhat spoiled the beautiful simplicity of his theorem by conceding that the Soviet-American relationship was made up "both of confidence and of competition, coexisting in a somewhat ambivalent manner."[94] If competition is part of the game, what is competition about if not for "marginal advantages," "increments of power," "tangible advantages," and "tactical gains"? In fact, if the theorem is valid, we hardly need a brilliant Secretary of State and a huge foreign-affairs bureaucracy and budget any longer; the nuclear era would by itself virtually insure a cessation of these petty annoyances and permit only the final, apocalyptic conflict. Unnoticed, the theory went all the way back in its implications to John Foster Dulles, who had never been one of Dr. Kissinger's favorite statesmen.

China and the "self-regulating mechanism": The role of China in the Soviet-American détente might also be profitably rethought. The once-popular "triangular theory" put China more or less on a par with the United States and the Soviet Union in order to account for the way they were reshuffling their relationships—China with the United States presumably against the Soviet Union, the Soviet Union with the United States presumably against China, and the United States with both of them, protesting that it was not against either.

The Soviets were certainly not above using the United States against China. We have been told on good authority that the Soviets on at least three occasions beginning in 1970 tried unsuccessfully to get an agreement with the United States to act jointly in the event of some vague "provocative action" on the part of a third nuclear power, which could only mean China.[95] Though the Chinese have never been so crass, they would certainly take help from anywhere and anyone if they found themselves in real trouble with the Soviet Union. The Chinese-American rapprochement, such as it is, derived in large part from the Chinese assessment that the Soviet Union was a greater threat than the United States.

Dr. Kissinger, it seems, had also chased the will-o'-the-wisp of a "self-regulating mechanism"—through China. In November 1972, he confided to the distinguished journalist, Theodore H. White, that "what the world needed was a self-regulating mechanism" and that the key to such a mechanism was China.[96] A "self-regulating mechanism" would imply that the United States, the Soviet Union, and China were so evenly matched that one would not dare to take on a second without the third.

The Soviet interest in a Soviet-American détente has often been attributed to the supposition that the Soviet leaders consider China a greater threat than the United States. This is another questionable proposition. It may have been true in the late 1960s, but the time has passed for it to be accepted uncritically.

One reason why the fear—as distinct from the hostility—of the Soviet Union toward China has diminished is the Soviet military build-up in the Soviet-Chinese border area. According to the best available information, the Soviet Union had fifteen divisions in this area in 1968; it had forty-five, including about eight tank divisions, in 1974.[97] This enormous increase in only six years was not accomplished at the expense of the Soviet armed forces in the West; it was achieved simply by adding more divisions to an already immense military machine.

The Chinese have given every evidence of knowing that they have more to fear from the Soviets than the latter have to fear from them. De Gaulle liked to believe that the Soviet Union needed the West, and the West had nothing to fear from it, because China had replaced the West as the main Soviet concern.[98] Whether or not de Gaulle was right in his time, the Soviets have had different ideas. They were faced, in essence, with the classical problem of the two-front war; de Gaulle assumed that they had to fall back on the classical solution of concentration; he gave the Soviets the option of concentrating their force in the East or West but not both. In effect, this constraint would put the Soviets at a disadvantage, at least to the extent that they could not afford to take risks in the West if they were tied up in the East. This kind of thinking has had a lulling effect on Western policy; it has also helped in making détente seem much safer than it has been.

Instead, the Soviet leaders chose to build up their armed forces on all fronts in order to give themselves the maximum freedom of action. The triangular theory was never very persuasive for the same reason that the pentagonal theory failed to be convincing—the balance was nowhere as "even" as President Nixon had supposed. The Chinese-American rapprochement may well be—and I think it is—a good thing in its own right, but it is not an insurance policy against the Soviet Union and it is least of all a "self-regulating mechanism."

The troubled partnership? This was the title, without the question mark, of Professor Kissinger's last book on European-American relations, published in 1965. It indicates how far back the trouble goes. I have put a question mark after the title to cast doubt not on the trouble but on the "partnership."

The term itself was first popularized by former President John F. Kennedy. When he spoke of Europe, he used such phrases as "partners in aid, trade, defense, diplomacy, and monetary affairs," "a partner with whom we could deal on a basis of full equality," "a full and equal partner," and "partners for peace."[99]

This rhetoric provoked some of de Gaulle's most wrathful discourses. If Kennedy was right about the equal European-American partnership, de Gaulle could not be right to declare against French and European dependence on the United States and against the lurking threat of an Anglo-Saxon–Soviet condominium. When the continental Europeans were excluded from the Test Ban Treaty negotiations of 1963, his anguish and anger exploded publicly. His separate détente with the Soviet Union two years later was partly a reply to that treaty and all that it implied to him.

One of those who substantially agreed with de Gaulle on this issue was Dr. Henry Kissinger. In addition to the Test Ban negotiations, he was disturbed by the attempt of the Kennedy administration in 1962–63 to deal directly with the Soviet Union on the status of Berlin. In the Gaullist vein, he protested: "The mere fact of bilateral negotiations raised the specter of a U.S.-Soviet accommodation at the expense of our allies." When Mr. Kennedy spoke of partnership on the basis of full equality, Dr. Kissinger instructed the President sternly: "Real partnership is possible only between equals."[100]

Much of *The Troubled Partnership* two years later was an extended commentary on these themes. It explored at length all the flaws in the concept of partnership from the European point of view. During those years Dr. Kissinger was Europe's most consistent and persuasive academic protagonist in the United States and a hard, relentless critic of U.S. policy; he almost never liked what any President or Secretary of

State said or did. If "consultation" was the issue, he countered that it "is far from a panacea"; it was least effective when it was most needed. If the Europeans were recognized as equal in fact, they would want to be more independent than partnership implied; if the United States insisted on retaining its dominant position, the political will of Europe would eventually be broken. About the most cheerful thing he could say was that we might get through "the transition from tutelage to equality" if we mustered enough "wisdom and delicacy," neither of which had been our strong points. In fact, his analysis was filled with such depressing contradictions that he finally took refuge, as we have seen, in the visionary call for an "Atlantic Commonwealth," far beyond the so-called Atlantic alliance.[101]

In his 1968 essay, only a year before he went to Washington as Presidential Assistant, Professor Kissinger still argued, more compellingly than ever, that European-American partnership was not feasible in the existing circumstances. He accused the Americans of invoking "leadership" and "partnership" only to support "the existing pattern" of inequality. He repeated his previous belief that Europe was no longer capable of playing a "global role." He regarded even more extensive consultation, always offered as a cure-all, as nothing more than a "palliative." Instead of partnership, he advised the United States to settle for "political multipolarity," by which he seemed to mean that differences in interest and policy should be accepted with understanding and tolerance. He criticized advocates of détente as being more concerned with atmospherics than with substance. He warned against mistaking a "benign Soviet tone" for the achievement of peace. In short, he was still the same old Kissinger, only more so.[102]

Then came the new Kissinger. In President Nixon's foreign-policy report to the Congress of February 1970, unmistakably written in Dr. Kissinger's familiar cadences, the first principle of American policy with respect to Europe was given as—"partnership." The term itself was used again and again throughout the report, even in headings: "Peace Through Partnership—The Nixon Doctrine" and "A New and Mature Partnership."[103] In the next foreign-policy report of February 1971, headings read: "Towards New Forms of Partnership" and "The Evolution of Partnership." A careful reader would have noted that we were merely in "the necessary transition to an equal partnership" which was "still in progress."[104] Evidently there were partnerships and equal partnerships, a distinction that had not been contemplated when Dr.

Kissinger had implied that there were only real and unreal partnerships ("real partnership is possible only between equals").

Had so much really changed between 1968 and 1970? The answer is that something had changed but not what the ritual use of the term "partnership" suggested. Instead of a change from non-partnership to partnership, Europe was increasingly neglected and shunted aside in favor of the deals with China and Russia. The pentagonal theory was conceived by the President, with or without Dr. Kissinger's assistance, to put Europe on more or less the same plane as the United States, Soviet Union, China, and Japan, "each balancing the other." This arrangement was hardly how a European-American *partnership* should have worked. The discrepancy was never explained.

In his "Year of Europe" speech in April 1973, Dr. Kissinger took over the term in his own name. He referred to "Atlantic partners," to "the principles of partnership," and to Japan as "a principal partner in our common enterprise." He also distinguished between the United States which had "global interests and responsibilities" and our European allies which had only "regional interests."[105] This distinction caused much resentment in Europe, where it was apparently not known or forgotten that he had been saying much the same thing for a decade. Nevertheless, Secretary Kissinger continued to make use of the term "partnership" and "our Atlantic partnership" in later speeches, even when he was trying to explain why the putative partners had been behaving so unpartnerly and why they should change their ways.[106]

If the use of the term were merely a verbal quibble, Dr. Kissinger would not have gone to so much trouble analyzing what was wrong with it when he was still a professor. In fact, the contradiction inherent in his "Year of Europe" speech takes us close to the heart of the matter.

The long-term trouble was the problematic relationship between the United States and Europe. As Dr. Kissinger had pointed out as early as 1963, *real* partnership required equality. Without equality, a so-called partnership could only have a leader and a follower, the dominating and the dominated. He was perfectly right to expose the self-serving shallowness of the Kennedy catchword. In the catchword was concealed a program, one that de Gaulle understood and, therefore, rejected.

How, then, could someone who had seen through this verbiage write it into President Nixon's foreign-policy reports to Congress without holding his nose and, worse still, bandy it about in his own speeches? It is tempting to ascribe this intellectual transmogrification to some venial political sin. The case, however, may be more serious. In April 1973, as we have seen, Dr. Kissinger was capable in one and the same important speech of combining a reference to "partnership" with a reference to an inequality of power and interest which, by his own say-so, made any respectable partnership impossible. Six months later, he told the Senate Foreign Relations Committee: "For the first time since World War II, all great nations have become full participants in the international system."[107] All? Full? Was he referring merely to the United States, the Soviet Union, and possibly China? Or to our great European partners, too? And if not, how could they be our *partners*?

One strongly suspects a profound confusion of thought. It is not an ordinary confusion; it arises out of the confusing circumstances in which the United States finds itself. In some situations, the U.S. policymaker is still able to think how strong the United States is compared to the lesser breeds; in other situations, the same person is forced to think how helpless the United States is to enforce its will, even on its friends, let alone its enemies. This duality has produced a kind of official schizophrenia which expresses itself in action and language. Dr. Kissinger has not been immune from the disease.

Americans are not the only ones. The French took the greatest umbrage when Dr. Kissinger consigned our European allies to the lower order of "regional interests." Of all the European powers, France still aspires most to play a world role. But what happened in October 1973 when the French were faced with the Arab-Israeli war and the Arab oil embargo? The French Foreign Minister Michel Jobert whimpered: "We count for little [*Nous pesons peu*]. We will try to count for more."[108] And what of West Germany which not so long ago was considered the "leading European power" and "the leading spokesman for Western Europe"?[109] The German Foreign Minister Walter Scheel has recently unburdened himself: "The Federal Republic is aware of the limits of her influence. She cannot overcome the existing differences between France and America on her own."[110] The British did not have to apologize for anything; they have known their place since November 1956.

The great gamble: To conclude, I wish to return to the beginning—the crucial effect of détente on our relations with our allies and antagonists. Nothing else is more important for deciding the fate of the United States and the world in the foreseeable future.

The decision on which of these relationships to foster came very early in the Nixon administration. One might not have expected it to go the way it did. In 1968, Dr. Kissinger noted with alarm that NATO was "in disarray," that the emergence of an economically resurgent but politically disunited Europe was inevitably bringing in "a difficult transitional period," and that "Atlantic relations, for all their seeming normalcy, thus face a profound crisis."[111] A year later, the first moves were made which, consciously or not, postponed facing the disarray of NATO, the difficult transitional period, and the crisis in Atlantic relations for at least four years. And when, finally, they came in for renewed attention, it was so late that the effort failed embarrassingly and merely called public attention to how intractable the difficulties had become.

Two decisions by the Nixon administration may prove to be of far greater long-range historical importance than anything else. I have already referred to the first—the willingness to take four years to end direct U.S. military intervention in the Vietnam war. The second was partially related but more far-reaching—the attempt to solve our problems through our antagonists, without, or even at the expense of, our friends. Conceivably, we might have tried to bolster both fronts simultaneously, but this effort was never seriously made. This onesidedness made it overly important that the détente with the Soviet Union should come off as a colossal, spectacular success. Even Dr. Kissinger lost his head long enough to hail the SALT I agreement as "without precedent in all relevant modern history." Since SALT I was in a sense the first agreement of its kind, that may not have been saying as much as Dr. Kissinger sought to convey.

The essence of the problem was once stated by Dr. Kissinger with remarkable clairvoyance. The situation at that time was not strictly comparable with the present one, but it was uncomfortably close. Words that seemed to be dealing with the past can now be read as prophecy:

> If the West is to act purposefully in this situation, it must develop a common policy and a specific program. The temptation for bilateral approaches is great. Each national leader, depending on his temperament, has visions of appearing as the arbiter of a final settlement or of adding Communist pressures to his own as a bargaining device within the [Atlantic] Alliance. This sets up a vicious circle. Since leaders generally do not reach eminence without a touch of vanity and since some stake their prestige on their ability to woo their Soviet counterparts, they tend to present their contacts with the Soviets as a considerable accomplishment. But the real issues have gone unresolved because they are genuinely difficult; hence they are usually avoided during summit diplomacy in favor of showy but essentially peripheral gestures. The vaguer the East-West discourse, the greater will be the confusion in the West. Moreover, each leader faces two different audiences: toward his own people he will be tempted to leave the impression that he has made a unique contribution to peace; toward his allies he

will be forced to insist that he will make no settlement in which they do not participate. Excessive claims are coupled with reassurances to uneasy allies which are in turn tempted to pursue bilateral diplomacy.

Where would it end? Here was how Dr. Kissinger saw it nine years ago:

> Such a course is suicidal for the West. It will stimulate distrust within the Alliance. The traditional Western balance-of-power diplomacy will reappear, manipulated by the Kremlin. Any Soviet incentive to be responsible will vanish. The Soviet leaders will be able to overcome their difficulties with the assistance of the West and without settling any of the outstanding issues. Since in the Kremlin—as in the West—there must be many who consider the status quo preferable to change, the result is likely to be diplomatic paralysis obscured by abstract declarations about peace and friendship.[112]

While many of these sentiments seem to be as fresh as ever, the parallels are, of course, not exact. Nevertheless, the real issues have certainly not been resolved, the Soviet incentive to be responsible in the Middle East vanished some time between May 1972 and October 1973, and none of the outstanding issues has been finally settled. There is something uncanny about the repetition of the suicide theme at the end of 1972 by the U.S. Ambassador to the European Community, J. Robert Schaetzel, just after his resignation: "What has been happening to U.S.-E.C. [European Community] relations is a kind of common death wish."[113]

No doubt we are still far from suicide or death. But we are no nearer safety and health if such grave warnings could have been issued by Dr. Kissinger nine years ago and by Ambassador Schaetzel less than two years ago. The central fact of the past five years is that détente with the East has beguiled us while deterioration in the West has beset us. It will not help at this late date to quarrel over which has been more to blame, Europe or the United States; there is more than enough blame for all. It is wasteful of energies for the United States to be exasperated with Europe or Europe to be exasperated with the United States; the accumulation of exasperation is part of the problem. Little is gained by adding up the resources of the European Community and finding that they exceed those of the Soviet Union or that their gross national product comes to about two-thirds that of the United States. Europe is like an optical illusion; it looks formidable only when it is viewed in the abstract as a whole; it shrinks and shrivels as soon as it is examined country by country in the light of each one's political and social reality. Only last month, Secretary of Defense James R. Schlesinger tried to inject some realism and clarity into our understanding of the position of the European states. He asserted that "contrary to the view that they are robust states with the strength to defend Europe by themselves, they are relatively weak states," and that "the most critical region in the world continues to be Western Europe."[114]

The policy of détente, whatever we may think of it, would not be so equivocal if turning toward the East had not been accompanied by turning away from the West. While lip-service was being paid to European-American "partnership," to the Atlantic alliance as the "cornerstone" of American foreign policy, and to concern about the resurgence of American isolationism, the concept of partnership became more and more of a mockery, the cornerstone was relegated to a corner, and ardent support for the policy of détente as it has worked out in practice has come from some of our most eminent neo-isolationists. There is a natural affinity between resurgent isolationism and illusory détentism; if we can persuade ourselves that we can solve our problems directly with our erstwhile enemies, why do we need to bother with allies? The great gamble inherent in this kind of détente is that we are going to be in worse trouble than ever unless détente pays off in continuous, long-lasting Soviet good-will and good behavior. For over four years, détente was pursued so single-mindedly and to the exclusion of so many other interests that it became a go-for-broke operation. The best criticism of such a policy may be found in Dr. Kissinger's past writings, which is why I have cited them so often.

Kto kogo? Who-whom? It was Lenin's favorite formulation of the crucial political question. It may be more freely translated as: "Who does what to whom?"[115] It is not a bad way of thinking about détente.

Commentary, June 1974

2

Kissinger's Apologia

I

In the first pages of the first volume of his memoirs, Henry Kissinger remarks with some bitterness about the way he was treated by Mc-George Bundy, his dean at Harvard and a predecessor as National Security Adviser to the President. It was "with a combination of politeness and subconscious condescension that upper-class Bostonians reserve for people of, by New England standards, exotic backgrounds and excessively personal style." By any standards, Kissinger's book is also exotic and excessively, if understandably, personal. It is numbingly long and stupefyingly detailed. It runs on and on for almost 1,500 pages; it needs over 400 pages to get through the first year of his service in 1969 alone. It is largely a chronicle of events, with set pieces on famous and infamous people whom he met or worked with, bits and pieces of potted history, and scatterings of familiar reflections and ruminations to leaven the lump. The main narrative pushes on relentlessly, often week by week or day by day and sometimes even hour by hour. Since this volume ends in 1972, we must be resigned to two or more volumes and more thousands of pages before Kissinger tells all. Dean Acheson, who served longer and participated in much greater history-shaking events, needed only one volume and a quarter as many pages as Kissinger's first volume to tell his entire story.

In at least one respect, the book is, by any previous standards, exotic. I know of no diplomatic memoirs that are so undiplomatically indiscreet. Some of Kissinger's pen portraits of colleagues in his own government, including the president under whom he served, can only be described as scathing. His frequently savage denigrations are scarcely alleviated by his habit of following them with a few kind words, as if to take the sting out of them or protect himself from the accusation of unmitigated malice. A typical exhibition of this technique of wounding and salving is his comparatively friendly treatment of former Secretary of Defense Melvin Laird. Laird was often "Byzantine" in his political maneuvers; his good humor was often "rascally"; he was the "probable source" of any newspaper story he complained about; he could be "maddening"; he was a "master-leaker of trivialities." But Laird was also "magnificent—strong, loyal, daring and eloquent" in crises. One gets the impression that Laird was not a man one would want to buy the proverbial second-hand car from. And the Secretary of Defense comes out relatively untarnished compared with the President and the Secretary of State who, besides Kissinger himself, are the key figures in the drama that slowly but inexorably unfolds.

The drama began when Richard Nixon unexpectedly invited Kissinger to become his Assistant for National Security Affairs in November 1968. I happened to exchange some words with Kissinger at a conference in Princeton that same week. Kissinger was still dazed by the appointment. I wondered aloud how long he would hold his new job. Kissinger said that he would be lucky to hold it for six months. I was not the only one to whom he spoke at this time in this vein. I tried to be more optimistic—he would not come out too badly if he held on to it for a year. No one who had known him in previous years (my own acquaintanceship with him went back to 1944 in the 84th Infantry Division) could have predicted that he would long survive in Washington's political jungle. Yet he not only survived; he managed, without any political constituency, by sheer force of intellect and personality, to outlast the President whose native habitat was in the darkest recesses of that jungle. He was appointed Secretary of State four years later by a jealous Nixon who already resented his subordinate's disproportionate share of credit for the conduct of foreign policy, which was Nixon's special pride and exclusive prerogative. Kissinger largely succeeded in extricating himself from the Nixon administration's disgrace and downfall. Nixon's successor, Gerald Ford, even found it necessary as almost his first order of business to announce Kissinger's retention in order to restore some confidence in the shaky new presidency.

Considering where he came from and how far he had to go, Kissinger's feat in Washington was an authentic *tour de force*. The same must be said of his memoirs, whatever opinion one may have of his ideas and policies. His book conveys much of the brute force, the intellectual virtuosity, and the insatiable appetite for power that enabled him to come out on the top, only slightly soiled, of a political dunghill. It is not for the average reader; I can sympathize with those reviewers who have dealt with it impressionistically; it would require another book to do justice to it substantively. Yet its very flaws contribute to its ultimate impressiveness—the inexhaustible self-absorption, the endless assault of detail, the craving for vindication. One thing is certain—no one who wishes to think or write about the world events of the 1970s can ignore it.

How did Kissinger do it? More of the answer than was previously accessible comes out, consciously or not, in these pages. The more he tells us about his triumphs and travails, the more disquieting they become.

II

The necessary condition for Kissinger's rise was an odd couple—Richard Nixon and William Rogers.

Kissinger's Nixon is a study in political pathology. There were, according to Kissinger, two Nixons—the one that functioned or malfunctioned most of the time in periods of relative stability, the other one that acted spasmodically when confronted by a crisis or critical decision.

The first Nixon was "weird" in his administrative approach. "He was almost physically unable to confront people who disagreed with him; and he shunned persuading people or inspiring his subordinates." He made decisions "inside his self-imposed cocoon." He saw himself as "the lonely embattled leader propping up faltering associates." Yet he distrusted his associates so intensely that he worked to tear them down. Obsessed by past resentments and suspicions of betrayal, he lived in a self-induced ambience of ubiquitous enemies. He resented and suspected most of all the members of his Cabinet and the bureaucracies that served them. At the same time he was incapable of giving direct orders to or imposing discipline on even his Cabinet. He was "petty in calm periods" and "small-minded in dealing with his associates." He was rancorous and vindictive—more so in victory than in defeat. The preoccupation of his White House with public relations was "monomaniacal." Nixon had such an uncontrollable tendency to give impetuous and irresponsible orders that he depended on his subordinates, Kissinger in foreign and H. R. Haldeman in domestic policy, to save him from himself by disregarding his instructions until he had cooled off. He dreaded meeting new people. In negotiations, which he tried desperately to avoid, "he was nervous to the point of anxiety." In dealing with foreign leaders, he sought refuge in laboriously memorized memoranda or escape into "general observations." His skill at avoiding unpleasant subjects was "finely-honed." He was so insecure that he constantly needed "reassurance" from the few persons close to him. He could be "maddening" in calm times.

Kissinger enjoys showing Nixon at his crassest. One story, with which Kissinger must have regaled countless dinner parties, has Nixon planning to go straight from a memorial mass for Charles de Gaulle at Notre Dame cathedral to the gastronomic pleasures of the restaurant Maxim's, a "mind-boggling" *faux pas* from which Kissinger rescued him. On another occasion, Nixon thought it appropriate to congratulate the Shah of Iran by citing one of former President Eisenhower's profundities to the effect that all successful political leaders had in common marriages "above themselves." Kissinger ends this tale with the punch line: "The King of Kings looked off into the distance with melancholy." Kissinger's president was surely, in Kissinger's words, a "flawed" and "strange" man. Has anyone who ever worked for a president described him in these terms? Exotic is one word for it.

The second Nixon emerged only in times of crisis or during the need for critical decisions. Kissinger gives him the saving grace of being able to make "lonely decisions" that were "extremely courageous" and demonstrated his "strategic grasp." Nixon was, to be sure, "not by nature courageous," but he "steeled himself to conspicuous acts of rare courage." The attribute of courage in crisis is the highest and almost the only praise that Kissinger bestows on Nixon, sometimes to take the sting out of his less admirable traits. Nixon in his own memoirs treats Kissinger much more gently, a restraint that he may now sorely regret.

Kissinger's Rogers is a study in political sadomasochism. The sadism was Nixon's, the masochism Rogers's. Kissinger says that Nixon told him at their first meeting before his appointment that he regarded Rogers as the "ideal man" for Secretary of State, for one reason because Rogers was unfamiliar with foreign affairs, for another because Rogers was "one of the toughest, most cold-eyed, self-centered, and ambitious men" Nixon had ever met. At that preliminary meeting, according to Nixon's memoirs, Kissinger advised him to build up a "national security apparatus" in the White House to coordinate foreign and defense policies and develop "policy options." Since Nixon planned in any case "to direct foreign policy from the White House," this recommendation suited both of them—Nixon to have a foreign-policy "apparatus" at his immediate disposal, Kissinger to be its coordinator and developer. Nixon's appointment of Kissinger was something of a fluke. He hardly knew Kissinger, but one of the things he says he knew was that Kissinger had made "disparaging comments" about him—a mild version of what Kissinger used to say about Nixon. Nevertheless, Nixon was sufficiently impressed by a single encounter with Kissinger to decide on the spur of the moment to offer him the post of National Security Adviser "in an uncharacteristically impulsive way." One of the things that must have endeared Kissinger to Nixon was the former's immediate advice to make the White House itself the headquarters of a foreign-policy and defense "apparatus."

Other presidents have appointed weak secretaries of state in order to direct their own foreign policy. But there has never been a case as shameful and indecent as that of Nixon's treatment of his old, "personal friend," William Rogers. In his memoirs, Nixon added indignity to injury by calling Rogers "a strong administrator" and "a resourceful negotiator." Rogers was given to administer a single area of policy, and that only for a time. If he was as tough, cold-eyed, self-centered, and ambitious as Nixon described him before Rogers took office, then Nixon deliberately set out to humiliate him.

The bone Nixon was originally willing to throw to Rogers was Middle Eastern policy. He chose this one, according to Kissinger, for thoroughly malicious reasons. If everything else was reserved for the White House, Rogers had to be given something with which to occupy himself. At the same time, however, Nixon believed that any active policy in the Middle East was then doomed to failure and to stir up domestic hostility against anyone identified with it. The ill-fated Rogers Plan, of December 1969, which Nixon says he knew all the time had no chance of being accepted by Israel and which made Rogers, "as Kissinger frequently reminded me, 'the most unpopular man in Israel,' " exactly suited what Nixon had in mind for Rogers.

Otherwise, Rogers and the State Department were deliberately and systematically deprived of every other area or policy that traditionally pertained to them. This move was initiated by Nixon almost immediately in February 1969 with respect to Soviet-American negotiations. Kissinger's and Nixon's divergent explanations of how it was accomplished show each of them retrospectively making the other responsible. Kissinger explains that Nixon "wished to establish his dominance over negotiations with the Soviet Union" and, therefore, "required the exclusion of Rogers, who might be too anxious and who might claim credit for whatever progress might be made"—this before Rogers was even given a chance to show what "a resourceful negotiator" he was. Nixon, on the other hand, relates that "Kissinger had suggested that we develop a private channel between Dobrynin and him"—and Nixon agreed. In any case, Rogers was left out of the first meeting between Nixon and Soviet Ambassador Anatoly Dobrynin. Rogers must have sensed what was happening because much of a weekend was spent, Kissinger says, "fighting off Rogers's pleas—basically not unjustified"—to attend. At this meeting, Nixon set up privately with Dobrynin the first of the notorious "back channels" that effectively cut the State Department out of Soviet-American policy and made it the monopoly of the White House, which, in practice, meant Kissinger and his "apparatus."

Gradually, the maw of Kissinger's "back channel" swallowed up one area, issue, and policy after another. After the Soviet connection came SALT I, the strategic arms limitation talks. The Vietnamese negotiations followed suit. China was next. If Kissinger had had his way, according to Nixon, Rogers and the State Department would not even have been permitted to gnaw away at the bare bone of the Middle East. Kissinger "bridled" at Nixon's assignment of all Middle Eastern problems to Rogers in 1969 and 1970 and tried to get them for himself too. By 1970, relations between Kissinger and Rogers had deteriorated to such an extent that, Kissinger says, the two of them could not engage in a "rational discussion." By the end of that year, Nixon almost automatically approved Kissinger's "tactical management of foreign policy" on a day-by-day basis, though the President still reserved for himself the ultimate decisions, especially in a crisis. By 1971, Kissinger succeeded in adding Middle East diplomacy to his laurels, leaving Rogers totally naked of responsibility for foreign policy and not even knowing most of the time what was going on. After 1971, Kissinger could not recall a single occasion when Nixon made any change in a negotiation once Kissinger had set it in motion.

This system led to situations that would be ludicrous if the consequences had not been so serious. Time after time, the President, Kissinger reveals, lied to his Secretary of State and, on occasion, to his Secretary of Defense as well. He lied to cover up decisions he had made months earlier without their knowledge. He lied to Rogers about Kissinger's first trip to China in 1971. He again lied to Rogers about Kissinger's trip to Moscow in 1972. He lied to both the Secretary of

Defense and Secretary of State about the number of American troops to be withdrawn from South Vietnam. Nixon even asked Soviet leader Brezhnev's cooperation to deceive Rogers.

The secrecy and duplicity with which Nixon, assisted by Kissinger, conducted foreign policy inevitably resulted in tragicomic confusion and cross-purposes. The American SALT negotiator, Gerard C. Smith, was more than once put in the humiliating position of bargaining with Soviet representatives without knowing what Kissinger had already agreed to. In 1971, Kissinger managed three negotiations in three months, and in all of these, as he put it, "the regular bureaucracy had not participated, indeed, was unaware" of their very existence. In one of them, U.S. Ambassador in Bonn Kenneth Rush followed Kissinger's orders "without the knowledge of his own State Department." During the India-Pakistan crisis of 1971, White House and State Department representatives "dealt with each other as competing sovereign entities, not members of the same team, and the President sought to have his way by an indirection that compounded the internal stresses of our government." In December 1971, we are told, neither the Secretary of State nor the Secretary of Defense nor anyone from their departments was permitted to attend a "crucial meeting, where, as it turned out, the first decision to risk war in the triangular Soviet-Chinese-American relationship was taken."

This Nixonian practice was not merely "weird"; it was a gross perversion of the American system of government. Kissinger observed and lent himself to it; he relates the circumstances with no more than an occasional expression of wonderment about how odd the whole procedure was. "Weird" is hardly the word for it; it was diseased. The disease permeates Kissinger's pages and contaminated all who came in contact with it.

III

We can now begin to get the answer to the question: How did Kissinger do it?

But first, there is another related question: Why did Richard Nixon subject his old, "personal friend," Bill Rogers, to such humiliation and degradation? Kissinger volunteers an explanation that must be read to be believed.

During the 1950s, Kissinger relates, Rogers was the "psychologically dominant partner" in the friendship with Nixon. Memory of his formerly dominant role may have reinforced Rogers's alleged "tendency" to disagree with Nixon and to refuse to do battle for him "at critical junctures." This background leads into Kissinger's extraordinary interpretation of the pathological relationship between the President and Secretary of State:

> In consequence he [Rogers] could not really grasp that in the new relationship his was the clearly subordinate position. Even less could he face the proposition that he might have been appointed, at least in part, because his old friend wanted to reverse roles and establish a relationship in which both hierarchically and substantively he, Nixon, called the tune for once.

In fact, Kissinger notes, Nixon started on this course immediately—the day after his inauguration—before Rogers had had a chance to show any evidence of the "tendency" ascribed to him. In Kissinger's own narrative, Rogers took all the indignities heaped on him for over two years without fighting back. Kissinger absolves himself by carefully noting that Nixon began to exclude Rogers from all important negotiations "at a time when it would have been inconceivable for me to suggest such a procedure." Very little then is left of the idea that Rogers brought his debasement on himself by failing to recognize that he was no longer the dominant partner or did not grasp his subordinate position. Moreover, even on Kissinger's showing, Rogers was not always wrong. He was admittedly right in January 1971 to protest against using South Vietnamese forces for an offensive in Laos.

The first stage of Kissinger's rise had little to do with his abilities, his nuances, or his concepts. It was made possible by Nixon's need to reduce Rogers to a figurehead. That done, Nixon had to fill the vacuum with someone else. Only Kissinger could benefit. As Kissinger himself recognizes: "This curious antiphonal relationship between the two men had the consequence of enhancing my position, but my own role was clearly a result of that relationship and not the cause of it." Nixon's vengefulness was Kissinger's opportunity.

Kissinger does not hide the fact that he took full advantage of the opportunity. After describing Nixon's administration as "an array of baronies presided over by feudal lords" beset by the zealous retainers of a central authority, Kissinger admits that he "became the beneficiary of this state of affairs." In the first phase, he explains: "Ironically, one reason why the President entrusted me with so much responsibility and so many missions was because I was more under his control than his Cabinet." As for Nixon's strategy of using him against Rogers, Kissinger acknowledges: "I do not mean to suggest that I resisted Nixon's conduct toward his senior Cabinet officer. From the first my presence made it technically possible and after a time I undoubtedly encouraged it."

Some presidents with weak secretaries of state have taken on much of the diplomatic burden themselves. But Nixon was unwilling or unable to be his own secretary of state. As Kissinger portrays him, he had no mind for the kind of diligent effort required for developing or enforcing policy. He was, for example, "bored to distraction" by the technical arguments put forward by different departments on the SALT I negotiations. "His glazed expression," Kissinger reports, "showed that he considered most of the arguments esoteric rubbish; he was trying to calculate the political impact and salability of the various options, of which only the broad outlines interested him." Beyond the "broad outlines" and most often before they were set, Kissinger took over. Except for the Middle East, and even that only until 1971, "Nixon would listen to the agencies for a while and then act from the White House; thus my office assumed constantly growing responsibilities."

Rogers was not the only victim of this eerie practice. Nixon also dealt with the other Cabinet members, except for former Secretary of the Treasury John Connally, through White House assistants. This system did not conform to the "bureaucratic politics model," which presupposes that official policy and action largely result from "bargaining" by different "players" in the government. In the triangle, Nixon-Kissinger-Rogers, the last was hardly a player at all; he was, in important matters, not even a spectator; he simply did not know what was going on. The appearance of division in high councils, Kissinger observes, makes White House politics "not so different from life at royal courts." The analogy with royal courts fits Nixon's administration better than any other "model" and is particularly apt for Kissinger's place in it. Initially, at least, he derived his power wholly from the favor of a miscreant lord in the White House.

This setup inevitably resulted in a vicious feud between Kissinger and Rogers. Pride supposedly prevented Rogers from admitting to himself that his old friend, the President, deliberately made many important decisions when the Secretary of State was off on foreign trips. Yet Kissinger adds that Rogers was not totally wrong to blame him.

Nixon distrusted State and wanted sensitive matters handled by the White House alone, but my presence made the two channel procedures possible and I was quite willing to step into the breach to conduct negotiations with my small staff and no interagency liaison. The procedures so painful to Rogers were clearly instigated by Nixon; it is equally evident that I nurtured them.

Nixon's version of this feud is characteristic of the man. He blandly remarks that no human organization could be free of personality and policy conflicts, such as those that took place among Rogers, Kissinger, and Laird. One might imagine from Nixon's account that Rogers and Kissinger just happened to hold low opinions of one another: "Rogers felt that Kissinger was Machiavellian, deceitful, egotistical, arrogant, and insulting. Kissinger felt that Rogers was vain, uninformed, unable to keep a secret, and hopelessly dominated by the State Department bureaucracy." These are the harshest words that Nixon puts in his book about Kissinger and Rogers, still playing them off against one another, as if he were not personally culpable and had not stacked the cards in favor of Kissinger. Nixon also adds this tidbit not found in Kissinger's book: "Kissinger suggested repeatedly that he might have to resign unless Rogers was restrained or replaced."

Ironically, Kissinger's subsequent tenure as Secretary of State made Rogers's ordeal at his hands a dangerous precedent. Kissinger protected himself by holding onto the post of National Security Adviser as well as that of Secretary of State, preventing anyone else from doing to him what he had done to Rogers. Since it would be unseemly for a Secretary of State to seem to accept Rogers's punishment as a model, Kissinger's memoirs are studded with *mea culpas* about the way he behaved and Rogers was treated. "Though I did not think so at the time," Kissinger writes, as if he had finally seen the light, "I have become convinced that a President should make the Secretary of State his principal adviser and use the national security adviser primarily as a senior administrator and coordinator to make certain that each significant point of view is heard."

At the time, however, Kissinger pretended that his role as National Security Adviser conformed to the latter specifications rather than, as he now reveals, to those of the President's principal foreign-policy adviser and operational head. When Kissinger tells of Ambassador Rush's instructions to act on Kissinger's orders without the knowledge of his own State Department, he comments guiltily: "It was an odd way to run a government." In another connection, Kissinger magnanimously places the responsibility for conditions that put State Department officials "in an extremely uncomfortable position" on "the personalities at the top, including myself." Moreover, the "personality clashes" between Kissinger and Rogers "did neither of us any credit." Still later, Kissinger apportions praise and blame for Nixon's method of government in this way—the President's "complex personality" contributed the "impetus" but "I, as the organizer of these procedures and their driving force, must, of course, share the responsibility for the shortcomings" as well as "perhaps undue credit for the successes." Even when Kissinger claims that Nixon's procedures "worked" in practice, he now professes to believe that they should not be repeated.

Kissinger's reference, becomingly modest, to the "perhaps undue credit" foisted upon him takes us to the second stage of his rising star. In late 1971, Kissinger became acutely aware of a change in Nixon's attitude. On his return from his first trip to China in October, Kissinger saw signs that "the President was becoming restive at the publicity I was receiving." By now he knew Nixon and his minions, Haldeman, Ehrlichman, and Ziegler, well enough to realize that his disembarkation at a remote corner of Andrews Air Force Base, "inaccessible to newsmen and photographers," was no accident. As Kissinger puts it plaintively, "it was not a heroic homecoming."

Nixon subsequently found other opportunities to teach Kissinger "a lesson in the limits of my authority." During the Vietnam negotiations in 1972, Kissinger virtually defied Nixon's wishes and substituted his own judgment for that of the President on how to deal with the North Vietnamese. Whoever was right, Presidential assistants are not supposed to be so headstrong and even insubordinate. Kissinger refers to his "solitary procedures," another way of saying that he went off on his own and confronted Nixon with accomplished facts. In return, the White House took pains "to distance itself" from Kissinger, because the President "was bound to become restless with an Assistant who was beginning to compete with him for public attention." Nixon became so "restless" that at one time he would not see Kissinger for several weeks. When *Time* magazine chose both of them as Men of the Year, Kissinger knew that Nixon would not be pleased and even tried unsuccessfully to remove his name. Not surprisingly, "Nixon's brooding disquietude with my newfound celebrity inevitably transmitted itself to his staff, only too eager to build him up and relishing the bonus of cutting me down to size after years of riding high."

In the second stage of Kissinger's meteoric career, then, Nixon replaced Rogers as the main rival. Nixon, according to Kissinger, first saw him as a "surrogate," then as a "competitor for public attention." That a presidential assistant—whose only strength, Kissinger tells us, is "the President's confidence"—could hold his own in such a competition makes one wonder about the power of the imperial presidency. Presidents have had competition from Cabinet members, whom they have had to get rid of, but this must be the first time that a president has had so much competition from a mere assistant, whom, in addition, he did not even dare to dismiss.

What made Kissinger do it? He drops a hint, though it is supposed to apply to someone else. "In contemporary America," Kissinger observes with reference to Nixon, "power increasingly gravitates to those with an almost obsessive desire to win it."

IV

Most of the reviews of Kissinger's book I have seen have been so impressionistic that they suggest how difficult it was for the reviewers to deal with it substantively. Even with more space at one's disposal it is impossible to do justice to all of Kissinger's themes—Chile, the Middle East, nuclear strategy, Cambodia, India-Pakistan, China, the Soviet Union, and Vietnam. I have chosen to limit myself to the last three in order to deal with these subjects more thoroughly than would otherwise be possible.

The "opening to China" by Nixon and Kissinger may well be their most important, enduring contribution. It was overdue, but that is no reason for taking credit away from them. In his book, Kissinger generously gives Nixon the main share of that credit, without neglecting to mention that he had come independently to the same judgment about China and designed many of the moves in that direction. Kissinger also makes clear that neither Nixon nor he took office with more than a nebulous idea about how to go about inaugurating a new China policy. The first move was made by the Chinese immediately after Nixon's election. Both sides maneuvered warily for another year before it was clear that they were going to make a serious effort to reach an understanding, and it took another year and a half to reach one.

The main question that arises is what Kissinger understood by a Chinese-American accord. Kissinger has some trouble making up his mind.

Back in July 1968, when he was still working to make Nelson Rockefeller the next president, Kissinger had written into one of Rockefeller's speeches the idea of engaging in a dialogue with Communist China in order to form "a subtle triangle of relations between Washington, Peking, and Moscow." It was—and is—one of Kissinger's conceits that such moves could be "subtle," as if no one were quite so clever as he is. This "triangular theory" suggested that China, Soviet Russia, and the United States were more or less equivalent power centers, each of which could try to play off one of the others against the third. Kissinger himself must have had some such arrangement in mind when he told Theodore H. White in November 1972 that "what the world needed was a self-regulating mechanism," the key to which was China.[1] If there were such a thing as a "self-regulating mechanism" in world affairs, this one would have had to be based on the assumption that the Washington-Peking-Moscow triangle was all that really mattered and that the three powers were so nearly matched in strength that one could not overcome a second without the aid of the third.

In this book, Kissinger recalls his triangular theory of 1968 with the following explanation:

> Our relations to possible opponents should be such, I considered, that our options toward both of them should be greater than their options toward each other. If we could free our diplomacy from the dead weight of two decades, each Communist superpower would have greater inducement to deal with us constructively.

This diplomatic recipe is a good example of Kissinger's occasional weakness for abstract formulas that get lost in muddled verbiage. Does "our options toward both of them" mean our options toward both of them together or toward each of them singly? It cannot mean the first because they were no longer together; once the split between them occurred we had options toward each of them separately, not both at once. But the real trouble is in the second sentence. It betrays Kissinger's intermittent yearning to have the best of all possible worlds. The facts of life, demonstrated abundantly in every day's newspaper, are that the closer we get to one of the Communist superpowers, the less likely the other is to "deal with us constructively." In practice, the more one of them deals with us "constructively," the more apt the other is to deal with us "destructively." We cannot have it both ways. This sort of spurious profundity cannot stand close examination.

The muddle gets progressively worse as Kissinger repeatedly tries to explain the new China policy.

On the one hand, Kissinger tells us that he belonged to the *Realpolitiker* school of thought, which argued that the Soviets were more likely to be conciliatory if they feared an American policy of rapprochement with China; it also urged that the United States should expand its contacts with China "as a means of leverage against the Soviet Union." With respect to Soviet-American negotiations in 1970, the China initiative gave the United States "an ace in the hole." On the Chinese side, he once told Nixon, "Washington was being brought into play as a counterweight to Soviet pressures." In briefings, Kissinger favored China over Soviet Russia because the former was the weaker party.

This interpretation can only mean that the United States and China were using each other, as well they might, against the Soviet Union.

On the other hand, Kissinger pushes a more conciliatory, benign line with respect to both Communist powers. The move toward China, he explains, was intended to shape a new "global equilibrium" to give the United States a "balancing position" to improve relations with both the Soviet Union and China. He also makes getting "the two Communist powers competing for good relations with us" the essence of the triangular strategy, as if the United States could shift from hostility to benevolence in its China policy without incurring the increased hostility of the Soviet Union.

This line of thought lands Kissinger in a flagrant contradiction. On page 763, he explains:

> Neither Peking nor Moscow was quarreling with the other to curry favor with us; they were currying favor with us because they were quarreling. We could not "exploit" that rivalry; it exploited itself.

According to this interpretation, the United States did not and could not make the Soviet Union and China into rival, quarreling powers, though it is less clear why we could not exploit that rivalry whether or not it exploited itself, whatever that may mean.

But on page 1076, Kissinger tells the reader who may have forgotten what he had been told some 300 pages earlier:

> If we appeared irresolute or leaning toward Moscow, Peking would be driven to accommodation with the Soviet Union. If we adopted the Chinese attitude, however, we might not even help Peking; we might, in fact, tempt a Soviet preemptive attack on China and thus be faced with decisions of enormous danger.

Here, what *we* do becomes most instrumental in determining the relationship between Peking and Moscow. *We* can drive China into the hands of Russia or provoke Russia into attacking China. What has happened to the Sino-Soviet hostility that had, on page 763, "followed its own dynamic"?

This kind of inconsistency haunts Kissinger's interpretation of the new China policy. He wishes to make it, as might be expected, an achievement of world-shaking significance. It betokened "a geopolitical revolution," "a new international order." But he also pronounces: "The China card was not ours to play."[2] If it was not ours to play, what in the world were we playing with in Peking? And if the United States did not have a China card to play, must we conclude that China did not have an American card to play either?

Kissinger's play is with words, not with cards. The question is what kind of China card we are playing with, not whether it is a card at all. There are cards and cards, some more valuable than others. What is the real difference between regarding China as "a means of leverage," "an ace in the hole," and a "card"? Reality does not change just because, or solely because, of a change of terms.

Something else is at stake here. The troublesome problem is a legacy of the triangular theory. The triangle of China, Soviet Russia, and the United States is not made up of equivalent sides. China does not threaten the Soviet Union anywhere as much as the Soviet Union threatens China. The Chinese have extremely limited military capabilities outside their own borders; the Soviets have vastly greater external capabilities. Much as the Chinese stick in the Russian craw and force the Russians to keep about forty-five divisions on the Chinese border, China represents much less of a deterrent to Russia on a world scale than the triangular theory would lead one to expect. It is not to denigrate the desirability of a Chinese-American understanding to recognize that the United States can potentially be more useful to China than China can be to the United States. So long as the Soviet armed forces are gigantic enough to permit a buildup on all fronts, including the Chinese, the Russians can enjoy maximum freedom of action. In most parts of the world, they have to worry much more about what the United States will do than what the Chinese will do.

The Chinese-American rapprochement was and is a good thing in its own right. It has considerable, but limited, effect on the Soviet-American relationship. It is a "card," but it is not "an ace in the hole," whereas Kissinger thinks it is "an ace in the hole," but not a "card."

v

The least candid, most untrustworthy portion of Kissinger's book deals with the Soviet Union and the policy of détente.

Until 1969, when he went to Washington, Kissinger held very severe and consistent positions on both. In brief, he was anti-Soviet and anti-détente. He was anti-Soviet in the sense that he considered the Soviet Union to be the most dangerous, most implacable enemy of the United States and all that it stood for. He was anti-détente because he viewed it as an insidious Soviet tactic to lull and gull the West in preparation for the next period of Communist expansion. He pursued these themes with sophistication and tenacity for about a dozen years before he was called on to do something about them.

How could someone with this background become converted to détente, and how does he explain it now?

The first surprise is the type of relationship that Kissinger soon established with the Soviet Ambassador in Washington, Anatoly Dobrynin. It can only be described as the coziest and chummiest imaginable. Few foreign ambassadors in American history have ever benefited so much from such close rapport and bonhomie. I do not mean to suggest that Kissinger and Dobrynin should have been at verbal swords' points, whatever the relations of their countries may have been. But what actually passed between these two went far beyond a civil working diplomatic association. Dobrynin was Kissinger's first "back channel," which sent the latter on his way to effective operational control of American foreign policy. He has rewarded Dobrynin with such fervent, effusive praise that it should stand the Soviet Ambassador in good stead for promotion in the Soviet hierarchy. Only one other person—Prime Minister Chou En-lai of China, who is written about with gushing veneration—gets higher marks from Kissinger. Despite Dobrynin's long service in Washington over almost two decades through every *Sturm und Drang*, despite "his unquestioning support of the Soviet line," Kissinger virtually nominates him for a future Nobel Peace Prize: "If someday there should come about the genuine relaxation of tensions and dangers which our period demands, Anatoly Dobrynin will have made a central contribution to it."

One can understand Kissinger's admiration for "a thoroughgoing professional" who "moved through the upper echelons of Washington with consummate skill" and whose "skill at putting his American interlocutor on the defensive was infinite." Such a Soviet operator might be considered more effective, slippery, and dangerous than any other, to be handled with the greatest care. Instead, Dobrynin was permitted to enjoy confidences and take liberties that he was never expected to reciprocate. After an important meeting between the Chinese and American ambassadors in Warsaw in January 1970, for example, Kissinger matter-of-factly records: "The day after the Warsaw meeting Dobrynin appeared at my office, seeking a briefing, undeterred by the fact that this was a favor Moscow never vouchsafed to us on any topic." Kissinger did not express surprise or administer a rebuke at such a question; he merely "evaded his request." Dobrynin would not have dared to ask the question at all if he and Kissinger had not had other such *tête-à-têtes*.

This "back channel" was more than a mutual admiration society; it was also a political commitment.

As Kissinger told Oriana Fallaci in the interview he now recalls with acute pain, he had set out to achieve three things: peace in Vietnam, rapprochement with China, and "a new relationship with the Soviet Union." That new relationship was consecrated in 1972 with the official sanctification of the policy of détente. The new relationship with the Soviet Union was the political side of his personal relationship with Dobrynin.

Kissinger invested so heavily in Soviet good will because he believed that Soviet cooperation was needed to solve the most acute foreign problems confronting the United States. Necessity was only one step away from availability, if "vested interests" could be created linking both sides. His theory of "linkage" was, therefore, critical for the success of this program. As Kissinger saw it, a Soviet-American understanding could not be based on a single issue, even one so important as arms control; a relaxation of tension had to encompass all outstanding issues. The Nixon-Kissinger foreign policy aimed at achieving nothing less than "fundamental settlements" through "an integrating conceptual framework." Though Kissinger had long detested détente and had even distrusted it when France and Germany had embraced it, he was converted to it by 1971. The summit meeting in Moscow in May 1972 made it "the integrating conceptual framework" without which, he insists, it is impossible to conduct a serious and fruitful foreign policy.

The summit meeting of May 1972, therefore, was not content with the first strategic arms limitation treaty (SALT I). The linkage to other outstanding issues came in another key document—the "Basic Principles of Relations Between the United States of America and the Union of Soviet Socialist Republics." It contained twelve basic principles that, in effect, tied the arms agreement, according to Kissinger, to "an agreed code of international conduct"—the code of détente. It was or should have been, in Kissinger's scheme, far more important than the arms agreement, which was in itself a highly problematic first installment. If either side broke the code, the whole point of an arms agreement was lost; and if the code prevailed, an arms agreement could be a welcome but unessential factor in keeping the peace.

Kissinger is apparently so embarrassed by his role in the codification of détente that his book comes close to distorting the record. He reduces his interest in the principles of détente to the merely "tactical," designed to intensify Soviet dilemmas, reduce Soviet influence in the Middle East, and "outmaneuver the 'peace' pressures" at home. If one takes this *ex post facto* rationalization seriously, détente was a weapon of the Kissingerian cold war, not a process of conciliation.

The real story of détente, SALT I, and the "Basic Principles" cannot be found in these pages. Détente stood or fell on the "Basic Principles," as Kissinger himself had previously interpreted them:

> They state that both sides will attempt to their utmost to avoid military confrontation and that neither will attempt to take unilateral advantage in situations, recognizing that the great nuclear powers cannot be pushed into a position that jeopardizes their basic survival without noting it and therefore recognizing that the attempt of traditional diplomacy to accumulate marginal advantages is bound to lead to disastrous consequences in the nuclear age.[3]

With one exception, this paraphrase closely followed the text of the "Basic Principles."[4] The exception was the theory of "marginal advantages." As Kissinger subsequently developed it, the theory held that the balance of power no longer fully applied in the nuclear age. Kissinger explained:

> The reason is that the determination of national power has changed fundamentally in the nuclear age. Throughout history, the primary concern of most national leaders has been to accumulate geopolitical and military power. It would have seemed inconceivable even a generation ago that such power once gained could not be translated directly into advantage over one's opponent. But now both we and the Soviet Union have begun to find that each increment of power does not necessarily represent an increment of usable political strength.[5]

The last sentence implied that the Americans and the Soviets had been moving toward a meeting of minds on the obsolescence of "marginal advantages" and "increments of power." If the Kissingerian theory was valid, there was nothing to worry about; even if the Soviets violated the understanding and grabbed for marginal advantages and increments of power, they could not be translated into "usable political strength."

Logically, the "Basic Principles" merely spelled out the theory of marginal advantages; the principles were not even needed if the theory operated as postulated.[6]

The reader of *White House Years* will not get a word about marginal advantages or increments of power, even though they played such a large part in Kissinger's thinking in the years of détente. Instead, he offers a version of détente that differs little from the familiar carrot-and-stick policy of "posing risks and incentives to encourage Soviet restraint." If that were all there had been to Kissinger's détente theory, he could hardly have been accused of originality. What made his version distinctive was that he gave it a theoretical foundation that made détente seem structurally sound and even built into the nature of the new international order. All this has mysteriously disappeared from a memoir that otherwise goes into the minutest of details.

Unfortunately for Kissinger's theory of marginal advantages, the Soviets were not converted to it. They showed their disrespect for his "integrating conceptual framework" by sending their Cuban proxies into Angola toward the end of 1975. If Kissinger had been right, the Soviets should have realized that a mere increment of power in such a faraway African country could not give them any "usable political strength." In that case, since the Soviet leaders were supposed to be so innately cautious and patient, they would have considered the Angolan intervention a waste of time and substance. Instead, Kissinger was converted to the Soviet point of view: he suddenly woke up to how usable this marginal advantage could be to the Soviets. Beginning in January 1976, he began to change his line somewhere between 90 and 180 degrees. He was apparently not prepared for such a change and for this reason may have reacted with unusual outrage. As late as April 1975, he had expressed the opinion that he expected the Soviet Union to move toward making relations with the United States better, not worse.[7]

The Angolan intervention brought out the new Kissinger, who remarkably resembled the old, pre-Nixon, Kissinger. In the first months of 1976, Kissinger announced the beginning of a new era—that "the U.S.S.R. has begun to define its interests and objectives in global terms" —as if the U.S.S.R.'s interest in Cuba since 1960, to go back no further, had been less global than its interest in Angola. He reincarnated the old doctrine of "containment" in so many words—"It is our responsibility to contain Soviet power without global war. . . ." He restored the balance of power to its traditional position of primacy in world politics. He saw a single marginal advantage or increment of power, not as the waste of effort that it had been in the previous theory, but as encouragement to seek further marginal advantages and increments of power—"If adventurism is allowed to succeed in local crises—an ominous precedent of wider consequence is set." He served notice that "cooperative relations" with the Soviet Union—he would have said "détente" if the term had not become politically taboo—could not "survive any more Angolas." Kissinger's strange Soviet interlude was over.[8]

We have gone beyond the bounds of *White House Years*, which ends at the beginning of 1973. The book cannot be understood solely in terms of its own period; it was written by the born-again, anti-Soviet, post-1976 Kissinger and reflects many of his latter-day preoccupations. One result is suppression of all evidence of his responsibility for the illusions of détente. This silence is the most deafening confession he could have made. He admits to some minor errors of judgment; he cannot bring himself to mention a major one.

Kissinger has, more recently, called for a policy that "must be pursued over an indefinite period of time."[9] Kissinger's own Soviet policy would have done better if he had followed this advice.

VI

Of all the subjects in his book, Kissinger dwells at greatest length and with most pathos on the Vietnam war. In the end, I am sure, it will far outweigh in importance anything else with which he had to deal.

One way to judge Kissinger's policy is to subject it to the test of his own guiding ideas or concepts. He has repeatedly put forward two, though not always with the same emphasis. They may, in his own words, be referred to as "nuances" and "geopolitics." He sometimes relies on one, sometimes on the other, without ever making clear how they fit together.

"Nuances" are just about the smallest change one can use in diplomacy. The dictionary says that nuance means: "A slight or delicate variation or difference in expression, feeling, opinion, etc." The important thing is that it should be slight or subtle. Such variations or differences do not by their very nature alter anything of substance or something of the essence. No serious or experienced negotiator would be taken in by them. Yet Kissinger has always given them a place of inordinate importance in his scheme of things. He has gone so far as to hold that nuances are all that really matter. On one occasion, he said:

"The difference between great policy and mediocre policy or substantial policy and average policy is usually an accumulation of nuances."[10] He has maintained that "intangibles" can determine the outcome of events.[11]

In this book, nuances again get co-star billing. One sentence reads: "I wanted to accumulate nuances for a long-range strategy." Now, there may be nuances in the way a long-range strategy is expressed, for expression is the chief function of nuances, but no accumulation of nuances can add up to a long-range strategy. Another example of muddled verbiage makes "nuances and interrelations" the test of foreign policy. By "interrelations," Kissinger explains, he means the "linkage" of events. In this passage, an accumulation of nuances is no longer enough to make up a long-range strategy or, as Kissinger also calls it, "an integrating conceptual framework." In any case, nuances and interrelations are not of similar or comparable status. Interrelations may be given this nuance or that, but the nuance is still bound to make no more than a slight or subtle difference to the interrelations. Only a dimwit would be won over to any interrelation because of the nuance given to it. Moreover, neither of them nor both together can do what Kissinger here asks them to do—satisfy the need for "an integrating conceptual framework." By themselves, nuances and interrelations beg the question; they need an integrating conceptual framework to give them function and direction. It is not enough to expound, as Kissinger does here, on the need for an integrating conceptual framework and then make it nothing more than a mix of nuances and interrelations in the abstract. Here, as elsewhere, there is much less in Kissinger's theorizing than meets the eye.

Despite his long infatuation with nuances, Kissinger in this book leans most heavily on "geopolitics." He defines the difference between Secretary of State Rogers and himself in terms of Rogers's "tactical" perspective and his own "strategic and geopolitical" approach. Again and again, he uses the term "geopolitical" as if it were his personal revelation or trademark. The United States, he laments, has "no geopolitical tradition."[12] For a word that is made to do so much work, however, Kissinger makes very little effort to explain just what should be understood by it. His one attempt is quite inadequate and even misleading: "By 'geopolitical' I mean an approach that pays attention to the requirements of equilibrium." It hardly helps to substitute an even more general and elusive term, "equilibrium," for "geopolitical." Geopolitics since Sir Halford Mackinder's time early in this century has always been based on a single factor—geography—as the main determinant of history. Equilibrium has no such concrete, clear-cut connotation. The mere reference to equilibrium does not tell us whether it is geopolitically sound or not. Traditionally, geopolitics has had more to do with world mastery than with equilibrium.[13] In any case, Kissinger cannot complain if we test his Vietnam policy by his own standards of nuances and geopolitics.

Curiously, Kissinger's view of the Vietnam war has never had anything to do with nuances or geopolitics. He came to his basic position on the war before going to the White House. He had given up the hope of military victory as early as 1966 after making two trips to Vietnam at the invitation of then Ambassador Henry Cabot Lodge.[14] It took him two more years to come forth with an alternative to military victory. In his article in *Foreign Affairs*, written in the summer of 1968, he implied that a wrongheaded geopolitical assessment had landed us in the Vietnam dilemma.

> Unquestionably, the failure to analyze adequately the geopolitical importance of Vietnam then [in 1961–62] contributed to the current dilemma. But the commitment of five hundred thousand Americans has settled the issue of the importance of Vietnam. For what is involved now is confidence in American promises.

What was also involved, he went on, were "credibility," "prestige," and ending the war "honorably," above all the last. In effect, we were not in Vietnam as a result of geopolitical imperatives; we were there because, as Kissinger also said a month earlier in 1968, we had created our own difficulties through a series of military and political "conceptual failures."[15] In a geopolitical perspective, it would have mattered little whether or not there were 500,000 Americans in Vietnam; the importance of Vietnam would have been settled by its geographical location. Whatever may be thought of Kissinger's argument that the 500,000 Americans settled the issue of the importance of Vietnam, geopolitics was involved only in the sense that they had been sent in defiance of geopolitical considerations.

Geopolitics is also no respecter of credibility, prestige, or honor. The geopolitical outlook is peculiarly hard-boiled and cold-blooded. It sweeps aside such vulnerable human sentiments as credibility, prestige, and honor. Its criterion is the conquest of space and power by whatever means may be necessary to achieve the goal. This is not to say that credibility, prestige, and honor are not important from some points of view; they are simply not geopolitical concepts; they are, in fact, as ungeopolitical or antigeopolitical as one can get.

In *White House Years*, Kissinger's position on Vietnam is essentially the same as that of 1968. For all his flaunting of geopolitics, his justification for what we were doing in Vietnam is primarily moralistic. His emphasis is on "our moral position," on avoiding "dishonor," on getting out "with dignity." The difference between the United States and South Vietnam in the later stages of the Paris negotiations was, he says, that "our goal was honor," their "problem was survival." Whatever one may think about this statement of the American goal, it belongs to a tradition of chivalry, not geopolitics.

Kissinger also has a more pragmatic rationale for the last four years of the American war in Vietnam—that "sacrificing our friends" would have shaken "the confidence of all who depended on us." He does not push this one as hard and as often as "honor," but it is worth considering whether there is anything to it.

Other people's "confidence" in the United States transfers the stake in Vietnam to the world outside. It implicitly admits that there was nothing in Vietnam itself to justify the American role in the war. By shifting the attention away from Vietnam, it is of a piece with the idea that the presence of 500,000 American soldiers settled the issue of the importance of Vietnam. In both cases, a geopolitical aberration is said to create reasons for increasing the cost of the aberration. On this reasoning, one could never cut the losses inevitably incurred by a miscalculation of such magnitude.

Here, again, we face a general, abstract, psychological term—"confidence." Even if the confidence of our other dependents and allies were shaken, we could not judge how much this factor should influence American policy in Vietnam without asking: How much was it shaken? For how long? In relation to what other reasons for retaining confidence in the United States? What other options did these allies and dependents have, even in the worst of eventualities?

All we get from Kissinger is shaken "confidence," as if this were an absolute. The real problem of Vietnam was concrete and relative. What was the expenditure of men and materiel in Vietnam worth in relation to American interests, domestic and foreign, as a whole? On this question, Kissinger has some surprises in store for the reader.

European public opinion as represented by the media, he concedes, opposed the war; European leaders, though they did not say so publicly, "wanted the war ended quickly" but also "wanted America's credibility unimpaired." The discretion of European leaders is easily understood; nevertheless, it cannot be doubted that Europeans looked on with increasing distress and disbelief as the United States spent itself in eight years of a hopeless war on the other side of the globe. If those eight years were not enough to attest to America's "credibility" as a faithful ally, how many more would have been necessary? What in any case does "credibility" in this intangible and abstract form mean in these circumstances? It is one of those words, like "geopolitics," that is being used as a substitute for thought and deserves to be put back in the dictionary for a rest.

If authority were needed to testify that the United States conducted its war in Vietnam at the expense of the rest of the world, two of the highest-ranking testimonials would come from President Nixon and Dr. Kissinger. In 1971, Nixon declared:

> Now, in terms of our world situation, the tendency is, and this has been the case for the last five to six years, for us to obscure our vision almost totally of the world because of Vietnam.[16]

In this book, Kissinger relates that he told Thieu in 1972: "We have fought for four years, have mortgaged our whole foreign policy to the defense of one country."

In the same year, Kissinger received some sage advice from Chinese Deputy Foreign Minister Ch'iao Kuan-hua, who presumably spoke with the approval of Kissinger's favorite statesman, Chou En-lai: "One should not lose the whole world just to gain South Vietnam."

It is in connection with China that Kissinger finally gets the geopolitical position of Vietnam straight. He writes: "The China initiative also restored perspective to our national policy. It reduced Indochina to its proper scale—a small peninsula on a major continent."

On that major continent, China is the geopolitical center of gravity. If China is permitted to develop its economic and military potential in coming decades, a geopolitician would presuppose that this small peninsula would be most likely to gravitate to the Chinese sphere of influence. In fact, the first American political theorist to work out a complete geopolitical system almost four decades ago assigned just such a role in the region to China.[17]

Still, Kissinger has given us some standards for judging his handling of the Vietnam negotiations. Did nuances matter or did geopolitics prevail? Was honor saved? Were our friends in Vietnam sacrificed or not? Could the settlement have restored the confidence of our allies and dependents in the world at large?

VII

By far the longest and most anguished part of the book deals with the negotiations that brought an end to the American intervention in Vietnam. Even if the outlines were clear before, Kissinger adds so much to our intimate knowledge of the events that there is nothing like it in the entire literature on the war so far.

Nuances, Kissinger soon found out, had no effect whatever on the North Vietnamese. From the beginning they were inflexibly determined to get all American forces out of Vietnam and to overthrow the South Vietnamese regime headed by President Nguyen Van Thieu. The masters of nuance in the Paris negotiation were, according to Kissinger, the North Vietnamese, not the Americans. For example, the North Vietnamese negotiators proposed a "coalition government" for South Vietnam, but in such a way that, as Kissinger understood it, it would effectively give the North control. Kissinger complains that this ruse deceived "many unwary Americans"; no such American gimmick ever deceived many unwary Vietnamese.

My favorite Kissingerian nuance is still another. What separated everyone in the Nixon administration from its moderate critics, Kissinger claims, was "not a philosophy but a nuance." The "philosophy" in question was American withdrawal; the nuance was a "lingering hope that Hanoi might at some point negotiate, paying some price to accelerate our total withdrawal." That Kissinger should want to pass off not only himself but everyone in the Nixon administration as secret doves, differing from other doves only slightly, by a nuance, would seem too farfetched to deserve serious consideration. Yet it is symptomatic of a deep strain that runs through the Vietnamese sections of the book—an "ambivalence," to which he confesses, and even a guilty conscience.

The "lingering hope" of "some price" to be paid by North Vietnam is thus made to justify four years of a futile and repulsive war. What was there to the hope? What was the price?

Kissinger had from the outset little or no hope that he could get any real concession from the North Vietnamese left to themselves. His hope originally rested on getting the Soviet Union to bail us out. His early strategy called for trading an improvement in Soviet-American relations for Soviet pressure on North Vietnam to make peace on acceptable terms.[18] Kissinger's proposed barter never had a chance. He even accepted with minimal protest the indignity of receiving no reply for months from Dobrynin, though no such letdowns seem to have spoiled their warm personal relationship.

What else was there to the lingering hope? There were, Kissinger points out, only two real choices—military escalation and Vietnamization. The former as a long-term strategy had been ruled out; it was, in any case, incompatible with the policy of piecemeal withdrawal. But the latter was equally unsatisfactory to Kissinger, who finally agreed to it with some reluctance. Yet, it is clear, he oscillated between these poles, never able to commit himself fully to either one. This equivocation more than anything else led to the interminably long, excruciatingly tortuous negotiations with North Vietnam and their disastrous denouement.

The heart of the matter was Vietnamization. It implied that the United States had become embroiled in a Vietnamese civil war, and that the only way to get out was to give the civil war back to the Vietnamese. The American problem from this point of view was less with North Vietnam than with South Vietnam. Even if the Nixon administration saw its duty as the preparation of South Vietnam for fighting its own battles, that preliminary period could not last forever. At some point it was necessary to make the Thieu regime in South Vietnam stand on its own and take the risk of defeat. The only other option, as Kissinger recognizes, was to resort to unlimited military escalation on the assumption that the war had to be won or lost by the United States. But Kissinger for one had ruled out such a perspective of American military victory years before.

Vietnamization did not have to be negotiated with North Vietnam. It was a means to get the United States out of the war, not to end the war between the Vietnamese. The United States could no more end the war between the Vietnamese by peaceful negotiation than by military force. Civil wars that go on as long and as ruthlessly as the one in Vietnam cannot be ended by a third party, which has paid so heavy a price for its interposition that it desperately seeks a way out. The negotiations in Paris, then, could not be about Vietnamization. They were undertaken to find a way to bring the war to an end and thereby save South Vietnam from the risks of Vietnamization.

We are now approaching the crucial point, which Kissinger does his best to obfuscate by hiding behind a screen of excess verbiage.

In the Paris negotiations, Kissinger holds that one thing was not negotiable—the survival of the Thieu regime in South Vietnam. That was the affair of American honor, credibility, prestige. The negotiable issues were the conditions for American withdrawal, short of abandoning the Thieu regime to its own fate. But there was one hitch. Thieu himself, who knew best, believed that American withdrawal under any circumstances was tantamount to the abandonment of South Vietnam and his regime. He had never accepted Vietnamization, but he had played for time or had hidden his true feelings in such a way that even Kissinger was misled. Thieu had to be bludgeoned into going along with the final settlement in Paris; his resistance was so great that Kissinger calls it "almost maniacal."[19]

What, then, made the settlement "honorable"? The entire case is essentially based on one point. Until the end of 1972, as Kissinger saw it, North Vietnam had always insisted that the United States should, directly or indirectly, abandon the Thieu regime and replace it with a North Vietnamese-controlled "coalition government." Once this demand was withdrawn in October of that year, the way was open for a deal between the United States and North Vietnam, the former to withdraw all of its forces, the latter to leave its forces in South Vietnam in place. The "peace with honor" rested, in the last analysis, on the North Vietnamese concession that it was not necessary to overthrow the South Vietnamese government in advance as the price of a cease-fire. Once Thieu realized that the United States was determined, one way or another, to withdraw its forces from Vietnam, even threatening to make a separate peace, he capitulated to the inevitable.[20]

But what if Thieu were right that his regime could not long survive the complete withdrawal of American forces? In that case, the withdrawal implicitly, if not explicitly, sealed the fate of the South Vietnamese government. If American honor depended on the Thieu regime's survival, and that survival depended on continued, indefinite American military presence in South Vietnam, the Paris agreement of January 1973 was no more than a token offering to American honor and Thieu's survival. Kissinger himself virtually admits that the peace terms gave the South Vietnamese government only a theoretical, rather than a practical, chance to survive because it lacked the will to do so without direct American military support. The terms, he writes, gave South Vietnam the means to survive "theoretically." The reality was something else: "But they did not of themselves provide the sinews of confidence and cohesion in Saigon to maintain the equilibrium which had in fact been achieved on the battlefield." Kissinger's use of the term "equilibrium" is almost always elusive and never more so than here; an equilibrium that left North Vietnamese forces in possession of much of South Vietnam was hardly calculated to last very long.

By dropping its demand for the dismantling of the South Vietnamese regime in advance, North Vietnam did pay "some price" for the American withdrawal. But, as Kissinger spends pages assuring us, only the demand, not the determination, was dropped. The price was no more than a face-saving device; it could not have been more as long as the survival of the Thieu regime depended on the presence of American armed forces. The wonder is not that the North Vietnamese agreed to drop their demand; it is rather that they took so long to do so. Kissinger finally came to see that Thieu and Tho (Le Duc Tho, North Vietnam's main negotiator) were alike in their tactics and behavior; they were also akin in that they understood each other better than Kissinger understood either of them.[21]

It is not altogether clear whether Nixon and Kissinger were deceiving themselves or deceiving Thieu. The problem arises because of something that Kissinger says was "inconceivable" to him at the time. It was the idea that the United States could not conceivably fail in months or years to come to make good the private assurances given to Thieu by Nixon that failure by North Vietnam to abide by the terms of the agreement would bring "swift and severe retaliatory action" and a response "with full force" by the United States. McGeorge Bundy has sufficiently shown how inconceivable it is that Kissinger should have found this idea "inconceivable."[22] The more intriguing question is: Why did Kissinger find it so inconceivable?

The answer is, I believe, that he was moved by a confusion of motives and forces, some of which is still reflected in his book. He rejected victory by military escalation. But from time to time he was willing to resort to a "military showdown" and thought that "going for broke" militarily should be seriously considered. He protests that "in all conscience" we could not impose "an unacceptable peace on our ally" and then tells in the most agonizing detail how he helped to impose a peace that our ally considered to be unacceptable to the point of near hysteria and tears of rage. He makes the American engagement in Vietnam a struggle over a principle—"that America did not betray its friends"— and ended the war in such a way that its South Vietnamese friends cried to high heaven that they had been betrayed. He was dead set against "a disguised form of victory" for North Vietnam, but that is what he eventually settled for. To avoid a disguised form of victory it was necessary, in his view, for the United States to "enforce" the agreement (which he mistakenly calls a "treaty"), as if a country that had found it politically impossible to maintain its forces in Vietnam could find it politically possible to send them back *en masse* to prevent a North Vietnamese takeover or, more realistically, to drive out the North Vietnamese after a takeover. He even makes a return of American forces to Vietnam inevitable or obligatory because North Vietnam's "single-minded quest for hegemony, we were certain, would continue after a settlement." Despite this, he pretends or deludes himself that the resolution of the Vietnamese civil war could have been left "to the free decision of the people" or amenable to "a genuinely free political choice by the people."

What has this jumble of inconsistencies, contradictions, vain hopes, and *non sequiturs* to do with the hard, cold doctrine of geopolitics?

The answer is that geopolitics had little or nothing to do with it. The real force that drove the United States out of Vietnam, Kissinger admits, was the popular American revulsion against the war. To obey the will of the people went against the grain; to resist it indefinitely was, however, impossible. The defense of "honor" and "prestige" could only permit a delaying, rearguard action. The decisive reason Nixon and Kissinger could not go along with Thieu to the bitter end was, as Kissinger puts it, that such a course "would have guaranteed the collapse of all remaining support at home." After Nixon's reelection in November 1972, "he was determined not to have his second term tormented like the first by our national trauma. . . ." One part of Kissinger, as he himself makes clear, sympathized with Thieu's position; another part recognized that the United States was tearing itself apart socially and politically on Thieu's behalf and could not go on doing so much longer. This duality more than anything else drives Kissinger into going over the ground of the Vietnam negotiations interminably, sometimes veering one way, sometimes another, never quite—I suspect—convincing himself or the reader.

In the end, American honor à la Kissinger could have been saved only if the United States had been able and willing to send back sufficient force to. Vietnam to save Thieu from collapse in 1975. This is the *reductio ad absurdum* of Kissinger's entire argument. If the U.S.–North Vietnam agreement of 1973 could not be expected to last, it followed that the United States had to be ready to renew the war in Vietnam at any time, in months or years, at a moment's notice—and Kissinger warned Nixon in advance that this was the logic of their course.[23] And why did the logic fail to work in practice? Kissinger's answer is that all would have worked out as planned "but for the collapse of executive authority as a result of Watergate." This can only mean, if it signifies anything more than a rhetorical last gasp, that the United States without Watergate would have "enforced" the Paris agreement by all means in its power, including the use of its own forces. Nothing else could have sufficed if, as we were already told, the real problem was that the American withdrawal caused the South Vietnamese to lose "the sinews of confidence and cohesion"—that, in effect, American forces had to carry the burden of the fighting as the *sine qua non* of the Thieu regime's survival. Honor wasn't saved. Dishonor, if it is understood to mean Thieu's collapse, was merely delayed. A country that as a result of popular revulsion could not stay in Vietnam could not expect to get back into it, Watergate or no Watergate. As for geopolitics, it was a bad reason for staying in but one of the best reasons for getting out of Vietnam.

VIII

Finally, something more must be said about the question with which we started: How did Kissinger do it?

Unusual personal qualities undoubtedly had much to do with it. Energy, stamina, even "megalomania" made his extraordinary career possible. He managed to embody a singularly potent combination—a sense of mission with a streak of opportunism. His intellectual facility impressed and intimidated. Yet all these personal characteristics hardly account for the extravagant adulation that he inspired. His record was not such as to merit the overwrought acclaim it drew from the media. Perhaps his greatest feat was to beat the President's media machine at its own machinations.

Kissinger has lots of fun with the frenzied efforts of Haldeman and Ziegler to get "photo opportunities" for the President on the evening television shows. He recounts a "bizarre interlude" at, of all places, the Vatican; a "monumental traffic jam" deliberately staged in the center of Belgrade; the anxieties of Nixon's advance men to get "exposure in prime television time" in China. But Nixon's publicity hounds were no match for Kissinger. Midway through his memoirs, Kissinger modestly remarks that "I was supposed to be skillful in dealing with the press." By the end, as previously noted, he had Nixon brooding about his "new-found celebrity." Lest readers miss all the nuances of his celebrity, Kissinger refers in the book's notes to "a good account" of the mood in the White House in William Safire's memoirs of his White House years. It tells of Haldeman's belated realization that "superstar" Kissinger was the President's chief competitor for the title of "#1 Peacemaker"; Kissinger himself "cheerily professed to be a megalomaniac"; Safire cheerily offers the opinion that Kissinger was no more than a "realistic megalomaniac." Kissinger's approach to the media, according to Safire, was "selective and flattering," and it drove the White House staffers nearly out of their minds with envy and rage.[24]

Kissinger's approach was different from that of Nixon's retainers. They worried about getting the picture of their chieftain to the *hoi polloi* on television news shows. Kissinger cultivated the *haut monde* of Washington's columnists and correspondents. The dean of the *New York Times* columnists sometimes wrote as if Kissinger had been dictating to him; he was even lured into deceiving his readers about Kissinger's alleged opposition to the Christmas 1972 bombing of North Vietnam.[25] (Kissinger admits only to the fact that he did nothing to counter the deception; it is "one of the episodes of my public life in which I take no great pride.") Two of Kissinger's hagiographers somehow managed to link him with George Washington; gave him credit for "humanizing" the Kremlin leaders for a whole generation of Americans; and paid him tribute for having "co-opted" many of his potential critics—including themselves, it may be added.[26] A usually sober British correspondent in Washington appointed him "the second most powerful man in America."[27] Another writer, favored with some twenty-five interviews with Kissinger and two of his closest aides, went even further—he had Kissinger "in real measure running the world" during the October 1973 Arab-Israeli war.[28]

Why did *they* do it? A full study of the way the usually disenchanted, hard-to-please Washington media mentality was wooed and won by Kissinger would be needed in order to get at the root of this phenomenon. One factor should not be missed. Kissinger as an intellectual in politics captured the allegiance and excited the imagination of a journalistic elite that is itself largely made up of intellectuals *manqués*. By selecting them as his chosen confidants and flattering them with his assiduous attention, he made them feel closer to the seat of power than ever before. Nixon's publicity peddlers tried to sell him from the bottom up; Kissinger sold himself from the top down. In the end, Kissinger's power over the American media may explain more about how he did it than his power over anything else.

POSTSCRIPT

I wish to call attention to an aspect of Kissinger's book that concerns the use of classified documents and is nothing less than scandalous. The book contains literally scores of direct references to and textual quotations from documents obviously of the highest classification. Some are only a sentence or two, some much longer.

I wondered how Kissinger could make use of classified documents on such a large scale and of such recent vintage. If they had been declassified for him, could I or any other scholar have access to them? Could one check up on how he used these documentary sources?

So I wrote a letter of inquiry to the Assistant Secretary for Public Affairs of the State Department. I received a reply dated January 16, 1980 from Deputy Assistant Secretary for Classification and Declassification Clayton E. McManaway. The essential paragraph in his reply reads:

> With regard to quotations from any classified Department of State documents in the book, the quotations themselves are declassified, but not the remainder of the documents from which the quotes were taken. References to or paraphrases of Department of State documents appearing in the book do not reflect a decision to declassify those documents, nor do references to DOS views, opinions or policy positions reflect a decision to declassify any classified documents underlying or setting forth those views, opinions or policy positions.

In effect only quotations were declassified, documents were not. By means of this dodge, no one else can gain access to these documents to determine how faithfully Kissinger made use of them. Most of Kissinger's quotations come from the White House and National Security Council documents. Only the State Department has so far replied to my inquiries, but no doubt the system in all is identical.

This system is a political and intellectual outrage. It is or should be particularly abhorrent to historians and other scholars. It enables political figures to control the history of their own deeds or misdeeds. No partial quotation can be properly understood without its context. Selective quotation is a frequent source of distortion and even falsification. The only remedy is to declassify any document of which a part has been declassified. What is declassified for one should be declassified for all. Whether or not the present classification system is good or bad is not here the question; the real issue is whether government officials should be permitted to make a mockery of it.

Dissent, Spring 1980

V

THE ARAB-ISRAELI WARS

1

From 1967 to 1973

I

Every Arab-Israeli war has been haunted by the previous one. In the end, each of these wars—1948, 1956, 1967, and 1973—may be thought of as extended battles in a long war. For this reason, a fuller understanding of one can contribute much to a fuller understanding of all. We are still too close to the war of 1973 to know nearly enough about its derivation and ramifications, but we now know a great deal more about the war of 1967—a great deal that casts some light on the present war and that has not been dealt with satisfactorily in the existing literature on the subject.

The ostensible Arab *casus belli* of 1973 was the recovery of the "occupied territories" taken over by Israel in 1967. In 1967, an ostensible *casus belli* was a different kind of "occupied territory"—that held by the United Nations Emergency Force (UNEF) on the Egyptian-Israeli border in the Sinai region as a result of the war of 1956. Until 1967, "occupied territory" in the Arab view meant the land which actually made up the State of Israel. In effect, the very existence of Israel was regarded by the Arabs as an "aggression." The Egyptian leader in 1967, President Gamal Abdel Nasser, stated the proposition bluntly: "Israel's existence in itself is an aggression" (May 28, 1967).[1] After 1967, Arab policy, or at least propaganda, shifted its ground; "occupied territory" came to mean the land won by Israel in 1967 and "aggression" the way the war came about. From war to war, the Arabs have sought to push back to the *status quo ante* in order to unravel the entire fabric of Arab-Israeli history. In 1973, they wanted to go back to 1967; in 1967, to 1956; and all the time to 1948, before the State of Israel was born. For this reason, the ostensible locus of the "occupied territory" has changed but its political significance or implication has not.

The term, "Israeli aggression," as applied to the 1967 war, became a banner, a war cry, an incantation, without which an Arab politician could hardly make a speech or an Arab diplomat compose a UN resolution. This slogan seemed necessary to give the Arabs a sense of outraged innocence, moral superiority, and unrestricted claim on the rest of the world. If the Israelis were really guilty of an unprovoked aggression in 1967, who could rightfully deny the Arabs their cries for simple justice or even fiery revenge? In those two words, "Israeli aggression," the Arabs put their entire moral and political case against Israel, as if the charge were self-evidently true; and, if true, nothing more needed to be said to condemn Israel before world public opinion.

How true is it? The answer should tell us much about one of the deepest manifestations of the Arab-Israeli conflict. It should also teach us something about the peculiar nature of political myths, especially how they arise after some wars to cover up the true reasons for defeat. This Arab myth is not the first of its kind; the German "stab-in-the-back" myth after World War I was very similar in purpose and fabrication. The legend of war guilt haunted Germany for years and contributed heavily to Hitler's victory in 1933. If the same legend lasts that long in the Arab world, the price may be equally high.

II

First, let us recall the main events leading up to the 1967 war. Memories have dimmed, and it is necessary to hold a few key dates in mind before we go on to inquire what the Arab leaders thought they were doing— and why.

In most accounts, the 1967 crisis began to come to a head on April 7, 1967, when Syrians and Israelis fought a one-day battle in the air and on the ground. It was the most violent flare-up since 1956. Nasser later claimed that this incident, followed by allegedly threatening anti-Syrian remarks by Israeli leaders, had precipitated his subsequent moves.

The first fatal military move came five weeks later, on May 14, with the large-scale massing of Egyptian troops in the Sinai region bordering Israel. This move was supposedly designed to relieve the purported Israeli pressure on Syria.

Two days later, on May 16, Egypt demanded the withdrawal of the United Nations Emergency Force (UNEF)—which was actually no "force" at all. The UNEF was merely a conglomeration of no more than 3,400 men from seven countries, over half Indian and Yugoslav, of whom about 1,800 policed 295 miles along the Egypt-Israel border and the Gaza Strip. It merely served as a buffer between the two sides, to keep them apart by its presence, not to "enforce" the peace.

Later, a controversy arose about whether Nasser had intended to demand the complete or only the partial withdrawal of the UN peacekeeping mission. If complete, the Egyptian takeover necessarily included the UN observation post at Sharm el-Sheikh, commanding the Straits of Tiran at the entrance of the Gulf of Aqaba. Sharm el-Sheikh was a critical piece in this deadly game because, as long ago as 1957, the then Israeli Prime Minister, David Ben-Gurion, had warned Egypt not to "block our historic and legal passage into the Gulf of Aqaba" if it wished to avoid another war. For ten years, this warning—plus the understanding that the United States stood behind it—had kept open the passage through the Gulf of Aqaba.

Then, on May 22, Nasser announced the closure of the Straits of Tiran, thereby blockading the port of Eilat, Israel's only outlet to the Red Sea. This act was the immediate *casus belli*.

The proximate, though of course not the deeper, causes of the war were, then, the unilateral expulsion of the UNEF and the closure of the Gulf of Aqaba. Both these moves assumed their overriding significance for Egypt and Israel because they represented a return to the 1956 war's *status quo ante*. As Nasser took pains to make clear, these actions were not ends in themselves; they were intended to begin the unraveling process. Or, as he put it: "If we were able to restore conditions to what they were before 1956, God will surely help and urge us to restore the situation to what it was in 1948" (May 29, 1967).

By May 22, then, Egypt had made its moves. The next two weeks were occupied with diplomatic maneuvers aimed at getting Egypt to reopen the Gulf of Aqaba to Israeli shipping or at deterring Israel from doing anything about it. When all such efforts failed, Israel struck on June 5. Its spectacular victory, ending in occupation of Egyptian, Syrian, and Jordanian territory, set the stage for the war of 1973.

The questions that arise and that have been dealt with most unsatisfactorily in the existing literature on the Arab-Israeli conflict are:

When did the Egyptians begin to think of making precisely those moves which led to the outbreak on June 5?

What were the calculations and motivations behind Egyptian policy in this period?

Who was chiefly responsible for the illusions and miscalculations which brought on the war?

In the light of what we now know, how meaningful is the legend of "Israeli aggression"?

If this legend has little to commend it historically, why has it persisted so tenaciously and what purpose has it served?

What are the larger implications of this experience for a better understanding of both the past and future of the Arab-Israeli conflict?

One of the main obstacles to an understanding of the 1967 war may be called the "Syrian myth." It alleged that Nasser was impelled to expel the UN mission, take over Sharm el-Sheikh, and close the Straits of Tiran because the Israelis were going to invade Syria.

Nasser himself was the chief author of this story. He repeatedly sought to give the impression that he thought of taking these actions when he learned that Syria was endangered.

Here is how Nasser put it the first time:

> On May 13 we received accurate information that Israel was concentrating on the Syrian border huge armed forces of about 11 to 13 brigades. These forces were divided into two fronts, one south of Tiberias and the other north of Tiberias.
>   The decision made by Israel at this time was to carry out an aggression against Syria on May 17. On May 14 we took measures, discussed this matter, and contacted our Syrian brothers (May 22, 1967).

Here is Nasser a second time:

> The circumstances in which we requested the withdrawal of UNEF are also known to all of you. Syria was threatened. There was a plan to invade Syria (May 28, 1967).

And a third time after the war:

> We all know how the Middle East crisis began in the first half of last May; there was an enemy plan to invade Syria . . . (June 9, 1967).

A fourth time:

> We all know that this crisis began with Israel's attempt to invade Syria (July 23, 1967).

And a fifth time:

> We received information about the Israeli mobilization against Syria. That is why we sent forces into the Sinai to deter them (interview in *Look*, March 19, 1968).

This is the rationale for Nasser's actions that has found its way into book after book and article after article. The most imaginative version may be found in the biography of Nasser by Anthony Nutting, whose book might make a good test case for a seminar on historical mythomania. Nutting claims that Israel deliberately lured Nasser into battle by means of calculated leaks and fictitious radio messages designed to convince the Russians, who in turn were to convince the Egyptians that a major Israeli assault on Syria was imminent. Thus Nasser's movement of Egyptian troops into the Sinai and his expulsion of the UN peacekeeping forces were all part of an "Israeli plan" or "trap."[2]

The whole elaborate structure of the myth of "Israeli aggression" in 1967 was based, then, on two interrelated points: Israel's alleged threat to Syria in mid-May, after which Nasser first thought of his countermoves in the Sinai and the Gulf of Aqaba.

All this might best be described as a "cover story." And, like other "cover stories" of the past few years, it came apart inadvertently, and in Egypt itself. A crucial portion of the real story has been available for over five years, but relatively little use has been made of it. What actually happened is still significant for its bearing on the present course of the Arab-Israeli conflict.

When the 1967 war ended, Nasser did not accept full responsibility for the Egyptian defeat. Instead, he shifted the blame onto the Egyptian military leaders, who, of course, fully deserved his wrath. After his top military leader, Field Marshal Abdel Hakim Amer, committed suicide in September 1967, Nasser staged a trial in February the following year of numerous officers and the former Minister of Defense, Shams Badran, who were accused of plotting to overthrow his regime. Badran, the chief defendant, insisted on talking about how the war had come about, despite efforts by the court to restrict his testimony to the postwar plot. Badran's testimony has never been disputed, and without it the genesis of the war cannot be fully understood.[3]

In December 1966, or January 1967, Badran related, he, Field Marshal Amer, and the Chief of Intelligence, Salah Nasr, made a trip to Pakistan. While they were there, the Defense Council of the Arab League met in Cairo.[4] At this time, it is necessary to recall, the main

Egyptian preoccupation was not Syria; it was Jordan. In the propaganda war then raging among the Arab nations, Egypt attacked Hussein as a reactionary monarch afraid to fight Israel, and Jordan retorted that Nasser was "hiding behind the skirts of UNEF" in order to avoid a confrontation. A Jordanian Prime Minister, Wasfi Tell, went so far as to charge that Nasser had made a secret agreement with Israel in 1957 to keep the UNEF in the Sinai area in order to give Egypt an alibi for staying out of the Palestine imbroglio. In this way, the UNEF was drawn into an internecine Arab struggle before the crisis of 1967 flared up.

Badran continued:

> So the idea occurred to the Field Marshal [Amer] that we ought to do something about it in order to forestall the campaign [of the reactionary Arab states]. So he said: Send a message to the President [Nasser], explaining our proposal—that we should remove the UNEF and occupy Sharm el-Sheikh, and that we have [army] units which are ready [for this purpose].

Nasser failed to reply because, Badran said, he was not yet convinced that the idea was a good one. Badran, however, pointed out to Amer that withdrawal of the UNEF from Sharm el-Sheikh would result in war. Amer replied that he wanted to occupy Sharm el-Sheikh only, without closing the Gulf of Aqaba, in order to deprive Egypt's enemies in the Arab world of a pretext for their hostile propaganda. Badran was skeptical. He thought that the anti-Egyptian propaganda would intensify if the Gulf were not closed and that Amer's proposal was merely "half a solution."

Let us stop here for a moment. We are now at the origin of the idea that led to the moves which precipitated the 1967 war. In December 1966, Field Marshal Amer was not concerned with alleged Israeli troop concentrations on the Syrian border or purported Israeli threats to invade Syria. He was motivated by an internecine Arab struggle in which Israel was used by each side as a weapon of propaganda against the other. In effect, Amer had given birth to an idea whose time had not yet come—but it was not long in coming.

The "Syrian myth" was necessary to conceal the fact that the idea of expelling the UNEF and taking over Sharm el-Sheikh had been in the air in Egyptian ruling circles ever since December 1966. Nasser himself made what seemed to be puzzling, contradictory statements on how the takeover of Sharm el-Sheikh and the alleged Israeli threat to Syria were connected. On one occasion he denied that Egypt had had any thought of war before May 13, 1967, the day he had allegedly learned of the Israeli threat, because "we did not imagine that Israel would dare to attack any Arab country" (May 22, 1967). Four days later, he told a totally different story which tied in more closely with Badran's testimony. This time he said that he knew taking over Sharm el-Sheikh meant a general war with Israel. Then he added that he had been authorized "to implement it [the Sharm el-Sheikh plan] at the right time; and the right time came with Israel's threats against Syria" (May 26, 1967).

By the time Nasser made his second statement, he had closed the Gulf of Aqaba to Israeli shipping, a step which had not been contemplated in Field Marshal Amer's original idea for the very reason that it was tantamount to bringing on a war with Israel. Nasser had taken over Amer's essential idea, but in a different form and for a different purpose. Sharm el-Sheikh now became symbolic of closing the Gulf of Aqaba to Israel instead of merely getting rid of the UNEF. And the purpose was no longer primarily to counter Jordanian propaganda; it was to challenge Israel to a direct confrontation.

Nasser later attributed his belief in an Israeli attack to Syrian and Soviet intelligence sources. Even if they were right, the attack, according to Nasser himself, should have taken place on May 17. When it did not, he presumably should have been satisfied that his military buildup in the Sinai had achieved its purpose. Nevertheless, it was after May 17 that Nasser made his most belligerent moves—occupation of Sharm el-Sheikh on the 18th and closure of the Straits of Tiran on the 22nd. Something happened during those days which hardened Nasser's resolve to transform Amer's original idea into a more far-reaching and complex scheme for taking on Israel.[5]

The inner story of what took place in Egypt's top command has not yet been fully told, and it still casts light on the fundamental considerations which have guided Egyptian policy.

III

So far, I have tried to get rid of an obstacle that stands in the way of understanding this Arab-Israeli conflict—the "Syrian cover story." Now I have come to what I consider to be the most important and most fascinating aspect of the entire sequence of events. Again, the key to Egyptian strategy may be found in former Defense Minister Badran's testimony.

A tip-off to what really happened first came from Nasser's chief journalistic confidant and mouthpiece, Muhammad Hassanein Heykal, editor of *al-Ahram*, in a series of post-mortem articles in October 1967. Heykal admitted that the Egyptians had ostensibly achieved their objective when the Israelis did not attack Syria on May 17 and that the Egyptian forces in the Sinai should have fallen back to "defensive positions." But he then let slip the reason why they failed to do so: "Some of us were dazzled by the spectacle of the force we moved into Sinai between May 15 and May 20" (*al-Ahram*, October 22, 1967).

Nasser had previously hinted at the same mood: "We are ready today," he had boasted (May 26, 1967). To visitors before the war, he had expressed confidence that his air force was more than a match for Israel's. He refused to listen to advisers who had warned him in advance that he was taking too great a risk.[6]

Badran told much more of the inside story. The Egyptian officers had been itching for a fight. Egyptian intelligence was confident that Egypt was superior in tanks, artillery, and air force. When Field Marshal Amer and Badran made a tour of inspection in the Sinai they were impressed by those "who were agitated and excited because they wanted to start operations." After Nasser spoke at an Egyptian air base in the Sinai on May 22 without actually declaring war, the officers were so disappointed that Amer felt a rising tension between Nasser and the officers. To calm them, Amer told them privately: "Don't worry, boys, you'll fight."

Meanwhile, a tactical dispute broke out in the Egyptian high command. The air force commander, General Sidqi Mahmud, wanted Egypt to strike first, a position with which Field Marshal Amer at first agreed. Nasser, who for his own reasons preferred to get the Israelis to make the first strike, soon won over the Field Marshal. The decisive reason for Nasser and Amer was that they thought an Egyptian first strike risked getting the United States into the war, while an Israeli first strike was calculated to keep the United States out. Badran related this exchange between Mahmud and Amer:

> Sidqi Mahmud objected and said: "I cannot accept an abortive operation because, for my part, it will paralyze me [i.e., the air force]." So the Field Marshal asked him: "Would you like to mount the first strike and face America or prefer to receive the first strike and face Israel only?" Sidqi Mahmud said: "All right, I agree." The Field Marshal asked him what the estimated losses would be. He [Mahmud] answered: "20 per cent."

The Egyptian decision to forgo a first strike was a deliberate one. It was not based on any intention to avoid war, because the Egyptians believed and knew that they had taken measures which made war inevitable. The Egyptians took a cold-blooded calculated risk because they were so sure of coming victory. This aspect of the Egyptian plan helps to explain why Nasser and Heykal tried so hard to goad the Israelis into making war.

"The Jews threaten war," said Nasser. "We tell them: 'You are welcome, we are ready for war' " (May 22, 1967). Six days later: "Today we are alone face to face with Israel, and if Israel wants war I would say it again, 'welcome' " (May 28, 1967). The following day: "We are now ready to confront Israel" (May 29, 1967). Heykal left nothing to the imagination: "Let Israel begin! Let our second blow then be ready! Let it be a knock-out!" (*al-Ahram*, May 26, 1967).

At the time these words seemed like vain boasting. They were more. The Israeli strike was an integral part of the Egyptian war plan. Nasser closely calculated the risks of war, took those which were sure to bring the Israelis in, and—until it was too late—calmly watched as his plans unfolded.

When he first sent Egyptian troops into Sinai on May 14, Nasser said that he had estimated the possibility of war at only 20 percent. On May 22, when he decided to close the Gulf of Aqaba, Nasser changed it to 50 percent. A few days later, he raised the figure to 80 percent (July 23, 1967). And on May 28, after the return of Badran from Moscow, where he had gone to confer with the Soviet leaders a last time before the showdown, Badran testified that Nasser had put the chances of war at 100 percent. Yet a day later, Nasser proclaimed: "Preparations have already been made. We are now ready to confront Israel" (May 29, 1967). The fatalism of the Egyptians on the outbreak of war was, by their own admission, complete a week before it broke out.

Moreover, Nasser even claimed to have known the date of the Israeli attack. He later declared that he had told a meeting of the Egyptian high command on June 2 that "I expected the aggression would take place on June 5 and that the first blow would be directed against our air force" (July 23, 1967). According to Badran's tantalizing testimony on this point, Nasser's source of information was American. We also know from the memoirs of the then Jordanian Prime Minister, Sa'd Jum'ah, that Hussein told Nasser on May 30 that he had had information from numerous sources, some of them foreign, that Israel was going to attack the Egyptian airfields by surprise on June 5 or 6.[7]

In short, Nasser's war plan called for goading the Israelis to attack first. He was totally mobilized and prepared. He knew the date. Curiously,

Nasser was telling the truth when he assured an American journalist after the war: "It was not at all in our plans to attack Israel. I promise you, we had no plans for this" (Arnaud de Borchgrave, *Newsweek*, February 10, 1969). He also told a French correspondent that he "did not want to begin a war in 1967" (Eric Rouleau, *Le Monde*, February 19, 1970). What he failed to say and by that time was anxious to conceal was that it was in his plans for Israel to attack, that he wanted it to appear that Israel had started the war, and that he had done exactly what he knew was necessary to achieve this objective.

Nasser's biographers have found it exceedingly awkward to face this inconvenient fact. Anthony Nutting portrays a Nasser so mindless of what he was doing that he could bring himself to believe that the Israelis would not fight a war alone and that, after Egyptian troops advanced to the Israeli frontier, "the matter would end there." The truth is that Nasser's entire strategy was calculated to make the Israelis fight alone, and that he repeatedly told his colleagues in the week before the war that the matter would not end there. Jean Lacouture has so little understanding of his subject that he assures his readers that Nasser "expected that Israel would passively submit to the Tiran blockade."[8] The evidence is overwhelming that Nasser understood how much the Israelis could take "passively" far better than that. Robert Stephens, a British journalist, blithely considers it "unlikely" that Nasser "was simply concerned to lure Israel into a first strike so that he could overwhelm her."[9] This is exactly what Nasser himself intimated more than once, what one as close to him as Heykal unquestionably implied before the war, and what Nasser's Defense Minister, Shams Badran, who was certainly in a position to know, spelled out in the most circumstantial detail after the war.

Even Lucius D. Battle, the U.S. Ambassador in Cairo until early in 1967 and Assistant Secretary of State for Near Eastern and South Asian Affairs during the war crisis, seems to have learned nothing and forgotten nothing. He recently offered the opinion that "Nasser thought there would be someone to pull the Arabs and Israelis apart—before a military debacle could befall him but after a political victory had restored his waning image. Certainly he knew he could not win" (*New York Times Magazine*, October 21, 1973). If, as we know from Nasser and Badran, Nasser told his generals that war was 80 percent and then 100 percent certain at a time when "he knew he could not win," he was a monster of irresponsibility and deceitfulness. Nasser was actually a man who had always calculated his chances carefully and had previously abstained from forcing a showdown with the Israelis because, as he had put it in 1965, he wanted the Arabs to be fully prepared in order "to determine the battle." If he decided to determine the battle in 1967, it was because he thought the Arabs were sufficiently prepared. There is more truth in the idea that Nasser would have wanted someone to save him before suffering a military debacle, but this is not the same thing as saying that he expected to suffer a military debacle. If this is what Mr. Battle still thinks in 1973, one shudders at the advice he was giving in 1967.

IV

Before turning to the implications of 1967 for 1973, it remains to inquire into the motivation of Nasser's war policy as a clue to that of his successor.

On the Arab side, 1956 haunted 1967. The lesson of 1956, for Nasser, was that Egypt had been saved and his reputation enhanced because Egypt had appeared to be the victim of an Israeli-French-British attack. The Suez adventure was Britain's last gasp as a great power willing or able to make its influence felt in the Middle East or elsewhere, and, by 1967, French policy toward Israel had turned from collaboration to hostility. There remained only the United States for Nasser to worry about—when he was not worrying about Israel.

The isolation of Israel, then, was a precondition for Nasser in 1967. He could not bring himself to believe that Egypt had much to fear from Israel alone. He read the events of 1956 as meaning that Israel could not hope to win unless backed by at least one great power. He thought that he could count on either an Egyptian victory in a one-to-one war or an Israeli backdown that would be the equivalent of an Egyptian victory without war. In effect, his objective was the fruits of war, with or without war. Isolating the battlefield was the key to his strategy in 1967, and for this grand maneuver to succeed, everything seemed to depend on how he handled the United States.

Nasser decided to forgo a first strike solely in order to isolate Israel. An Egyptian first strike, he thought, vastly increased the danger of U.S. intervention; an Israeli first strike vastly decreased it. His motivation, then, had nothing to do with avoiding a war with Israel; it was solely guided by his best judgment of how to win it.

Significantly, Nasser's first impulse after he knew that he had lost the war was to blame active U.S. intervention for his defeat. In his desperately ludicrous telephone conversation with Hussein on June 6, the second day of the battle when he already knew some of the bad news but not all of it, it was Nasser who had the idea of putting out a phony story about imaginary attacks from American and British aircraft carriers. It took him almost a year to withdraw this alibi for the Egyptian debacle (in the interview in *Look*, March 19, 1968). This legend was more than a purely arbitrary, senseless canard; it betrayed in a distorted fashion what had long been in his mind as the necessary precondition for an Israeli victory.

Nasser, in fact, succeeded in achieving the isolation of the Middle East battleground. To this extent, his strategy was not badly designed. If it failed in the end, the fault was elsewhere.

In order to encourage an Israeli first strike, Nasser had to believe in the decisive superiority of his own armed forces. They had to be able to take a first strike with minimal losses and hit back with crushing effect. For this reason, it was so vital for Field Marshal Amer to get the Egyptian air force commander's estimate of Egyptian losses in the opening Israeli attack. When Sidqi Mahmud answered "20 per cent," the necessary relationship of forces for a successful Egyptian counterattack against an isolated Israel appeared to be satisfied. Heykal had made known the Egyptian strategy before the war: "As of now, we must expect the enemy to deal us the first blow in the battle. But as we wait for the first blow, we should try to minimize its effect as much as possible. The second blow will then follow. But we will deal this blow to the enemy in retaliation and deterrence. It will be the most effective blow we can possibly deal" (*al-Ahram*, May 26, 1967). Six days before the war, the then Jordanian Prime Minister who accompanied King Hussein to Cairo heard Field Marshal Amer saying that the fight against Israel would last only a few days and "be a picnic." This highly placed Jordanian source summed up the fate of the two aspects of Nasser's strategy as follows: "Nasser was deceived by Egyptian intelligence regarding the Israeli power and Israel's real aims. He also had the illusion that he had won the diplomatic campaign against the United States and Britain."[10] In his post-mortem speech after the war, Nasser implicitly admitted that the military side of the war had been miscalculated: "Here we should acknowledge with complete honesty and complete dignity that the military fight did not proceed the way we expected or desired" (July 23, 1967). And at his trial, former Defense Minister Badran testified that, if all had gone as planned and Egypt had lost only the 20 percent that it had expected, "there was no one [in the Egyptian air force] who believed that the Jews would have any capability left to mount an operation against us," owing to the vaunted superiority of the Egyptian air force and the excellence of the Egyptian war plan. Indeed, Badran still would not concede that Israel alone had beaten Egypt. He attributed Israel's victory to the Americans, who had allegedly given the Israelis the benefit of American aerial reconnaissance, down to "every nail in every [Egyptian] airplane."

Unlike President Kennedy, who had assumed full responsibility for the Bay of Pigs fiasco in 1961, Nasser unloaded all the blame onto his generals. To one American correspondent he complained: "What helped the Israelis the last time was not so much their cleverness, but the conceit and complacency of our generals. They felt Israel would never attack. They even overestimated their own strength. And because of that, they failed to take elementary precautions" (*Newsweek*, February 10, 1969). In another interview, he forgave himself: "I was not handling military matters before the 1967 war" (*Time*, May 16, 1969).

When an enemy's "aggression" and "first strike" become part of one's own war plan, something strange and ominous has obviously happened to the meaning of these terms. Even in 1973, when the Israelis were clearly the victims of an Arab first strike, the Arabs and their Soviet backers persisted in a bizarre propaganda campaign against "Israeli aggression." Is what has happened in the Middle East a portent of what may come elsewhere? Has "aggression" virtually lost its meaning in the circumstances of modern warfare? Does it have any relationship to the "first strike" any longer?

At minimum, the Arab propaganda about the "Israeli aggression" in 1967, let alone that in 1973, deserves to be rejected with derision and contempt. If ever a war was willfully and knowingly provoked, it was the 1967 war. In this respect, the two wars are different only in form, not in substance. The Egyptians decided to give the first strike to Israel in 1967 and to take it for themselves in 1973 for exactly the same reason—they thought it was best for them. In so doing, they have set precedents of such gravity and peril, not least to themselves, that the whole problem of war and peace in the entire world may never be the same again.

v

In a number of other ways, the wars of 1967 and 1973 seem to be as closely related as were the wars of 1956 and 1967.

It is almost as if the Arabs asked themselves in 1973 what the Israelis had done in 1967 and had then decided to do likewise. The Arabs obviously concluded that it had been a mistake to make the Israelis deliver the first strike in 1967. They were going to do it themselves in 1973. The Arabs were surprised by the sheer weight and intensity of the opening Israeli attack in 1967. They were going to start off with an equally massive movement of men and materiel in 1973. The Arabs were impressed by their failure to wage a simultaneous, multi-front war in 1967, enabling Israel to deal with Egypt first and turn on Syria and Jordan afterward. They were going to synchronize major offensives from Egypt and Syria, holding Jordanian and other Arab forces in reserve, in 1973.

Jordan's role in 1967 has been widely misunderstood, and a similar misunderstanding in 1973 is less excusable. It was generally thought that Hussein had waited until the last minute to make up his mind about getting into the 1967 war and that he did so only after he was convinced that Egypt was sure to win.

We now know from Hussein himself that this was not the case.

Two books on Hussein have appeared, with his blessings, since the 1967 war. The first, published originally in French in 1968, is largely made up of Hussein's own words. The second, by an English writer, published in 1972, was also written with Hussein's cooperation. Both tell more or less the same story of how Hussein got into the war.[11]

As soon as Nasser announced the closure of the Gulf of Aqaba on May 22, 1967, Hussein decided that war was inevitable. In the next two days he made his decision: to get into it. On May 26, Hussein called in the Egyptian ambassador in Amman and asked him to arrange a meeting with Nasser. The latter accepted Hussein's overture on May 29; Hussein flew to Cairo the following day; a reconciliation took place between the former enemies; Nasser assured Hussein that his forces were superior to the Israelis'. Hussein later insisted: "Nasser never appealed to us. We were the ones who appealed to him."

That Hussein was totally unprepared to play the role of an effective Egyptian ally does not change the political significance of his behavior, especially for the United States, which has consistently supported him. In the event of an Arab-Israeli war, Hussein is sure to take Jordan into it, whatever the state of his preparedness. If he ends up on the losing side, he is equally sure to come to Washington for another handout. He behaved in 1973 exactly the same way that he had behaved in 1967. Hussein went to Cairo on September 10 of this year; he released hun-

dreds of political prisoners, including Palestinians who had tried to overthrow him, on September 18; and war broke out on October 6. When
this one is all over, we may expect to be told how he knew everything in
advance and had made up his mind long before anyone had guessed
what he was up to.

As for the other Arab countries, the 1973 war was far better coordinated and prepared than that of 1967. When Nasser arranged to have
the 1967 conflict, he still had about 50,000 troops in Yemen, where he
was virtually fighting a war against King Faisal's Saudi Arabia, which
was supporting the Yemeni royalists. In 1973, Egypt had lost so much
ground in the internecine Arab struggle for power that it no longer posed
a threat to Saudi Arabia and, indeed, was happy to accept Faisal's
advice as well as his money. Nasser went into the 1967 war with barely
more than a rickety military alliance with Syria, to which Jordan even
more dubiously attached itself. Sadat went into the 1973 war after
mobilizing the entire Arab world for military, financial, and diplomatic
support.

Nevertheless, the inter-Arab aspect of every Arab-Israeli war should
not be neglected or underrated. The Arab world is far from being a
unity; ancient as well as modern rivalries and grudges persist behind
the façade of solidarity. Nasser once aspired to leadership of the entire
Arab world, and he used such causes as the Yemen civil war and the
anti-Israeli *jihad* to serve his ends. Every war that Egypt fights against
Israel weakens her in relation to the other Arab powers. In any case,
Egypt cannot have it both ways. Saudi Arabia's Faisal is paying Egypt
not only to fight Israel but also to spend Egyptian energies that might
be—and have been—directed against him. For Faisal, it is tails I win
and heads you lose.

Arab propaganda in 1973 also seems to have learned something from
1967. In the previous war, the candor of the Arab spokesmen, who
either threatened to turn the clock back to 1948 in the manner of Nasser
or promised to leave no Israeli survivors alive in the raw language of
Ahmed Shukairy, then head of the Palestine Liberation Organization,
clearly backfired. This time, the Arabs decided to be more restrained in
their declared demands and to use more evasive formulas, such as restoring "the legitimate rights of the Palestinians." In 1967, candor came
before the war; in 1973, it was put off until the end of the war—assuming that the Arabs would then be in a position to be candid about what
"the legitimate rights of the Palestinians" are.

As for Israel, its successful surprise attack in 1967 ironically contributed to the success of the Arab surprise attack in 1973. The Israeli intelligence and preparedness failure in this war was, at least in good part, a product of the same kind of underestimation of the enemy that proved so costly to the Egyptians in the previous war. The initial Israeli setback had its deeper roots in the changed social conditions in Israel after 1967, the widespread disdain for the Arab ability to wage a co-ordinated, modern war, and a pervasive sense of satisfaction with the post-1967 status quo. General Hubris seems to have changed sides. Nasser's complaint about Egyptian "conceit and complacency" may be just as close to the truth in its Hebrew translation—except that the Israelis had enough back-up leadership and reserve stamina to turn the tide of battle.

VI

In his news conference on October 12 of this year, six days after the present war started, Secretary of State Henry Kissinger made a strange and disturbing statement. Of the Soviet role, he said: "If you compare their conduct in this crisis to their conduct in 1967, one has to say that Soviet behavior has been less provocative, less incendiary, and less geared to military threats, than in the previous crisis."

In 1967, the Soviet leaders were certainly provocative and incendiary, but they were also more confused and constrained by more limited military capabilities. They peddled the still unexplained story about Is-raeli troop concentrations on the Syrian border which helped to give Nasser the thought of putting into effect Field Marshal Amer's six-months'-old idea of chasing out the UN forces and taking over Sharm el-Sheikh. Subsequently, the Soviet commitment to Egypt and Syria was twofold. Without Soviet war materiel and training programs, the Arabs could not have contemplated going to war. But there was another essen-tial function which the Soviets promised to perform. As explained by Nasser to Jordanian Prime Minister Sa'd Jum'ah, "The contact between our people and the Soviet leaders has assured us that they will come quickly to our support in the event of U.S. intervention."[12] Thus Nasser took out an additional insurance policy with the Soviet Union against the United States. Overconfident of the success of Arab arms, he was more interested in keeping the United States out of the battlefield than in bringing the Soviet Union in.

Yet the Soviet Union pursued a policy of limited liability, to the disappointment of Nasser when his plans went awry. He later blamed the Soviets as well as the United States for misleading him about their ability to hold Israel back (July 23, 1967). Another deep grievance was their failure to fly in more planes on an emergency basis or provide the Egyptian forces with air cover as soon as the extent of the Egyptian losses was known. According to Nutting, Nasser told his former Vice President, Abdel Latif Boghdady, that the Soviets "had been frozen into immobility by their fear of a confrontation with America."[13] In any event, the Soviets did not attempt to keep the Egyptian army going with a large- or small-scale resupply operation in 1967.

This, too, changed in 1973. The Soviets were again in on the war at the start, but experience had taught the Arabs to keep them in, at least for the purpose of resupply, during the war. The Soviet role was far more provocative, far more incendiary, far more geared to military action in 1973 than it had been in 1967. There was nothing in 1967 comparable to at least two Soviet actions in 1973—the huge, prompt resupply effort for Egypt and Syria, and the *démarches* to Iraq, Algeria, and other Arab countries urging them to get into the fight against Israel with the express admonition that the advanced Soviet equipment had been given to them for this very purpose. If only for these reasons, Kissinger's excessive solicitude for Soviet sensibilities may or may not have been good diplomacy but it was certainly bad history.

Let us now go back and try to reconstruct, in its main lines, how the Soviet Union was implicated in the Arab decision to go to war again.

Nasser at first needed a breathing spell and hoped against hope to retrieve his fortunes through the United Nations and joint U.S.-USSR pressure on Israel. In March 1969, he launched what he called a "war of attrition" against Israel; it cost him dearly and he called it off in July. By the end of 1969, his frustration could no longer be contained. On November 6, he made a speech in which he for the first time talked of using force again "to open our own road to what we want, over a sea of blood and under a horizon of fire."

At this time, however, Nasser had not yet made a new deal with the Soviets, and without it he was helpless to convert his words into deeds. This dilemma sent him to Moscow from June 29 to July 17, 1970, one of his longest stays in the Russian capital, when he succeeded in getting the Soviets to install the first SAM-3 missiles near the Suez Canal, though the Soviets still insisted on training Egyptians to use them. Soon afterward, Nasser accepted the so-called Rogers Plan, named after the former U.S. Secretary of State, providing for an Egyptian-Israeli cease-fire for ninety days to set the stage for intensive peace negotiations. In effect, Nasser was preparing to move either way, though his faith in the Rogers Plan must have been minimal.

A cease-fire agreement was signed on August 7, 1970. It prohibited military build-ups or offensive action within a zone at least thirty-two miles wide on each side of the canal. The United States and the Soviet Union were co-signatories, and an American spokesman defined the understanding in unmistakable terms:

> The depth of the cease-fire was described as sufficient to assure Israel that neither Egypt nor the Soviet Union would expand military positions— especially the Soviet SAM-2 and SAM-3 anti-aircraft missile sites—into the 32-mile belt along the canal during the truce.
> The informed sources said that the Soviet Union had given the United States a "categorical commitment" to abide by the requirement not to build up positions in this zone during the truce. This enabled President Nixon to give Israel firm assurances on this point.[14]

This categorical commitment and these firm assurances were worthless as soon as they were made. Even such kindly chroniclers of Nasser as Jean Lacouture and Anthony Nutting admit that the missiles were installed in violation of the August 7 cease-fire.[15] We now know that the U.S. government knew all about the violations and failed to live up to its assurances. Senator Henry M. Jackson has revealed that he tried to persuade Kissinger, then the President's national security adviser, to recognize that "the accumulated result could do irreparable harm to Israel's security" and to insist on the removal of the missiles.[16] His efforts were fruitless.

Nasser died in September 1970. It was the end of the Arab-Israeli postwar Phase 1.

Nasser's successor, Anwar el-Sadat, also needed a breathing spell before he was ready to go to Moscow.

Sadat permitted the cease-fire to last until March 1971. Then came the following timetable:

March 1–2: Sadat in Moscow.

March 7: Sadat ends the cease-fire.

March 20: A special "War Preparation Committee" headed by Sadat orders nationwide measures to mobilize the national resources for the eventuality of war (*al-Ahram*, March 21, 1971).

March 22: Abdel Mohsen Abul-Nur, Secretary General of the Arab Socialist Union, Egypt's only political organization, declares at a rally at Aswan that "the only way for us now is a military solution" and "our armed forces are now ready to force him [Israel] to withdraw" (*New York Times*, March 25, 1971).

March 24: The *New York Times* correspondent in Cairo, Raymond H. Anderson, writes: "A new wave of weapons and military equipment deliveries from the Soviet Union has reached the United Arab Republic in the last few weeks, according to reliable Western sources, coinciding with stepped up, widely publicized measures by the Egyptian leadership to prepare the country for war" (*ibid.*).

The fullest and bluntest expression of Egyptian thinking came, as usual, from Muhammad Hassanein Heykal on March 26. In an article entitled "The Inevitable War," he wrote that "this war will be long, fierce, and complicated, but there is no alternative." As if the Egyptians were merely trying to improve on their 1967 strategy, he concluded: "While the stage is prepared by political means, the Egyptian military forces are ready to start war against Israel—a war which is inevitable, as I have already said. It is inevitable against Israel, but it is avoidable against any other factor [in the situation] except for Israel."

In an interview later that same year, Heykal incautiously acknowledged that Egypt was after far more than the post-1967 "occupied territories." Speaking to an Arab publication, he said: "It's not enough to return to the borders of 1967. Adjustments are needed which it is unlikely that Israel will make." As Nasser's literary heir, he also stated: "He [Nasser] wanted the Arab world, and the whole world, to realize that a peaceful settlement was impossible, so that it would no longer be a subject for discussion. As a result, the Arab world will organize itself and prepare for a long struggle on many fronts."[17]

After these bold words, the Egyptian leadership hesitated for a few months owing to more diplomatic maneuvering. By the beginning of last year, however, the original decision to go to war was reaffirmed, as Sadat disclosed in a speech on January 13, 1972:

We have reached the conclusion that the battle has been forced upon us. We took this decision in 1971, but a little fog descended upon us and we had to find our way all over again.

On January 25, 1972, he reiterated:

We must be prepared for battle since we have adopted the view that the problem can only be solved by force.[18]

After this, the only open questions were the preparation, the timing, and the tactics. There is reason to believe that the final, operational decision did not come until last summer, but the political decision goes as far back as two years ago. Unlike Nasser, Sadat did not intend to telegraph the blow. Since he was determined to strike first, there was no need for a complicated escalation of threats and stratagems to get the Israelis to do anything. In fact, the less the Israelis did, the better. Having made their decision, the Egyptians were faced with many complex problems vis-à-vis the Soviets, the other Arab countries, and the non-Arab world, especially the United States. Without going into the details here, it is enough for our purpose to note how long ago the fundamental Arab decision was made and how closely it followed another mission to Moscow.

Whenever Arab statements are cited, the question of Arab "rhetoric" arises. Should it be taken seriously or are Arabs peculiarly addicted to hyperbolic bombast? Whenever an Arab spokesman says something particularly provocative or outrageous, there is always someone who says that "they never really mean it." One writer has maintained that the Israeli case has been more "believable" because of Arab "irrationality" and that Arab leaders invariably tell Arab audiences merely "what they *wish* to hear."[19] I have even heard the foreign minister of an Arab country instruct a group of Americans that Arabs are allergic to Western rationalism and that, if Westerners wish to deal with Arabs, they must adopt the seemingly irrational Arab mode of thinking. Former Ambassador Battle has related that one of the first things Muhammad Hassanein Heykal told him was: "Don't try to understand us. We don't understand ourselves."[20] But in that case, why should anyone try?

Whatever one may think about Arab rhetoric and rationality, Arab politicians who know the West perfectly well are not above taking advantage of what may well be nothing more than a patronizing or apologetic attitude on the part of some Westerners. It enables them to operate on the basis of a political double-bookkeeping system—one version for their own people and the same words but in a bowdlerized version for the West. I am inclined to agree with an acute Israeli student of Arab ideas and attitudes, Dr. Yehoshafat Harkabi, a former chief of Israeli army intelligence and now a lecturer at the Hebrew University in Jerusalem. Dr. Harkabi has this to say about the difference between private and public utterances in the West and in Arab countries: "If in the United States a private statement is an indication of real intentions, the reverse seems to be true, very often, in Arab countries, where public proclamations are more significant than soft words whispered to foreign journalists. Even if the masses cannot impose their will on their leaders by democratic processes, the importance of the public declarations lies in the fact that they create commitments and arouse expectations that the leadership will practice what it preaches."[21]

Certainly, both Israelis and Westerners would have been better advised and more nearly forewarned if they had taken Arab public proclamations and declarations quite literally since at least 1971. Too many Westerners treat the Arabs as if they were irresponsible, irrational, petulant children who go into a tantrum every time they do not get what they want. Even if some Arabs invite it, this Western attitude does no one any good, least of all the Arabs, whom it encourages to indulge in irresponsible histrionics.

VII

Ever since the so-called Soviet-American détente was consecrated in Moscow by President Nixon in May 1972, the ambience of détente has been incxtricably linked with the latest phase of the Arab-Israeli conflict.

The Americans were admittedly caught off guard by the outbreak of the 1973 war. They were "burned"—to use Treasury Secretary Schultz's elegant phrase—as much in the Middle East as in the celebrated "grain deal." We still do not know whether the Russians were ablc to get such a favorable deal simply because they were so much smarter than the Americans or whether the latter were unusually complaisant owing to a bureaucratic understanding that détente meant keeping the Russians happy by giving them more or less what they want, at least in the economic sphere. The American rationale has seemed to be: give now, get paid later.

This bad American habit of going from cold to hot in Soviet-American relations did not start with Mr. Nixon. The pattern was set by so vastly different a President as Franklin D. Roosevelt. If a Roosevelt and a Nixon can lurch from one extreme to another in this highly inflammable area, something is deeply wrong.

When Roosevelt decided to recognize the Soviet regime in 1933, his hopes were high. Soon disappointed, he lost interest and Soviet-American relations in the 1930's settled down to a low level of economic exchange and diplomatic intercourse. With the Soviet attack on Finland in 1939, however, Roosevelt went into his most extreme anti-Soviet phase. He privately expressed disgust at "this dreadful rape of Finland." He told Ambassador Joseph C. Grew in Tokyo that "people are asking why anyone should have anything to do with the present Soviet leaders because their idea of civilization and human happiness is so totally different from ours." He stated publicly in February 1940 that "the Soviet Union, as everybody who has the courage to face the facts knows, is run by a dictatorship as absolute as any other dictatorship in the world."

Yet, after Russia entered the war the following year, his attitude changed miraculously, though nothing had changed in Russia's internal setup. By September 1941, he tried to convince Pope Pius XII that freedom of religion in Russia was a real possibility. He advised newsmen to read the article in the Soviet Constitution guaranteeing freedom of conscience, as if the reality could be found there. He boasted that he "got along fine" with Stalin. He told both Under Secretary of State Sumner Welles and Cardinal Spellman that the difference between the United States and Soviet Russia was going to be reduced from a ratio of 0 to 100 to one of 40 to 60.[22]

Those who choose to remember only Roosevelt's wartime attitude toward Russia have oversimplified him. A President who could change so drastically from the anti-Soviet 1939–mid-1941 period to the pro-Soviet late-1941–1944 period could easily change back again. Yet the disturbing fact remains that Roosevelt could not conduct a policy of wartime cooperation with Russia without sowing illusions about the Soviet regime.

A somewhat similar phenomenon has accompanied the Nixon policy of détente. Nixon, like Roosevelt, has made his Soviet policy a personal one. Roosevelt imagined that he alone was capable of dealing cozily with Stalin and that he alone could cajole concessions out of "Uncle Joe," as Stalin was endearingly called. Now we have Mr. Nixon telling us, at his news conference on October 26, that "it's because he [Brezhnev] and I know each other and it's because we have had this personal contact that notes exchanged in that way result in a settlement rather than a confrontation." Oddly, this personal contact did not prevent a confrontation from erupting before it resulted in a "settlement," as ill-timed and ill-defined as any in recent years, extorted under the menace of unilateral Soviet military action. The two most persuasive "notes" that Mr. Nixon communicated to Mr. Brezhnev were unwritten and unsent—the first on October 13, when Mr. Nixon decided to start the resupply effort to Israel, and the second on October 25, when he took what were delicately called "certain precautionary measures" of a military nature. If there is one area in our foreign policy which should be essentially *impersonal*, it is that dealing with the Communist powers, Communist China as well as Soviet Russia. Roosevelt's personal diplomacy with Stalin was one of his costliest aberrations. There is much less excuse for Nixon and Kissinger to repeat it with Brezhnev and Chou En-lai.

But this is only part of the trouble. One of the most delusory documents in American diplomatic history was signed on May 29, 1972, by Richard Nixon, President of the United States of America, and Leonid I. Brehznev, General Secretary of the Central Committee CPSU. It was grandiosely entitled, "Basic Principles of Relations Between the United States of America and the Union of Soviet Socialist Republics." As a compendium of illusions and effusions, it reminds one of the "Atlantic Charter" of 1941, which Kissinger had the misfortune to recall nostalgically earlier this year. The second and third "basic principles" of the charter of détente are particularly pertinent to the Arab-Israeli war:

> SECOND. The USA and the USSR attach major importance to preventing the development of situations capable of causing a dangerous exacerbation of their relations. Therefore, they will do their utmost to avoid military confrontations and to prevent the outbreak of nuclear war. They will always exercise restraint in their mutual relations, and will be prepared to negotiate and settle differences by peaceful means. Discussions and negotiations on outstanding issues will be conducted in a spirit of reciprocity, mutual accommodation, and mutual benefit.
>
> Both sides recognize that efforts to obtain unilateral advantage at the expense of the other, directly or indirectly, are inconsistent with these objectives. The prerequisites for maintaining and strengthening peaceful relations between the USA and the USSR are the recognition of the security interests of the Parties based on the principles of equality and the renunciation of the use or threat of force.
>
> THIRD. The USA and the USSR have a special responsibility, as do other countries which are permanent members of the United Nations Security Council, to do everything in their power so that conflicts or situations will not arise which would serve to increase international tensions. Accordingly, they will seek to promote conditions in which all countries will live in peace and security and will not be subject to outside interference in their internal affairs.

What has all this to do with the Arab-Israeli war of 1973? The answer is that the main Soviet effort to prepare the Egyptian and Syrian armies for war took place after this declaration of principles was signed. I do not mean to oversimplify Arab-Soviet relations over the years. They have had their ups and downs; Sadat brought in hordes of Soviet "advisers" and technicians in 1971 and sent most of them out in 1972. Yet the two sides managed to patch up whatever differences they may have had, and Soviet planes, tanks, missiles, and the myriad of other war materiel poured in to enable the Arab armies to take the offensive. The upshot seems to be that the Soviets have invested in their Arab proxies too heavily since 1955 to let go so easily; whatever their difficulties and rebuffs may have been, the Soviets have not permitted them to stand in the way of a long-term policy which has now persisted for eighteen years despite upheavals in the Soviet leadership.

After Mr. Nixon and Comrade Brezhnev signed their names to these beautiful sentiments, détente became the chief political capital of the Nixon administration. The more the President was forced to wallow in the Watergate and associated ignominies, the harder Mr. Nixon tried to sell the blessings of détente. It was almost the only thing he could sell, and he repeatedly tried to change the subject from Watergate to détente.

In Washington, it became almost indecent to say anything nasty or naughty about the two great Communist powers. They order this matter better in China. On August 24 of this year, Premier Chou En-lai delivered a report to the Tenth National Congress of the Chinese Communist party in which, détente or no détente, he referred scathingly to both the United States and the Soviet Union. They were "contending for hegemony," "are in a sorry plight indeed," "want to devour China, but find it too tough even to bite," and—this for U.S. imperialism alone—it has "started to go downhill" and "has openly admitted that it is increasingly on the decline." If such a speech were made by President Nixon or Secretary Kissinger about China, their whole "structure of peace" would seem to come tumbling down, and Washington would quake with rumors of the return of hot, cold, or lukewarm war.

The trouble, of course, is not détente. It is the illusions that détente has fostered or that have been fostered in the name of détente. Unfortunately, détente with illusions is worse than no détente at all; one-sided détente is worse than no détente at all. While Mr. Nixon and Dr. Kissinger were basking in the warmth of détente, the Russians were heating up a war in the Middle East. While a new academic doctrine was developing that the Soviet Union had become a conservative, status-quo power that abjured risks and renounced upsetting the existing balance of forces, the Soviet Union was preparing to take incalculable risks to upset the precarious balance in one of the most sensitive areas in the world. If the President and Secretary of State had not developed a case of un-wonted bashfulness on the subject of Soviet Russia, they might have asked some embarrassing questions about how the USSR had lived up to the "Basic Principles."

Had the USSR tried to prevent "the development of situations [in the Middle East] capable of causing a dangerous exacerbation of their rela-tions"? Did the USSR do its utmost "to avoid" this military confronta-tion? Was the approaching war in the Middle East ever discussed with the United States "in a spirit of reciprocity, mutual accommodation, and mutual benefit"? Had the USSR sought "to obtain unilateral advantage at the expense of the other [U.S.], directly or indirectly"? Did the USSR do everything in its power "so that conflicts and situations [in the Mid-dle East] will not arise which would serve to increase international tensions"? Accordingly, did the USSR "seek to promote conditions [in the Middle East] in which all countries [including Israel] will live in peace and security and will not be subject to outside interference [viz., Russian tanks, planes, and missiles] in their internal affairs"?

No such questions have been raised, at least publicly, about a docu-ment only a year and a half old. President Nixon was so far from realizing how close the Soviet-backed Arabs were to war that he decided to blame both sides indiscriminately and to disclaim being pro-Israel or pro-Arab only a month before the outbreak of hostilities. This "even-handedness," as it was called, might have made sense if General Secre-tary Brezhnev had come out with more or less the same thing. In the circumstances, it was an invitation for the Russians and Arabs to catch the American leaders unawares. After the outbreak, Kissinger still thought it necessary to compare Soviet behavior in 1973 favorably with Soviet behavior in 1967 and to characterize the former as not yet "ir-responsible," as if he were waiting for the Russians themselves to attack Israel before entertaining the thought that they might have gone too far. It took him a little while to realize that it was pointless to make excuses for Russian irresponsibility. When Kissinger rushed off to Moscow at the behest of General Secretary Brezhnev, he could not fail to give the impression that the Russians could turn the war on and off as they pleased. They may even be blaming him for having unwittingly misled them about the price the United States was willing to pay for the privi-lege of participating in a détente with them.

Secretary Kissinger might usefully reread some of Professor Kissinger's old writings, especially an article on the 1962 Cuban missile crisis. Eleven years ago, President Kennedy was also caught by surprise and then reacted strongly. Now President Nixon has told us that the 1973 Soviet-American confrontation was the worst since the missile crisis. In the earlier case, Kissinger was not satisfied with mere self-congratulation. He asked some deeper questions, which might also be asked now. He admonished that "even this success does not free us from the need to understand how we arrived at the point where such a dramatic and risky action was necessary." He wanted to know "what tempted the Soviets into so rash, so foolhardy an adventure"? Or, as he also put it, "with the stakes so high, what made the Soviets believe that they could get away with it?"

Part of the answer, Kissinger indicated, pointed in the direction of U.S. policy before the missile crisis. "Over the past decade," he suggested, "Khrushchev may well have become convinced that the United States would never run risks to protect its interests, either because it did not understand its interests or because it did not have the appropriate doctrine for using its power."[23] A similar line of thought might well be pursued now. What was there about previous U.S. policy that had given Khrushchev's successors the idea that they could take such an exorbitant risk in the Middle East and expect to get away with it? Soviet moves of such gravity are not taken in a vacuum; they reflect, among other things, a perception of U.S. policy. Was the policy of détente, as publicized and practiced before October 1973, an "appropriate doctrine" for warning off the Soviet Union from "so rash, so foolhardy an adventure"? We were once instructed by Professor Kissinger that "the test of statesmanship is the adequacy of its evaluation *before* the event" (emphasis in original).[24] By this test, his statesmanship in this instance was somewhat less than adequate.

If, as the usually sober and trustworthy International Institute for Strategic Studies in London estimates, the Egyptians had as many as 1,000 Soviet "advisers and instructors," the Syrians 3,000, and the Iraqis 1,500, and the Egyptian army closely followed Russian tactical procedures, on top of the fact that the immense accumulation of war materiel was entirely Soviet, the Soviet Union was up to its neck in this war. Some people like to make a distinction between whether the Soviets encouraged the Arabs to go to war and whether they merely acquiesced in it. The practical difference is negligible. The Soviets encouraged it by acquiescing, and they would have discouraged it by refusing to acquiesce. They have, at minimum, a veto power over any Arab action on this scale. If they choose not to exercise it, they might as well push the button to let it go on. In fact, the vast and expensive effort the Russians must have made to render this war possible required a major decision on the part of the Soviet leadership many months ago. By its very nature, that decision entailed secrecy and deception, made all the more necessary because it was in flagrant violation of both the letter and spirit of that charter of détente solemnly signed in May 1972 at the insistence of the Russians.

The starting point for any reconsideration of U.S. policy in the coming months is that the Soviets prepared this war under cover of the détente. It was the 1973 edition of the Soviet-Arab strategy for isolating Israel and the Middle East battleground. In the division of labor between the Arabs and the Soviets, the former are supposed to do the fighting and the latter to run diplomatic and other interference. If this is still not enough to insure an Arab victory, the Soviets are then expected to blow the whistle, call off the game, strong-arm the Security Council, and, in the event of an imminent Syrian-Egyptian military collapse, stave it off by all possible means, even to the extent of threatening to take over the war from its Arab proxies. A détente which permits the Soviets to play such a double game is doomed to end in disillusionment and recrimination.

In his news conference on October 26, President Nixon tried to answer criticism of the détente by arguing that "without that détente we might have had a major conflict in the Middle East. With détente, we avoided it." This is a most peculiar interpretation of what détentes are for. In Mr. Nixon's view, a détente can apparently take us to the very brink of a major conflict, as if that were not the business of a détente to avert. But if the major conflict is avoided by a last-minute display of precautionary power, credit for the allegedly happy ending should go to the détente. The awkward fact is that the dénouement of October 22–25 was the result of the oldest of old-fashioned power plays on both sides. If this is what détente signifies, the word has become meaningless, and we might as well trade it in for something less pretentious and disarming. When President Kennedy faced up to Khrushchev in 1962, he did not find it necessary to pretend that it had anything to do with something like détente.

The Israelis have reason to be grateful to the United States for the aid which they received when they needed it most. After a week of bureaucratic wavering and division, President Nixon acted with forcefulness and decision. For the future, however, the policy before October 13 is more alarming than the policy after that date is encouraging. If U.S. policy is going to be based on deals with Soviet Russia, it will have to find a way to stop the Russians from underwriting Arab wars instead of stopping wars that do not go according to the Russian-Arab plan. If détente is helpless before the first and operates only in the second fashion, it will be dishonored the same way another perfectly good word, "appeasement," was dishonored before World War II.

Judging from Brezhnev's speech to the World Peace Congress in Moscow on October 26, the task of salvaging détente from the wreckage of this war will not be easy. Listening to Brezhnev, one might imagine that nothing worth mentioning had happened in the Middle East before October 22, the day the Security Council voted the first cease-fire. Here was the leader of a great nuclear power, which had aided and abetted a reckless, perfidious aggression against Israel on Yom Kippur, unctuously accusing Israel of "perfidiously" violating Security Council decisions, continuing "aggressive action" against Egypt, and exhibiting "the recklessness of the peace-violators." One would have given much to hear someone at this "peace" congress ask Mr. Brezhnev why he waited until the Egyptian army was on the verge of collapse before he bethought himself to denounce the violation of peace in the Middle East. Or to inquire how a nation which as a result of World War II had acquired 272,500 square miles of territory with a population of 24,168,000—a territory as large as Jordan, Lebanon, Syria, and Iraq combined, with a population two-and-a-half times as large—could without shame tell any other nation that "acquiring territories through means of war" was impermissible.*

The 1973 war has also had far more serious international repercussions than the previous one, not least in the United Nations. Rarely,

---

* As a result of World War II, the Soviet Union acquired the following territories and population, some of which had been former conquests of the Czarist Empire, which the Bolsheviks had disavowed in 1917, and some of which had never belonged to Russia at all:

	Sq. miles	Population
Lithuania	24,000	3 million
Latvia	20,000	2 "
Estonia	18,000	1.1 "
Eastern Poland	68,000	10 "
Bessarabia and Bukovina	19,000	3.7 "
Moldavia	13,000	2.2 "
East Prussia	3,500	0.4 "
Carpatho-Ukraine	5,000	0.8 "
West Karelia	16,000	0.5 "
Petsamo	4,000	0.004 "
Tannu Tuva	64,000	0.06 "
Southern Sakhalin	14,000	0.4 "
Kurile Islands	4,000	0.004 "

perhaps never, has the world organization been so crudely used to provide a fig-leaf for naked great power. Fig-leaves, to be sure, have their uses or they would not have been invented. It was undoubtedly better for the UN to furnish a small-power cease-fire force than to have direct Soviet and American armed intervention in the area. That Sadat begged for the latter showed that, in desperation, he had become more interested in bringing the Soviets in than in keeping the Americans out. Nevertheless, the convenience of the UN's role is small consolation for the damage that was done to the organization and that it did to itself. Its members, if they have any consciences left, will long have to account for the fact that they did nothing to restore peace when Israel was in danger but hurriedly passed one "peace resolution" after another, with hardly any time to know what they were doing, as soon as Egypt was in danger. This war may well be to the United Nations what the Italo-Ethiopian war was to the League of Nations.

VIII

From war to war, the essential Arab strategy has become increasingly clear. Gimmicks will not make it go away, and UN resolutions have mainly served to exacerbate it.

The essence of that strategy was put in five words by former President Nasser to Eric Rouleau: "Time works in our favor" (*Le Monde*, February 19, 1970). This idea, giving impetus to every successive war, has been the *leitmotif* of Arab and Soviet propaganda for a long time.

The result is that the Arab countries want to end as well as to start wars in their own way. As we have seen, it has pleased them to give and also to take the first strike. As soon as they get into trouble, however, they expect someone else—the Soviet Union, with or without the United States, the United Nations, the oil-consuming nations—to get them out of it. The manufacture of myths about why they lost—Israel was the "aggressor," the United States intervened in some unfair fashion, the Soviet Union did not do enough—becomes a national passion. After the 1948 war, the young Egyptian officers, of whom Nasser was representative, blamed a corrupt regime. After the 1956 war, Nasser blamed Britain and France. After 1967, he blamed the United States, his generals, his allies.

In order to make every defeat inconclusive, it is necessary to act as if the defeat did not really take place. Other countries have, after all, fought wars and lost. But when has a country sought to dictate the terms of peace negotiations to the victor? The answer is that the Arabs are not yet interested in a peace, and they consider themselves to be the ultimate victors. In defeat, they yet feel it necessary to act as if they were going to have the last word. For this reason, the Arabs have always been interested in a cease-fire, whatever it may be called, not in a definitive peace. A cease-fire implies that a battle has been lost; a peace might imply that a war has been lost. The language which Arabs use to convey their intent should not deceive us. Its form is psychological, but its content is political. It would be "humiliating," we hear interminably, to negotiate with Israel while Arab land is still occupied by the Israeli army. If the Arabs have to be spared all humiliation, it would be necessary to undo far more than the 1967 war; that kind of psychological therapy would go right back to the equally disastrous and humiliating 1948 war. Among themselves the Arabs consider the very existence of Israel to be their real "humiliation"; the surrender of the post-1967 occupied territories in advance of negotiation would only be a start toward relieving Arab humiliation on the installment plan. To negotiate on the basis of only one side's psychological propensity is obviously an absurd and futile exercise.

These tactics flow from the Arab assumption that "time works in our favor." It sometimes takes the form of boasting that the Arabs can afford to have a war every few years, and Israel cannot. Or that Israel can only fight a short war, and a long one is sure to favor the Arabs. The trouble with such theories is that, even if there is some truth in them, there is rarely a military problem, providing it is sufficiently clear, for which there is absolutely no answer. The French, for example, were convinced that the Germans could not break through the Maginot Line in World War II. Whether or not the French were right, the Germans disappointed them by going through Holland and Belgium, thereby outflanking the Maginot Line. The history of warfare is full of such "challenges and responses." The idea that the Arabs can have as many wars as they please may well be their mental Maginot Line. It gives the Israelis the moral and psychological advantage of always fighting what may be the last war, while the Arabs need not go to the bitter end because there is still another and better war in the offing. The most serious flaw in the theory, however, is something else. *It inevitably escalates the level of every war.* From 1948 to 1973, each Arab-Israeli war has increased in scope and costliness. The Israelis cannot tolerate an infinite series of wars; the Arabs have provoked every war at a greater disadvantage than the last one. The whole theory of time working inevitably and inexorably in favor of the Arabs is a formula for the most destructive war yet.

If the 1973 war is not the last Arab-Israeli conflict, the next one is sure to be worse. If Soviet-American-UN diplomacy can come up with nothing better than a retreaded version of all the gimmicks that failed in the past—the UNEF in another guise, the slippery UN resolution of November 22, 1967, indirect "negotiations," ambiguous formulas and face-saving evasions—the result will again be a cease-fire rather than a peace.

And if it is to be a cease-fire in all but name? Arab strategy in 1967 and 1973 has virtually made meaningless the terms "aggression" and "first strike." It is too much to expect any Israeli government and high command to take chances next time. The lesson of 1967 for Egypt was that Israel should not have the first strike, and the lesson of 1973 for Israel is that Egypt should not have the first strike. From now on, the finger will always be on the trigger. Let us pray that the lesson for both sides is that they must reconcile themselves to each other's existence, to the realities that have been brought about by a unique and singular set of circumstances, to the realization that the entire fabric of Arab-Israeli history cannot be unraveled.

Commentary, December 1973

2

The Road to Geneva

In one way or another, every phase of the Arab-Israeli conflict has been linked with the United Nations. The current Geneva conference is but the latest in this tradition—with a difference. In the past, the UN was Israel's benefactor and the Arabs' affliction. Now the sides have been reversed. The Israelis have come to distrust the UN so much that they grudgingly agreed to give it a minimal role at Geneva; the Arabs are so fond of the UN that they wanted its role to be maximal.

For a state with Israel's unique background, the change has been peculiarly painful and damaging. It was the General Assembly's resolution of November 29, 1947, providing for an Arab and Jewish state in Palestine, that opened the way for the formal establishment of the state of Israel on May 14, 1948. After five Arab armies invaded Palestine and tried to strangle the new state at birth, a UN mediator, Dr. Ralph Bunche, helped to bring about the armistice agreements of 1949. In these first years, the Security Council tried repeatedly to restrain the Arabs. Egypt closed the Suez Canal to Israeli shipping in 1949 on the ground that, despite the armistice, it considered itself to be in a state of "belligerency" vis-à-vis Israel. Two years later, the Council called on Egypt to put an end to this restriction of the canal and held that it was "unreasonable" for Egypt to behave as if it were still an active belligerent. In 1954, when Israel protested against Egypt's blockade of the port of Eilat, Israel's only outlet to the Red Sea and the East, the Security Council upheld Israel, only to run into a Soviet veto. Though the UN did not open the Suez Canal for Israel or lift the blockade of Eilat—Israel never achieved the first and obtained the second in 1956—at least the UN did what it could. It passed resolutions, which the Arab nations ignored or defied.

Today the UN is Israel's affliction and the Arabs' benefactor. The Soviet veto for the Arabs has given way to the U.S. veto for the Israelis. The change that has taken place in the UN accounts for much of this change in Israel's position. The growth in UN membership from 51 to 135, together with the increasing prevalence of bloc voting, has altered the UN so much that its founding fathers would hardly recognize it. Where Israel is concerned, the bloc set-up works almost automatically against it. The Arabs start with their own eighteen votes. They are sure to pick up eight more from the non-Arab Muslim countries. Then come the twelve inevitable votes from the Communist countries. Twenty-six African nations, which do not now have diplomatic ties with Israel, unwaveringly back the Arabs as part of their dues in the Afro-Asian bloc, and they carry most of the other African nations along with them. About a dozen other "nonaligned" nations, such as India and Yugoslavia (for whom nonalignment has come to mean nonalignment with only one side), make no effort to hide their pro-Arab commitment. In Western Europe, France and Spain are consistently hostile to Israel, and Britain does not lag far behind. If most or all of the Latin-American bloc, as part of its lip service to the "Third World," goes along, as it usually does, the Arabs can count on at least two-thirds of the General Assembly on almost any issue that lines them up against Israel.

At the time of the October 1973 war, the Security Council was equally one-sided. Of the five permanent members, Communist China and Soviet Russia were so hostile that they did not have diplomatic relations with Israel. The competition between them took the form of seeing which one could be more pro-Arab than the Arabs. Of the remaining three permanent members, the Arabs could count on France, if not Britain too. Three of the ten non-permanent members, Sudan, Yugoslavia, and Indonesia, had no diplomatic relations with Israel, and a fourth, India, virtually belonged in the same category. The 1974–75 Security Council is even worse from Israel's point of view. Of the five non-permanent members whose terms expired at the end of 1973, only two had no diplomatic relations with Israel; of the five that replaced them, four (Byelorussia, Cameroon, Iraq, and Mauritania) have no diplomatic relations with Israel. The Israeli diplomat who remarked that Arabs could get a majority in the UN for a resolution declaring that the earth is flat was exaggerating only a little.

In a previous article,[1] I referred harshly to the UN's role in the

October 1973 war. The trouble with referring to the UN as a single entity is that the organization does not live a life of its own. The UN may be international in form, but it is national in content; it is no more than the member states, and especially the permanent members of the Security Council, choose to make it. Whatever it was intended to be, it has become little more than an international forum in which member states ruthlessly pursue their national interests according to certain rules or principles which they recognize, ignore, or violate as they see fit. The UN is not a "supranational" government with any power of its own; it is not the "conscience of mankind," dispensing a higher law equally to all. Whenever Israel is concerned, a disturbing pattern of behavior has developed. It should disturb the most those who wish the UN the best.

II

The pattern emerged clearly in 1967.

When Egypt began to mass troops in the Sinai region bordering Israel on May 14, and especially when Egypt demanded the withdrawal of the United Nations Emergency Force (UNEF) on May 16, and even more so when Egypt closed the Straits of Tiran and blockaded the Israeli port of Eilat on May 22, a crisis was clearly on its way. What happened in the UN?

On May 23, Canada and Denmark requested an immediate meeting of the Security Council to deal with the Middle East crisis. On May 24, the Soviet representative, Nikolai T. Fedorenko, prevented the Council from even taking up the subject. He accused the Western powers of "artificially heating up the atmosphere" and insistently pooh-poohed the seriousness of the situation.[2] As late as May 29, Fedorenko accused the U.S. representative, Ambassador Arthur J. Goldberg, of uselessly engaging in "histrionics of all kinds."[3] Until war broke out on June 5, the Soviet representative sought by one means or another to prevent serious discussion of the issue in the Security Council.

While the Soviet representative was running diplomatic interference, the Egyptian representative, Ambassador Mohammad Awad el-Kony, made head-on verbal attacks on Israel to justify Egypt's actions. He did not deny that they were acts of war, especially in the case of the blockade of Eilat. Nor were the Soviets in a good position to justify the blockade, because that would have set a precedent for the unilateral closure of the Dardanelles by Turkey, blockading the Soviet ports in the Black Sea. Ambassador el-Kony boldly defended Egypt's action on the ground that "a state of overt war" had existed and continued to exist between the Arabs and Israelis.[4] It is a mistake, then, to think that the Egyptians did not knowingly commit acts of war before June 5. A blockade of an international waterway, such as the Gulf of Aqaba, was an act of war—and the Egyptians did not try to hide that fact as long as they were confident of victory.

Thus, at least two things took place in the Security Council before the 1967 war. First, the Soviets immobilized the Council in the period of aggressive Egyptian actions. Second, a double-bookkeeping system operated as soon as the Egyptians were thrown on the defensive.

The second point is particularly striking because the charge of "Israeli aggression" came to have such importance for the Egyptians. The Egyptian rationale for blockading Eilat on May 22 was equally a rationale for the Israeli attack on June 5. If the one was a justified act of war because a state of war already existed, the other was no more than a justifiable response. So long as the Egyptians thought that they were sure to win the war, they wanted the world to know that they had started it. If the Egyptians had not miscalculated and had won the war, they would have dated it from May 14 or at latest May 22, not June 5.

But as soon as their plans misfired, and the war was lost in six days, the Arabs filled the air with cries of "Israeli aggression." Forgotten was Ambassador el-Kony's proud boast that a "state of war" had always existed between Israel and the Arab states and that it gave Egypt the "legitimate right" to blockade the Straits of Tiran, an admittedly aggressive act. Now the Arabs were innocent victims of an unprovoked Israeli aggression which had broken the peace and harmony of the Middle East. In this way a double standard was smuggled into the Middle East conflict and has plagued it ever since.

III

After the 1967 war broke out on June 5, neither the Arabs nor the Israelis asked the Security Council to intervene. The Arabs were at first too confident of victory. As for the Israelis, they were determined to push back the 80,000 or so heavily armed Egyptian troops on their Sinai border and to reopen free passage of the Straits of Tiran. The Security Council met on June 5 without result. The legal position was obviously double-edged. As a fair-minded account by the former Indian ambassador to the UN, Arthur Lall, put it, the UN charter outlaws "not only the use of force or aggression but the threat of force." On the latter count,

Egypt had made threats of force repeatedly in the previous days. When did hostilities begin? When the Gulf of Aqaba was blockaded by Egypt or when Israel responded to it? Only the Soviet Union demanded unconditional condemnation of Israeli "aggression,"· and it was supported by no more than two members, all the way by Bulgaria, less forcefully by Mali. On the second day of the war, June 6, the Egyptians knew that they were in trouble. "Late that afternoon," Lall relates, "the Egyptians informed the Soviet Union that they would accept a cease-fire unless they received immediate military assistance. It was clear, however, that such assistance could not be given."[5]

So the Arabs shopped around for a quick cease-fire to save them from further military disaster. A resolution limited to calling for an immediate cease-fire was unanimously voted on the early evening of June 6. But the fighting raged on after the Council's belated awakening to the seriousness of the situation. Still another Soviet-sponsored cease-fire resolution, this one with a specific time limit, was unanimously adopted on June 7. With an Arab military collapse approaching, the Arabs and their Communist allies had changed their attitude toward UN intervention. For at least three weeks before, and for thirty-two hours after the fighting started, they had blocked every effort to bring the issue before the Security Council. Now, suddenly, Security Council resolutions were flaunted as if they had the force of absolute, peremptory, self-enforcing law. For years, the Security Council had passed resolutions obnoxious to the Arabs without the slightest effect on their behavior. This time it was different. The vaguest call of the Security Council for a cease-fire was touted as if it had come from on high.

Another innovation became a bad habit in the Security Council. As Arthur Lall has noted, "condemnation" has no place in the tasks allotted to the Council in the UN charter. "Unfortunately," he observed reproachfully, "it has become a tendency of certain organs of the United Nations to overlook the charter injunctions relating to conciliation and the harmonizing of the actions of nations, and to substitute for these approaches that of condemnation. It may, of course, be a matter of opinion as to whether condemnation is a more effective approach toward achieving settlements than the approach of skillful urgings, even demands, and quiet pressures. However, the essential point is that the charter rejects the former approach in favor of the latter, and whatever individual governments may say or do in their bilateral dealings, in the organs of the United Nations they should adhere to the charter's approaches."[6]

The chief specialist in these "condemnations"—always, of course, against Israel—was the Soviet Union. While the Egyptians were satisfied for the moment to get no more than a cease-fire, the Soviet representative Fedorenko, held out for an Israeli withdrawal from Arab territory; the "main task," he said, was to condemn Israel as "the aggressor."[7] But Fedorenko failed to get Israel condemned as the "aggressor" or ordered to withdraw its forces. As matters stood when the Security Council adjourned on June 14, only a cease-fire had been agreed on by all parties. As Lall noted sadly: "The Council had missed its most constructive opportunities when it had failed to act in May, and thereafter it had never really caught up with the flow of events in the region."[8] And if it failed to act in May, as he makes clear, the Soviet Union was primarily responsible.

But this was only the beginning of the diplomatic battle that followed the military struggle.

IV

We have now come to the magic number: 242.

After several futile attempts to reach an agreement acceptable to all sides in the dispute, the Security Council met again in November 1967. It did not seem like a propitious moment. The Arab states had come together at Khartoum two months earlier and had arrived at an intransigent formula vis-à-vis Israel: no peace, no recognition, no negotiations. Nevertheless, the mood in the Security Council favored one more big try to reach a settlement.

The Arab states, in line with the Khartoum formula, were merely interested in getting Israel out of the occupied territories. For Israel, the occupation of the territories won in June was still a somewhat unreal, fortuitous experience. Most Israelis were as yet less interested in keeping all or some of the territories than in using them to get the Arabs to recognize the state of Israel within "secure borders." All outside efforts at the November meeting were bent on incorporating and reconciling these two main Arab and Israeli aims.

After a number of false starts by the Afro-Asian bloc, the Soviet Union, and the United States, the winner was—Resolution 242. The chief impresario was the British member, Lord Caradon, who gave a classical exhibition of diplomatic unflappability. The diplomatic struggle accompanying the military battle since 1967 has been based on this resolution. The present Geneva conference was set in motion by Resolution 338 of October 22, 1973, which in turn implements Resolution 242. Thus everything that has happened in the Arab-Israeli conflict in the past six years goes back in one way or another to Resolution 242. How it was concocted and why it was adopted constitute one of the most curious operations in recent diplomatic history.

Caradon's stratagem was to give something to everyone, and everything to no one—in such a way that no one knew whether he had anything.

In the preamble, Caradon managed to write a paragraph which began with something for the Arabs and ended with something for Israel. The first portion emphasized "the inadmissibility of the acquisition of territory by war" and the second "the need to work for a just and lasting peace in which every State in the area can live in security." Egypt, which had acquired the Gaza territory (that had not been Egyptian) and Jordan, which had acquired the territory on the West Bank of the Jordan River and the Old City of Jerusalem (that had not been Jordanian) by war in 1948, blithely hailed the principle of the "inadmissibility of the acquisition of territory by war" because, in their interpretation, it was aimed solely at Israel. As for the Soviet Union, it had acquired through World War II 272,500 square miles of territory, with a population two-and-a-half times as large as Jordan, Lebanon, Syria, and Iraq combined, but was not inhibited from voting for this lofty principle for someone else.[9] Israel enjoyed reading the words "a just and lasting peace" and "security," which had evaded it for so long.

But preambles are merely the appetizers of UN resolutions. The main courses come in the operative paragraphs. The Egyptians wanted most the withdrawal of Israeli armed forces from Arab territory. So Caradon gave them the first operative paragraph, which provided for the

> Withdrawal of Israel armed forces from territories occupied in the recent conflict.

This combination of words was not as clear and simple as it may seem. For a previous Soviet resolution had stipulated that Israel "should immediately and unconditionally withdraw all its forces from the territory of those States [United Arab Republic, Syria, and Jordan] to positions behind the armistice demarcation lines [i.e., before June 5, 1967]." And another Latin-American draft resolution had urgently requested Israel "to withdraw all its forces from all the territories occupied by it as a result of the recent conflict."

Caradon's formula omitted four key words: "immediately," "unconditionally," "all," and "the." By omitting "immediately" and "unconditionally" in the Soviet text, it implied that the withdrawal might not be immediate or unconditional. By omitting the first "all," before the mention of Israeli "forces," it implied that not all of them might be withdrawn—or, as in the previous case, at least left the question open. But the crucial excision was made in the reference to "the territory," in the Russian text, or to "all the territories," in the Latin-American text. By removing "the," and even more so, "all the" before the word "territories" in his final text, Caradon deliberately left open the possibility that the Israeli withdrawal might be partial rather than complete. The Israelis could accept it because it might be partial; the Arabs could vote for it, albeit less enthusiastically, because it might be complete. In short, what Resolution 242 did not say was fully as important as what it did say.

To make matters even more complicated and dubious, the equally authoritative French version of Resolution 242, owing to the exigencies of the French language, translated "territories occupied" as *"des territoires occupés,"* making it possible for an interpretation to include the word "the" before territories. Thus, in effect, the English version seemed to favor the Israelis, the French version the Arabs.

The Israelis, of course, wanted recognition of their state within secure borders. So Caradon gave them the second operative paragraph:

> Termination of all claims or states of belligerency and respect for and acknowledgment of the sovereignty, territorial integrity, and political independence of every State in the area and their right to live in peace within secure and recognized boundaries free from threats or acts of force.

This paragraph also bears close scrutiny. It will be noticed that the state which was in contention, Israel, was not mentioned by name as deserving respect for its "sovereignty, territorial integrity, and political independence." Did or did not the reference to "every State" include Israel? It might or it might not, depending on whether Israel was accepted as a valid, legitimate state. True, Israel was a member in good standing of the United Nations. On the other hand, the Arab states had ostentatiously refused to recognize Israel's rightful statehood. Israel in fact wanted to be mentioned by name. But Caradon's resolution bypassed the issue by using the much more general formulation, giving the Arabs the possibility of denying Israel the right to be accepted in their minds as a "State in the area."

However, assuming that Israel was such a state—and for the United Nations as such, its status was unquestionable—the most important words in the resolution were the "right to live in peace within secure and recognized boundaries." Without the reference to such boundaries Israel would probably not have accepted this resolution. For two things were inextricably meshed. One was the abstract acceptance of the state of Israel. But what and where was this state? What boundaries did it have? Without a clear and final delineation of its boundaries, Israel's acceptance as a state could mean anything or nothing. By challenging its boundaries concretely, the Arabs could make a mockery of accepting the state of Israel abstractly. As we shall see, the problem of "boundaries" is one of the most vexed and venomous of all aspects of the Arab-Israeli conflict. Resolution 242 demanded its solution without in the least resolving it.

Resolution 242 included three more major operative paragraphs:

Guaranteed "freedom of navigation through international waterways in the area." This stipulation was supposed to reopen the Straits of Tiran and the Gulf of Aqaba to Israeli shipping.

"A just settlement of the refugee problem." Each side, of course, wanted such a settlement, but whether they could agree on what was "just," which the resolution did not define, was something else.

And the designation by the Secretary-General of the UN of a "Special Representative to proceed to the Middle East to establish and maintain contacts with the States concerned in order to promote agreement and assist efforts to achieve a peaceful and accepted settlement in accordance with the provisions and principles in this resolution." On this provision hinged all the others. Everyone knew that Resolution 242 was merely the beginning of a long and tortuous process. This process was made all the more difficult by the Arab refusal to negotiate directly with Israel. As in 1949, the UN resorted to an intermediary to get the process going indirectly.

Alas, we are not yet finished with Resolution 242. Something more was needed before the diplomatic tapestry could be woven.

First, there apparently were private, behind-the-scenes, unwritten understandings. The most important of these related to the most hotly disputed clause about the "withdrawal of Israel armed forces from territories occupied in the recent conflict." What did the omission of "all" and "the" before "territories" mean? An Arab delegate later revealed that the Arab delegations had been privately given the explanation that the omission of these words "really related to the possibility of minor and mutually agreed rectifications of the frontier."[10] He complained that Israel subsequently wanted more "substantial changes" than the

Arabs had been led to expect. There was, evidently, some kind of private understanding about some frontier changes, even if opinions might differ about which were minor or major.

On the other hand, the Egyptian delegate, Mohammad Hassan el-Zayyat, claimed that Lord Caradon had privately told the then Egyptian Foreign Minister, Mahmoud Riad, that "the words 'territories occupied' meant all territories occupied." El-Zayyat also claimed that the U.S. delegate, Arthur J. Goldberg, had given a private assurance that "not an inch of Egyptian territory is going to be touched."[11] Both Caradon and Goldberg have gone on record denying that Resolution 242 meant any such thing.[12] In the fall of 1968, according to former Under-Secretary of State, Eugene V. Rostow, who was then in charge of the Arab-Israeli conflict at the State Department, Soviet ambassadors both in Washington and at the UN indicated that they could agree to "insubstantial" modifications of the pre-1967 borders as part of a "package deal." The next day, however, they reversed themselves.[13]

The former Indian ambassador, Arthur Lall, who was in a good position to know, tells us what went on behind the scenes between the Soviets and Arabs before the resolution was voted on. The Arab delegates came to the Soviet representative, V. V. Kuznetsov, to complain about the British version. "They insisted that the wording read either that Israeli forces would be withdrawn from 'all the territories,' instead of 'territories' occupied by Israel, or that Israel would 'withdraw to the positions of 4 June 1967.' In addition, the Arabs were unwilling to accept the phrase 'recognized boundaries' also occurring in the first operative paragraph." But the Arabs changed their minds the next day because they "concluded that it was better to get a resolution backed by all fifteen votes in the Council than to insist on a resolution which might not be adopted or might obtain the bare minimum of nine votes." They also tried to prevail on Caradon to substitute "all the territories" for "territories" in the crucial clause on Israeli withdrawal. He soothingly told them that his draft represented "a delicate balance" which could not be upset.[14]

It is obviously not safe to rely on anything but the actual words in the resolution. Yet some private give-and-take undoubtedly played a part in getting agreement on the resolution.

Of one all-important aspect of the resolution there can be no doubt. It was a "package deal."

If it had not been such a deal, the Arabs could have claimed—as they proceeded to claim anyway—that it was necessary or possible to put into effect the first operative paragraph on Israeli withdrawal, in which they were primarily interested, before or without putting into effect the other operative paragraphs in which the Israelis were primarily interested. As a matter of fact, the order in which the various provisions were listed had nothing to do with priority or preeminence. The resolution was to be taken as a whole or not at all.

This point was clearly made by Lord Caradon at the time. He called the resolution "a balanced whole."[15] What he meant by this was later spelled out by him and other authoritative British officials who, after all, knew best what they had put together. In an interview on February 10, 1973, Caradon gave this explanation: "Withdrawal should take place to secure and recognized boundaries, and these words were carefully chosen: they have to be secure, and they have to be recognized. They will not be secure unless they are recognized." Other British explications have emphasized the term "concurrently" to stress how the parts of Resolution 242 were linked together. The Secretary of State for Foreign and Commonwealth Affairs, Michael Stewart, stated in the House of Commons on November 17, 1969: "The resolution speaks of secure and recognized boundaries. Those words must be read concurrently with the statement on withdrawal."[16] A British member of the Security Council, K. D. Jamieson, reiterated as late as June 11, 1973, that "we for our part have always considered that there is a close interconnection between all the elements of the settlement envisaged in resolution 242 (1967)."[17] Assistant Secretary of State Joseph Sisco, in charge of Middle East affairs, has stated: "The Security Council did not call for unconditional Israeli withdrawal to the armistice lines [of 1949] as had been the case at the time of the 1956 war in Sinai. Rather, it called for 'withdrawal . . . from territories occupied' in the 1967 war as part of a package settlement in which the parties would agree to respect each other's right to live in peace within secure and recognized boundaries."[18]

It should be clear by now what Resolution 242 did and did not say.

Ah, but no—nothing about Resolution 242 was—or is—that easy.

When the members of the Security Council explained their votes on November 22, 1967, the disparity between their explanations was so great that one might have imagined that they were talking about different things. Although he did not rule out "mutual territorial adjustments," the Indian member, Gopalaswami Parthasarathi, maintained: "It is our understanding that the draft resolution, if approved by the Council, will commit it to the application of the principle of total withdrawal of Israeli forces from all the territories—I repeat, all the territories—occupied by Israel as a result of the conflict which began on 5 June, 1967." To which Lord Caradon coyly responded that only the resolution itself was binding but that "all of us, no doubt, have our own views and interpretations and understandings." Foreign Minister Abba Eban of Israel cautioned: "The representative of India has now sought to interpret the resolution in the image of his own wishes. For us, the resolution says what it says. It does not say that which it has specifically and consciously avoided saying." But this advice did not stop the Soviet member, Kuznetsov, from declaring that "we voted for the United Kingdom draft resolution, as interpreted by the representative of India, whose views we share." Heedless of everything that had been said by the United Kingdom delegate, he continued, "We understand the decision to mean the withdrawal of Israel forces from all, and we repeat all, territories belonging to Arab States and seized by Israel following its attack on those States on 5 June 1967." The Bulgarian member, Milko Tarabanov, echoed Kuznetsov. The Egyptian representative, Mahmoud Riad, insisted that the "full withdrawal of Israel forces from all territories they have occupied as a result of their aggression on 5 June" was the first step to be taken and that other steps could then follow. The Jordanian representative, Abdul Monem Rifa'i, called "the immediate and complete withdrawal"—neither of these qualifiers was in the resolution—the "essential step." The U.S. member, Arthur Goldberg, gently chided: "The voting, of course, has taken place not on the individual views and policies of various members, but on the draft resolution. I, and I assume other members of the Council, voted for the draft resolution and not for each and every speech that has been made." But he then slightly opened the door to the possibility of multiple interpretations: "I hastily add that I have voted for my own speech, and I assume others have done likewise with respect to their speeches." Finally, the Israeli representative, Abba Eban, apparently aiming at the French version, informed the Council that he was communicating "nothing except the original English text of the draft resolution" to his government.[19]

From all this one might gather that a private understanding had been reached to permit members of the Security Council to vote for the resolution unanimously but to interpret it individually. This diplomatic technique for obtaining unanimity was such that it was sure to breed future confusion and contradiction. Nevertheless, this arrangement was probably the only course if unanimity was desirable or necessary to make any progress at all.

When the Security Council met in June 1973, however, arbitrary reinterpretations of Resolution 242 came from both sides. The Soviet member, Y. A. Malik, proclaimed that a complete Israeli withdrawal was "a primary prerequisite for peace in the Middle East" and "the key question of a Middle East settlement."[20] On the other hand, the Israeli representative, Yosef Tekoah, held that "the question of secure and recognized boundaries" was "the central problem."[21] Both sought shelter under Resolution 242, which had clearly and deliberately refrained from making withdrawal or boundaries "primary," "the key," or "central." My impression is that by sheer repetition the Arabs and Soviets have come out ahead in this propaganda argument. Most people who read or think about Resolution 242 probably have the impression that it exclusively or mainly "orders" Israel to withdraw completely from the occupied territories.

And yet, all diplomatic activity since 1967 to settle the Arab-Israeli conflict has been based on the shifting sands of this resolution.[22]

V

Whatever Resolution 242 said or did not say, its fate depended on what the UN's Special Representative did or did not do. As representative, the Secretary-General appointed the Swedish ambassador to Moscow, Gunnar Jarring, who set up his headquarters in Cyprus.

The failure of the Jarring mission was one of the preconditions of the 1973 war. Why it failed is still critical for a full understanding of the deepest, most irreconcilable issues underlying the entire Arab-Israeli conflict.

The divergent interpretations of Resolution 242 were quick to emerge. Israel advised Jarring that the best way "to promote agreement" as provided for in the resolution was through direct negotiations, the first step of which should be an Israeli-Egyptian meeting to discuss an "agenda for peace." Egypt—and Jordan too—replied that such discussion was out of the question so long as Israeli armed forces had not withdrawn from the occupied territories. The essential "ambiguity" built into Resolution 242 began to torment Jarring by the end of 1967.

The next gambit took the form of "indirect negotiations." After some attempt to make "indirect negotiations" lead to "direct negotiations," Israel accepted the indirect approach without conditions. But again the fundamental differences, especially the dispute over complete Israeli withdrawal, emphasized the hopelessness of Jarring's task. There is no need here to go into all the ingenious efforts made by Jarring to get around the main stumbling blocks. By the end of 1970, after three years of frustration and disenchantment with all sides, he seemed to have reached the end of the road.

Early in 1971, Jarring decided to make one final, desperate effort. What had thwarted him, he thought, was the question of priorities. The Egyptians wanted to get a commitment on complete Israeli withdrawal before they did anything else, and the Israelis wanted to be sure of their security before they gave up anything. Jarring decided that the way to break the deadlock was to approach both sides to make "parallel and simultaneous" commitments. On February 8, 1971, Jarring sent proposals to this effect to Israel and Egypt. From Israel, in the main, he asked for a commitment to withdraw its forces from the occupied territories, and from Egypt he essentially wanted "respect for and acknowledgment of each other's right to live in peace with secure and recognized boundaries." This time, Jarring had most trouble with Israel. On the most vital point of withdrawal, the Israeli reply of February 26, 1971, was willing to accept only the following: "Withdrawal of Israel's armed forces from the Israel-United Arab Republic cease-fire line to the secure, recognized, and agreed boundaries to be established in the peace agreement. Israel will not withdraw to the pre-5 June 1967 lines."[23]

What was the trouble? Israel made known its objection that Jarring had overstepped the bounds of his authority as set forth in Resolution 242. In it, the special representative had been enjoined "to promote agreement and assist efforts" of the states themselves to reach a peaceful settlement. Jarring, however, specified that Israel was to withdraw to "the former international boundary between Egypt and the British Mandate of Palestine." The extent of the withdrawal had been deliberately left open in the resolution; Jarring had taken it on himself to spell it out. This was not a merely technical or formal deviation; for Israel, it went to the heart of the matter. Israel had agreed to the resolution in order to negotiate the precise boundaries with Egypt. Now Jarring had done all the "negotiating" by himself and had confronted Israel with a *fait accompli*.

Neither side was totally satisfied with the map of withdrawal as drawn by Jarring. Egypt's reply demanded Israeli withdrawal from the Gaza Strip as well as from Sinai, even though the former had not been Egyptian territory during the British Mandate of Palestine. But the Israeli problem in this respect was probably more serious. Jarring's plan entailed only the Israeli-Egyptian border. Even there, Israel was supposed to get "respect" and "acknowledgment"—at most a promissory note that might be exceedingly difficult to collect on—in return for giving Egypt an immediate commitment on a definite delineation of the Israeli withdrawal. This exchange, from the Israeli point of view, was flagrantly one-sided. Israel had agreed in Resolution 242 to some form of withdrawal in return for "secure and recognized boundaries" not on one side but on all sides. Jarring, however, could not deliver Jordan at the same time as Egypt, and Syria was out of the question altogether—Syria had never even accepted Resolution 242. If Israel was truly "to live in peace within secure and recognized boundaries free from threats or acts of force," as the resolution required, its existence could not be separated from its boundaries, and its boundaries could not be decided only on the Egyptian front.

Jarring no doubt had opted for the piecemeal approach because he could not bring off a "balanced whole." Whatever his motives, he had transmogrified Resolution 242 in such a way that his plan was far more acceptable to the Egyptians and their Soviet backers than to the Israelis. Jarring had jarred loose the "package deal" and had spilled the pieces on the floor, hoping to pick them up and put them together as in a jigsaw puzzle one at a time. Whether he would have succeeded is more than doubtful, but he was never given the chance.

By March 1971, Jarring's mission was virtually dead. Those who imagine that Israel lost its great opportunity to make peace by not accepting Jarring's plan in 1971 have not fully understood why it failed.

VI

In 1968, in the first months of Jarring's mission, the influential Egyptian editor, Muhammad Hassanein Heykal, put into words what he must have thought was a very witty idea:

> If somebody says, for example, let's assume that Israel would demand recognition of the former cease-fire lines as permanent and recognized boundaries, the answer would be the following: What could prevent us in such a situation from stating that according to our own conception, the secure and recognized boundaries are one Jewish synagogue in Tel Aviv and ten meters around it?[24]

If this were written about almost any other country, it might stir up a little amusement or, at worst, annoyance. In Tel Aviv, it can inspire real consternation. The reason is not that Israelis are so very different from other people. The cause is buried deep in Israel's peculiar history.

At this point, we must step back a quarter of a century in order to go forward to the present. History has haunted the Arab-Israeli conflict in every phase and at every step, and never more than from 1967 to the present.

The Jewish state envisaged in the original UN partition plan of 1947 was a minuscule geopolitical monstrosity. The plan divided Palestine into seven parts, three Jewish and three Arab, each virtually disjointed, plus Jerusalem, which was to be "internationalized." A condition of the partition was the economic union of the Jewish and Arab parts. The largest Jewish part consisted of the Negev, then a wasteland.

As if this were not enough, the UN plan also gave the Jewish state the "wrong" parts of Palestine. The Jewish parts were made up of those districts in which the Jews had been able to settle and own land, not where God had presumably put them in biblical times. "The nursery of the Jewish race and the Jewish religion," as Cecil Roth put it, had been the Kingdom of Judah, which the UN plan allotted to the Arabs. David was anointed King of Judah in Hebron—an Arab center in the UN plan and still so today. Tel Aviv was made up of little more than barren and swampy dunes at the beginning of the twentieth century, disconcertingly situated in ancient Philistine territory.

If the Arabs had permitted the 1947 partition plan to go through, even temporarily, it is doubtful whether Israel could have survived until the present. Despite misgivings and dissension, the Jews accepted the plan. Confident of their superior numbers and arms, the Arabs did not. The result of the war that followed in 1948 was the enlargement of the Jewish state by about one fourth. But the Jewish state was not the only one that benefited territorially from the war. Instead of going ahead with the projected new Arab state in Palestine, Egypt and Transjordan proceeded to divide the remaining territory among themselves. Egypt gobbled up the Gaza Strip, which it never made part of the state of Egypt but ruled through a military governor. The Emirate of Transjordan, as it was then called, refused to give up the West Bank of the Jordan River and the Old City of Jerusalem, despite the bitter opposition of the other Arab states, and soon changed its name to the Hashemite Kingdom of Jordan. All these territorial changes, according to the armistice agreements of 1949, were supposed to be provisional and temporary. Article XII of the Egyptian-Israeli General Armistice Agreement of February 24, 1949, for example, stated that the provisions "shall remain in force until a peaceful settlement between the parties is achieved." But such a peaceful settlement was never achieved because the Arab states would never agree to negotiate one with Israel.

So the armistice agreements of 1949, not the UN partition plan of 1947, became the *de facto* basis of Arab-Israeli relations. No one, and certainly not the Soviet Union, objected to this change. No one denounced Israel as an aggressor because it had turned back the armies of five Arab states and had forced them to sign armistice agreements. No one was scandalized because the Arabs were compelled to pay a penalty for provoking and losing a war. As a result, the armistice agreements of 1949 set a precedent for territorial changes brought about by wars provoked by the Arabs themselves—a precedent which the Arabs have insistently tried to revoke by provoking more wars.

Nevertheless, the armistice agreements of 1949 left a difficult and dubious legacy which is still the crux of the Arab-Israeli conflict. The trouble with those armistice agreements was that they were nothing more than—armistice agreements. From 1949 to 1967, the boundaries of Israel were not secure and were not recognized because they were not confirmed by a peace settlement. Indeed, since Egypt considered itself to be at war with Israel despite the armistice agreements and, the Egyptians even argued, by virtue of them, secure and recognized boundaries could not result from the armistice agreements of 1949 any more than they could derive from the cease-fire lines of 1967. Ironically, the claim to Palestinian territory by Egypt and Jordan is just as tenuous as they regard Israel's claim to be, since they are equally dependent on the armistice agreements of 1949 for any title to that land. By challenging Israel's boundaries, Egypt and Jordan logically call into question their own. Yet only Israel has been asked to justify being where it is.

History, then, has exerted a tormenting pull on both sides—on the Arabs to reduce Israel to an empty shell, on the Israelis to realize the Zionist dream of restoring the Jews to their ancient "homeland." This pressure could have been held back if both sides had been able to reach some kind of stable territorial settlement. If such a settlement had been based on the UN partition plan of 1947 or the armistice agreements of 1949, it would not have been fully satisfactory to either side. But at least they would have arrived at some fixed points in their relationship. By never going beyond the armistice agreements or cease-fire lines, everything always remained open, uncertain, unhinged. When Israel asks to be a secure and recognized state, it asks for secure and recognized boundaries. Or conversely, without secure and recognized boundaries,

Israel cannot be a secure and recognized state. Arabs and others are sometimes willing to pay lip service to Israel as a state but never to what boundaries that state has. This is the "dirty little secret" of the Arab-Israeli conflict.

The secret has been fairly well kept from the general public—except, of course, in Israel, which has almost been fixated by the problem of boundaries. The impression must still be widespread that the Arab leaders wish nothing more than Israeli withdrawal to the pre-June 5, 1967 boundaries and that all would be well if only the Israelis agreed.

This myth should not have outlived the session of the Security Council in June 1973. Unfortunately, few bother to go through the dreary pages of Security Council discussions, though they sometimes contain the most devastating revelations of what official policies really are.

The Security Council met on June 6, 1973, to consider the Middle East problem as a whole for the first time since November 1967. Almost six years after Resolution 242 had been unanimously adopted, the Arab states had come to the conclusion that it was too ambiguous for their purposes and that it needed modification in their favor in order to serve as a diplomatic bludgeon against Israel. They also had had time to harden their position on the resolution's critical reference to "secure and recognized boundaries."

The Egyptian press had already foreshadowed that position, which went far beyond any possible interpretation of Resolution 242. On February 25, 1971, Heykal had written in *al-Ahram*:

> There are only two specific Arab goals at present: elimination of the consequences of the 1967 aggression through Israel's withdrawal from all the lands it occupied that year, and elimination of the consequences of the 1948 aggression through the eradication of Israel.
> The second goal is not, in fact, specific but abstract, and some of us make the mistake of starting with the second step instead of the first. On the basis of the conditions I have mentioned, it is possible to believe in the possibility of attaining the first goal. As for the second goal, we should learn from the enemy to move step by step.

So, according to this highly authoritative spokesman and confidant of Egypt's top leaders, the goal in Resolution 242 was only the first step. If that were achieved, the second goal would be to go back to 1948 when Israel was established as a state.

An even more authoritative Egyptian spokesman and top leader, President Anwar el-Sadat, made another significant allusion to the first and second steps on February 17, 1972:

> Nor do we have the right to compel the Palestinian people to accept the Security Council resolution because the land is their land, both those areas occupied in 1948 and the remainder of Palestine occupied after 1967 (*al-Ahram*, February 18, 1972).

From this, the Egyptians were clearly thinking far beyond Resolution 242, which seemingly concerned only the post-1967 occupied areas. In the background, but already emerging publicly, was another resolve to undo the 1948 war in the name of the "Palestinian people."

All this came out openly in the Security Council in June 1973. At the very first meeting on June 6, the Egyptian representative, el-Zayyat, called on the Council to:

> Resolve that all the rights and aspirations of the Palestinian nation be respected, including their right to live in peace within secure and recognized boundaries in their homeland of Palestine as it was before the partition, as it was under the Mandate.[25]

Now the familiar terms, "homeland" and "secure and recognized boundaries," were made to apply to the "Palestinian nation" rather than to Israel. And the homeland of the "Palestinian nation" was so defined —"before the partition, as it was under the [British] Mandate"—that it antedated even the UN plan of 1947, when the state of Israel had not yet been established.

On June 11, the Sudanese representative, Khalid, also brought up 1947 in a somewhat more veiled form:

> The truth of the matter is that the June [1967] war is a consequence of the unresolved crisis since Israel burgeoned its way into a State in 1947 [*sic*]. Any reference to the Armistice Agreement vexes Israel, because going back twenty-five years helps clear our thinking, though it does not necessarily mean that we are unaware of the facts created by war and current international diplomacy. The present cannot be divorced from the past. It is one piece with it. It is the prelude of the future.[26]

On the same day, another Egyptian representative, Abdel Meguid, again opened up the question of boundaries in this provocative fashion:

> The logic of the representative of Israel surprises us, to say the least. He speaks about "safe and recognized boundaries" for Israel. Of what boundaries is he talking: those of 1947, 1948, 1949, 1956, or 1967? When

certain States recognized the State of Israel they recognized it with boundaries that were defined in the partition plan—in other words, within a
territory that had been allocated to it by a United Nations resolution, and
nothing more.[27]

On June 13, the Egyptian, el-Zayyat, took the position that Egypt
gave the Palestinians the right to decide the fate of Israel, again going
back to 1947:

It is up to them [the Palestinians], if and when they desire, to put the
territorial and political boundaries between them and the Jewish State—
if and when they desire to accept the partition resolution of 1947, which
they deem to be unjust.[28]

This strategy of "two stages"—one Egyptian, the other Palestinian—
is now so deeply rooted in Egyptian thinking[28a] that it was expressed
by Heykal in *al-Ahram* on October 19, 1973, just before the present
cease-fire agreement:

The issue at present is not connected with the liberation of the Arab territories occupied after June 5, 1967, but concerns the Israeli future in
a deeper sense and in the long run—even if this is not obvious right now.
The issue is as follows: If the Arabs would be capable of liberating the
territories occupied after June 5, 1967, by armed force, then what is there
to prevent them in the next stage from liberating Palestine itself by armed
force?

This Egyptian line clearly threatens the state of Jordan as well as the
state of Israel. King Hussein of Jordan knew what he was doing at the
end of November 1973 when he refused to attend the Arab leaders'
"summit meeting" in Algiers which issued a declaration that, among
other things, called for "Re-establishment of the full national rights for
the Palestinian people." This formula could only mean the dismember-
ment of Jordan by means of a new Palestinian state in the West Bank,
or the overthrow of the Hashemite regime and takeover of all Jordan by
the Palestinians. This threat to the present state of Jordan logically
flowed from the strategy of returning to the boundaries of 1947—if at
all—in the case of Israel. By going so far back, the other Arab states
undercut all claim of Jordan to the West Bank, which dated only from
the military invasion of 1948. Hussein now has far more to fear from
his Arab neighbors than from Israel, though he has been living dangerously by playing the game of his would-be executioners.

In effect, the Arabs had fully worked out their political and military strategy by the time they came to the Security Council in June 1973. It was, basically, a strategy of "stages." The reason they could not live with Resolution 242 as a "package deal" was that it precluded a strategy of stages. When they could not get what they wanted out of 242, they went back to the Security Council in 1973 to get something stronger. In July, they almost got what they wanted.

The last diplomatic struggle in the UN before the outbreak of war took place over a draft resolution known as document S/10974, submitted by eight co-sponsors (Guinea, India, Indonesia, Kenya, Panama, Peru, Sudan, and Yugoslavia) on July 24. The vote two days later showed how much had changed in the UN since November 1967.

S/10974 changed Resolution 242 in at least three basic respects. It substituted "the territories" for "territories" in the second operative paragraph dealing with Israeli withdrawal. It substituted "the legitimate interests of the Palestinian people," the new code term, for what had been "a just settlement of the refugee problem." And it substituted a piecemeal approach for the "package deal," which had been the essence of Resolution 242.

The vote on S/10974 was 13 to 1 (with China not voting). Since the one vote was cast by the United States, the draft resolution was vetoed. Only the Australian and British members expressed some discomfort in going along with the majority.

As has now been admitted, Egypt was already actively preparing for its attack when this vote was taken. If the diplomatic isolation of Israel was one of the preconditions of the attack, Egypt had succeeded in its purpose. Since all those who voted for S/10974 knew in advance that the United States was going to cast a veto, it also represented an advanced state of U.S. isolation in the UN.

This action was but a prelude to what happened in the UN after the war actually broke out.

VII

Before we see how the UN—or, more exactly, the members of the Security Council—dealt with the October 1973 war, let us try to reconstruct, as best we can, how the war came about.

There is one firm bit of evidence from an unimpeachable source, Major General Sa'ad ad-Din al-Shazli, the Egyptian Chief of Staff. He has disclosed that the planning of the war took nine to ten months before the outbreak of hostilities.[29] This would put the initiation of active Egyptian war preparations at the beginning of 1973.

A most circumstantial account has been given by the Middle East correspondent of *Le Monde*, Eric Rouleau. Long *persona grata* in Egypt, Rouleau has had unrivaled Arab sources, though, of course, we cannot be sure of every detail in the story that he has put together.

Rouleau draws particular attention to one occurrence, unnoticed at the time. In July 1972, about 20,000 Soviet advisers and technicians had been expelled from Egypt. But, Rouleau informs us, an important Soviet military mission came back to Egypt on February 1, 1973. The arrival of the new Soviet military mission would coincide with the date of Egypt's initial war preparations given by General al-Shazli.

The actual date for the outbreak of hostilities, according to Rouleau, was probably fixed in July or August 1973. In any case, Sadat is said to have referred to the "imminence" of war on several occasions in August 1973. No one, it seems, took him seriously. The first operational military measures, such as moving forward Egyptian infantry forces, were taken on September 3. Sadat and Syrian President Assad discussed these military preparations in Cairo on September 10. U.S. intelligence sources allegedly learned on September 26 that Egyptian forces had been put on the alert. When the Americans, it is said, tried to warn the Israelis, the latter refused to be alarmed and interpreted the troop movements as "routine maneuvers." On October 3, Sadat and Assad informed the Soviet ambassadors in Cairo and Damascus that war was imminent. Soviet planes were immediately sent to evacuate the families of Soviet "advisers" in Egypt and Syria. U.S. diplomats allegedly interpreted the evacuation as evidence of another Soviet-Arab break. Until the morning of October 4, the exact timing of the Arab attack was a closely guarded secret, known only to four men, the presidents and war ministers of Egypt and Syria. At 2 PM on October 6, the attack was launched across the canal by 8,000 men and hundreds of tanks.[30]

An American version places the Egyptian decision "to resume war with Israel" in March 1973, and the final operational decision to invade the Sinai "sometime in early August," the operation itself being set for "sometime in October." The March decision, according to this account, came because Sadat was disappointed with the result of the mission to Washington the month before by his foreign-policy adviser, Hafez Ismail. After March 1973, Sadat was mainly bent on lining up the support of other Arab states and camouflaging his war preparations.[31]

A reliable Israeli source has reported that the Israeli Chief of Staff,

Lieutenant General David Elazar, doubted until the early morning hours of October 6 that war was imminent. A single item of intelligence from one source, not yet revealed publicly, caused the Israeli General Staff to change its evaluation of the situation. Soon after 4 AM that day, General Elazar proposed a preemptive air strike and asked permission to mobilize reserves. The first request was rejected, the second granted. A top state of alert was ordered at 11 AM, too late to save the limited Israeli forces at the canal and in the Golan Heights from being taken by almost absolute surprise.[32] As Prime Minister Golda Meir later put it: "What happened was a disaster. It is no secret, and no one intended, or intends, to keep it a secret. We misinterpreted the information we had."[33]

Still another version, in the *Sunday Times* (London), says that the order to prepare to reopen hostilities was given by President Sadat in November 1972. The actual planning, however, began the following February, which would coincide with the arrival of the Soviet military mission. By September 10, Egypt, Syria, and Jordan were lined up together militarily and diplomatically. Egyptian tanks began assembling the last week of September; Syrian tanks and heavy artillery moved to forward positions on October 1. Though these movements were being closely watched, Israeli—and influenced by it, U.S.—intelligence was not convinced that war was imminent until 4 AM on October 6 when, according to this account, "Israeli and American monitors picked up the unmistakable radio traffic patterns of final Arab preparations for war." When General Elazar proposed a preemptive air strike, Prime Minister Meir is supposed to have asked: "How many friends would we have left if we did that?" Two hours later, Mrs. Meir summoned the U.S. ambassador, Kenneth Keating, who, it is said, reinforced her decision against the preemptive strike by warning her, in effect, that "if Israel struck first, world opinion would make it hard for America to supply Israel with war material."

This British version also purports to give the inside story of a bitter U.S.-British falling-out during the war. The Israelis, it is said, asked for U.S. arms as early as October 7, the second day of the fighting, and were turned down by Secretary Kissinger. His first diplomatic stance was to call for a cease-fire based on a return to the pre-October 6 positions; it never had a chance because the Egyptians were ahead and had no intention of withdrawing. Four or five days later, Kissinger presented another cease-fire proposal, but this time based on pinning down both warring sides to the positions held at the time; now the Israelis were unhappy because it meant giving up all hope of driving the Egyptians back across the canal. By October 12, Secretary Kissinger and Ambassador Dobrynin had concocted a plan to get Britain to sponsor a resolution in the Security Council for just such a cease-fire "in place." Unfortunately, the British ambassador in Cairo, Sir Philip Adams, checked this plan with Sadat and found him totally uninterested in it owing to what still seemed the favorable prospects of the Egyptian army. When the British refused to act as front men for the U.S.-USSR scheme, which fell through on October 13, "Kissinger blew up"—if we may believe this account which apparently derives from British sources. Obviously we need to learn much more before we can know what to believe about this entire sequence of events.[33a]

The UN, of all parties, should have had no doubt which side had started the war. Even if it knew nothing about Yom Kippur, the state of Israeli mobilization, or the Egyptian-Syrian preparations, it had its own observers on the spot. The first report from the war fronts came through on October 6 at 12:14 GMT (two hours earlier than Cairo time): "General heavy activity along Israel-Syria and Suez Canal sectors. Further information will follow." The second report at 12:21 was still inconclusive. But the third at 13:40 read: "General heavy air and ground activity continues along all sectors. Egyptian ground forces have crossed the Suez Canal in vicinity of OP's Copper, Yellow, Pink, Red, and Blue. Syrian forces have crossed the area between the limits of the forward defended localities indicating the cease-fire lines in the vicinity of Quneitra and near OP November. Detailed summaries of incidents now under preparation." A more detailed report was made at 2 PM, confirming that Syrian and Egyptian forces had taken the initiative.[34]

It has been reported without denial that "sizable segments" of the U.S. intelligence community continued to believe for as much as eight hours after the outbreak of hostilities that Israel, not the Arabs, had launched the attack.[35] If so, "sizable segments" of the U.S. intelligence community should have their heads examined or were too predisposed against Israel to think clearly.

From all this, it is abundantly clear that the key Arab war decisions antedated the meetings of the Security Council in June–July 1973. Even if the United States had not vetoed S/10974, it is hard to see what the Arabs would have gained immediately, inasmuch as its provisions were not self-enforceable. A 13–1 vote was not much worse than a 14–0 vote if the diplomatic isolation of Israel was the objective. The United

States might even have cast a favorable vote without doing much more for Egypt. Some Egyptian comments have sought to give the impression that the vote on S/10974 was the last straw, after which war was inevitable. In fact, the diplomatic struggle over S/10974 was a propaganda operation which led to the war because it was so successful, not because it was such a failure.

As for the Soviet Union, the available evidence indicates that it must be judged by Lord Salisbury's rule that "those who have the absolute power of preventing lamentable events, and, knowing what is taking place, refuse to exercise that power, are responsible for what happens." The Soviet Union certainly had the power to prevent this war, because it had to furnish the enormous quantity of arms that made it possible. The Soviet military missions with the Egyptian and Syrian forces certainly knew what was taking place, advised both Arab commands in their planning, and trained the Arab military in the use of Soviet equipment, much of it of the latest vintage.[36] The Soviet Union is not in the habit of giving away thousands of tanks, and hundreds of planes, missiles, rockets, and artillery pieces without having a good idea of what is going to be done with them. Even if the Soviet ambassadors in Cairo and Damascus were not officially informed that war was imminent until October 3, Soviet military intelligence had other sources of information, and there is reason to believe that preparations for the airlift and resupply operation had been set in motion considerably before October 3.

These are some aspects of the situation that should be kept in mind as we follow what happened in the UN after October 6.

VIII

The UN did not react to the October 1973 war the way it had reacted to the June 1967 war. When the earlier war broke out on June 5, none of the combatants asked for a cease-fire, but their reticence did not stop the Security Council from voting for a cease-fire twenty-four hours later. In 1973, the combatants again did not ask for a cease-fire, but this time the Security Council did not vote for a cease-fire until seventeen days later.

In those seventeen days, this is what happened in the Security Council:

October 8: This first meeting of the Security Council after the outbreak of war was requested by the United States, which, however, did not present any cease-fire resolution, no doubt because it would have been a futile gesture. The Egyptian representative, el-Zayyat, accused Israel of "aggression" on October 6 and pretended that the Israelis had attacked at points where the UN did not have observers. The Chinese member, Huang, was so sure of what had happened in the Middle East that he denounced Israel for having "flagrantly launched on 6 October fresh military attacks on a large scale in expanded aggression against Egypt, Syria, and the Palestinian guerrillas." In a demonstration of how little ideology may have to do with reality, the Chinese spokesman accused the Soviet Union as well as the United States of "conniving at and supporting the Israeli policies of expansion and aggression." It remained for the Soviet Union's Malik to reveal why the Security Council had done nothing and was not likely to do anything until the Soviet Union was ready and willing to let it do something. Reminiscent of Fedorenko's obstructionism before the June 1967 war, Malik coolly criticized the Security Council for having come together at all and insisted that no new decision or resolution was called for on the part of the Council.[37]

So the first session of the Council after the outbreak of war was an almost total waste of time in an atmosphere of almost total unreality. Meanwhile, in Washington, a U.S. government spokesman reported that the Soviets were already providing a "massive" airlift of military supplies to Egypt and Syria.

October 9: The Yugoslav member, Minic, went further than anyone had yet dared to go by threatening possible "sanctions" to punish Israel for its "aggression." The Syrian representative, Ismail, repeated a false report that Israeli planes had bombed the Soviet embassy in Damascus and had killed thirty of its members. Malik then outdid himself. "This bloody act is similar to the acts of Hitler when entire cities and villages were removed from the face of the earth," he shouted. And then this: "Like savage, barbaric tribes, in their mad destruction they [the Israelis] have annihilated, destroyed, and tried to remove from the surface of the earth cities, villages, the cultural heritage of mankind. They have ravaged entire civilizations." He accused Israel of responsibility for "world inflation and the rise of prices throughout the world." When the Israeli representative Tekoah tried to express his sympathy for all the human losses suffered in the war, including those at the Soviet cultural center in Damascus, which had been hit, Malik heatedly interrupted him with the words: "The Soviet delegation is unwilling to hear excuses and condolences from a representative of the murderers and international gangsters"—and stalked out of the chamber. At this, according to the

Washington *Post*'s correspondent at the UN, Anthony Astrachan, "diplomats crowding the Council chamber burst into applause. Other diplomats said later that there had been a feeling of lynch mob and pogrom in the chamber of peace."[38]

Other than that, very little of importance happened at the second meeting of the Security Council.[39]

October 11: For the first time, an Arab representative, Baroody of Saudi Arabia, the UN's licensed jester, virtually gave up the pretense of an Israeli attack on October 6 and fell back on the plea that it was "immaterial" which side had started the present conflict. Malik, however, was less inhibited. He continued to inveigh against Israel as the "aggressor country," whose representatives at the UN were trying to justify "the barbarous murders of peaceful populations." He compared them to the Hitlerites: "This was how they 'Coventrified' Coventry; that was how they destroyed thousands of towns in the Soviet Union and tens of thousands of villages." Tekoah replied to Malik: "You mentioned, in your usual manner, Goebbels and his methods. If my memory does not fail me, there was a time when Goebbels was Stalin's ally; and if my memory does not fail me, you were brought up in the so-called Stalinist school." Malik spoke again, perhaps thinking that he had gone too far: "Do not speculate on these feelings of anti-Semitism. Do not accuse me of this. My best friends are Jews. I can mention their names here: Brodsky, Chernjak, and Shub."

Apart from these pleasantries, very little worth preserving happened at the third meeting of the Security Council.[40]

October 12: This relatively short meeting was taken up with tired charges and counter-charges, as if all the speakers knew that nothing they said could change anything.[41]

October 13–20: No meetings of the Security Council.

Yet it was while the Council was not in session that the crucial turn in the war occurred. On October 13, the Israeli position was so precarious that President Nixon decided to start the resupply effort to Israel. On October 15, a small Israeli force turned the tide of battle by crossing the canal and establishing a foothold on the West Bank. According to Rouleau, it took the Egyptian high command in Cairo three or four days to realize how serious the situation had become. On October 16, President

Sadat was so little cognizant of the true state of affairs at the front that he still spoke of liberating all of Sinai. On the same day, Soviet Prime Minister Kosygin arrived in Cairo. Evidently the U.S. resupply effort had shaken the Soviet leaders sufficiently to make them more amenable to renewed U.S. overtures for a cease-fire. Rouleau says that Sadat very probably was not fully conscious of the seriousness of the Israeli break-through until the 18th. Only on the 19th, in a meeting with Kosygin, was Sadat willing to accept a cease-fire in principle.[42] When Kosygin returned to Moscow later that same day, the men in the Kremlin must have received the news from Egypt with something akin to consterna-tion. For they proceeded to send messages of such grave import to Washington that Secretary of State Kissinger, who was preparing to leave for Peking shortly, abruptly changed his plans and rushed off to Moscow in the early morning hours of October 20. One can only assume that Dr. Kissinger would not have acted with such unseemly haste if the Soviet messages had not been extraordinarily alarming. What these messages were, we still do not know and have been given no hint.

This sequence of events was the reason there were no meetings of the Security Council between October 13 and 20. It was also the reason why the Council was called together at 10:15 on the night of October 21. Now that the Soviets and their Egyptian clients were hell-bent on getting a cease-fire without delay, the Council could meet again.

October 21–22: On the seventeenth day of the war, the fifth meeting of the Security Council opened on the night of October 21 with the presentation by the U.S. member, John Scali, of a joint U.S.-USSR resolution, the product of the previous two days of hard bargaining in Moscow by Secretary Kissinger and General Secretary Brezhnev. It was made up of three interrelated parts: 1) A cease-fire in place within twelve hours after adoption of the resolution; 2) implementation of Resolution 242 "in all its parts" immediately after the cease-fire; and 3) "negotiations [to] start between the parties concerned" aimed at estab-lishing "a just and durable peace in the Middle East" immediately and "concurrently" with the cease-fire and "under appropriate auspices." It was also explained by Mr. Scali that the cease-fire applied "not only to the parties directly concerned but also to those who have joined in the fighting by sending units," and that both sponsors had agreed that there should be an immediate exchange of prisoners of war.

In the discussion, Baroody of Saudi Arabia used the occasion to defend the Germans during and after the Weimar regime for having considered the Jews to be "their enemy" and for having believed that they had "been sold out by the Jews." The Indian, Sen, revealed that members of the Security Council had been informed only at 7 PM that evening that a meeting was planned and that he had received definite word only at 8:30 PM that the meeting was to be held. The members were thus given only about three hours for consultation among themselves and no time at all to get guidance or instructions from their governments. As Sen put it, "The United States and the Soviet Union have come to an agreement the details of which are not fully known and perhaps cannot and should not be known to us now or in the foreseeable future," and "the two Powers, however great and however powerful, have come to an agreement and we have to underwrite it quickly." The Chinese member, Huang, also protested against the methods of the two superpowers: "This practice of imposing one's view on the Security Council is most unreasonable and is one we cannot agree to." Nevertheless, the vote at about 1 AM on October 22 went 14 to 0 in favor of the resolution (with China not voting).[43]

Resolution 338 of October 22, as it came to be known, was clearly a "trade-off." Egypt got the cease-fire which it desperately needed. Israel got a reinstatement of Resolution 242 as a "package deal" in the words "in all its parts," a promise of "negotiations," and a U.S.-USSR commitment, not in the resolution, for an immediate prisoner exchange. And so Resolution 242, with all its ambiguities and contradictory interpretations intact, was reincarnated in Resolution 338 but with something added that Israel had never obtained before—"negotiations" between "the parties concerned," whatever that might come to mean.

For all but two members of the Security Council, the night of October 21–22 was probably the most humiliating experience in UN history. After seventeen days of doing nothing in the face of an Israeli "disaster," the Security Council suddenly shook itself out of inertia in order, as a Chinese member rightly put it,[44] "to rubber-stamp" a U.S.-USSR deal with hardly enough time to know what it was doing, when the Egyptians were facing disaster. The double standard had never operated more ruthlessly.

October 23: This sixth meeting of the Security Council was requested by Egypt because the proclamatory cease-fire provision of Resolution 338 had not been implemented and Israeli forces had succeeded in cutting off the Egyptian Third Army on the east bank of the canal. Each side accused the other of having violated the cease-fire agreement. According to Rouleau, the Israeli advance across the canal had resulted in the first signs of "panic" in both Cairo and Moscow. It would seem that the two top Egyptian commanders, including General al-Shazli, offered to resign, and Sadat himself thought of giving up the Presidency. If we may trust Rouleau, the Russians reacted with an "unaccustomed firmness" that surprised the Egyptian leaders. The Russians undertook to resupply the Egyptian Third Army by air if necessary, and allegedly told Sadat: "We will not permit a new defeat; we will be at your sides until the end and whatever the consequences may be."[45]

The Russians, who had now put their own power and prestige on the line, moved on three fronts—in Cairo to bolster Egyptian morale, in Washington to put additional pressure on the Israelis, and in the UN to give their next move a semblance of international legitimacy. In Washington, Secretary Kissinger and Ambassador Dobrynin worked out a new UN resolution urging the embattled forces in the Middle East to return to the original line of October 22 and requesting the UN Secretary-General to send observers to supervise the cease-fire. Unfortunately, no one knew where the original line had been. The resolution of October 22 had been drawn up so hastily that no provision had been made to implement it. To make matters worse, the Russians in the UN decided to take things into their own hands. They presented Ambassador Scali with a draft resolution which had changed a few key words from the version agreed on by Kissinger and Dobrynin in Washington. "Urges" was changed to "demands" in the provision pertaining to the return of the forces to the mysterious line of October 22, and the line itself was defined as that which had prevailed at the time of the vote by the Security Council, without the leeway of twelve hours clearly set forth in Resolution 338. This contretemps delayed the Council meeting on October 23 until agreement was reached to go back to the original Kissinger-Dobrynin version.[46]

For thirteen of the fifteen members, the meeting itself was in some ways even more humiliating than the previous one had been. Most of them had been ready to swallow their pride and go along with the first U.S.-USSR gang-up, but the second one, so soon after, was almost too much. Malik chose to behave in his most insufferable bully-boy fashion. His main victim was none other than Chiao Kuan-hua, the deputy foreign minister of the People's Republic of China. Malik took it upon himself to demand a vote on the new resolution without any prior discussion. When the Chinese representative protested, Malik repeatedly interrupted and tried to cut him off. The meeting degenerated into such a brawl that the presiding officer had to suspend it for ten minutes, the first such occurrence in the history of the Security Council. The Chinese member was finally able to complete his statement, which took about half an hour. The vote was 14 to 0 (with China not voting). Malik still could not leave the matter alone. When he spoke after the vote, he temporarily forgot that Israel was supposed to be the enemy and showed off his considerable repertoire of insult at the expense of the Chinese.

Several members could no longer repress their indignation. The Sudanese member, Khalid, started off by saying: "When we accepted the cease-fire resolution [of October 22] we did so in trust, and therefore refrained from discussing its implications. We marked the hasty manner in which it was conceived, we marked the hasty manner in which it was presented to us, we marked our rejection, as loyal members of this Organization and as a nonaligned country, of any concept of condominium that reduces this Council to a rubber stamp." The Indonesian member, Anwar Sani, observed: "Two days ago we were asked to vote on a draft resolution practically without being given time to study it properly." He expressed regret that his delegation had not asked how the previous cease-fire resolution was going to be implemented. The Peruvian member, Pérez de Cuellar, spoke of Resolution 338's "obvious lack of clarity" and suggested that the continuation of military action could be attributed "precisely to the lack of clarity in resolution 338 (1973) and also to the excessive speed with which it was adopted." Sadly, he confessed: "Once again we have adopted, almost without considering it, a draft resolution submitted by the United States and the Soviet Union." Then Huang of China revealed that his delegation had been asked to vote on the latest resolution without even having seen it.[47]

In truth, the first cease-fire Resolution 338 of October 22 was a diplomatic monstrosity. It violated every conceivable requirement for a successful cease-fire. As the British member of the Security Council, Sir Donald Maitland, soon observed, "It is unfortunately clear that a cease-fire in such a complex military situation could not have been self-policing. If the cease-fire is to be maintained, there must be proper arrangements on the ground to supervise it, of the sort which have been tested and have on the whole proved effective over the years."[48] Resolution 338 made no such arrangement. Instead, it was rushed through as if the United States and the Soviet Union could wave a magic wand and, by their joint fiat, bring to a sudden halt a war that had been raging in a Middle Eastern desert for seventeen boiling, bleeding days. Of the ten Arab states that had participated in the war against Israel, only one, Egypt, had accepted the cease-fire. The response of Syria had so little to do with what was actually in Resolution 338 that it approached the ludicrous.[49] Syria had never accepted Resolution 242; it did not, in fact, accept Resolution 338; it did not agree to attend the Geneva conference. Yet no Security Council resolution was ever passed or offered condemning or even gently reproaching Syria. Instead, an intense and incessant propaganda campaign was launched against Israel for having committed the crime of *lèse-majesté* by not stopping in its tracks as soon as the Soviet Union decided to save the Egyptian army from disaster.

The road to Geneva was paved with Resolutions 242 and 338. They were the best the diplomatic mind could devise.

IX

What is there to be learned from this history, if it is not to be repeated?

One of the chief factors that makes this conflict so difficult to resolve is its asymmetry. The areas and populations of the combatants are so disproportionate that the perspective of each side must be fundamentally different. Israel cannot possibly swallow up Egypt, let alone the rest of the Arab world. The Arabs can very easily conceive of swallowing up Israel. Loss of territory means totally different things to Egypt and Israel—to the former, loss of territory; to the latter, the very basis of existence. If Israel had suffered the 1967 defeat, it would not be here today or it would have survived in such a puny, mangled state that the Arabs could have finished it off at will. But Egypt could survive an unprecedented debacle and immediately prepare for another, greater battle. Even though the Arabs have feared and fought against Israeli "expansionism," they well know that, even for Israeli extremists, it has logistical and historical limits. No such consolation can reassure the Israelis.

The Arabs cannot deny that this asymmetry exists; it is what gives them confidence in ultimate victory. As a consequence, any peace settlement which does not take this factor into consideration cannot be fair or "just" to both sides.

Yet the Arabs also face a problem with some Israelis' version of the strategy of stages. The more extremist or religious Zionists have regarded each war, even if forced on them, as a stage in the reclamation of the biblical land of Israel and the relocation of the Jews in the "right" places. In a postwar self-examination of Israeli "illusions" bred by the 1967 victory, Foreign Minister Abba Eban recently cited "the illusion that Israel's historic legacy was exclusively a matter of geography and not also, and principally, a heritage of prophetic values of which the central value was peace" and "the fallacy that to see anything temporary in some of Israel's positions west of the Jordan was tantamount to alienation from the biblical culture."[50] As long as the Arabs refused to settle for any boundaries, Israelis were almost irresistibly tempted to set those boundaries by themselves on the basis of historic legacy and military security. Though the Israelis did not threaten the Arab world the way the Arabs threatened Israel, that is not to say that the Arabs have not felt threatened, if to a much lesser degree, and much of it self-inflicted.

No diplomacy can do much about a holy war. A strategy of stages based on immemorial claims is a prescription for protracted conflict. The only way out of the dilemma is to start with the present and the living and not with the past and the dead. It is too late for Arabs to say that so many Jews do not belong in Palestine; they are there, and they cannot be removed or dispossessed without another Holocaust. It is too late for Israelis to say that the West Bank does not belong to the Arabs; they are there, and they cannot be removed or disregarded without incalculable suffering. The trouble with history is that it is non-negotiable, and diplomacy is negotiation or it is nothing.

Without seeking to negotiate the Arab-Israeli differences here, it may be useful to clarify the terms of such a negotiation. Secretary Kissinger has given his understanding of what the Geneva conference is all about: "The question then is where are the borders and what are the security arrangements, and this is what is going to be negotiated in the next phase in accordance with Security Council Resolution 242."[51] On the Israeli side, Defense Minister Dayan has asserted: "The central issue is the borders of the state of Israel."[52] However difficult its implementation may be, the concept of "borders" is at least sufficiently clear and concrete to provide a basis for meaningful negotiations.

Those who have accepted Resolutions 242 and 338 on the road to Geneva have implicitly agreed to negotiate in good faith on "secure and recognized boundaries," as stated in Resolution 242, and "a just and durable peace," as in Resolution 338. There can be no negotiation if the Egyptians simply demand that the Israelis withdraw to the pre-June 5, 1967 borders, or if the Israelis take the position that they have already negotiated their borders with God. There must have been something wrong with the 1967 borders if they were such as to provoke a war on June 5. And, even if the borders should be God-given ones, the Jewish God has never been strong on security for His chosen people.

Something can also be gained from a closer examination of the term "secure and recognized boundaries." The two adjectives have become inseparable, but they need to be clearly differentiated. Boundaries can be recognized without being secure, and they can be secure without being recognized. Moreover, it is much easier to know what recognized boundaries are than what secure boundaries are. In the present circumstances, Israeli security depends on so much more than boundaries that the very notion of secure boundaries is far more complex than it may seem to be. Israeli security cannot be separated from, but neither can it be reduced to, Israeli territory.

Unfortunately, the very term, "secure boundaries," lends itself to some misconception. Security in this world is relative, but the term tends to make it appear to be absolute, as if boundaries by themselves can be secure or not secure instead of more or less secure. Surely the 1949 boundaries were more secure from the Israeli point of view than the 1947 boundaries in the sense that they were easier to defend. The post-1967 boundaries seemed to be easier to defend than the previous ones, and yet they proved to be harder to defend because they lulled the Israelis into a false sense of security. The idea that Israel could have had security after the 1967 war by unilaterally withdrawing to the former boundaries is hardly credible; those were the very boundaries that had brought on the war in the first place. These examples of the security problem should be enough to show how tricky and deceptive the concept of security can be.

Until now, however, Israel has had neither recognized nor secure boundaries. It may be useful, as a starting point, to agree on the principle of recognized boundaries before tackling the more difficult question of secure boundaries. If, as heretofore, the Arabs refuse to recognize any boundaries for Israel, there is little point in trying to get them to recognize more secure boundaries.

The Israeli craving for security is historically understandable, but it will never be satisfied simplistically or to the exclusion of other factors. The Arabs, on the other hand, were not satisfied with any previous boundaries, and it is up to them to negotiate in good faith on boundaries before any progress can even be hoped for. If there is going to be negotiation in good faith at Geneva, the old issues in the UN are bound to arise again. Is negotiation in accordance with Security Council Resolution 242 going to take the form of a "package deal" or will it degenerate into a demand for a unilateral and arbitrary "priority" that favors only one side? Is Israeli withdrawal to be separated from agreeing on more secure, recognized boundaries? Is a strategy of stages going to be pursued, making impossible any prospect of a "durable peace"? These are some of the questions that were never satisfactorily answered in the Security Council and, therefore, must still seek for answers in Geneva. Diplomacy may be able to help but, like psychoanalysis, diplomacy helps those who want to be helped.

Commentary, February 1974

3

How Not to Make Peace
in the Middle East

I

Why did the negotiations for a peaceful settlement between Egypt and Israel break down? Why has the breakdown been so difficult to overcome? The search for an explanation cannot be limited to the negotiations themselves; it can even be hindered by sticking too closely to the day-by-day "peace process." The issues that led to the breakdown of the negotiations did not arise at Camp David and could not be settled by the negotiations at Camp David.

To get our bearings, we need to step back and view the negotiations from a greater distance. It is necessary to step at least as far back as 1967. For the Six-Day War in June of that year produced the hard territorial problems which the negotiations sought to resolve. What to do with the Sinai? The West Bank? The Gaza Strip? The Golan Heights? The Israeli settlements? These and other questions did not exist before June 1967. How they came to be is the starting point of any serious effort to find answers for them.

Mustafa Amin, a leading Egyptian commentator and confidant of President Sadat, recently provided an additional reason for going back to the 1967 war. *The New York Times* of December 24, 1978, reported him as having written: "This may be the first instance in history where a thief claims compensation for his own crime."

Mustafa Amin's allusion to the Israeli occupation of Arab territory after the 1967 war was not novel or original. It was typical of the steady journalistic diet fed Arab readers for the past decade. If all that had happened were no more than simple thievery and the criminal were so clearly identified, there would be very little more to say about it.

But the matter is hardly so simple. In fact, we now have it on the highest Egyptian authority how unsimple and how double-edged is the charge that a "crime" was committed in 1967.

The Egyptian authority is Anwar el-Sadat. His autobiography, *In Search of Identity*, appeared in English and other languages last year. In it he tells of the events leading up to the 1967 war. Although he leaves out a good deal, what he includes is enough.

Sadat relates that his predecessor, Gamal Abdel Nasser, knew that war with Israel was inevitable if the Straits of Tiran, leading to the Israeli port of Eilat in the south, were closed. The United Nations Emergency Force had been stationed at Sharm el-Sheikh in 1957 for the precise purpose of keeping the Straits open. In May 1967, according to Sadat, Nasser convened a meeting of his top leaders, including Sadat, at which he declared: "Now with our concentrations in Sinai, the chances of war are fifty-fifty. But if we close the Straits, the war will be a 100 percent certainty." Nasser then turned to his Minister of War, Abdel Hakim Amer, and asked whether the Egyptian armed forces were ready. Amer assured him that everything was "in tiptop shape."

With the Straits closed, Sadat writes, "war became a certainty." Nasser also knew that the Israelis were going to aim their first blow at the Egyptian air force; he deliberately took that risk because he was assured by the Air Force Commander, General Sidqi Mahmoud, that the Egyptian losses would come to no more than 10 percent of the air force. Nasser even correctly guessed the exact timing of the Israeli attack. He expected it to come at latest by June 5. He was right.

We have long known all this and more from other sources.[1] Yet it is reassuring to have Sadat himself confirm how Egypt decided with calculated premeditation to set up a situation which could only lead to war.

If ever a war was deliberately instigated, it was instigated by Egypt in June 1967. Of this there cannot be the shadow of a doubt—except on the part of the present ranking Middle East expert on the National Security Council.[2]

But Sadat hardly told the whole story, or even the most important part of it. What he does not mention in his memoirs is the war aim that Nasser repeatedly and unequivocally announced to the world before the outbreak of hostilities.

On May 26, 1967, Nasser said: "The battle will be a general one and our basic objective will be to destroy Israel." On May 28, 1967, he said: "Israel's existence in itself is an aggression." On June 1, 1967, Ahmad Shukairy, then head of the PLO, at that time subsidized and controlled by Egypt, was asked what would happen to native-born Israelis if the Arab armies were successful. "Those who survive will remain in Palestine," he replied. "I estimate that none of them will survive."

It may be contended that Nasser's words should not have been taken seriously. Nasser's threats, however, were more restrained than popular Arab propaganda. We will never know whether Nasser would have gone as far as his henchman, Shukairy, but he fired up his armed forces for the battle with the language of the *jihad*—the holy war of Muslims against non-Muslims, which must end in death, conversion, or submission to Islam. The least that Nasser promised his followers was that the state of Israel would cease to exist in the event of an Egyptian victory.

The war, of course, ended with Israel in possession of Sinai and the Gaza Strip. That is how Israel became a "thief" and committed the "crime" to which Mustafa Amin referred.

We also know from the highest Jordanian authority, King Hussein, how Israel happened to occupy the West Bank. Two books, neither of which has been published in the United States, contain his version of how he got into the 1967 war. The story, told largely in Hussein's own words, is this:

Hussein decided that war was inevitable as soon as Nasser announced the closure of the Gulf of Aqaba on May 22, 1967. It took him only two more days to decide to get into it. Hussein flew to Cairo on May 30 for a reconciliation with Nasser as the prerequisite for joint Egyptian-Jordanian action. Nasser assured Hussein that his forces were superior to the Israelis'. Hussein's own words are: "Nasser never appealed to us. We were the ones who appealed to him."[3]

On the eve of the outbreak, Israel promised Jordan immunity from the war if it would stay out. One such message was transmitted through then Under Secretary of State Eugene V. Rostow to the Jordanian Ambassador in Washington. But Hussein was tempted by the jackal's share of the easy victory held out by Nasser. After joining in the attack and getting punished for it, Hussein justified his poor showing on the battlefield by leading Nasser to believe that Jordanian forces had been attacked by hundreds of American war planes.[4]

And that is how Israel became the "thief" of the West Bank.

. . .

As for Syria, its leaders claimed to be in the vanguard of the struggle to destroy Israel. Hafez al-Assad, then Syrian Defense Minister and now President, was particularly outspoken. He anticipated Nasser by saying early in 1967: "The mere existence of Zionism in Palestine constitutes an aggression, and aggression and peace cannot coexist in the same territory." In the same speech made to army units, he declared: "The people's revolution has decreed that the enemy shall be humiliated until zero hour strikes, after which no enemy will remain in Palestine." The Syrians actually attacked Israel on the morning of the first day of the Six-Day War and were, in fact, the only Arab force to stage an abortive raid into Israeli territory during the entire war. The bulk of the Syrian army was stationed on the Golan Heights, from which the Israeli settlements below had long been terrorized. This Syrian force was virtually wiped out in the last two days of the war.

Which was how Israel became the "thief" of the Golan Heights, too.

Without keeping in mind how Israel came to occupy the Sinai area, the West Bank, the Gaza Strip, and the Golan Heights in 1967, the conflict over them becomes a travesty. I do not mean to suggest that the way Israel came to occupy these territories answers the question whether Israel should keep all or any part of them. That is a much more complex problem, involving other factors in past and future Arab-Israeli relationships. But the original basis of the Israeli occupation in a war of self-defense, deliberately provoked by Egypt, cannot be ignored or falsified without making it impossible to understand the events leading up to the Camp David agreement and beyond.

II

Why were all attempts to get serious negotiations started so futile until Sadat went to Jerusalem in November 1977?

One reason stands out. Again we have Sadat to thank for confirming it in one short sentence in his speech to the Israeli Knesset: "We used to reject you." Just before making this frank admission, Sadat had said: "You want to live with us, in this part of the world." Rejection, therefore, had meant that he and his fellow Arabs had *not* wanted Israel to live in that part of the world. Other rationales, such as Israeli withdrawal from occupied territory or recognition of a new Palestinian state, had been used in diplomatic negotiations or for public consumption. But this one—the survival of Israel—had always gone to the heart of the matter.

When Sadat also said, "We welcome you among us with full security and safety," he for the first time broke away from the "rejectionist" Arab front to which he had in principle belonged. There was nothing else in Sadat's speech that differed from the previous Arab negotiating position. Sadat himself recognized where the break had come. Immediately after his word of welcome, he added: "This in itself is a tremendous turning point, one of the landmarks of a decisive historical change."

It was. But it also cast a lurid light on what the real issue had been from the birth of Israel in 1948 to that 20th of November almost thirty years later. For this reason, the rest of the Arab world responded to Sadat's initiative with execration. The one thing for which Sadat could not be forgiven was his acceptance of Israel's existence and survival as a nation, even if that acceptance was not unencumbered.

For Sadat named a price for the "tremendous turning point" and the "decisive historical change." He went out of his way to stress that he had not come for a separate peace between Egypt and Israel. He spoke of "our land" that could not be the subject of bargaining or even open to argument. He demanded "complete withdrawal from the Arab territories occupied after 1967." He made the Palestinian Arabs, not the Egyptians, "the crux of the entire problem." He specified that Israel had to accept a new Palestinian state. On everything but the tolerated existence of pre-June 1967 Israel, his conditions were maximalist. If he had left out his acceptance of Israel's existence and had not chosen to announce it in Jerusalem, his speech would have been unexceptionable from the point of view of the past Arab position.

Almost all attention was subsequently paid to Sadat's concession of Israel's national survival. This one-sidedness was understandable. The circumstances were so dramatic, not to say theatrical, that no one wished to spoil the effect. One could even believe that if the Egyptian acceptance of Israel was possible, everything else was possible. It was as if the fine print in a contract had been ignored.

Thus one important implication of Sadat's approach was by and large overlooked in the general euphoria. To take Sadat's speech seriously meant accepting him as the representative of the entire Arab world. He spoke as if he was not worried about what he could get for Egypt and even knew what he could expect to get. He devoted most of his speech to what he wanted for the other Arab states and interests. This assumption by him of Arab leadership was something of a tour de force. He asked to be accepted by Israel as the representative of the entire Arab world in the very act of breaking with that world on what it considered to be the essence of the Arab-Israeli conflict.

That Sadat had this representative role very much in mind was soon confirmed by Prime Minister Menachem Begin. Sadat, he related, told him in Ismailia, where they met in December 1977, that he "represents the Arab cause and he would like to see a solution to the problem of the Palestinian Arabs." Begin accepted Sadat as just such a representative. The future negotiations were mortgaged to this understanding.

It was a peculiar understanding. Sadat did not have a mandate to negotiate for any state other than Egypt. He had, in fact, mortally offended the other Arab leaders by going to Jerusalem without consulting them,[5] by offering a deal with Israel for which they vilified him and even threatened his life, and by appointing himself to negotiate for them. It was a wonderful trick, if he could get away with it.

Sadat evidently calculated that the other Arab states would have to come in with him sooner or later. This calculation was by virtue of Sadat's strategy hardly more than a possibility. Sadat set up a situation which made it most humiliating for Assad of Syria to follow along meekly in the Egyptian leader's footsteps. The PLO would have had to violate the dictates of its own "Covenant," something it had stubbornly refused to do despite all sorts of bribes and blandishments in the past. Sadat had not consulted his paymasters in Saudi Arabia, for the good and sufficient reason that they would not have countenanced his initiative. Jordan's Hussein, seeing all choices as dangerous, had become a perennial fence-sitter. The more extreme "rejectionists," such as Iraq and Libya, were certain to cry out for revenge.

In any event, Sadat's strategy of pulling off a diplomatic coup by himself and somehow imposing it on the other Arab states left him vulnerable to their disapproval and retaliation. If all of them, including the Palestinian Arabs, refused to go along, he faced the prospect of going back to the other Arabs or going forward with Israel, in which case, whatever the appearance, he would have the separate peace he had renounced. When Sadat, inferentially, volunteered to represent all Arab interests at Jerusalem and did so outrightly at Ismailia, he presented no credentials for assuming this role other than the vision in his own head of what an Arab peace with Israel could or should look like.

Sadat's offer to Israel sought to hold in tandem Egypt's national interest and Egypt's interests in the Arab world. A separate peace with Israel would substantially serve Egypt's national interest but only by risking the sacrifice of Egypt's putative role as leader of the Arab world. Sadat clearly assumed, with good reason, that he could have a separate peace for the asking. He rejected that prospect in his Jerusalem speech with such dispatch and finality that he was obviously determined to emphasize that he was not ready to give up Egypt's pan-Arab calling. All he was ready to do was to work it out in a different way; yet the difference was so hazardous that it could jeopardize both of his objectives—the Egyptian and the Arab.

Some observers could not believe that Sadat was aiming at anything other than a separate peace, suitably camouflaged. Israelis hotly debated whether Sadat merely wanted to have a "fig leaf" for his separate peace. Meanwhile Sadat had one inestimable advantage if there was to be any negotiation at all. There was no one else for the Israelis to bargain with.

III

Begin's response to Sadat's challenge also broke with the past. The Israeli counter-proposals never received the appreciation they deserved. They were virtually taken for granted, even though they were, in fact, startling, most of all in Israel itself.

At their meeting in Ismailia in December 1977, one month after the Jerusalem visit, Begin offered Sadat at one stroke the return to Egyptian sovereignty of all occupied Egyptian territory in the Sinai, including the key post at Sharm el-Sheikh, guarding the entrance to the Straits of Tiran, the immediate *casus belli* of the 1967 war. There was one qualification—that the Israeli settlements in the so-called Rafiah area, representing no more than 1 per cent of the Sinai, should be linked to Israeli administration and defended by an Israeli military force. This qualification was withdrawn, despite a great deal of embarrassment and anguish in Israel, when Sadat announced that he would not permit "one square centimeter" of Israeli settlement within Egypt's international borders. In the end, Egypt was offered the return of its entire territory and everything in it.

This offer was not something that should have been taken for granted. No such flat, unconditional offer had ever been made or even contemplated by any Israeli government before. Sadat did not even have to enter into negotiations to get back the whole of Egyptian territory. By holding out for the Sinai unconditionally, Sadat was able to get Israel to throw in three strategically important airfields in eastern Sinai, the major naval base at Sharm el-Sheikh, the oilfields which Israel had developed and which supplied it with 20 per cent of its oil needs, and ultimately the dismantlement of the Israeli settlements on the eastern coast adjoining Gaza. Begin and his chief lieutenants, Moshe Dayan and Ezer Weizman, considered the move to be their most original and imaginative achievement. They boasted that their Labor Party predecessors would never have dared to make it. Indeed, it was widely criticized in Israel as premature and unnecessarily generous.

It is well to recall once more how Egypt had lost the Sinai to Israel. It had been lost in 1967 in a war deliberately provoked by Egypt with the open aim of extinguishing the Jewish state. The Egyptians had started a second war in 1973 to get it back and had nearly succeeded before they were turned around, narrowly avoiding total military disaster, thanks in part to pressure exerted on Israel by the United States. The issue was not merely that it was Egyptian territory that had been lost; it was also how Egypt had lost it.

Again, I am not suggesting that it is wise or necessary for Israel to hold on to the Sinai or any other part of the occupied territories in perpetuity just because they were won in a demonstrably defensive war. But I am concerned that this Israeli offer should not have been taken for granted, as if all past history were not full of countless examples of the opposite, including in the relatively recent past the vast territory acquired by the Soviet Union as a result of World War II and the even more recent seizure by force of almost half of Cyprus by Turkey.

The brute fact is that Begin was offering Sadat the fruit of war without war. Such an offer may well have been ultimately advantageous for both sides, but that is no reason for disregarding or discounting the rich prize freely tendered to the Egyptian side.

If Begin expected gratitude from Sadat for the offer of virtually total withdrawal from the Sinai, he received none. Sadat responded in the spirit of his Jerusalem speech—that he was not interested in a separate peace and that his responsibility for representing all other Arab interests took precedence over or was indistinguishable from Egypt's national interest. As a result, Begin might have saved himself the trouble of offering to give back the Sinai in advance of any serious negotiation on all other aspects of the Arab-Israeli conflict.

In effect, Sadat forced the issue of the Palestinian Arabs to the forefront. Here also Begin and especially Dayan thought that they had something new and original to offer.

IV

Compared with previous Israeli positions, the so-called Begin plan for the West Bank and Gaza Strip presented in late December 1977 was new and original.

Labor governments had proposed a "compromise" solution. Their compromise, however, was "territorial." It implied some sort of division of the West Bank, generally between Israel and Jordan, leaving the heavily populated areas under Arab sovereignty with an outlying, peripheral area going to Israel. Most Israeli settlements had been set down in this latter area. The emphasis in this plan was on "security."

Begin's old position had made Israeli withdrawal from Sinai and the Golan Heights negotiable but not withdrawal from the West Bank, which he always referred to as Judea and Samaria to emphasize the area's Jewish origins. "I believe that Judea and Samaria are an integral part of our sovereignty," Begin said as late as May 22, 1977, six months before Sadat's visit to Jerusalem. "It's our land." In principle, this was Begin's "hard-line" position. In reality, he made very little change in day-to-day conduct on the West Bank, except for authorizing a handful of new settlements by Israeli extremists. The emphasis in this approach, however, was on "sovereignty."

As long as Begin claimed the West Bank totally for Israel, the Laborite position could appear to be "dovish" because it entailed keeping only a part of the West Bank. In fact, neither conception had the slightest chance with the Arabs and amounted to little more than the Israelis talking to themselves. The West Bank's administration was actually a peculiar kind of tacit Israeli-Jordanian admixture, with security entirely in Israeli hands while Jordanian books were used in the schools, Jordanian law prevailed in the courts, and Jordan's old retainers in the West Bank received their accustomed stipends.

Begin's new plan did not fall into either of these two previous categories. It is worth more attention than it has received because parts of it later reappeared in different form in the Camp David agreement. In essence, the Begin government separated "administration" from "security." Under administration it included everything from education and finance to the administration of justice and supervision of local police forces.

While the Israeli military government was to be abolished, Israeli armed forces were still to remain in charge of security.

To this extent, the inhabitants of the West Bank and Gaza were to be given control over their own affairs with the exception of the armed forces. On all other matters, however, the plan pointed in the direction of Jordan.

One provision, curiously, permitted residents of the West Bank and Gaza to choose either Israeli or Jordanian citizenship. Those who opted for Jordan could be elected to the Jordanian parliament, sitting in Amman. Negotiations between Israel and Jordan were provided for to settle questions arising from the vote in the Jordanian parliament by West Bank–Gaza residents, and other matters into which Jordan was to be drawn. Israeli citizens were to be allowed to acquire land and settle in the West Bank and Gaza, but only those Arabs who opted for Israeli citizenship could acquire land and settle in Israel.

Finally, the plan addressed itself directly to the question of "sovereignty." At this point, too, Begin backed down from his previous hard, fixed position. His proposal declared that Israel stood by its right and claim to sovereignty over Judea, Samaria, and the Gaza district. But it recognized that other claims also existed. To reach agreement, it proposed to leave open the question of sovereignty and to review the entire matter after a five-year period.

The Begin plan presented such a complex set of conditions that sovereignty might ultimately go to the local Palestinian Arabs as an outgrowth of their "administrative" responsibilities, to an Israeli-Jordanian condominium, or to the Israelis alone. Yet, despite all the possible combinations and permutations, it was held together by a basic conception of the future of the Jewish and Arab inhabitants of Palestine.

This conception is chiefly identified with Dayan, who first put it forward in the early 1970s when he was still a Laborite in good standing. The main idea behind it is that Jews and Arabs should "live together" from the Mediterranean to the Jordan. It differs from the Laborite conception of a territorial division of the West Bank between Israel and Jordan in some manner that would leave a formal border between them. It also differs from what may be called the Egyptian conception—to create a formal border between pre-June 1967 Israel and a new Palestinian state or some autonomous Palestinian "entity" within Jordan. It differs from both of them by putting the main emphasis on some way of "living together" rather than on some way of living separately. Begin was apparently won over to this approach, judging from an interview on December 18, 1977, in which he said that "we should live together"— Dayan's favorite slogan.

In an interview on April 30, 1978, Dayan himself explained what he had in mind:

So now this time we come forward with an absolutely different concept about it, not dividing the West Bank between Jordan and Israel, but living together, both the Arabs and Israelis living in the West Bank, the way we live in Jerusalem now (and no one really is now recommending dividing Jerusalem) so we say the same thing about the entire West Bank.

Dayan's analogy with Jerusalem left something to be desired. Jerusalem is under total Israeli sovereignty, as the West Bank might or might not be. As anyone who visits Jerusalem can see, the city is united juridically, not socially. There was some movement toward "living together" after the 1967 war, but it was reversed after 1973. Nevertheless, Dayan's aim of "living together" may well be as good a definition of peace in Palestine as is possible, for tomorrow or the day after if not for today. His conception, at any rate, helps to explain some of the complexity of the so-called Begin plan for Palestinian "self-rule" of late December 1977.

It was, from an Israeli point of view, a genuine innovation. It avoided both the Laborite formula of dividing the West Bank and Begin's old dogma that the West Bank belonged by ancient prescription to Israel. It was so unconventional that it succeeded in throwing the "hawk-dove" lineup in Israeli politics into disarray. Some former Laborite doves now began to attack Begin for having given away too much. Begin's hawkish followers began to feel the ground under them slipping away because the Palestinian Arabs were offered too much autonomy, while Israeli sovereignty in the West Bank and Gaza would be moot for five years. Begin himself became temporarily unclassifiable as he alternately resorted to old-time Beginisms and anti-Beginisms. "Our preoccupation, our worry, is security," he told the Knesset on July 2, 1978, just the way Laborites used to talk. On July 23, 1978, he attacked the Laborite leader, Shimon Peres, on the ground that the latter was ready to give up parts of Judea, Samaria, and the Gaza Strip. "I am not," Begin protested, while his critics were shouting and wailing that he was ready to give up practically everything.

From the Arab point of view, Begin's plan never had a chance. In June 1978, Sadat presented his own plan for the West Bank and Gaza.

Like Begin's, it provided for a five-year "transitional period." But whereas Begin had merely stipulated a review of the entire procedure after five years, Sadat demanded that "the Palestinian people will be able to determine their own future" after a maximum of five years. Sadat also injected Jordan into his plan by proposing that the future would be decided by representatives of Egypt, Jordan, Israel, and the Palestinian Arabs. Begin's plan would not have touched the existing Israeli settlements or Israeli armed forces. Sadat required them to be removed at the very beginning of the transitional period, during which Jordan would supervise the administration of the West Bank and Egypt of the Gaza Strip. Jordan and Egypt would thus have had five years of administering the two areas before the final adjudication.

Sadat's plan never had a chance with the Israelis. It was followed by the stalemate broken three months later at Camp David. Still, both the Begin and Sadat plans had elements which could be juggled or compromised. Most noteworthy in view of later developments was the agreement on a five-year transitional period before a final decision on sovereignty. Jordan was brought into both schemes. The inhabitants of the West Bank and Gaza were drawn into varying degrees of immediate management of their own affairs. There were plenty of significant differences, but they were the stuff of which diplomatic compromises are made.

v

All during this period, the initiative belonged to Sadat. He had seized it in Jerusalem, and he held on to it with skill and tenacity.

His trump card throughout was U.S. policy. The relationship of forces in the Arab world vis-à-vis Israel was such that Sadat could not hope to prevail without the backing of Washington. By going to Jerusalem on his own, Sadat had found himself almost totally isolated in the Arab world. Egypt alone was in no position to enforce its demands on Israel. Egypt plus the United States was something else. Every move by Sadat was calculated primarily with an eye on the United States.

Sadat himself said as much repeatedly with disarming candor. Sometimes he said that the United States held 100 percent of the cards. Sometimes he reduced the figure to a mere 99 percent. The implication of this favorite observation was clear. If the United States held 100 percent or 99 percent of the cards and Israel none or 1 percent, Sadat was inferentially negotiating with the party that held all those cards, not with the party without them. Thus Sadat's strategy was to get the United States to make up for what Egypt lacked. He set up and worked within a triangle—Egypt-Israel-United States. His success or failure was made to depend on his manipulation of the United States. This schema was designed as if all that mattered was American "leverage" on Israel. It left out of the account Egypt's leverage on the other Arab states.

Of greatest interest to Sadat must have been President Carter's choice of Zbigniew Brzezinski as his National Security Adviser.

Brzezinski is no exception to the rule that political intellectuals give literary hostages to fortune before they reap political rewards for their intellectual labors. In his case, efforts to find out what he had in mind for the Middle East before he took office have focused on the report issued by a Brookings Institution Study Group, of which he was a prominent member, in December 1975. But it was signed by fifteen others, some of whom did not agree with him on everything. For Brzezinski's position on the Arab-Israeli conflict before it became advisable for him to watch his words for their immediate political effect, it is necessary to turn to an article, "Peace In An International Framework," which he—together with François Duchêne of England and Kiichi Saeki of Japan—published in the Summer 1975 issue of *Foreign Policy*. This article put Brzezinski on record as advocating, among other things, that:

1. The United States should overtly take the initiative to present the substance of an international framework for an eventual settlement.

2. The solution had to "treat the whole problem" at once, not piece-meal.

3. Israel should trade occupied territories for Arab acceptance of the pre-June 1967 borders.

4. The result of such a trade-off would most likely be a PLO-dominated state on the West Bank and Gaza Strip. Such a state was seen on one page of the article as coming "probably" and on another page "almost certainly."

5. The Soviet Union must be drawn into the negotiations. It was needed to provide a "joint guarantee by the superpowers" of any territorial settlement. No peace treaty was feasible without Soviet participation.

One more tenet was perhaps the most revealing of all. It appeared in this form:

But the United States is also keenly aware that its relations with the Arab world impinge on its status as a superpower, and its support of Israel cuts across American *raisons d'état*.

This oracular pronouncement must be understood in terms of a long-standing argument in American policy-making circles about where the true American *raisons d'état* are located—in Israel, the Arab states, or some combination of both. The article by Brzezinski *et al.* shifted them sharply over to the Arab side. The Arabs were said really to matter so far as America's "status as a superpower" was concerned; *Israel cut across American raisons d'état*. The implication was inescapable—we may sympathize with Israel but we must in the final analysis support the Arabs, or at least get their support. This assessment was slipped in unostentatiously, though its implications informed the entire argument. With the exception of the stress on Soviet participation, there was nothing in the article that Sadat could not accept.

Despite this open manifesto on how to settle the Arab-Israeli conflict only a year before the presidential campaign and his choice of Jimmy Carter as his standard-bearer, Brzezinski's views were conspicuously absent from candidate Carter's campaign commitments in 1976. Carter denounced the Ford administration for having "tried to make Israel the scapegoat for the problems in the Middle East." He came out for "defensible borders," the Israeli code term for substantial changes. He rejected a Soviet-American imposed settlement. He told the Israelis that he himself would not relinquish direct control of the Golan Heights or Old Jerusalem. He advised them not to deal with the PLO. He put almost the entire onus for peace on the Arabs, from whom he demanded recognition of Israel, diplomatic relations, and a peace treaty as the "heart" of the matter.

After the election, most of these professions of deeply held convictions were consigned to the famous "dust heap of history," which in American politics receives another delivery in only as much time as it takes to get from the campaign to the election. All through 1977, the Middle East policy of the Carter administration moved in directions suspiciously similar to those which Brzezinski had charted in 1975.

1. The United States decided to adopt a more overt, operative role leading to a settlement. "We are not just an idle bystander," said President Carter on September 16, 1977. "We are not just an uninterested

intermediary or mediator." A few days later came word from Brzezinski that the United States had "the legitimate right to exercise its own leverage" and was not "just an interested bystander, not even a benevolent mediator."[6]

2. The United States was committed to an all-inclusive "comprehensive" settlement, extending from Egypt to Syria. President Assad was persistently wooed; systematic efforts were made to find out what would be acceptable to him. As late as July 5, 1978, Carter called Assad "a major force for peace in the Middle East for many years."

3. Israel's "defensible borders" turned out to be just what they had been in the previous Nixon and Ford administrations. On March 9, 1977, Carter came out for "some minor adjustments in the 1967 borders." (A "minor adjustment" is understood to be something on the order of the reunification of a village cut in half by the 1949 armistice lines, which are all that the 1967 borders are based on.)

4. On a PLO-dominated state in the West Bank and Gaza, the official policy began to move by degrees toward Brzezinski's 1975 prescription. On March 16, 1977, the President for the first time came out for a Palestinian "homeland." On September 16, he endorsed a Palestinian "entity," preferably associated with Jordan. Repeated efforts were also made to get the PLO to say the right words or even to pretend that they had done so in order to gain admittance for them at a reconvened Geneva conference.

5. The climax of all this American activity was the Soviet-American statement of October 1, 1977. It anthologized almost every important recommendation in Brzezinski's 1975 article. It called for a "comprehensive" settlement "incorporating all parties concerned and all questions." It recommended joint Soviet-American "guarantees" of any settlement. It maintained that a reconvened Geneva conference, no later than December 1977, was the only way to achieve a solution. It edged even closer to the PLO by employing the Arab formula of "the legitimate rights of the Palestinian people."[7]

In large part, this statement followed the line that had been urged by George W. Ball, Professor Stanley Hoffmann, and Nahum Goldmann as well as by the Brzezinski-Duchêne-Saeki article and the Brookings Report. What they had in common was the premise that the United States and the Soviet Union had to arrive at a prior agreement on the terms of a settlement in order to make an agreement by the parties themselves feasible.[8]

Not only that. The Soviet-American statement came as close to imposing a settlement on the interested parties as could be conceived of in the circumstances, despite official protestations to the contrary. The logic behind it had been worked out in the 1975 article by Brzezinski *et al.* It had envisaged a statement negotiated by the United States and the Soviet Union to provide a joint guarantee for a return to the pre-June 1967 borders. Such a statement, it had delicately hinted, "would put great pressure on the Arabs and the Israelis, especially if it were then endorsed by Western Europe and Japan" (p. 16). The United States and the Soviet Union did not have to present their statement as an imposed settlement; their "great pressure" was expected to do it for them.

Instead of great pressure, there was great shock in Egypt, Israel, and not least the United States.

The Soviet-American statement of October 1 was negotiated so secretively that neither Sadat nor Begin had been taken into Washington's confidence. Sadat let it be known that he was appalled by American sponsorship of Soviet intervention in a matter which primarily concerned Egypt, without full Egyptian cognizance of what had been afoot. Israel was infuriated because the Carter administration had issued the statement with no advance consultation, in flagrant violation of a previous commitment dating from September 1, 1975, to consult fully and to seek to concert position and strategy with Israel in advance of any effort to reconvene the Geneva conference. Begin and Dayan were permitted to see the statement only twenty-four hours before it was issued. Congressional opinion, also taken by surprise, reflected incredulity and hostility. The most enthusiastic public support for the statement came from Syria and the PLO.

This diplomatic coup was the culmination of months of policy planning and weeks of diplomatic negotiations—"long weeks," President Carter later said. It could not possibly be attributed to a fit of absent-mindedness. Anyone who wants to know what the original Carter-Brzezinski-Vance policy for settling the Arab-Israeli conflict really was need only read this statement; the Soviets astutely recognized that that policy was good enough for them and their Arab clients. If such a coup was worth pulling off at all, however, it should have been followed by an exhibition of that "great pressure" which a Soviet-American statement was supposed to generate.

Pressure there was, but in the end it was not great enough. The

Israelis protested bitterly and succeeded in getting some minor concessions. They were told that they did not have to accept the Soviet-American statement in advance of a reconvened Geneva conference. They obtained some nominal changes in the PLO's presence at the conference. But the Carter administration would not budge on essentials; the President still insisted at the end of October that the Soviet-American statement was a "major move in the right direction." American policy was hell-bent on going to Geneva and working in conjunction with the Soviet Union, with or without Egyptian and Israeli approval and cooperation.

One surprise begat another. While Washington was preparing to go to Geneva in December, Israel and Egypt quietly began to put out feelers to each other. Sadat's bolt-out-of-the-blue bid on November 9 for an invitation to Jerusalem was his way of rejecting Geneva. Begin's invitation and Sadat's speech in the Knesset—all within eleven days—came so quickly that all control of events was lost by Washington, which was reduced to watching them unfold on television. As significant as anything that was said in Jerusalem was what was left unsaid—that the road to peace led from Cairo to Jerusalem, not from Washington to Moscow.

The effect of Sadat's Jerusalem speech was almost magical. The Soviet-American statement was put in cold storage. The new Geneva conference was indefinitely postponed. The plan to bring a recalcitrant Syria, an immobile Jordan, and a disinfected PLO into early, all-inclusive negotiations was sidetracked. The Soviets were again relegated to the sidelines.

Thus was a year of American policy-making for the Middle East undone. The only thing our policy-makers and planners could take credit for was that they had unwittingly helped to send Sadat to Jerusalem.

The first reaction in Washington to Sadat's visit was compounded of bewilderment, embarrassment, and hesitation. But it would be a mistake to think that the American-Soviet statement was simply written off. It represented too great an investment and too deliberate a decision to be permanently abandoned. Instead, after a suitable period of recuperation and reflection, a determined effort was made to recover the ground lost without direct reference to the statement itself.

The most ambitious effort along these lines was made by Brzezinski, who now introduced the concept of three concentric circles. In the first, the United States supported an Egyptian-Israeli settlement. In the second, the "moderate" Palestinian Arabs and Jordan would be brought in. And the third was reserved for Syria and the Soviet Union, preferably at a comprehensive, reconvened Geneva conference. What the Soviet-American statement had contemplated achieving at one stroke, Sadat's visit was now supposed to accomplish in three stages.

Another way to achieve the same end was to make Sadat the negotiator for all the other Arab states. As we have already seen, Sadat had assigned this role to himself, and Begin had gone along with him. Now Carter also associated himself with it. In an interview on January 6, 1978, after meeting with Sadat, Hussein, and King Khalid of Saudi Arabia, Carter asserted that he—and Hussein—felt "that Sadat is adequately representing the Arab position." Hussein and Khalid allegedly supported Sadat "unequivocally." Even more, Sadat was "almost uniquely trusted" not only by his own people but by the rest of the world, including "to a substantial degree" the Israelis. Only Syria was still inscrutable. But if Sadat could adequately represent the Arab position, we were in effect returning to the long sought "comprehensive" agreement.

Unfortunately, Hussein did not say that Sadat represented him. Khalid did not say that Sadat represented him. Carter said it for them. It remained to be seen how right the President was or how gullible he had been.

At about the same time, Sadat was given the opportunity to find out where the real "leverage" was.

The Begin plan for Palestinian "self-rule" had been submitted to the United States before it was made public at the end of December 1977. Carter told Begin, according to the latter, that he considered the plan "a fair basis for negotiation to achieve peace." Publicly, Carter confirmed that he had been decidedly encouraging. In an interview on December 28, he agreed that Begin's plan "certainly is a realistic negotiating position" and declared that Begin "already has shown a great deal of flexibility." Begin had every reason to think that the Americans would back the Israeli proposals as a basis of negotiation with Egypt.

The test of American "leverage" came when Sadat categorically rejected the Israeli plan. Thereupon the Americans also discarded it. The lesson was not lost—that Sadat's "leverage" upon American policy was greater than American "leverage" upon Sadat's policy, and that Sadat's "leverage" on American policy set in motion American "leverage" upon Begin's policy. The 100 or 99 percent of the cards that the Americans held, according to Sadat, was apparently to be played only in games between the United States and Israel.

Another example of how this "leverage" worked was given in a speech on April 5, 1978, by Alfred L. Atherton, Jr., who had just been appointed U.S. special negotiator for the Middle East. Atherton was discussing the provision in Security Council Resolution 242 of 1967, which was to assure Israel of secure and recognized borders. Atherton explained why such borders were not achievable:

> But borders that might give Israel the greatest sense of security in geo-graphic and military terms are not those acceptable to Israel's neighbors. They could not, therefore, provide true security.

This reasoning was an American version of a familiar Arab argument. The Israelis might get a greater sense of security if their borders were substantially changed, but it would not be true security unless the Arabs decided what those borders should be. Inasmuch as the Arabs at best wanted no change from the pre-June 1967 borders, the Israelis therefore could not get a greater sense of security in geographic and military terms. Thus the United States had to accept the Arab demand for Israeli "withdrawal"—not qualified on this occasion by "substantial" or any other adjective—to the pre-June 1967 borders. There may be good reasons why Israel should agree to a total withdrawal, or to something substantially or insubstantially less, but this reason is surely not among them. It is, in effect, a rationale for giving the Arabs a veto power over both Israeli and American policy. Yet it was seriously propounded by the leading State Department official in direct charge of Middle East affairs.

By mid-1978, American "leverage" was demonstrated in still another way. It concerned Begin's proposal of December 1977 for Palestinian "self-rule"—still the official Israeli position. By this time, Israelis and Egyptians were deadlocked over, among other things, the outcome of the transition period. Was the decision on Palestinian sovereignty in the West Bank and Gaza to be left open after the five-year period, as the Israelis proposed, or were the Palestinian Arabs to decide the issue at the end of this period, as the Egyptians urged?

In June 1978, the United States virtually took over the negotiations. It sent a questionnaire to Jerusalem, the nub of which was the question whether Israel would be willing to negotiate a final status for the occu-pied territories after a five-year transitional period. The response reiterated the original Israeli position—that "the nature of future relations between the parties will be considered and agreed upon" at the end of the period. The Carter administration clearly intended its question as a signal to the Israeli cabinet that only an affirmative answer would be considered satisfactory. No other supposition can account for the reaction in Washington to the Israeli reply. The State Department spokesman publicly expressed "regret that the Israeli replies did not fully respond to our questions." In a news conference on June 26, President Carter censured the Israeli responses as "very disappointing." He was clearly incensed.

On this occasion the Carter administration might just as well have issued instructions to Jerusalem on how to respond. The trouble with the Israeli response was that it was fully responsive but not according to Washington's intention or liking. In fact, the Israeli response would not have been so "disappointing" if it had been less responsive. Another peculiar aspect of this diplomatic exchange was the way it was flaunted in public. A request for information between governments is usually made discreetly. This incident was played up as if the Carter administration was determined to humiliate the Israeli government by getting it to reverse itself upon American demand or face a public dressing-down by the combined disciplinarians in the State Department and the White House.

If this sort of American "leverage" upon Israel had worked, there would have been no need for the command performance at Camp David in September. Not that the United States was without leverage; it was merely without sufficient leverage to make Israel give up what it considered a vital interest. The distinction was critical to the success—and later breakdown—of the agreements reached at Camp David. The basic reasons for both went back to Sadat's visit to Jerusalem.

In his speech almost a year before, Sadat had anticipated no trouble reaching agreement between Egypt and Israel, which, he said, was not the problem. He proved to be right. The Egyptians correctly surmised that the Israelis would not permit their few settlements in the Sinai to stand in the way of an Egyptian-Israeli peace, however painful it might be to remove them. But most of Sadat's Jerusalem speech had been spent on his role as representative of the entire Arab world in its disputes with Israel, and the Camp David negotiations hinged on this aspect of Egyptian policy. Thus the "Framework for Peace in the Middle East" was three times as long as the "Framework for the Conclusion of a Peace Treaty Between Egypt and Israel." The presupposition of the former was that Egypt did or could represent the Arab states and interests in the Middle East. Without this presupposition, the agreement made little sense.

The Middle East framework made no secret of this assumption of pan-Arab representation on the part of Sadat. It was intended, the text said, "to constitute a basis for peace not only between Egypt and Israel, but also between Israel and each of its other neighbors which is prepared to negotiate with Israel on this basis." To make sure that no one missed the point, the document reiterated: "Egypt and Israel state that the principles and provisions described below should apply to peace treaties between Israel and each of its neighbors—Egypt, Jordan, Syria, and Lebanon." And once more, the framework invited "the other parties to the conflict" to negotiate peace treaties simultaneously with Egypt and Israel "with a view to achieving a comprehensive peace in the area." One can imagine Sadat's reaction if Assad of Syria or Hussein of Jordan had made a deal with Israel and told Egypt to go and do likewise.

The most troublesome part of the Middle East framework, dealing with the Palestinian Arabs, had Sadat implicitly negotiating not only for the Palestinian Arabs but for Jordan. Sadat's ostensible aim had been to gain recognition for "the legitimate rights of the Palestinian people"—and this language was incorporated in the framework. Sadat had also held out for a determination—not merely a review—of the final status of the West Bank and Gaza within a transitional period not exceeding five years. Begin's greatest concession came at this point, though he could claim that he had not promised any particular outcome of this determination. The entire process was, however to be controlled from the outside—by Egypt, Israel, and Jordan. The three, according to the document, first had to agree on the "modalities for establishing an elected self-governing authority in the West Bank and Gaza," defined in the next paragraph as merely an "administrative council." The Egyptian and Jordanian delegations might—not would—include Palestinian Arabs. Jordan was brought into the exercise at every opportunity. After the "modalities" were agreed on, the next step was to be negotiations to determine the "final status" of the Palestinian Arabs. These negotiations were again to be carried on by Egypt, Israel, and Jordan, this time joined by the elected representatives of the West Bank and Gaza. Arab immigration into the West Bank during the transitional period was also to be decided by this quadrumvirate.

Nothing in the Palestinian framework committed Israel—or any other party—to any particular outcome or "final status." Nothing in the Egyptian-Israeli peace framework referred to the Palestinian framework or to Egyptian treaties with other Arab states. The peace framework was so worked out that it concerned Egypt and Israel only, and therefore could be controlled and carried out by them. The Palestinian Arab framework was so put together that it had to have the cooperation of at least two other parties—Jordan and the Palestinian Arabs. If Sadat was not really representing them, that framework was bound to come apart at the seams.

There was reason for this singular solicitude for Jordan on the part of Egypt, Israel, and the United States. However much they differed, the three of them agreed on one thing—that the new Palestinian Arab homeland or entity or self-governing authority should in some way be linked to Jordan. This was the only kind of "linkage" actually built into the West Bank–Gaza framework. And all the while, Hussein could not make up his mind whether to say yes or no. The autocratic Jordanian state could easily be disrupted by permitting an "authority" in Palestine to be "self-governing," and Palestinian Arab "self-government" could easily end up without much authority by linking itself to the autocracy in Amman.

Egypt, Israel, and the United States wanted the Jordanian link as a form of insurance against a PLO-controlled Palestinian state. Israel wanted this link the most, but Sadat had also resorted to the double-talk of an "independent" Palestinian state "linked with Jordan." Carter had never gone further than a Palestinian homeland or entity "in a very strong federation or confederation with Jordan." Meanwhile, no one had heard from Jordan how much independence it was willing or able to grant a state or entity which was also a constituent part of itself. At the same time, the Camp David formulas had, without Jordan's approval, assumed Jordan's participation in the determination of the Palestine Arabs' "final status."

The Jordanian link in the Camp David framework again put Sadat's representative function to the test. If he had had a prior understanding with Hussein, or could count on his support without it, the framework might not have crumbled so quickly. But Hussein had been sulking all the while, as decisions were made for him thousands of miles away. He finally asserted himself by publicly posing fifteen querulous questions about the Camp David agreement.

One would imagine that the answers should have come from Sadat who, after all, signed the agreements and supposedly represented the Arab side. But no, Assistant Secretary of State Harold Saunders rushed off to Amman to answer the King's questions. Saunders succeeded only in making a bad situation worse. He failed to satisfy Hussein, and he infuriated Begin. The Israeli Prime Minister understood Saunders's answers to imply that the Camp David framework was tantamount to a commitment to establish Arab sovereignty over the West Bank and Gaza after the five-year transition period. Begin had given way on the issue, but not that much; he had agreed that the "final status" would be determined within five years, not what that status would be. And so Begin sent off a letter to Washington protesting that Saunders had distorted the plain language of the agreement. Saunders's indiscretion strengthened the already disturbing suspicion that the American side had never been wholly happy with the Camp David agreements and was trying *ex post facto* to smuggle into them more of what the Egyptians had originally demanded.

In effect, the Palestinian framework of the Camp David agreements was a self-destructive diplomatic instrument. It needed little help from the outside to explode from within. Once Jordan and the Palestinian Arabs let it be known that they would not play their allotted roles, the framework fell of its own weight. Only those who had not read the fine print could imagine that Egypt, Israel, and the United States were enough to make it stand up without Jordan or the Palestinian Arabs, not to mention Saudi Arabia and other Arab states. The verdict was in, even as President Carter's standing in the public-opinion polls shot up for his seeming diplomatic triumph and Prime Minister Begin went to Stockholm to receive a peace prize he had not earned.

VI

And yet, there was something about the Camp David agreements that let a glimmer of reality into the murk of the Arab-Israeli conflict.

The glimmer came through the crack between the Israeli-Egyptian framework and the West Bank–Gaza framework. The separation of the two frameworks was itself a decision of utmost significance. It implied that the negotiators formally distinguished between what was binding and what was contingent. A separation between the two frameworks did not mean that they were unrelated. It meant that they were not necessarily related. They were related, if only because Israel was central to both of them, and one could help the other to succeed. But Israel was not central to both in the same way, and one could also hurt the other. If they had been necessarily related, there would have been no need for the two frameworks at all, or there would have been a built-in connection between them. In the latter case, the Camp David agreements would have been only as strong as their weakest link. The only way out of this predicament was to separate the two.

This move was clearly understood by the Americans at Camp David. A "senior White House official," whose disguise deceived no informed reader, told reporters that each of the frameworks "stands on its own." President Carter clearly distinguished between the legal and the psychological relationships when he said: "The two discussions on the Sinai, which relate to Egypt and Israel only on the one hand, and the West Bank–Gaza Strip discussions on the other, are not legally interconnected, but I think throughout the Camp David talks and in the minds of myself, Prime Minister Begin, and President Sadat, they are interrelated." In agreements of this sort, there is a world of difference between what is legally interconnected and what is mentally interrelated.

One word has bedeviled this subject. It is "comprehensive." Sadat, Begin, and Carter have all paid tribute or lip service to this shibboleth, which Carter seems to cherish the most. The term lends itself to different interpretations in different circumstances, so that it is hard to know just what is meant by it. The Egyptian-Israeli framework was a comprehensive peace treaty between Egypt and Israel, but not comprehensive enough to take in the West Bank and Gaza. The other framework was designed to be comprehensive for the West Bank and Gaza, but still left out Syria. A truly comprehensive settlement of the conflict would have to embrace all the neighboring states and perhaps even get the blessings of Saudi Arabia. Such a settlement is not considered possible in present circumstances even by the most wild-eyed advocates of comprehensiveness *à outrance*. In practice, no one expects a truly comprehensive agreement by all interested parties at one stroke; all that is immediately attainable are degrees of comprehensiveness—which is the same as degrees of non-comprehensiveness.

The trouble with a fully comprehensive agreement in these circumstances is that it is illusory in practice, not that it is wrong in principle. The more comprehensive an agreement sets out to be, the more it has to take in Arab states that are the most intransigent. Comprehensiveness thus negates itself. What is important here is not how comprehensive an agreement is, but how effectively an agreement can be carried out within its own terms.

The French saying that "the best is the enemy of the good" may be reworded in the Arab-Israeli context as "the impossible is the enemy of the possible." The Egyptian-Israeli peace treaty was possible because the issues were not intractable and, above all, because Sadat had a mandate to negotiate them. The West Bank–Gaza treaty was not possible at this time because the issues were much less tractable and, above all, because Sadat did not have a mandate to negotiate them. Yet in order to get the negotiations started at all, it was necessary to assume or to pretend that Sadat represented the Arab and not merely the Egyptian side.

But Sadat did not and could not represent the Arab side. His self-appointment as representative of the other interested Arab states inevitably excited their resentment and hostility. Hussein spoke for them rancorously in an interview which appeared in *The New York Times* on January 12, 1979. Sadat had to understand, Hussein told Christopher S. Wren, that "it is not a situation where Egypt is a shepherd and the rest are a herd that can be moved in any direction without question." The implications of Sadat's representative role were never clearly understood, or at least never made understandable to the wider public. For Sadat was not merely reaching agreements with Israel, whether for a peace with Egypt or disposition of the West Bank and Gaza issues. He was not merely protecting his Arab flanks. He was doing both, but he could not do them both without at the same time imposing Egyptian leadership on Arab states, which were put in the position of taking or leaving an agreement which he had negotiated for them.

The intractability of the non-Egyptian issues in the Arab-Israeli conflict is not merely the result of willfulness or pettiness. With the best will in the world on all sides, the issues would still be cruel and painful. Words cannot make them go away, and good intentions cannot change the realities on the ground. One of the greatest obstacles to a settlement of the Arab-Israeli conflict is the assumption that all such differences are amenable to rational, practical arrangements. This sort of remote-control optimism makes a settlement all the harder by making agreement seem too easy and by encouraging a susceptibility to gimmicks and shortcuts.

Take the pre-June 1967 borders of Israel, which are so much in dispute. They are merely the armistice lines of 1949, where the opposing armies happened to come to a halt. The West Bank was taken by Jordan by force of arms. The Jordanians had invaded the West Bank in 1948 in defiance of the UN partition plan in order to prevent the emergence of an independent Palestinian Arab state called for by the plan. In all the years since then, only two states, Great Britain and Pakistan, and no other Arab state, had ever recognized Jordanian sovereignty over the West Bank. On July 29, 1977, Secretary of State Vance acknowledged that it is "an open question as to who has legal right to the West Bank." Legally, then, the position of the West Bank could not be more ill-defined. If forcible occupation is illegal, Jordan had no more right to it than has Israel—and Israel at least has the justification of having occupied it in a war of self-defense.

The geopolitical aspect of the pre-June 1967 borders also resists easy manipulation. The hardest strategic nut to crack is the fact that the 1949 armistice lines left Israel with a waist about ten miles wide at the narrowest point between Arab territory and the Mediterranean sea. Israel's largest city, Tel Aviv, was only about fifteen miles from the Arab lines. The Gaza Strip under Egyptian military control—never legitimized as part of Egypt—was situated at the tip of the traditional southern invasion route into Palestine. The Golan Heights provided the Syrians with a fortress-sanctuary from which to harass the Israeli settlements below. None of these strategic monstrosities left by the 1949 armistice lines can be ameliorated by "insubstantial" territorial changes. But if the changes are "substantial," they must cut into territory that Arabs inhabit or consider their own.

Anyone who has ever set foot on the Golan Heights knows how little leeway they permit. From one direction on a clear day one can see the Israeli city of Haifa on the Mediterranean coast; from the opposite direction, the Syrian capital of Damascus. The plains below on both sides of the Heights are virtually defenseless, or at least desperately difficult to defend against an enemy entrenched overhead. Both sides have too little space at their disposal. The space factor in any Arab-Israeli conflict governs the time factor; there is just too little room for taking risks or making serious compromises so long as tensions remain high.

The most frequent suggestion by outsiders of a way out of this impasse has been "guarantees" by the superpowers. Unfortunately, Israel's position is such that guarantees would not be worth the paper they were written on. Among other reasons, the time factor in any Arab-Israeli war is against them. Israel won the 1967 war in the first two days and almost lost the 1973 war in the first three days. An effective guarantee would have to go into effect immediately, which would be possible only if the guarantor's protective forces were in place in sufficient numbers with sufficient arms on all fronts before the outbreak of hostilities. Israel, in effect, would give up responsibility for its own self-defense, and American soldiers would conceivably have to die instead of Israeli soldiers (it is too great a strain on the imagination to see Soviet soldiers dying to save Israel). Any threat to the guarantee would set off an international hubbub over who was to blame, whether and how to make the guarantee work, and what sort of resolution to pass in the United Nations. Those who advocate a guarantee make no provisions for enforcing it, want foreign soldiers to swarm all over the area, or assume that it would not have to be enforced.[9]

The problem of Israeli settlements in the West Bank is another vexing dilemma. At the heart of it is a question which is rarely considered: Should there be any Jews in the West Bank? And if so, where and how?

There are about 500,000 Arabs in Israel itself out of a population of about 3,500,000. If the same proportion of one-seventh of the population of about 700,000 in the West Bank were permitted for Jews, the latter would number about 100,000. This figure is so unrealistic that no one gives it a thought, for which very reason the imbalance in any proposed distribution of Arabs and Jews in Israel and the West Bank is all the more glaring.

The Jewish communities in the West Bank happened to be the oldest in Palestine. The oldest of all Jewish communities was situated at Hebron, south of Jerusalem, where David was first anointed King of Judah. It survived the destruction of both Temples but not Arab violence in 1929 and 1936. Only one Jewish family remained in Hebron when Jordan took over in 1948 and made the entire West Bank *Judenrein*. The Jewish return to a suburb of Hebron, now called Kiryat Arba (the older name of Hebron), with a population of a few hundred, came after the June 1967 war. Kiryat Arba is atypical in that it is a relatively large Jewish community owing to its biblical associations for the Orthodox; it is typical in that it is still a small, self-enclosed Jewish enclave in a hostile Arab environment.

What constitutes historical justice here? Who is to say?

A few of the other Israeli settlements in the West Bank are like Kiryat Arba—a return to places where Jews lived before 1948. But many are not real settlements by long-term homesteaders; they are military-farming outposts for young people organized by "Nahal," a youth branch of the Israeli army. Others are civilian settlements of various political colorations. At latest count, there were forty-eight Jewish settlements in the West Bank with a total population of about 4,500, most of whose support comes from those who work in Israel and commute morning and evening. Gush Emunim, the extremist religious faction, claims fifteen of these settlements, few of whose residents work in them and some of whom merely spend the weekend there. If the number of existing settlements and settlers were doubled, the result would still be nothing but small, barbed-wire-enclosed Israeli enclaves drawing their sustenance from Israel itself and numbering fewer than 10,000 Jews. Meanwhile, Israelis worry about the natural increase of the Arab population in the Galilee and the reluctance of Jewish immigrants to settle in that part of Israel in sufficient numbers to offset the growing Arab concentrations.

The tenacity with which these settlements are espoused by many Israelis and opposed by most Arabs tells us something else about this problem. It is not altogether amenable to ordinary diplomacy or practical politics. Its roots are too deeply historical, religious, and in some cases irrational. In present circumstances, isolated settlements are the only way for Jews to live in the West Bank, which also happens to be the Judea and Samaria that constituted the original Jewish homeland. The only way is, however, more symbolic than real. In the 1973 war, the settlements on the Golan Heights demonstrated the difference between symbols and realities, when the hard-pressed Israeli army had to deflect soldiers desperately needed elsewhere to pull out the settlers at the first sign of danger.

Whatever one has in one's head, the reality is paradoxical on the ground. If the West Bank is Jewish territory, it is a peculiar kind of Jewish territory on which Arabs live and will continue to live almost exclusively. If it is Arab territory, it is a peculiar kind of Arab territory which was previously denuded of Jews by coercion and violence, was lost in a war provoked by Arabs, and is so situated that in the wrong hands it could mortally endanger both Jordan and Israel. The worst thing about the problem of the West Bank is that it is so tormentingly intractable; it would be much easier to resolve if it were only the product of ill-will or stupidity.

What, one may ask, has all this to do with the Camp David agreements? The answer is that it has everything to do with them.

As I have tried to show, one of those agreements, dealing with the future of the West Bank–Gaza area, was fatally flawed. But its faults should not blind us to its chief virtue. It recognized that this problem was one that had to be dealt with circumspectly and experimented with in order for there to be a chance of finding a solution with which all interested parties could live.

The old Labor-party compromise of partition could never work, because it was totally unacceptable to the Arabs and made no provision for anything but an Israeli-Jordanian future for the Palestinian Arabs. The Camp David arrangement was a different type of compromise. It was based on the provisional distinction between Palestinian-Arab civil autonomy and Israeli security, the former very broad in scope, including a strong local police force, the latter limited to a thinned-out Israeli military deployment—numbering only 6,000 soldiers—within specified security locations. For such a compromise, the five-year transition period was minimally indispensable. It would have given all sides an opportunity to move toward a new relationship without feeling totally hedged in. The negotiations for a final status were set to begin almost midway through the transition period—no later than three years. If "peace process" has any meaning, this arrangement was just such a process.

It was, moreover, a genuine compromise. It was especially a compromise on the part of Prime Minister Begin. He was the one who gave away the most. How much he gave away can be seen by comparing the open-ended Camp David agreement with the 1977 election platform of Begin's electoral Likud bloc, which called for "Jewish sovereignty alone between the sea and Jordan." Not a single one of Begin's chief lieutenants in his own party went along with him in favor of the Camp David agreements; several of those who had been closest to him attacked him the most savagely; he was put in the curious position of being saved from defeat by the opposition. Sadat compromised by agreeing to leave some Israeli security forces in place in the West Bank for the time being, to postpone the final status for up to five years, and to exclude the disposition of East Jerusalem, on which the sides were too far apart. But the compromise was uneven. What the Israelis gave up, they actually had; what the Egyptians gave up, they had merely wanted. We may now come back to Dayan's formula of "living together." It can be misused, as it is misused when it is applied to the Israeli settlements in the West Bank. These settlements are evidence of just the opposite. They are in the West Bank only in a geographic sense; socially, they might just as well be in Israel; their inhabitants live farther apart from their Arab neighbors than Jews and Arabs live apart in Israel.

Yet the ultimate validity of the idea cannot be rejected. Whatever the juridical arrangements, Jews and Arabs can have peace in the small, cramped space of Palestine only by "living together" in some manner. There is no other way to make any arrangement work, and any peaceful arrangement must finally be judged by how it contributes to living together, not by largely unrealizable abstractions—whether Israeli or Arab —about sovereignty in the West Bank.

Can Jews and Arabs live together some day in the whole of Palestine? In this matter, optimism is futile, pessimism fatal. When it comes to staying alive, people do what they must—not always, but often enough to give some hope for the survival of the human race. The Camp David framework for the West Bank and Gaza, shorn of its flaws, offered some hope for a peaceful future for Jews and Arabs in Palestine. That much cannot be said for the all-or-nothing proposals for an Arab-Israeli settlement.

VII

The first loser as a result of the breakdown of the Camp David agreements was Egypt.

It was a classical case of giving up a bird in the hand by chasing a bird in the bush. The bird in the hand was the Egyptian-Israeli peace settlement. It would have been no mean feat of diplomacy to regain all that Egyptian territory without war. But the bird in the bush lured Sadat into an effort to bulldoze his way to a West Bank–Gaza settlement without assured cooperation from the Palestinian Arabs, Jordan, or any other Arab state. That Begin and Carter played along with Sadat in his pretense that he could represent all Arab states and interests does not make him any less responsible for putting himself and them in that position.

That Sadat chose to reopen the Camp David negotiations at all was far more important than the grounds he gave for reopening them. These grounds, moreover, undermined the most realistic aspects of the agreements and magnified the most illusory.

The necessarily loose connection between the Egyptian-Israeli framework and the West Bank–Gaza framework was undercut by the demand for a rigidly set, time-bound linkage between the two. To make matters worse, another linkage was proposed making the Egyptian-Israeli peace treaty subject to the vicissitudes of Egypt's treaties with other Arab powers, which have never repudiated the political doctrine enunciated in 1967 by Nasser and Assad, the latter with far more power today, that the very existence of Israel in itself is an "aggression."

The West Bank–Gaza framework had been built around the basic design of a five-year transitional period, which was to proceed by stages with Jordanian and Palestine-Arab cooperation. All previous proposals, Egyptian as well as Israeli, had provided for a five-year interval. When Sadat insisted on rushing ahead with the elections for the West Bank–Gaza administrative council—the first Egyptian proposal made the intervening period as short as three months, then altered it to six, and finally to nine—without Jordan and with no sign of support by the Palestinian Arabs, he was short-circuiting the transition period to the point of ensuring that nothing of lasting value could come out of it.

Sadat did not need the oppositionist Baghdad summit meeting of Arab states, including Saudi Arabia and Jordan, on November 2–5, 1978, to tell him that he had lost his gamble at Camp David. The West Bank–Gaza framework had been so constructed that it could not work without prior agreement with, or almost immediate acquiescence by, Jordan and the Palestinian Arabs. When they refused to go along, before the Baghdad meeting, the framework fell apart. What the Baghdad meeting did, by uniting "extremists" and "moderates" against Sadat, was to serve notice that Egypt had to be humiliated and punished for breaking ranks, attempting to serve its own interest, and presuming at the same time to represent the Arab world. The message of the meeting was not that Sadat's version of peace with Israel is wrong; it was that any peace with Israel is wrong. It was not merely a verdict on the past; it was also a mobilization for the future. For that mobilization, Egypt was told that it could no longer count on being the dominant factor, as it had liked to think of itself. The point of the exercise was to confront Egypt with the choice of having peace with Israel or peace with the other Arab states, but not with both. It is too often forgotten that the Arab-Israeli conflict is not the only one going on in the Middle East; there is also an inter-Arab conflict, sometimes reflected in the jockeying for position against Israel, sometimes quite apart from Israel.

Sadat's greatest problem is that his policy tends to outstrip his power. He seeks to manipulate forces much greater than those at his disposal. Ironically, he has found it much easier to manipulate the United States than his Arab brethren.

The second loser as a result of the breakdown of the Camp David agreements was the United States.

The American performance was not one to be proud of. Nothing could have been more embarrassing than the outcome of the policy consecrated in the Soviet-American statement of October 1977. To make a deal with the Soviet Union that neither Egypt nor Israel nor much of the U.S. Congress could tolerate must set some sort of record for wrong-headedness. After Sadat's end run to Jerusalem, the Carter administration had to limp along after him. When Sadat's momentum finally gave out after Camp David, the chief executive of the United States completely lost his bearings. By saying that the Egyptian-Israeli differences over Sadat's new demands were nothing more than "tiny technicalities, phrasing of ideas, legalisms" which had "absolutely no historical significance," President Carter unwittingly confessed that the full meaning of Sadat's turnabout had eluded him.

In its initial spasm of disappointment, the Carter administration turned the full force of its wrath on the Israeli government. After recovering from shock, the masterminds of U.S. policy came up with a "compromise"—they stretched Egypt's new demand for nine months between treaty signing and West Bank–Gaza elections to twelve months, as if they did not understand what the real issue was. Mechanically tacking on another three months could make no difference so long as Jordan and the Palestinian Arabs refused to cooperate. Without one or the other, and probably both, a hasty election imposed by Egypt, Israel, and the United States was sure to make the existing confusion worse.

The Carter administration would have been better advised to expend some of its wrath on Jordan. If any Arab country is beholden to the United States, it is Jordan.[10] The Camp David framework was composed as if there were good reason to believe that Jordan could be counted on. Yet Hussein had burned his fingers so often that he could least afford to take chances. His reflexive disposition is to stay on the fence or join forces with the prospective winner. Hussein's defection to the anti-Sadat camp did more to undermine the Camp David agreements than any other single action or inaction. It was at the same time a stunning defeat for and blatant affront to the United States. That Hussein can get away with this ambidexterity without the slightest sign of official disapproval or a whimper of protest from the American press suggests that some American leverage has been misdirected.[11] Now that Hussein has been flirting with Syria and even the PLO, one wonders how much longer he can count on American indulgence. To be sure, he has not always guessed right. He jumped the wrong way in 1967; he may be jumping the wrong way again.

The fundamental problem facing American policy in the Arab-Israeli conflict is whether, as Brzezinski thought, "Israel cuts across American *raisons d'état*." The State Department's Middle East specialists tried to prevent American recognition of Israel in 1948 with essentially the same argument, and the attitude has survived underground or above ground ever since.[12] The upheaval in Iran should especially bring this thesis into question. The resurgence of militant Islamic orthodoxy on the Iranian model threatens the *raisons d'état* of the United States in the entire region more than any other single force. It cannot be held back by the movement of an American battle fleet toward the Persian Gulf (recalled) or a visitation by F-15's to Saudi Arabia (unarmed). The reaction of the Saudi rulers to the events in Iran should be most disturbing in Washington. If all the Saudi rulers could think of was to blame the United States for the Shah's debacle, they have not begun to understand the social and political conditions which can also erupt in Saudi Arabia and have shown how ready they are to turn on the United States for an alibi. In comparison to most Islamic states, Israel stands out in the area as a rock of steadfastness. I do not mean to propose that Israel should be the only state in the Middle East befriended by the United States. I mean that it is self-defeating to befriend other states at the expense of Israel rather than in addition to Israel.

The third loser was Israel.

The Camp David agreement was extremely costly to the Israeli political system. It tore up each party and left wounds that may be difficult to heal. Begin suffered a major ideological split in his own party and gave up a lifetime of political consistency. In the opposition, the former dovish spokesman, Yigal Allon, turned hawkish, and only the critical support of the Labor-party leader, Shimon Peres, saved the Camp David agreements from parliamentary disaster. The Gush Emunim fanatics and their fellow-travelers resorted to actions and language that amounted to civil disobedience.

The political turmoil which the Camp David agreements provoked might have been a cheap price to pay for a peace with Egypt and a transition period in the West Bank and Gaza with a reasonable chance of success. But when they were quickly frustrated by Sadat's equivocations, the damage to Israeli political institutions was not matched by any equivalent reward.

The U.S.-Israeli relationship was also subjected to unprecedented strain. Sadat's entire strategy was based on the 100 or 99 percent of the cards that the United States was supposed to hold against Israel. On this account, he could always make the United States responsible for anything he did not get from Israel; the Carter administration tried its best not to disappoint him and, in any case, considered that it had far more "leverage" to move Israel than to influence Egypt. As a result, Israeli resistance to Egyptian demands could be translated into Israeli defiance of American desires, and Egypt could sometimes exercise a virtual veto power over American policies. The classic instance in the first case was Israel's rejection on the same grounds of both Egypt's nine months and America's twelve months for the West Bank–Gaza electoral timetable. In the second case, a classic example was Carter's initial praise for Begin's West Bank–Gaza self-rule plan of December 1977 as "a long step forward" and then his backing away as soon as the Egyptians made known their refusal to consider it.

Because, at times of hard bargaining, Israel was not negotiating with Egypt alone but rather with Egypt backstopped by the United States, the future Israeli negotiating position may have been seriously compromised. Prospective negotiations as a result tend to start from what Israel has already conceded and turn on what more Egypt wants. Made-in-America "compromises" usually give the Egyptians much or most of what they want and thereby raise the level of Israeli concessions to only a little lower than the original Egyptian demands. All the post-Camp David demands by Egypt were designed to provide Egypt with escape clauses for scaling down Egyptian obligations without any compensatory way out for Israel. So long as this type of bazaar diplomacy goes on, with tacit and sometimes open U.S. connivance, the end for Israel is never in sight.

The paradox in the Israeli position is that it may well be true that only Begin could have made the concessions necessary for the Camp David agreements and that Begin could make them only by acting as if he were his old political enemy, David Ben-Gurion. The tension between David Begin and Menachem Ben-Gurion is so great, however, that it may not be able to stand the strain of much more pulling and hauling.

We may yet look back at the Camp David agreements as having been in essence the most that Israel could give and the least that Arabs could accept. If so, sturdier frameworks for peace between Israel and its Arab neighbors need a better understanding of what was right and what went wrong at Camp David.

Commentary, March 1979

VI

"NEO-CONSERVATIVES" IN REVIEW

1

Podhoretz's Vietnam War

Norman Podhoretz likes to be the fugleman of the latest political revelation. For this reason, his reconsideration of the Vietnam war may be an awful portent.* It could be the signal for a corrosive campaign to reopen the wounds of the war and envenom American political life once again. We may not even be spared an American stab-in-the-back legend of the kind that haunted the German Weimar Republic during the 1920s.

Podhoretz's research is almost exclusively research into books by other people. Paragraph after paragraph is constructed out of quotations and citations, fourteen of them from my own *Abuse of Power*. His book thus comes out as potted history—but potted for a purpose. It is the purpose that makes the book worth more than cursory notice.

As a potted historian, however, Podhoretz leaves much to be desired. It is a thankless task to correct an author's mistakes, for they take longer to correct than to make. An example will show what I mean. It concerns so fundamental a matter as the Tonkin Gulf resolution of August 1964. If Podhoretz after almost eighteen years can still twist it to mean what it was never intended to mean, the time has again come to set the record straight.

Former Senator J. William Fulbright, according to Podhoretz, "pointed out that the resolution would indeed empower the President to involve the United States in a major land war." In fact, Fulbright pointed out no such thing. Without further explanation, a reader would gather that Fulbright and the Senate were culpable of implicitly authorizing and accepting the subsequent involvement of the United States in a major land war in Vietnam.

* Norman Podhoretz, *Why We Were in Vietnam* (New York: Simon and Schuster, 1982).

Podhoretz could not have written this sentence in good faith if he had himself studied or even read the debate in the Senate. Senator Daniel Brewster of Maryland questioned Fulbright about whether there was anything in the resolution that would authorize, recommend, or approve the landing of large American armies in Vietnam. Fulbright replied: "There is nothing in the resolution, as I read it, that contemplates it. I agree with the Senator that that is the last thing we would want to do." Fulbright also said: "Speaking for my own [Foreign Relations] committee, everyone I have heard has said that the last thing we want to do is to become involved in a land war in Asia."

Senator Gaylord Nelson of Wisconsin asked whether the resolution authorized a complete change in the previous policy of refraining from "a direct land confrontation with our army as a substitute for the South Vietnam Army or as a substantially reinforced U.S. Army to be joined with the South Vietnam Army." Fulbright answered: "I do not interpret the joint resolution in that way at all." Pressed again to say what the resolution actually authorized, Fulbright said that "when we try to confine ourselves and say that this resolution either prohibits or authorizes such action [to put a large land army on the Asian continent] by the Commander in Chief in defense of this country, I believe that is carrying it a little further than I would care to go."

Here and elsewhere, the problem arises because Podhoretz did not do his own research. He depended in this case, as his citations show, on a deeply flawed book by Guenter Lewy, *America in Vietnam*, which has misled him more than once.* Anyone who had taken the trouble to consult the debate in the Senate would have known that the Tonkin Gulf resolution was presented in an effort to deter the North Vietnamese, not to encourage the involvement of the United States in a major land war in Vietnam. Fulbright later regretted having supported a resolution so loosely worded that he could not even tell the Senate just what it prohibited or authorized. Unfortunately for Fulbright and the country, it opened the way for President Johnson to take exactly the action that Fulbright had assured the Senate he and the entire Foreign Relations Committee opposed. It opened the way by not explicitly forbidding Johnson's action, a rather different matter from expressly empowering

---

* For an extended consideration of Lewy's book, and its bearing on the question of the "morality" of the Vietnam war, see pp. 157–167 of my essay, "Ghosts of Vietnam."

it. The debate made absolutely clear what the Senate's intention was and was not. It was not what Podhoretz says it was.

More important than factual offenses, which would take another small book to compile and correct, are some of Podhoretz's ideological fixations. One basic issue concerns the very nature of the Vietnam war.

For Podhoretz, it is important that the conflict should have been a "foreign aggression," not a civil war. He seems to think that it had to be restricted to South Vietnam in order to have been a civil war. It was not a civil war, he insists, because an aggression from North Vietnam was responsible for it.

This strange theory treats North Vietnam as if it were not inhabited by Vietnamese. Vietnam was one country until it was temporarily divided by the Geneva Agreements of 1954—temporarily, because they provided for general elections in 1956 to unify the country. South Vietnamese President Ngo Dinh Diem refused to honor that agreement and even created a Committee for the Liberation of North Vietnam. South and North Vietnam never accepted the division of the country; both pledged themselves to reunify it by all possible means.

How, then, could a war between South and North Vietnam *not* be a civil war? North Vietnam was not a "foreign country." The control of the southern Vietcong by the North Vietnamese did not make either of them less Vietnamese. To be sure, it was not a "pure" civil war any more than the Spanish Civil War had been a pure civil war; entire Italian fascist divisions fought on the Spanish fascist side without changing the fundamentally Spanish character of the civil war. Yet much of Podhoretz's case rests on the dubious proposition that the Vietnamese conflict was not a civil war.

His case also rests on an equally muddled view of why the United States intervened in the war. One of his notions is that the American motivation was selfless and spiritual. The United States went into Vietnam "for the sake of an ideal." It was "self-evident that the United States was doing the right thing in trying to save South Vietnam from Communism."

It was hardly self-evident. Saving South Vietnam from Communism was never enough to justify American intervention, let alone on the scale of 1965–1972. Intervention was justified on much larger grounds. President Eisenhower had had Vietnam in mind when he first propounded the "domino principle" in 1954. That "principle" continued to be the chief rationale for the increasing American commitment, as it is in the case of El Salvador today. Then Vice President Nixon had even predicted that if Vietnam fell the United States would have to fight a major war to save the Philippines or Australia. President Johnson's dominoes went as far as Singapore and Indonesia. The dominoes, not South Vietnam, provided the raison d'être of the war. There was too little at stake and too much at risk in South Vietnam to make its political fate the self-evident proof that the United States had done the right thing.

Podhoretz also presents another theory. Elsewhere he maintains that the United States originally sought to prevent a Vietnamese Communist victory because it "could be tantamount to an expansion of Soviet power." Even if this statement were not fanciful, it would mean that the "ideal" had somehow turned into a worldwide struggle for power.

It happens to be more of Podhoretz's fanciful history. Strange as it may seem in retrospect, the official American line was that we were fighting Chinese, not Soviet, expansion in Vietnam. High State Department officials even tried to put across the idea that the United States was fighting in Vietnam to enable "Moscow's doctrine of peaceful coexistence," as one put it, to prevail over "Peiping's assertion that armed struggle is a more productive Communist course." We were, according to this reasoning, virtually fighting with Moscow and against Peiping, even though Moscow had become the prime supplier of war materiel to North Vietnam. Almost to the end, U.S. policy counted on the Soviet Union to help pull U.S. chestnuts out of the fire in Vietnam. Former Secretary of State Henry Kissinger clearly and repeatedly described in *The White House Years* how he sought to trade an improvement in Soviet-American relations for Soviet cooperation to make North Vietnam settle the war on acceptable terms.

Podhoretz, too, has his own domino theory. "Everyone was wrong," he believes—except, now, himself. His new theory is that the war was finally vindicated by the later appearance of Cuban troops in Angola and by similar occurrences in the next few years in Ethiopia, Mozambique, South Yemen, and Afghanistan. He makes no effort to explain what the connections between these far-flung events were. His theory implies that the Soviet Union would not have gone into Afghanistan, for example, if the United States had won the war in Vietnam or, conceivably, was still fighting there. Eight years separate the U.S. withdrawal from Vietnam and the Soviet invasion of Afghanistan. Whatever the pressures on the Soviets in Afghanistan, it is hard to see how or why they would have changed in the least whatever had happened in

Vietnam. The missing link here is not merely evidence; it is simple plausibility.

Despite his apparent bravado, Podhoretz's vindication of the Vietnam war is curiously restricted and defensive. On all grounds but one, he makes no effort to justify U.S. intervention. The only way, he concedes, "the United States could have avoided defeat in Vietnam was by staying out of the war." The U.S. Army and Officers Corps were "unfitted for the kind of war they were called upon to fight in Vietnam." The American people were never "enthusiastic about the war." The final abandonment of South Vietnam demonstrated that "saving South Vietnam from Communism was not only beyond its [America's] reasonable military, political, and intellectual capabilities but that it was ultimately beyond its moral capabilities as well." These devastating admissions are scattered throughout the book and make one wonder why, if they were true, anyone would want to vindicate an unwanted, unnecessary, and unwinnable war.

Podhoretz's last stand in favor of the war is restricted to morality. In his most blustering style, he proclaims that "nothing is easier to refute than the moral case against the American intervention in Vietnam." Or again—"stupid though the American way of war no doubt was in the political context of Vietnam," it cannot "reasonably be considered immoral." It was not immoral for him, because, as we have already been told, the United States intervened solely "to save South Vietnam from Communism" and simply "for the sake of an ideal." His Vietnam war does not exist in a real world, tainted with struggles for power and geopolitical forces. His war exists in an ideal realm of anti-Communism, no matter where, by what means, at what price, or against whom.

Yet Podhoretz was let down by the very real Americans who had to live up to his idealization of the war. He laments that the war was ultimately beyond the "moral capabilities" of the United States. The entire enterprise was doomed because we failed to provide a "moral justification." The political and military arguments of the Johnson administration "floated aimlessly in a moral vacuum." In his very last paragraph, Podhoretz concludes that he is "fully, painfully aware" that "the American effort to save Vietnam from Communism was indeed beyond our intellectual and moral capabilities," though it was still, as President Reagan called it, "a noble cause."

There is something theological in this dualism between the nobility of the cause and the lack of nobility of the human beings called upon to realize it. In the real world, nations should not try to do what they are incapable of doing. In Podhoretz's world, nations get the highest marks for trying to do what they are unable to do, despite the evil they may do to themselves and their enemies in the effort.

No one who has questioned the American role in the war, especially its morality, can hope to escape Podhoretz's wrath. Among those who get the roughest treatment are Susan Sontag, Mary McCarthy, and Frances FitzGerald. They were gullible and fatuous enough in their treatment of the Vietnamese Communists to merit this ridicule. If an ignoble prize were given for the Higher Inanity, Susan Sontag's account of her pilgrimage to Hanoi would certainly deserve to win it—as she herself has apparently come to realize. About twenty others make Podhoretz's black list, from Noam Chomsky to the late Hans Morgenthau, the latter his once-revered mentor and valued contributor. Despite all the unpaid research I did for him, I earn Podhoretz's displeasure for having alluded to the war's "shamefulness" and "immoral conduct."

But one sinner is mysteriously missing.

He is Norman Podhoretz. Podhoretz was editor of *Commentary* throughout the Vietnam war. From 1965 to 1972, the years of America's massive intervention, at least a half-dozen articles on the war appeared in *Commentary*. Every one of them, without exception, was explicitly or implicitly critical of U.S. policy. As early as May 1965, the late George Lichtheim offered some advice that might still do Podhoretz some good: "No country in the world, least of all South Vietnam, can go on forever subsisting on anti-Communism." In March 1968, an article by me referred to the war as "a political debacle, a military folly, and a moral disgrace." In May 1969, Lionel Abel thought "our policy in Vietnam wrong, in both political and moral terms." In May 1971, Nathan Glazer, now a fellow neoconservative, had an article entitled "Vietnam: The Case for Immediate Withdrawal." The "moral damage," wrote Glazer, "has been enormous, greater in some ways than the impact of any war in the history of the nation." One article sympathetically considered the antiwar tactics of Dr. Benjamin Spock and the Reverend William Sloane Coffin.

Article after article in *Commentary* in those years questioned the morality of the Vietnam war. Podhoretz did not object to this view at a time when the debate raged and a strong stand one way or the other could have had practical consequences.

But the cream of the jest—if it is a jest—is still to come.

Podhoretz himself began to write a monthly department of comment in June 1970, in the midst of the war. It took him twelve issues to get to the subject of the war, in May 1971. In an article entitled "A Note on Vietnamization," he revealed that he had delivered a speech in the fall of 1969 in which he had urged "an immediate American withdrawal," using arguments similar to those in Glazer's article. But Podhoretz, who never does things by halves, ended his article by going beyond the advocacy of withdrawal. He announced that he now found himself "unhappily moving to the side of those who would prefer just such an American defeat" to anything but complete withdrawal.

As late as 1979, in *Breaking Ranks*, Podhoretz was still willing to admit that the Vietnam war "could only be fought in ways that were bound to seem, and sometimes actually were, immoral and atrocious." No reader of *Why We Were in Vietnam* could possibly imagine that this book was written by a onetime defeatist who not so long ago agreed that immoralities and atrocities were at least sometimes necessarily committed in that venomous war.

Everyone has a right to change his mind. But no one has a right to be so smug and sanctimonious, lashing out at those with whom he had essentially agreed only yesterday—and to keep that a secret from the reader.

If Podhoretz had not kept this secret from his readers, he would have had to accept some personal responsibility for the U.S. failure in Vietnam along with all the other opponents of the war. "The truth is," he now exhorts ominously,

> that the antiwar movement bears a certain measure of responsibility for the horrors that have overtaken the people of Vietnam; and so long as those who participated in that movement are unwilling to acknowledge this, they will go on trying to discredit the idea that there is a distinction between authoritarianism and totalitarianism.

We need not discuss that distinction here. But if there is one thing Podhoretz does not do in this book it is to acknowledge his role in the antiwar movement and—to follow his own reasoning—his measure of responsibility for the horrors that have overtaken the people of Vietnam.

He was far from candid about his own role in his previous autobiographical book, *Breaking Ranks*, but full self-disclosure was demanded of him in this book, in view of his savage denunciations of others, including some who had taken a less extreme position than he had done. In *Making It*, Podhoretz's "dirty little secret" was the lust for fame and success, which he seemed to think it shocking to reveal. In

Why We Were in Vietnam, he has another dirty little secret, which he does not seem to think it shocking to conceal.

As history, Podhoretz's version of the Vietnam war cannot be taken seriously. Its significance must be sought in the present rather than in the past. It represents a trend of selective moralistic zealotry which, if permitted to spread, will give both anti-Communism and neoconservatism a bad name. It opens the door to a viciously dangerous stab-in-the-back legend by inferentially blaming the horrors of the war on those who opposed it rather than on those who waged it. An even more explicit stab-in-the-back type of accusation was made in *Commentary* in April 1980 by Charles Horner, who was subsequently appointed a Deputy Assistant Secretary in the State Department.

The specter of a German-style stab-in-the-back legend cannot be dismissed. It is being actively propagated by retired U.S. military officers of the highest rank, of whom the most aggressive and blatant is General William C. Westmoreland, former field commander in Vietnam and Army Chief of Staff. In an address at the U.S. Army Command and General Staff College in April 1979, published in its official organ, *Military Review*, January 1979, Westmoreland blamed the United States for having "betrayed and deserted" South Vietnam and named "partisan politicians, intellectuals, the media and 'crusading groups,'" together with "members of Congress and other political leaders," as most responsible for the betrayal and desertion. Much of Podhoretz's argumentation coincides with the line in Westmoreland's book, *A Soldier Reports*, and in this address to the Army's school for future commanding officers.

Anyone who wishes to understand what went wrong in Vietnam and elsewhere would do better to take a hint from Edmund Burke. In one of his most famous speeches, delivered 207 years ago, before another failed war, he observed that "a great empire and little minds go ill together."

The New Republic, March 10, 1982.

2

Mrs. Kirkpatrick's Theories

Intellectuals in politics live dangerously. They run the risk of being neither good intellectuals nor good politicians. During the nineteenth century, American intellectuals were extremely rare in government; the great break in this tradition came in the 1930s with the New Deal. Now, however, politicized intellectuals go back and forth between universities or research institutes and governmental office. They are always on call; Washington is their promised land; they get there only to find that they are intellectually not what they once were.

The latest star performer among intellectuals in politics is Jeane J. Kirkpatrick, formerly of Georgetown University and now Ambassador to the United Nations. She is the second academic intellectual to serve in that post; Senator Daniel Patrick Moynihan was the first. Both owed their appointments to articles they wrote for *Commentary* magazine, which has proven to be, among other things, a highly specialized employment agency.

Mrs. Kirkpatrick's new book* offers an opportunity to see how she has developed from an academic intellectual writing about politics to an intellectual embroiled in politics. It is not an easy book to review, because it is made up of an introduction and eleven essays or articles, one going back almost twenty years, that do not add up to a sustained argument. Yet they permit some insight into her political and intellectual metamorphosis.

Mrs. Kirkpatrick came to the United Nations with a considerable body of noteworthy academic work behind her. It might almost seem to have destined her for some such job. In 1971, she put on *Leader and*

---

* *Rationalism and Reason in Politics* (New York: American Enterprise Institute/Simon & Schuster, 1982).

Vanguard, a book on the Peronist movement in Argentina, the very country that has preoccupied her at the United Nations. Two years later she edited *The Strategy of Deception*, dealing with Communist propaganda and tactics; her own contribution solidified her reputation as a militant anti-Communist, if any such assurance were needed. In 1974, she published the first major study of women in American political life; its title, *Political Woman*, might now be her own job description. And in 1976, she produced another large book, *The New Presidential Elite*, of particular interest in view of her present occupation and associations.

The "new elite," according to this study, came into its own during the 1972 Presidential election. It arose in both parties, but mainly in the Democratic Party through the McGovern campaign. As Mrs. Kirkpatrick saw it, the older, dominant political type was party-oriented, moderate in policy and long on political experience. The "new breed" or "new class" of political intellectuals, as she also called them, was more likely to have weak and recent party ties, to conceive of politics as an arena of clashing values and to hold far more extreme political views.

The famous irony of history has caught up with Mrs. Kirkpatrick. If she were writing the same kind of book today, she would have to shift her focus from the Democratic to the Republican Party, which the most recent new-class political intellectuals have infiltrated. Indeed, she would be writing about herself and her embattled band of so-called neoconservatives.

If Mrs. Kirkpatrick had known that she was destined to play a large political role, she might well have written differently about new-class intellectuals. In *The New Presidential Elite*, she defined the new class as one motivated by "pure issue concern," resulting in weak institutional loyalties and strong "personalist politics." These attributes might describe her today. But she was still in her academic phase six years ago, so that she held back from passing explicit judgment on this phenomenon. Nevertheless, she clearly implied that the new class was a potentially dangerous excrescence on the body politic.

In 1977, Mrs. Kirkpatrick was less discreet. In "Why the New Right Lost," another *Commentary* essay included in this current book, she criticized the rightist variety of the new class on the ground that the ideological perspective in politics bred "intolerance of diversity, impatience with compromise, and the kind of intransigence characteristic of sectarian, rule-or-ruin politics." In her 1979 piece "Politics and the 'New Class,' " when she was more concerned with the leftist variety, she went so far as to express the belief that "politics featuring large roles for intellectuals is especially dangerous to human liberty." She accused intellectuals of a tendency "to find reality wanting" and of a "marked proclivity for moralistic politics." The new class was clearly the enemy for her before she became a charter member of its neoconservative subdivision.

This was her position just before Richard V. Allen, then foreign-affairs adviser to candidate Ronald Reagan, read her article in *Commentary* and brought it to Mr. Reagan's attention, thereby setting in motion a series of tête-à-têtes that ultimately brought her to the United Nations at the new President's express behest. It is odd to read the ominous warnings against the new class in this book by one who now belongs to it. Something apparently happened to Mrs. Kirkpatrick's viewpoint when the new class shifted its main attention from the Democratic to the Republican Party, and she was given the opportunity to play a large role in politics.

A similar transformation seems to have taken place in her views on foreign policy.

As late as 1978, in "On the Invocation of Universal Values," Mrs. Kirkpatrick came out in favor of President Carter's "emphasis on human rights" and "its irreducible role in American foreign policy," though she had reservations about the way he had expressed it in his speech at the University of Notre Dame in May 1977.

By November 1979, however, she mounted a frontal attack on the Carter foreign policy all along the line. Her article "Dictatorships and Double Standards" implied that there was no place in practice for human rights in American policy; it was hard to see when she would ever approve of applying such a standard. As she has since revealed, she began to make a serious study of the human-rights policy only after other people had read her 1979 article in that light, and the more she studied, the less she liked it. Others criticized the Carter policy because it flip-flopped so much; she made it seem uniformly and deliberately malevolent.

The article that gives this book its name merits closer examination. In it, Mrs. Kirkpatrick puts forward the thesis that has become most closely associated with her thinking on foreign policy, and it raises several issues that beg for more serious discussion than they have received.

Its leading idea hinges on the distinction between authoritarian and totalitarian regimes. According to Mrs. Kirkpatrick, authoritarian regimes, such as Shah Mohammad Reza Pahlavi's in Iran and Anastasio Somoza Debayle's in Nicaragua, merely seek to preserve "traditional" societies. Totalitarian regimes, such as those in the Soviet Union and in Nazi Germany, seek to transform and regulate the whole of society—the economy, culture and human personality. The distinction is by no means original with her. It has, in my view, a basic theoretical or abstract validity. The troublesome question is how she interprets and applies it.

She describes the Shah and Somoza as "traditional rulers of semi-traditional societies." Neither, she maintains, "attempted to alter significantly the distribution of goods, status, or power." She wastes no indignation upon any aspect of their rule or sympathy for their peoples, because she regards these rulers as merely heads of a "traditional autocracy." Somoza's "operation," as Mrs. Kirkpatrick calls it, was nothing more than that of "an efficient, urban political machine," oddly equipped with a private army. If she can be believed, Somoza's government was something like the old Tammany Hall, with a little more clout.

Since Mrs. Kirkpatrick uses the Shah and Somoza as her two prime cases, it is fair to test her viewpoint with them. In each case, the reality was far from her version of it. The Shah and Somoza virtually tore their traditional societies apart.

It was not traditional in Nicaragua for the dictator to own about 50 percent of all property, including most of the profitable industries. Somoza's downfall came about because he neither knew where to stop nor wanted to. When he and his closest associates shamelessly enriched themselves with the international aid that poured in after the devastating earthquake in Managua in 1972, they set in motion the forces that led to their disaster. The corruption and repression reached such an intolerable level that the traditional middle and upper classes were appalled and alienated. The children of these same classes provided the initial leadership of the guerrilla movement that arose against Somoza. If he had been as truly traditional as Mrs. Kirkpatrick describes him, it would have been most unlikely for the Catholic hierarchy to have played such an outstanding role in condemning and undermining his regime.

The case of the Shah is even further from Mrs. Kirkpatrick's traditional model. If anything undid him, it was his attempt to change Iran too much and too fast and—once resistance to his rule began to threaten him—too brutally. The source of the fanatical opposition led by the Ayatollah Ruhollah Khomeini was precisely the traditionalism that Mrs. Kirkpatrick perversely locates in the Shah.

Mrs. Kirkpatrick needs this historical mythology in order to exempt the Shah and Somoza from all responsibility for their own downfalls and to place the entire blame on American policy. She writes as if the two rulers were innocent victims of sheer American rancor. It is not enough for her to say that, once crises had broken out in Iran and Nicaragua, the Carter administration floundered and lost its way. For her, the Carter policy was directly and wholly responsible for both debacles. One might imagine that unfriendly words in Washington about violations of human rights in Iran and Nicaragua were enough to topple both regimes.

In fact, the deeper and more lasting causes for the downfalls of the Shah and Somoza were generated inside their own countries, not in the United States. Mrs. Kirkpatrick short-circuits the entire process and does not see beyond the last, diseased phase.

What would Mrs. Kirkpatrick have done? She hints at the answer by nostalgically recalling that "once upon a time a President might have sent Marines to ensure the protection of American strategic interests." Once upon a time, of course, the world was not what it is now. When the Marines were sent to Nicaragua, they occupied the country for almost twenty years before putting the Somozas, father and son, in power. The notion that any American President, including Ronald Reagan, could in the present period send enough Marines to occupy Nicaragua or Iran long enough to protect American strategic interests in that fashion is so farfetched that this presumably glorious past seems hardly worth evoking.

In this connection, however, Mrs. Kirkpatrick raises a larger issue: Should the United States support a foreign dictatorship because it is "authoritarian" rather than "totalitarian"? She seems to believe that anything short of totalitarianism is good enough to merit American support. No other type of oppression elicits indignation from her. The level of American tolerance is thus to be determined by totalitarianism alone, as if it were the only form of despotism.

The problem is complicated by the way in which Mrs. Kirkpatrick deals with an alleged difference between authoritarian and totalitarian dictatorships. It is supposed to be the ability of "right-wing autocracies" to evolve into democracies, whereas no revolutionary socialist or Communist society has ever been democratized. She points to Spain as an example of right-wing evolution, sees in Brazil the initial steps in that direction and even conceives that the same thing might have happened in the Shah's Iran and Somoza's Nicaragua.

We thus have a political law established chiefly on the basis of a single case, which can hardly be thought typical, since Spain was democratic before it became "authoritarian" with the help of two foreign totalitarian regimes. Spain in any event had to wait twenty-six years for the death of its authoritarian ruler, Generalissimo Francisco Franco, and its stability is still threatened by his followers. It is questionable whether Spain's authoritarians—if they should be called that rather than fascists—evolved into democrats. There is a difference between the idea of Franco Spain's evolving into democracy while Franco was still alive and the fact that his system was supplanted after his death. The difference seems to escape Mrs. Kirkpatrick.

In reality, authoritarian states of the type of Batista's Cuba and Somoza's Nicaragua are more likely to breed revolutionary change than to evolve into democracies. In these cases, the initial opposition tends to be democratic, but as the peaceful tactics of the moderate party bring on increased repression and frustration, the ensuing stage of military struggle produces a more extremist leadership and a more revolutionary program.

The other part of Mrs. Kirkpatrick's theory—that totalitarian regimes have never been democratized—is also open to question in the extreme form in which she states it. She makes no mention of Yugoslavia, which, whatever else may be said about it, has for years evolved away from the traditional totalitarian model. More significantly, nothing is said about the abortive efforts of Czechoslovakia, Hungary and Poland to break out of the Communist straitjacket—in the case of Czechoslovakia an attempt initiated by the then Communist leadership.

Mrs. Kirkpatrick's thesis would make it appear that these countries—and perhaps others in Eastern Europe, if they were permitted to go their own ways—have been held back from democratizing themselves, or from at least going part of the way, by their loyalty to totalitarianism rather than by the crushing weight of Soviet military power. We cannot be sure how the "Prague Spring" would have evolved if the Soviets had not intervened, but surely it was more promising than anything that has happened in Brazil or was likely to happen in the Shah's Iran or Somoza's Nicaragua.

To make matters even more puzzling, Mrs. Kirkpatrick also tells us that the new totalitarian leaders "bear a remarkable and discouraging resemblance to the old tyrants." This can only mean that there is not as much difference between authoritarian and totalitarian leaders as she elsewhere contends. Indeed, the common bond is their tyranny, whatever ideological pretensions one or the other may have. Mrs. Kirkpatrick takes the ideological Potemkin villages of Communist regimes more seriously than anyone in them does.

. . .

The last thing written for this volume was apparently the introduction. It brings forth Mrs. Kirkpatrick's latest and greatest enemy—rationalism. My dictionary says that "rationalism" means "the view that reason and experience rather than the irrational are the fundamental criteria in the solution of problems." Mrs. Kirkpatrick, however, chooses to twist the word out of all recognition. She makes it mean the "failure to distinguish between the domains of thought and experience." In effect, rationalism for her implies an astonishing lack of rationality.

Once she has spotted the real enemy, Mrs. Kirkpatrick fires off her most devastating ideological weapons against it. It is, in her view, most responsible for all that is evil and destructive in this century. Rationalism encourages utopianism; rationalism has an affinity with tyranny; rationalism is largely to blame for totalitarianism. To believe her, Adolf Hitler would have been the perfect rationalist.

What does Mrs. Kirkpatrick propose to put in the place of rationalism? She is a devotee of "non-rational factors such as sentiment, habit, and custom." She celebrates "the intractability of human behavior, the complexity of human institutions, and the probability of unanticipated consequences." She is opposed to changing institutions because it means "radically changing the lives of people who may not want their lives changed."

Here we have a clue to Mrs. Kirkpatrick's ideological blinders. People *may* not want their lives changed; on the other hand, they *may* desperately want them changed. People *may* be so miserable, oppressed or despised that they *may* become victims of totalitarian demagogues and utopian visionaries in a vain effort to change their conditions. One does not need to be a conservative to recognize that sentiment, habit and custom cannot be ignored or abolished in any sound social theory or practice. It is something else to make them all-embracing and self-sufficing.

Once Mrs. Kirkpatrick decides which side she is on, she is a formidably single-minded partisan. She gives no consideration to the danger that we would condemn society to immobility and decadence if we put all our hope and faith in sentiment, habit and custom. There is nothing "neo" about this conservatism; it is so old, in fact, that it can be resurrected as if it were a daring discovery.

The New York Times Book Review, July 25, 1982

VII

THE PAST IN THE PRESENT

1

Prophets of the "Cold War"

The first and most famous prophet of the post–World War II "Cold War" between Russia and America is often thought to be Alexis de Tocqueville. He was not. There were others who preceded him and who came much closer to the basic idea, and they also help to put into better perspective what Tocqueville actually did say about the destinies of Russia and America. If there is still so much admiration for and wonder at Tocqueville's pronouncement, these largely forgotten prophets should be of very special interest.

Tocqueville's prognosis in the last sentence of the first part of his *Democracy in America* in 1835 has long been something of an enigma. The forecast that "each," Russia and America, "seems called by some secret design of Providence one day to hold in its hands the destinies of half the world" appears to come out of nowhere.[1] The reader is not prepared for it by anything he has previously been told. Russia is only once mentioned briefly in another connection.[2] Tocqueville paid relatively little attention to America's foreign interests, affairs, or policies. Indeed, he seemed to have forgotten by the end of the second volume of 1835 what he had written earlier. In his first reference to foreign affairs, he had remarked that America had "no external interests" and was unlikely to exercise "a powerful influence on the world's destiny" because it was not controlled by an aristocracy, which he thought was necessary for such a role.[3] But in his climactic passage at the end of the volume he professed to believe that America would one day "become the leading naval power on the globe" and "rule the seas, as the Romans were [born] to conquer the world." He placed America in 1835, with

Russia, "in the first rank of nations."[4] And then came the even more famous prophecy that America and Russia were fated to hold the destinies of half the world in each of their hands. It is hard to see how America could fail to be a powerful influence on the world's destinies, with or without an aristocracy, if it were to become the world's leading naval power, rule the seas, and take over the destinies of half the world while Russia took over the other half.

It is important to be clear about what Tocqueville did not say. He did not say or even imply that America and Russia were bound to clash or compete after each had achieved its semi-global destiny.[5] He was content to give each of them half the world and leave it at that. Just what he meant by "half the world" for each of them is more obscure. He gave some hint of the geography of the American half but none at all of the Russian half.

He predicted that, in the near future as the life of nations goes, the "Anglo-Americans" (as he called them) would cover "the whole of the immense area between the polar ice and the tropics, extending from the Atlantic to the Pacific coast." By this area he seems to have had in mind just about what the United States did finally occupy in the next decade, since he went on to define the area as eventually three-quarters the size of Europe.[6] It is reasonable to suppose, however, that he was here predicting the ultimate extension of the United States itself, not the entire half of the world which it was going to "hold in its hands." Tocqueville's American half was probably a sphere of influence taking in North and South America.

The Russian half is even more problematic. In his day, the question at issue was whether Russia was going to make itself the master of Western Europe. Asia and Africa were still outside the range of Russian ambitions and could not have been envisaged in either half. Tocqueville's expression of the division of the world between Russia and America is so loose and metaphorical that it is hard to know just what he had in mind.

In any case, there was nothing new about either the Russian or the American half of Tocqueville's prognosis.[7] This was not one of Tocqueville's presentiments, however, that attracted mention from his contemporaries. The most famous British review of Tocqueville's book by J. S. Mill (*London Review*) did not bother to mention it. Neither did J. G. Lockhart's equally lengthy essay (*The Quarterly Review*).[8] In the United States, the *American Quarterly Review* gently reproved Tocqueville for sometimes stepping "boldly into the region of prophecy, whose misty and uncertain confines we cannot overpass."[9] The *United States Magazine and Democratic Review*, the drumbeater of "manifest destiny" in the 1840s, cited Tocqueville's last paragraph without comment.[10]

The only significant exception that I have been able to find appeared in the *Revue des Deux Mondes*. It was written by a friend of Tocqueville's, François de Corcelle, who, however, protested against just this point. He was appalled by the idea that Russia would hold half the world, including Europe, in its hands. "No," he expostulated, "half the world will not be its prey" because the Russian "giant" lacked the right kind of "moral life," which was the sole condition for "high and powerful destinies." Corcelle caught the fatalistic note in Tocqueville's prognosis and did not like it, at least so far as Russia was concerned. Corcelle wanted European and American democracy to work together against Russia's "servile barbarism," a far closer approximation to the attitudes that animated the future Cold War.[11]

A somewhat different reason for rejecting Tocqueville's division of the world was given two decades later by Count Adam de Gurowski, a Polish émigré in America. Gurowski was a disillusioned pro-Russian Panslavist who became a fervent admirer of American democracy.

> It has become very common of late [he wrote in his book *Russia As It Is*, published in New York in 1854] to compare the growth of America with that of Russia; to look for a similitude in their development and progress: and finally to divide the future of the two hemispheres between these two ascending states.

Gurowski would have none of this Tocquevillian perspective on the ground that there was "only one right line" towards the future and it was represented by free America, not despotic Russia. He claimed that as early as 1836, soon after the appearance of Tocqueville's first two volumes, he had already put himself on record as having allotted to Russia a different destiny—away from Europe towards Asia. He particularly looked forward to the Russian conquest of Turkey and even expected the Czarist court to move to Constantinople. This transplantation, he believed, would prove fatal to the Czarist regime but would lead to the salvation of the Russian people to whom Western ideas and culture would then make their way freely and irresistibly. In this curious way, Gurowski avoided the implied Tocquevillian takeover of Europe by Russia, settled the long-festering "Eastern Question," restored Europe to political supremacy over the Slavic world, and inferentially

conducted both Russia and Europe along the "one right line" of ultimate American influence and example.

Apart from this response to Tocqueville's futurology and testimonial
that it had become "very common of late" in the 1850s, Gurowski's
grand design helps to recapture the visionary intellectual climate of the
second quarter of the nineteenth century in which Tocqueville—as well
as the Saint-Simonians, Fourier, Marx, and many others—thought and
dreamed.[12]

Gurowski was not the only European émigré in the United States in
the 1850s to instruct Americans on Russia's destiny as well as their
own. Two German émigrés, Theodore Poesche and Charles Goepp, put
out a book in 1853 entitled *The New Rome; or The United States of the
World*, in which, among other things, they held that Russia must conquer all of Europe after which it would come into final conflict with the
United States.

> The choirs are marshalled on each wing of the world's stage, Russia leading
> the one, the United States the other. Yet the world is too small for both,
> and the contest must end in the downfall of the one and the victory of the
> other.

So much for the novelty of the post–World War II theories of "con-
vergence" and inevitable "struggle for the world"!

II

The real fame of Tocqueville's prognosis came more than a century
later, brought on by the demonstrations of Russian and American power
during and after the Second World War.

The sentence of 1835 was read again and remarkable previsions were
found in it. In 1942, in the midst of the War, one American writer
discovered that Tocqueville had foreseen the "Union Now" movement,
which called for the unification of democratic countries the world over
in preparation for a future world government. He also claimed that
Tocqueville had "looked beyond the Russian Revolution and foreseen
America and Russia holding the balance of power at Armageddon." The
prospect of Armageddon was a strange extrapolation from Tocqueville's
rather bare and matter-of-fact statement about the two halves.[13]

Soon after the Second World War, Charles de Gaulle called attention
to the fact that only Soviet Russia and the United States were now first-
rate powers. Both were impelled to expand, he said, by virtue of their
advantages—"abounding in men and resources, compact in territory,

naturally protected, one by vast oceans, the other by its own size"—and, as always, justified themselves in terms of political doctrines, which really were, in the last analysis, "a thrust for power." Just this development had been foreseen by Tocqueville, de Gaulle asserted, quoting at length from the famous last sentence in the first part of *Democracy in America*. De Gaulle thought that Tocqueville's description of the future was somewhat "schematized" and, as a result, an exaggeration of what had become a reality, but that it was necessary to acknowledge that events had substantially confirmed Tocqueville's vision.[14]

In 1949, the German writer, Ernst Jünger, interpreted Tocqueville as having forewarned that Germany would split into "Atlantic and continental" parts, an implication more Jünger's than Tocqueville's.[15] The latter had not given Germany any such option to escape from Russia's future half of the world.

In his large study of *America as a Civilization*, published in 1957, Max Lerner also thought that Tocqueville had accurately anticipated the post–World War II "polarizing forces" of Russia and America.[16]

In 1962, in one of his major works, *Peace and War*, Raymond Aron, that most complete of contemporary Tocquevillians, was moved to exclaim:

> How many times, in recent years, has de Tocqueville's famous parallel been quoted as to the two peoples destined, by a mysterious decree of Providence, each to dominate one half of the world, the one by the plow and the other by the sword!

Aron then went on to add one more misinterpretation to Tocqueville's famous parallel. "Alexis de Tocqueville," according to Aron, "was the first, a century ago, to give a classic form to the antithesis *Washington or Moscow*."[17] There is no such antithesis in Tocqueville's work. The thesis there is clearly Moscow *and* Washington. Tocqueville gave each of them half the world without the slightest hint that any other country was offered a choice. Aron is not the only one who has strangely misread Tocqueville in this passage or who has read into it a phenomenon of his own times, not Tocqueville's.[18]

Whatever Tocqueville's "antithesis" was, what inspired him to juxtapose Russia and America? We know where Tocqueville got some of his other ideas. For example, the statement that America would one day "become the leading naval power on the globe" can be traced to his lengthy conversations with one of his American informants, Joel Roberts Poinsett, the US Minister to Mexico from 1825 to 1829. Tocqueville kept careful notebooks of his conversations and observations. He spent five days with Poinsett, who at one point told him: "The future of the United States as to commerce is immense. We are certainly called to become the first maritime power in the world." Later, Tocqueville drew up a memorandum for himself in which he repeated Poinsett's statement in almost the same words. Finally, he put it in his book, again in almost the same words.[19]

Nowhere in Tocqueville's *Cahiers* does he record even bringing up the subject that might have led him to think those thoughts about Russia and America. Nowhere in them does he ever jot down a word about American foreign interests or foreign affairs. He records conversations with the distinguished Everett brothers (Alexander and Edward), both deeply engaged in foreign affairs, and with former President John Quincy Adams, with whom he might have discussed such a major event of the preceding period as the so-called Monroe Doctrine, promulgated during Adams's tenure as Secretary of State. Instead, his notes tell us that he talked to Alexander Everett about imprisonment for debt and to Adams about slavery and religion. Thus we have no clue from Tocqueville's notebooks why he was led to make his comments on the lack of American "external interests" and the destinies of Russia and America. The two volumes that make up the second part of Tocqueville's great work, which some consider the more important half, published in 1840, completely ignore the subject of American foreign affairs, as if he had no further interest in the subject.

But the juxtaposition of Russian and American destinies was not exactly literary *terra incognita* before Tocqueville's pronouncement. For about half a century previously, now almost totally forgotten writers had played variations on the theme, coming much closer to authentic prophecies of the twentieth-century "Cold War." Tocqueville, who read voraciously in preparation for his youthful masterpiece, could not have been ignorant of all of them. The theme was so much in the air that even Tocqueville's particular handling of it was not wholly original with him. The other prophets may give us a clue to what had inspired Tocqueville's famous prognosis as well as being interesting and important in their own right.

III

There are two leading contenders for the honor of having first foreseen the emergence of Russia and America as the coming rising powers. One did not go as far as Tocqueville, the other went much further.

The first was an American, Silas Deane of Connecticut. Deane was the first American foreign agent dispatched to France in 1776 to get aid for the American Revolution. On June 7, 1777, he sent a letter to Charles William Frederick Dumas, a native of Switzerland, who lived for the most part in Holland and served as an American secret agent.

Deane's purpose in this letter was to evoke the specter of British domination of the entire world as an argument for obtaining aid in Europe from countries that shared the fear of British rule. Britain, he asserted, could become "mistress of the world" by means of securing the "friendship and alliance of the United States." With Russia added, he went on, "it is easy to foresee that Great Britain, America, and Russia united will command not barely Europe, but the whole world united."

In one sentence, Deane brought Russia and America together: "Russia, like America, is a new state, and rises with the most astonishing rapidity." But all this build-up of Russia and America was designed to warn of what would happen if Britain were permitted to use both of them for its own aggrandizement.

Like a Colossus, with one foot on Russia and the East and the other on America, it [Britain] will bestride, as Shakespeare says, your poor European world, and the powers which now strut and look big *will creep about between its legs to find dishonorable graves.*[20]

This letter has been misinterpreted. A superficial reading makes it appear that Deane's message was "that the time would come when Great Britain, the United States, and Russia would dominate the world."[21] In fact, Deane was interested in forecasting the domination of the world by Great Britain if it was able to use Russia and America for its own ends. Deane directed attention to the rise of Russia and America, but not for their own sakes; he made them subordinate to his anti-British propaganda. By wrenching a few words from Deane's letter out of context, he has been made a forerunner of the Tocquevillian prognosis, which left Britain out altogether in favor of a Russo-American division of the world.[22]

Deane himself came to a bad end. In 1778 he was charged with embezzlement, though it was never proven; he then lost faith in the American Revolution, became a defeatist, and spent his last years reproached as a traitor in England.

Another early American forecast of Russo-American relations is not in the direct line of the Tocquevillian thesis but is nevertheless of some interest. Francis Dana was the first American Minister to Russia, commissioned in 1780. Three years later, he expressed the view that "in the nature of things" the future relations between Russia and America would be commercial rather than political.[23]

By far the closest approximation to Tocqueville's prevision first came from Catherine the Great's agent in Paris, Baron Friedrich Melchior von Grimm, better known for his literary and critical correspondence. After the French Revolution, Grimm and Catherine carried on a lengthy exchange of letters, in which they commiserated with each other on the parlous state of Europe. Catherine was most gloomy about the prospect. In a reply, dated December 31, 1790, Grimm made this remarkable prediction:

> Two empires will then divide among themselves all the advantages of civilization, of the power of genius, of letters, arts, arms and industry: Russia from the Eastern side, and America, having freed itself in our time, from the Western side, and we others, peoples of the center [*noyau*], will be too degraded, too debased, to know what we have been other than by a vague and stupid tradition.[24]

Almost a half century before Tocqueville, Grimm had hit on the essence of the Tocquevillian formula—the Russo-American division of the world. Tocqueville could not have known of Grimm's prophecy; it was not published in St. Petersburg until twenty-two years after Tocqueville's death. Just what Catherine made of Grimm's prophecy we do not know; she never replied to it.

There is also a tradition that Napoleon was an early prophet of the same idea. It originated with Count Emmanuel de Las Cases, who accompanied Napoleon to his last imprisonment on the island of Saint Helena. In his famous *Mémorial*, Las Cases has Napoleon say: "In the present state of things, all Europe can be in less than ten years *cossack* or completely *republican*."[25] Later writers took Napoleon to mean that Europe would come under the sway of Russia or the United States. Abbé de Pradt, of whom more later, took the liberty to change Napoleon's timing of the event. "In fifty years," Napoleon had said, according to de Pradt, "Europe will be cossack or republican."[26] Heinrich Heine, the German poet and sometime political commentator, understood Napoleon to have referred directly to Russia and America, though he was appalled by the prospect: "Napoleon's words on Saint Helena that the world would in the near future become an American republic or a Russian universal monarchy is a most discouraging prophecy. What a prospect!"[27] Cassius Marcellus Clay, the U.S. Minister to Russia in the 1860s, attributed to Napoleon the belief that Russia and America would eventually be the two great powers "in the world's history."[28]

Las Cases had started something which might have surprised Napoleon as it went through various incarnations for the rest of the century.

IV

Of all the early prophecies, the first one that is likely to have come to the attention of Tocqueville, albeit in a peculiar form, appeared in a book by an Englishman living in America. His name was John Bristed; his book was *The Resources of the United States of America*; it was published in New York and London in the same year, 1818. A German translation appeared in 1819, a French in 1826 and again in 1832. The indications are that it was one of the most widely read and internationally circulated books on America of the period. Bristed's career encompassed half a dozen fields. He started out in England, studying and practicing medicine, then law. He came to New York City in 1806 at the age of twenty-eight, already the author of some books, including one novel. In New York, he practiced law, gave lectures, edited a magazine and wrote more books, including the one on American resources. He returned to England in 1828, became an Episcopal clergyman, and devoted himself mainly to religious and philanthropic activities until his death in 1855.[29] The title of the book on American "resources" does not prepare the reader for what is in it. Bristed was a discursive, rambling, idiosyncratic writer who went much further afield than this title suggests.

At the very outset, Bristed informed his readers that "no circumstances can prevent these United States from becoming, eventually, and at no distant period, a great and powerful nation, influencing and controlling the other sovereignties of the world." Tocqueville's half a world was modest in comparison. Midway through his book, Bristed rhetorically announced that Britain's child and rival, America, "is rapidly emerging into unparalleled greatness; is flaming upwards, like a pyramid of fire, so that all the Western horizon is in a blaze with the brightness of its ascending glory." He claimed to see that America was playing a waiting game—"to wait and nourish the growing resources of the Union" until the existing European coalition of the Holy Alliance of Russia, Prussia and Austria had broken up. Then, he warned, America would "gradually bear down all possible opposition from any single foe."

Bristed next turned to Russia. He reflected the post-Napoleonic dread of Russia that swept through Europe as Alexander I took upon himself the defense and restoration of legitimacy and monarchy all over the world. The mood in Europe after 1815 was not unlike that after 1945. "Is *Russia* now, and for the time to come, deemed formidable to Europe?" Bristed asked. He had a solution to the Russian menace: "Behold another and a greater Russia *here*. With a better territory, a better government, and a better people, *America* is ripening fast into a substance, an attitude of power, which will prove far more terrible to the world than it is ever possible for the warriors of the Don or the defenders of Moscow to become." Many pages later, he was more pessimistic about stopping Russia. "It is doubtful," he reflected, "if she [Russia] be allowed a few years of peace to organise her resources, to consolidate her strength, to develop her schemes, whether or not a coalition of the other European States could stop her progress towards universal dominion in that quarter of the world." In the end, Bristed forgot that America was supposed inexorably to get the best of Russia and called on Britain "to save Europe once more."[30]

Fleetingly, Bristed had brought the already formidable Russian power and the ripening American power into confrontation. It was not the way Tocqueville would go about it. Bristed had America breaking out of its half of the world to challenge Russia in the other half; Tocqueville had been content with an essentially static model, with America in one half and Russia in the other. In this sense, Bristed was much more clearly an incipient prophet of the next century's "Cold War."

But Bristed's story has a surprise ending that may cast more light on Tocqueville's prognosis. Tocqueville and his friend, Gustave de Beaumont, came to the United States for nine months in 1831–1832. If Tocqueville had not read the 1826 translation, *Histoire des Etats-Unis*, before leaving for America, he could hardly have ignored the 1832 edition upon his return. In any event, something peculiar happened to a key passage in Bristed's work in its transition from English into French.

Here is the passage again in English:

Is *Russia* now, and for the time to come, deemed formidable to Europe? Behold another and a greater Russia *here*. With a better territory, a better government, and a better people, *America* is ripening fast into a substance, an attitude of power, which will prove far more terrible to the world than it is ever possible for the warriors of the Don or the defenders of Moscow to become.

Here is how this passage came out in the French translation:

La Russie est devenue formidable en Europe; l'Amérique peut l'imiter dans l'autre partie du globe: elle marche rapidement vers une attitude de puissance qui deviendra bien plus redoutable au monde entier, que jamais les Cosaques du Don ou les défenseurs de Moscou n'ont pu l'être.[31]

The French translator, for a reason we can no longer guess at, performed an operation on Bristed's first two sentences which brought them into consonance with Tocqueville's prognosis. That Russia and America would both become formidable in their own parts of the world was merely a weaker version of the idea that each would "hold in its hands the destinies of half the world." The rest of the passage seems to explain why America can "imitate" Russia in "the other part of the world," not why America (as Bristed intended) was waiting to become strong enough to take on all comers.[32]

In any case, Bristed can take credit for having been an early prophet of both the "Cold War" and, through his French translation, of Tocqueville's prognosis. For an almost totally forgotten book, that is no small achievement.

V

Our next precursor could only have come out of the late eighteenth and early nineteenth centuries. He is Dominique-Georges-Frédéric Dufour de Pradt, better known as the Abbé de Pradt. Only a Balzac could do justice to such a character.

He was ordained a priest at the age of twenty-four; appointed a clerical deputy to the Estates General in Paris in 1789 at the age of thirty; spent a decade as a counter-revolutionary émigré; enjoyed the next decade as a favorite of Napoleon; went back to the Bourbons for a short stretch; and finally, after 1815, settled down for two decades to a successful career as a self-appointed spokesman of the liberal opposition. At various times, he served as Chief Army Chaplain, Archbishop of Malines, Ambassador in Warsaw, and Grand Chancelier of the Légion d'Honneur. As a politician, he was a Talleyrand *manqué*, much better at getting important appointments than at keeping them. Stripped of all his honors and titles, first by Napoleon, then by Louis XVIII, he was forced to live by his wits as the outstanding political chronicler of his age—much the best thing that ever happened to him.[33]

No one, except de Pradt himself, can have read all that he wrote. He produced forty-six books, some in more than one volume, and innumerable articles.[34] In just one year, 1817, he put out four books. One volume was reprinted nine times in France alone. Three editions of any one of his books were not uncommon. A reprint edition of his entire works, some of them dating back thirty years, came out in 1828. He was translated into Spanish (at least nine volumes), English (at least five), German (three). Three different Spanish translations were made of one book. He was so influential that he has been called "the Walter Lippmann of his age." No politically minded contemporary could have ignored de Pradt's literary industry.[35]

Leading political figures in the United States read and reckoned with de Pradt. John Adams's library contained one of de Pradt's most important books. Jefferson lent one of them to John Adams and John Quincy Adams. The younger Adams knew enough about "the equivocal character of the Abbé's reputation" to denounce him to Jefferson for his "treachery" to Napoleon and his "time-serving obsequiousness to the Bourbons"—both of which were true. Jefferson replied somewhat guardedly that Adams had given him a fuller understanding of de Pradt's character but still managed to express admiration for his eloquence and ingenuity. Of another book by de Pradt, Jefferson later wrote to de Pradt's American translator that he had found it ambiguous but again put in a good word for de Pradt for having given him "great outlines and profound views" of the subject. One American historian has argued, probably mistakenly, that Jefferson owed de Pradt ideas with which Jefferson had anticipated the Monroe Doctrine, and so de Pradt, through Jefferson, was putatively a progenitor of the famous doctrine.[36] Henry Clay was more generous to de Pradt, whom he quoted in a speech with the recommendation that "no man could read [de Pradt] without being enlightened and instructed."[37] We are going to find that one of the possibly basic sources of the Tocquevillian prognosis was an American review in 1830 of a major work by de Pradt.

So much for the man. The importance of his ideas on the destinies of Russia and America can hardly be appreciated without knowing something about his life and the popularity in its time of his enormous literary output. De Pradt's ideas on the two destinies were never worked out thoroughly or consistently. He often seemed to forget in one work what he had written in another or even in the same work. Yet he had some favorite themes to which he returned, not always in the same way, again and again.

One of them, dealing with the United States, came out as early as 1817, just before Bristed's book. De Pradt stressed that the US had increased so much in territory, population and wealth that "history presents nothing equal among nascent peoples in antiquity or modern times." He was so impressed by American growth that he expounded: "The future of America is incalculable; it is clearly destined to change the face of the world." Sooner or later, he was sure, the US would dominate all of North America.[38] From this time on, de Pradt never wavered in his conviction that the United States was bound to become a great power with which Europe would have to reckon.

In 1819, de Pradt announced that Russia was "the dominant power on the continent" of Europe. He brought Russia into juxtaposition with the United States by considering them both as "vast countries, until then strangers to the rest of the world," but immediately added that the United States "already carried a preponderant weight in the affairs of the world."[39] In later works, he repeatedly envisaged Russia and the United States as bearing down on Europe from opposite sides, with Russia the immediate danger and the United States in need of more time to act as a counterbalance. In 1822, he again paid his respects to Russia. It was the only independent state on the Continent and "thus dominates Europe." Henceforth and for a long time to come, he feared, the history of the Continent could be summed up in these words: "Tutelage of Europe by Russia." He viewed England as then playing the role that the United States would be seen playing a century later—as "protector of the liberties of Europe against the colossus of the North." His thought developed along the following lines: the struggle was between Eastern absolutism and Western constitutionalism. What Europe needed was a power in the West capable of counterbalancing Russia; but it did not exist. The US took no part in European quarrels, still preferring to increase its population, fortify itself, and cover the seas with its ships of commerce.

In 1823, he returned to the charge. Russia would make itself the "regent" of Europe. Its power was "excessive [*démesuré*], colossal, pressing down on all." Russia was able to "crush" Europe, to "wipe out its very existence." In 1825, he saw South America following in the footsteps of the USA which, he thought, had already demonstrated its naval prowess in the War of 1812. As a result, he had a vision of

America as "a great naval power," which would become "the liberator of the seas and the avenger of Europe." He exhorted Europeans to think of America as "an entire world, destined to attract towards it the rest of the world."[40]

De Pradt could be wildly visionary, to the point of exasperation. He could also be subtly realistic. In 1828, for example, he refined his idea of Russian supremacy in Europe. He explained that Russia was not necessarily going to expand territorially. It was enough for Russia to possess an "immense power," which carried with it "a kind of virtual supremacy." He pointed out: "Already, before anything is resolved upon by any other government, the first question is: What will be thought of this at St. Petersburg." The rest of the passage is worth quoting:

> It is not improbable that this new authority may be exercised, for a time, with all the forms of the most polite usage, but it will not be for that reason the less real. Russia may not perhaps, like ancient Rome, order her ambassadors to insult foreign sovereigns at their own courts—command one to make war, and another to make peace—attempt to settle the domestic concerns of royal families, or declare her allies inviolable; but a look from her will carry terror, her intimations will be regarded as orders, and her displeasure felt as a disgrace and a misfortune. Such is the mildest form in which the supremacy of Russia over Europe can possibly be exercised. The pride of the Western politicians may lead them to affect to doubt the reality of this state of things; but their unwillingness to acknowledge it does not alter the case, which the lapse of a few years will make but too plain to every one.[41]

Over a century later, this state of affairs would be called "Finlandization."

It was in his book, *On the Permanent System of Europe with regard to Russia and Eastern Affairs*, published in 1828, that de Pradt came closest to pitting Russia against America. As the foremost anti-Russian publicist in the France of his day, de Pradt here suggested that the salvation of Europe might eventually lie in the rapid growth of American power. "There the avengers, the liberators of Europe, will be found," he prophesied, and added: "Europe offers the image of two camps facing each other, the Russified East and the West."[42]

In these works from 1817 to 1828, de Pradt dealt with Russia and America unequally. Russia for him was already a fully-formed "colossus," bearing down with all its weight on Europe. America was still in a stage of formation, strong and willing enough immediately to play a preponderant role in North America or the Western hemisphere. But de

Pradt held out the promise that it might not stop there. What a reader of de Pradt could not miss was the shadow cast by these two extra-European powers over their respective halves of the world. De Pradt never formulated their future destinies with the one-sentence precision of Tocqueville, but he made the potentiality of Russian and American hegemonies the insistent message of his books. De Pradt's contribution was to make Europeans more conscious than ever before that Russia and America had in some sense pre-empted the future.

VI

One of the more distinguished Americans with whom Tocqueville talked in September 1831 was Alexander Hill Everett. It was this Everett who invited Tocqueville and Beaumont to dinner to meet the former President John Quincy Adams, Edward Everett, and an English guest, Sir James Colleton.[43] The older of the two Everetts, Alexander, had had an outstanding diplomatic career and was notable for two books on foreign affairs. It seems strange that Tocqueville should have found nothing touching on this subject in his talk with Alexander Everett to record in his notebooks; but it would be even stranger if Tocqueville had not known of Everett's books and had not given them some thought. For Alexander Everett's books were the first of their kind by a native American.

Everett was born into one of the first families of Boston. His father was the minister of a leading Boston church. He graduated from Harvard in 1806, the youngest member of his class and also the one with the highest standing. John Quincy Adams took him into his office for the study of law; he became and remained Adams's favorite protégé. When Adams went to Russia as American Minister in 1809, Everett went along as his private secretary. From 1815 to 1824, while Adams was Secretary of State, Everett was secretary of legation and then chargé d'affaires at The Hague. During this period he wrote his first book on foreign affairs and an essay on population. During Adams's presidency Everett served as Minister to Spain, 1825–1829, and put out his second book dealing specifically with American foreign affairs. When Tocqueville met him, Everett had retired from the diplomatic service and was editing the *North American Review*, the foremost American political and literary organ of its time. In 1845 he was named the first American envoy to China but died soon after arriving in Canton.

Everett's first book, *Europe*, published in 1822, was unlike anything an American had yet written. It was a systematic, knowledgeable survey of European politics, country by country, "with conjectures on their future prospects," based on reading and experience. It was so well done that (as the *North American Review* noted) English reviewers thought that the book, which was signed "by a Citizen of the United States," could not have been produced by an American.[44] He had read his de Pradt and his Schmidt-Phiseldeck, the latter a then-renowned, German-born, Danish official and editor whose book, *Europe and America*, was published in 1820.[45] Everett cited the latest European magazines and newspapers.

Alexander Hill Everett has deserved better from posterity. The almost 700-page *Harvard Guide to American History* has room for scores of obscure writers and books but no space for him. He is equally unknown to the almost 1,200 pages of the Library of Congress's *A Guide to the Study of the United States of America*. I have not been able to find him mentioned in any history of American diplomacy or foreign affairs, even those ostensibly devoted to ideas and issues as well as to policies and events. Yet, at the time, Ralph Waldo Emerson praised Everett's *Europe* as "the most considerable American book that has been published, the most removed from our business-like habits, the most like Burke."[46] One hundred and ten years after his death he was rediscovered in a different connection by Professor Hans Kohn, who devoted five pages to him in his *American Nationalism*, published in 1957. Professor Kohn had such a high opinion of Everett that he considered him "better equipped to see the United States as a nation among nations" than George Bancroft of vastly greater fame.[47] But it was left to a contemporary German scholar, Heinz Gollwitzer, to recognize that Everett was worth all of seventeen pages in his *Ideengeschichte* of world politics. Gollwitzer chose Everett above all others as "statesmanlike intellectual, and a political figure with a broadly cultivated horizon" who best revealed how an American of his time understood the development of international relations.[48]

In *Europe*, the subject demanded far more consideration of Russia than of the United States. Everett fully agreed with de Pradt about Russia's domination of Europe:

> There is evidently nothing in Europe capable of making head against such a power as this. Not all Europe, combined in opposition, will be able to resist its progress, whenever this vast machinery is seriously brought to bear upon the independence of other nations by an able and ambitious emperor.

He acknowledged "the irresistible preponderance of Russia in the European balance of power" and expected that "at no distant period it may very probably obtain an actual military dominion over the rest of Europe." Unlike de Pradt, however, Everett was less pessimistic about the outcome of Russian dominion. He professed to believe that the Russian ruling class was as civilized as that of Europe, so that liberal political institutions, but not civilization itself, would suffer at the hands of the Russians. "It is merely a change of power from the hands of one cultivated and civilised government to those of another, and will produce no unfavourable effect on the general state of society," he wrote reassuringly. He even welcomed Russian domination because it would allegedly put an end to the division of Europe and bring about European consolidation under Russian rule.[49]

Everett dealt with the United States in this book only as a commercial power. He boasted that America's "commercial greatness" had risen to such heights that "all preceding maritime states dwindle into nothing in comparison." The United States were commercially already "the rivals and may perhaps be the successors of England." A European reader might have wondered when politics would follow economics.

The *North American Review* criticized Everett for exaggerating the force of Russia and contended that he was wrong to consider it "to be superior to that of all the other European states combined." It also thought that he had overrated the advantages of consolidating Europe under Russian rule. But it acknowledged that Russia

> is powerful indeed; at this time the most powerful state on the continent, and it is by no means the true policy of the others to encourage her growth; but she is not yet a counterpoise for them all.[50]

Americans did not need Tocqueville, thirteen years later, to tell them how close Russia was coming to holding the destinies of the European world in its hands.

In his companion volume of 1827, *America*, Everett dealt at greater length with his native country but did not neglect Russia. By this time he had added the United States to Russia and Great Britain as "the three prominent and first rate powers of the civilised and Christian world." Geography, good government, industry, wealth and knowledge had given the United States "at this early period of their national existence, the lofty position of a leading power among the nations." He was now sure that America was bound to outstrip England. By the time he had finished the book he had made the United States "at no very distant period, a more populous, wealthy, and powerful community than any the world has ever seen" and more important politically than all of Europe combined—by the close of the nineteenth century.[51]

As for Russia, Everett now changed his mind about the benevolence and advantages of its rule over Europe. Much closer to de Pradt's vision, he saw Russia as an immense military empire "advancing with giant steps to the conquest of the west." A Russian victory would mean "a return to barbarism." But he came through with a surprise ending. If Russia were to be prevented from imposing its barbaric rule on the West, it would come about "because the principle of civilisation and improvement will be powerfully sustained by aid from abroad, that is, from America." Everett, in effect, put his hope in a future European-American alliance against Russia.

This was not Tocqueville's perspective. Everett did not limit America's power to half the world. He projected it to Europe and beyond, at least by the end of the nineteenth century. Nevertheless, the emphasis on Russia and America as the two coming great powers, with an embattled Europe increasingly dependent on American aid against Russia, contributed to a climate of opinion which was differently reflected in Tocqueville's prognosis. Everett, like de Pradt, came much closer than Tocqueville to the prophecy of a future "Cold War."

Another Everett—the more famous Edward—made one more attack on the subject after Alexander had assumed the editorship of the *North American Review*. In 1830, Edward Everett—pastor, Harvard President and professor, Governor of Massachusetts, Minister to Great Britain, Secretary of State, US Senator—reviewed two of de Pradt's books which had appeared during the previous two years. In his review, he agreed with de Pradt that Russia was likely to turn its power against Europe. He was, however, less harsh in his view of Russian expansionist policy, on the ground that its most important territorial acquisitions had been gained as a result of a war forced upon it by Napoleonic France. But he went along with de Pradt's view that Russia threatened "the independence of the western nations of Europe." He also shared much of de Pradt's pessimism about the outcome and reluctantly agreed that efforts to contain Russia would mostly be "hopeless."[52]

Edward Everett's review of de Pradt appeared in the issue of April

1830. Tocqueville arrived in the United States in May 1831. Soon after their arrival in New York, Tocqueville and Beaumont began to haunt two libraries where they had at their disposal books and periodicals. When Tocqueville saw Alexander Everett at the end of September 1831, he identified him as "former minister of the United States in Spain and distinguished writer."[53] He soon met Edward Everett. Is it likely that Tocqueville would by the time he met the Everetts not have become acquainted with their recent work, in which he would have read the views of both de Pradt and the two brothers on the destiny of Russia? Even if Tocqueville had by some chance failed to inform himself of the Everetts' works in the New York libraries and in subsequent reading, was it likely that the Everetts themselves would have made no mention of them during their talks with Tocqueville? Owing to the silence of Tocqueville's notebooks and letters on this score no final answer to these questions is possible. Still it is safe to say that the likelihood of Tocqueville's ignorance of the Everetts' works cannot be very great.

VII

We have three more precursors, all French and all closest to Tocqueville in time.

The first was Saint-Marc Girardin, a professor of literature, who was also a prolific and influential political commentator. One of his favorite themes was the threat of Russia to the West, especially to France and England. Another was the need to win over Germany for a decisive struggle against the Russian enemy. In a preface to a collection of political and literary essays on Germany entitled *Notices sur l'Allemagne*, published in 1831, the same year that Tocqueville set out for the United States, Saint-Marc Girardin combined these themes with a striking, pre-Tocquevillian allusion to the United States.

Saint-Marc Girardin argued that only an alliance of France, England and Germany could prevent Europe from being dominated "under the yoke of Russia." He forcefully advocated the political unification of Germany, forty years before it was actually achieved, as the necessary condition for Germany to play its destined role in the struggle between the "despotic civilization" of Russia and the "liberal civilization" of France and England.

But what if European civilization should be too weak to resist Russian domination? At this point, Saint-Marc Girardin suddenly suggested that it would then be necessary "to look towards America." A "prophetic instinct," he went on, had led peasants of Baden and Württemberg to leave their native lands and settle on the banks of rivers in the New World. And then came this rather plaintive question: "Does Europe, alas, have to divide its heritage in two parts—to Russia, its soil; to America, its spirit?"[54]

Later commentators interpreted this somewhat cryptic *cri du coeur* to mean that Saint-Marc Girardin had anticipated Tocqueville by foreseeing "a partition of the world" between Russia and America.[55] If so, the division of Europe would be most unequal, with Russia getting physical possession and America an intangible *"esprit."* Nevertheless, despite the vagueness of this stab-in-the-dark, Saint-Marc Girardin had raised a fateful question about the future division of the European heritage between Russia and America. Though Saint-Marc Girardin was widely read in France at the time, we have no way of knowing whether Tocqueville read this work or, if he did, what he thought of this curious version of how Russia and America might one day divide Europe between them.

The second Frenchman anticipated Tocqueville and went even further in the very year that Tocqueville published his first volume. This time it was Philarète Chasles, another Parisian literary critic and political commentator, well known as a friend of Balzac. In 1835, Chasles wrote:

> There are two countries whose power grows daily, and our children will perhaps witness the gigantic conflict between them: North America on one side and Russia on the other; republican federation and despotism; industry and war; and antagonism the like of which has rarely presented itself and which is developing on a scale of which the empires of Sesostris, Tamerlane, Cyrus or Charlemagne gave us no idea.[56]

Here again, the similarity is stunning, though Chasles added the element of a potential Russo-American conflict. But Chasles' divination appeared in a forgotten French periodical and was not exhumed by a scholar for over a century and a quarter.

The third, however, is by far the most important, a rival of Tocqueville's insight as well as a precursor.

VIII

Michel Chevalier belonged to the converts to Saint-Simonianism after the master's death in 1825. Comte Claude Henri de Saint-Simon, the founder of the school, had already indicated to his disciples what to think of the future of the United States. At the age of nineteen, Saint-

Simon had joined the French forces fighting in the American War of Independence; he later claimed that he had made an important contribution to the British defeat at Yorktown; it gave him reason, he thought, to regard himself as "one of the founders of the liberty of the United States." In *Letters to an American*, written in 1817, Saint-Simon boasted that he had recognized ever since the American Revolution that it had

> signalled the beginning of a new political era, that the revolution would necessarily bring about an important progress in civilisation in general, and that in a short time it would cause great changes in the social order then existing in Europe.

In an unpublished work, Saint-Simon credited Americans with a "political capacity" superior to that of the English and advised that the United States should be regarded "like a child which had grown up and which from now on ought to be listened to in the council which deliberates on the general interests of the great family."[57]

Chevalier was a young engineer won over to Saint-Simonianism in 1830 at the age of twenty-four. He gave up his original career to become a leading journalist and activist of the movement, soon to become a cult. After spending six months in jail as an alleged threat to the régime of Louis Philippe, he received a commission from the Minister of the Interior, Adolphe Thiers, later Premier and President, to investigate the new means of communication and transportation in the United States. His mission was not unlike that of Tocqueville and Beaumont which was to look into the American prison system. With this trip to the USA, Chevalier broke his ties with the Saint-Simonians and struck out on his own as a leading economic thinker and doer. The Collège de France appointed him professor of political economy in 1840; he sat for a short time in the Chamber of Deputies, later for a longer period in the Senate; he was the main French instigator and signatory of the first European commercial agreement between France and Great Britain in 1860. Heinrich Heine called him "one of the most noble characters."[58] Chevalier is another prophet who has been obscured in Tocqueville's shadow.

Chevalier came to the US in 1834, two years after Tocqueville had left. As against Tocqueville's nine months, however, Chevalier stayed for almost two years. By chance, parts of Chevalier's book were published before the appearance of Tocqueville's first half in January 1835. About one-third of Chevalier's book, which came out in 1836, began to appear in 1834 in the semi-official *Journal des Débats* in the form of letters from North America. Tocqueville studiously avoided reading Chevalier's reports in order to be uninfluenced by them; Chevalier for his part does not seem to have known of Tocqueville's work until he came to the end of his own stay in America at the end of 1835.[59] Thus both wrote independently at almost the same time and in much the same circumstances. Both were the same age, thirty, when their books came out.

That Chevalier's work is worthy of standing beside Tocqueville's masterpiece has occasionally been recognized, though few American scholars have taken the hint.[60]

Chevalier's work complemented Tocqueville's and sometimes anticipated it. One of the oft-remarked weaknesses of Tocqueville's treatment was his ignorance of or lack of interest in the economic substructure of American society and institutions. Chevalier, an engineer by profession and then still a social radical in transition from the school of Saint-Simon, took an interest in material aspects of American life which Tocqueville largely ignored. Moreover, some of his views of America's future were no less prescient than Tocqueville's.

Like Tocqueville, Chevalier foresaw that the United States was bound "without delaying long" to extend from sea to sea (though he did not venture to say anything about north-to-south). The United States was reserved for "high destinies" of the utmost importance to the "general progress of the human race." Chevalier, in the manner of his time, divided Europe into two main branches—the Latin and the Teutonic, with England and America belonging to the latter. The Teutonic, he warned, was forging ahead of the Latin; but the latter was also beset by a third group, the Slavs, led by Russia, which threatened to put the Latin nations in third place.

Chevalier was filled with anxiety about the future of a Europe pulled between East and West. In an early letter to the *Journal des Débats* (dated in his book 24 April 1834), Chevalier raised the question of what Europe would be in a hundred years, that is, by 1934, five years before the Second World War. He speculated that Europe would be "divided, enfeebled by internecine struggles," forced to "bow our heads that we still carry so high and so proudly." And then what? What countries would take Europe's place? Here, suddenly, Chevalier strikingly anticipated Tocqueville.

Chevalier's answer to his own question was—Russia and America, "the two great figures which are rising today at both ends of the horizon." They were "two young colossi who watch each other from one shore of the Atlantic to the other and touch each other on the banks of the Pacific Ocean." Would they not, he wondered, "soon divide among themselves the dominion of the world?"[61]

Of the two colossi, Chevalier seemed to think that America was more likely to play the dominant role:

> The Americans are the most enterprising of men and the most ambitious of nations: if we continue for too long to be completely absorbed by our sterile disputes, they would be the people to come upon us unexpectedly to take away from us the precious burden of the destinies of the human race and put themselves in first place.

Chevalier was also greatly concerned about what he called "the struggle between the East and the West," which he called "the most general fact in the history of the civilisation to which we belong." In this struggle, too, he thought that the Americans might best be able to reconcile the two.

In his last letter (dated October 22, 1835) Chevalier passed judgment on the general foreign policy of the United States. It differed markedly from Tocqueville's view, which had practically obliterated foreign policy from the American scene for the foreseeable future. "The foreign policy of American democracy," wrote Chevalier, "is profoundly egoistic; national ambition is characteristic of growing nations." He specified: "The ambitions of the United States are without limits; they aspire to the suzerainty over South America; they covet one by one the provinces of Mexico." The Americans, he thought, greatly resembled the Romans, though he would not go so far as to suggest that the Americans were also "destined to become the masters of the world." While the Americans had "faults" which shocked foreign nations, he reflected, they also had formidable "qualities" which Europeans were advised to emulate in order to "maintain our rank in the world in spite of them and everyone else."[62]

There were obvious similarities and differences between the views of Tocqueville and Chevalier on the destiny of America. Both anticipated the "manifest destiny" of the next decade. Both, in fact, used the very term, Tocqueville in the plural, Chevalier in the singular. Tocqueville saw it extending from the polar regions to the tropics and from the Atlantic to the Pacific, Chevalier from sea to sea and more particularly through the domination of South America and absorption of Mexico. Both resorted to an analogy with the Romans—Tocqueville when he thought of the Americans making themselves "master of the seas," Chevalier more generally, stopping just short of making Americans "the masters of the world." The Roman analogy was to become especially popular after the Second World War.[63]

But most remarkable was the thought common to Tocqueville and Chevalier and which they put into print within a few months of each other: that Russia and America were going to divide the world between them. Yet, for all the similarity, there was a difference. Tocqueville did not clearly put the rise of Russia and America in the context of the decline of Europe. He merely observed that all other nations had apparently reached their "natural limits"; only these two were still growing. Chevalier explicitly linked the rise of Russia and America to the decline of Europe. If Europe wished to avoid such a fate, it had to learn from America. He held out some hope, but not much.

The two precocious and formidable Frenchmen made up their minds about America's destiny in the midst of the Jacksonian era, which American historians have traditionally regarded as excessively concerned with internal problems and politics. Tocqueville was more distinctly influenced by the seeming American withdrawal from foreign affairs. Chevalier speculated more freely and adventurously, not only about the meeting of East and West but also the role of the United States in bringing together the North and South. The Jacksonian introversion did not stop thoughtful Europeans from looking ahead to where all this build-up of raw power was likely to go.

There were prophets aplenty of America's destiny as a great power in the first decades of the nineteenth century. I have chosen to discuss those who, like Tocqueville, juxtaposed Russia and America. Of these, it may be said that they fall into two groups, both ancestors of similar schools of thought since the Second World War.

One—to which Bristed, de Pradt, and Alexander Everett belong— more nearly prophesied a Russian-American "Cold War." Their thinking was imbued with fear of Russia—de Pradt most of all and Everett almost as much in his second book. They had largely lost faith in Europe's capacity to withstand Russian pressure and anxiously looked about for a "counterweight." In the distance they saw the United States, growing furiously in population, wealth, and territory. They did not want Russia and America to divide the world between them; they wanted America to help Europe drive Russia back to its own world— outside Central and Western Europe. They looked on America's future domination of its half of the world with complacency, but they did not want or did not expect America to remain satisfied with it. In varying degrees they were anti-Russian and pro-American.

The second school of thought—to which Tocqueville belonged and to a lesser degree Chevalier—might be described in present-day terms as "bi-polar." Instead of conflict, they foresaw a division of the world. Not that Tocqueville's political sympathies were equally divided between Russia and America. He saw America as combating the wilderness and barbarism, Russia as combating the civilization of the West. America stood for freedom, Russia for servitude. Nevertheless, Tocqueville allotted to each of them "the destinies of half the world." There he stopped. He did not attempt to say what would happen next or whether they would be content with their portions of the world. Chevalier is harder to pin down. If one goes no further than the letter dated April 24, 1834, the similarity with Tocqueville is remarkable, even if Chevalier put the idea of a division of the world as a question rather than as an affirmation. But Chevalier also suggested elsewhere that Americans might put themselves in "first place" in the place of Europeans. To some extent he may be said to have had a foot in both camps.

One way or the other, the two decades after 1815 produced some extraordinary anticipations and approximations of theories and realities that came out in full force after 1945. The odd thing is that the prophet who least well anticipated the post–World War II "Cold War," Alexis de Tocqueville, has received almost all the honor and attention. Tocqueville's work is great enough to stand without this gratuitous glorification. The other prophets have waited long enough for some share of the glory.

IX

The real prophets of the "cold war" came in the mid-nineteenth century, a decade or two after the works of Tocqueville and Chevalier. The same thought seems to have occurred at approximately the same time in the United States and France.

One of these American prophets was Waddy Thompson, a Congressman from South Carolina, who was appointed first Minister to Mexico in 1842 and later disapproved strongly of the Mexican war. In 1847,

Thompson put out a book entitled *Recollections of Mexico* in which, towards the end, he ventured far beyond what his title would have led his readers to expect. He unexpectedly took on the relationship of Great Britain, Russia and the United States.

> England has no single motive for a war with us. It is not of this country that she is jealous, but of the northern despotisms of Europe, and mainly of Russia, and has been so since the seizure of the fortress of Oczacow, in 1788. And well may England and all Europe tremble under the shadow of that terrible military despotism now holding one-eighth of the territory of the globe, and continually extending its limits and its power. All the wars of the present century which have weakened other European powers have resulted in the aggrandizement of Russia. The government is not only a despotism, but essentially a military despotism. The studies in which her people are educated are principally those of war and diplomacy. Russia and the United States are antipodes and antagonists. The wise and far seeing statesmen of England see this and calculate, as well they may, upon our sympathy, in a conflict with Russia.[64]

Thompson was well ahead of his time. Some of his phrases might strike a responsive chord a century later. His purpose was to herald a conflict between England and Russia, not between the United States and Russia. In such a struggle, he wanted the United States to side with England. But his line of reasoning led him to make an assertion that foreshadowed the ideological battles of the "Cold War" in the late twentieth century: "Russia and the United States are antipodes and antagonists." Meanwhile, he was satisfied to put England in the front line in the effort to hold back "the aggrandizement of Russia."

Another better-known American made a somewhat ambiguous prediction about future Russo-American relations a decade and a half later. In 1861, the first year of the Civil War, William H. Seward, Lincoln's Secretary of State, gave some advice to Cassius Marcellus Clay, the newly appointed American minister to Russia. Seward suggested that America and Russia might remain good friends—but apparently not forever. Their friendly relations, he forecast, would continue

> until, each having made the circuit of half the globe in opposite directions, they shall meet and greet each other in regions where civilization first began, and where, after so many ages, it has become now lethargic and helpless.[65]

These words have been interpreted to mean that Seward expected some sort of Russo-American struggle or rivalry to take place some time in the future in or over China. Meanwhile, he instructed Clay "to confirm and strengthen" the traditional relations of "amity and friendship" with Russia. In 1867, Seward's policy was rewarded by the purchase of Alaska from Russia for $7,200,000, a deal then known as "Seward's Folly." Over a century later, China did appear to be a focal point of Russo-American antagonism.

Meanwhile, some French prophets expressed even clearer forebodings. In 1847, the same year as the appearance of Waddy Thompson's book, the French statesman and historian, Louis Adolphe Thiers, was heard holding forth on the future of Russia and America. His conversation was preserved by the French critic, Charles Augustin Sainte-Beuve, in the following form:

> There are only two young peoples left: Russia over in the East; it is barbaric, but it is great . . . Old Europe will sooner or later have to reckon with that youth, for Russia is a youth, as the common man puts it. The other youth is America, an adolescent and intoxicated democracy, which acknowledges no obstacle. There lies the future of mankind, between those two huge worlds. One day, they will clash; and struggles will take place, of which the past cannot give us an idea, at least for the mass and the physical shock; for gone is the age of great moral accomplishments.[66]

Thiers was by this time expounding views that were already familiar —Russia and America as "young peoples" on the march. But his premonition that their clash would be unprecedented in its "mass and the physical shock" was less common. The devastation of atomic and nuclear warfare was still a century away; he must have been thinking of the immense bulk and growth of both countries as reason enough for fearing the unprecedented consequences of a conflict between them. Yet such a foreboding reads with peculiar mordancy a century later.

Another such French opinion showed up in print seven years later. It was offered by Emile Montégut, then a well-known essayist and translator. In an article published in July 1854, entitled "On the Idea of Universal Monarchy," he maintained that the dream of universal monarchy, which had been prevalent in ages past, had not vanished. In pursuing this thought, Montégut pointed to Russia and America:

> Two colossal nations, still weak, but weak only because they have not had the time to gather and concentrate their forces, are in their turn caught in that vertigo of domination: America and Russia. Of those two ambitions, only one is at present to be feared, that of Russia. Never was an immoderate ambition revealed under such dangerous and clever forms.

Montégut believed that Russia represented a danger to Europe not only because of its armies but even more because of its spirit and ideas. Europe, he thought, was too fond of comfort and too passionately devoted to equality, whereas "the Russian spirit consists in the hatred of the individual and in his absorption into the State, to the advantage of despotic power." Thus Russia still embodied "the ambition of universal monarchy." But Montégut did not advise Europe to get the help of America to protect itself against Russia. Instead, he exhorted Europe that the way to vanquish Russia was to "purify ourselves, strip ourselves of what may, in us, offer her sway, not just over our bodies, but over our souls."[67] Such counsel was not uncommon a century later—that the real defense against Russia was political and intellectual, not merely military.

Another cry of alarm against the Russian menace that touched on the American role came from the French scholar and philosopher, Ernest Renan. He had always regarded Russia rather than Germany to be the enemy of France and Europe; the Franco-German war of 1870 and its outcome for France provoked him to warn that Germany was doing Russia's work and would live to regret it. In a letter to David Strauss, the German historian of religion, he fearfully evoked "the day when Bohemia, Moravia, Croatia, Serbia, all the Slavic populations now under Ottoman rule, who need only a leader to command them, will be gathered around that huge Muscovite conglomerate." He asked what the Germans would have to say if the Slavs should come and lay claim to Prussia proper, to Pomerania, Silesia and Berlin, as well as if they should settle along the Oder and the Elbe. Three-quarters of a century later, these anxieties were less farfetched and alarmist.

Renan, like Saint-Marc Girardin, favored a cultural union between Germany, France and England to safeguard the future of civilization, as he understood it. This union, he also reflected, might perhaps lean on the young American Republic. That was as far as he went to bring the United States into the European defense system against the Russian menace.[68]

Tocqueville's successors in this prophetic vein may be said to have drawn an implication from his prognosis. What they got from him, and what he got from his predecessors, we cannot know. Most likely, the basic idea of a Russo-American division of the world or that of a Russo-American struggle for world power was in the air ever since Baron von Grimm, the true original, had thought of the first version in 1790. It may well be argued that a division of the world between Russia and

America fatally implied a subsequent struggle for supremacy between them. Such a division was bound to be dangerously unstable. If only by implication, then, Tocqueville may be regarded as a forerunner of those nineteenth-century prophets of the "Cold War." Still, we cannot be sure what he would have thought. One of the most curious aspects of his famous augury is that he lived for almost another quarter of a century and never so much as touched the subject again.

Encounter, February 1979

2

Intellectuals in Politics

"Intellectuals in politics" immediately raises two questions: What intellectuals? What politics?

Instead of trying to define these terms, which are so broad and loose that they defy exact definition, I prefer to start by name-dropping. To begin with, the names are Woodrow Wilson, Raymond Moley, Patrick Daniel Moynihan, Henry A. Kissinger and Zbigniew Brzezinski. These names indicate the type of American intellectual with which I will be largely concerned. Three things can be said about them immediately. They went into politics, full-time or part-time, after they had established themselves professionally as intellectuals. The intellectual in politics is most often the professor in politics. And politics here does not refer merely to the realm of ideas or intellectual influence; it requires actual service in government. There are other types, such as intellectuals in revolutionary politics, but they are so different that they need a quite different approach.

The late Richard Hofstadter wrote an admirable book called *Anti-Intellectualism in American Life* (1963), much of which dealt with anti-intellectualism in American politics. He may have chosen anti-intellectualism rather than intellectualism because he thought that the former had deeper historical roots. Intellectuals in American politics are, in fact, a relatively recent phenomenon, limited almost wholly to the present century. Their history remains to be written.

In the eighteenth and early nineteenth centuries, from Thomas Jefferson to John Quincy Adams, the United States had intellectual politicians rather than intellectuals in politics. The distinction is important. The intellectual politician is a type of politician; the intellectual in politics is a type of intellectual. One makes his career in politics; the other comes to politics after making an intellectual career. The most happy reconciliation between intellectualism and politics was achieved by the intellectual politicians in the first half-century of American life. It was not to be approached for another century.

Beginning with the Jacksonian Era in the 1830s, intellectualism and politics drifted apart. Despite a few notable exceptions, intellectuals considered politics alien, politicians considered intellectuals politically useless. The historian George Bancroft served as Secretary of the Navy and Minister to Great Britain and Germany. Edward Everett, a professor of Greek at Harvard University, was later Governor of Massachusetts, Minister to Great Britain, and US Senator. Henry Cabot Lodge was an assistant professor of history at Harvard before becoming a Senator. One nineteenth-century President, James A. Garfield, not one of the most distinguished, was for a short time a teacher of classics and president of Hiram College, a small institution in Ohio. With one exception, these careers signified no trend. The exception was a tradition even in the nineteenth century of appointing intellectuals to diplomatic posts. But Presidents varied even in this respect, and it was at most a marginal affair.

The intellectuals' distaste for politics was, for most of the nineteenth century, matched by the politicians' disdain for intellectuals. An intellectual-political movement, known as "the genteel reformers," arose in the post-Civil War period but had little success. A Tammany Hall boss in the last quarter of the nineteenth century put the case against intellectuals in politics in this way:

> Some young men think they can learn how to be successful in politics from books, and they cram their heads with all sorts of college rot. They couldn't make a bigger mistake. Now, understand me, I ain't sayin' nothin' against colleges. I guess they have to exist as long as there's bookworms, and I suppose they do some good in certain ways, but they don't count in politics.[1]

It is said that the first—or one of the first—American uses of the term "intellectual" appeared in a letter by the philosopher William James in 1899.[2] James used the term in a context that had a direct bearing on the American attitude toward intellectuals in politics. Commenting on the Dreyfus case in France, James sympathized with the French intellectuals' "aggressively militant" role and hoped that they would grow "stronger and stronger." But then he turned around and thanked God for an America in which "intellectuals"—he still thought it necessary to put the word in quotation marks—could stay out of all corrupting "big institutions," which he blamed for Captain Dreyfus's ordeal. Except for the American "party spirit," James believed, American sources of corruption were trivial compared with the European. He did not say so in so many words but he seemed to imply that American intellectuals should stay out of politics and instead "work to keep our precious birthright of individualism" and seek fulfillment in "free personal relation." His emphasis on "freedom from all corrupting institutions" must have included the political in view of his conviction that "the only serious permanent force of corruption in America is party spirit."[3]

Nevertheless, it was at the turn of the century that the institutionalization of intellectuals in American politics began. Its birthplace was the state of Wisconsin where, under the leadership of Governor Robert M. La Follette, the outstanding political figure of the Progressive movement, the first successful experiment in achieving a symbiosis between a university and a government was attempted. A comprehensive program was worked out to put academic "experts" of the University of Wisconsin at the service of the state government. Scientists, engineers, agronomists, economists, historians, political scientists and the like were systematically called on for advice and information. The Wisconsin system was nominally non-partisan; in fact, it was the servant of Progressive politics, which was the only kind of politics willing and able to engage in such an experiment. Thus the Wisconsin experience produced a familiar type of intellectual in politics—the reformer working for a reform movement.

The next great step forward by an American intellectual in politics was taken by Woodrow Wilson. In fact, he took the greatest step forward that any American intellectual has ever taken—right into the White House. Wilson was an authentic intellectual if ever there was one— Professor of Jurisprudence and Political Economy, President of Princeton University, author of basic works on the American political system. The story of how Wilson became a politician suggests the function sometimes reserved for intellectuals. When he was approached in 1910 to accept the Democratic nomination for Governor of the State of New Jersey, his stepping stone to the presidency two years later, he examined his overworked conscience to find a good reason why he should give in to the temptation. He came up with the idea that " a new day had come in American politics." He interpreted the proposition, in effect, as the opening of a new era in American politics—the era of the intellectual in politics. Wilson later realized that he had naively deceived himself. His biographer notes that the New Jersey politician who masterminded Wilson's nomination "hoped to use Wilson as a respectable front behind which he could operate." It was not a role that Wilson could or would play, but he might never have started on his political career if some politician had not chosen him to play it.

I do not imagine that Wilson was the last intellectual whom politicians have intended to use as a "respectable front." But Wilson learned fast. One of the first things he had to do to win the governorship was to repudiate virtually everything he had stood for on the issue of trade unionism, which he had previously opposed.[4] In short, he had to learn how to act like a politician, not an intellectual, to gain power. For better or worse, however, Wilson unlearned this lesson in the course of his Presidency. He was always more the schoolmaster than the politician. The more power Wilson had, the less he was willing to compromise—a trait attributed to his intellectualism but perhaps more attributable to his character.

Far more than Wilson personally, the First World War opened the political door to intellectuals.

> The war itself, ironically, raised many of them to heights of influence as no domestic issue could [Hofstadter observed]. Historians and writers were mobilized for propaganda, and experts of all kinds were recruited as advisers.[5]

They became so prominent that one Republican Senator protested that "this is a government by professors and intellectuals." He warned, not for the last time, that "intellectuals are good enough in their places, but a country run by professors is ultimately destined to Bolshevism and an explosion."[6] The high point of this academic invasion came in 1919 when a group known as "The Inquiry" was organized to prepare the ground for American policy in the peace negotiations. It brought together 150 scholarly experts from many different fields, ranging from history to ethnology, aided by a staff of several hundred more of similar backgrounds.

The First World War, then, might have been the decisive breakthrough of American intellectuals into political or at least governmental service.

They were welcomed in unprecedented numbers and variety. Some lessons can be drawn from this experience. One is that the first large-scale incursion of American intellectuals into political life needed a national crisis which united the nation, including the intellectuals. The second is that intellectuals were drawn into government in large numbers when the functions or responsibilities of government were enormously enlarged. By vastly expanding the reach of government in the economic and social as well as the military sphere, the First World War temporarily created a need to tap a new and sizable reservoir of special training. Such a reservoir for a quick, massive infusion existed only in the universities and other schools. That a professor was President did not hurt, but another war showed that it was not necessary to have a professor as President to produce the same result.

The First World War did not constitute the decisive breakthrough, because it was immediately followed by national disillusionment and Wilson's repudiation. The next administrations of Presidents Harding, Coolidge, and Hoover went back to the older system of using intellectuals selectively and even exceptionally. This wartime and postwar experience introduced an aspect of intellectuals in politics that has forcefully struck students of the subject. It is the cyclical nature of the phenomenon. This was the first time that American intellectuals went in and out of the revolving door of politics. For the first one hundred and fifty years of the Republic, then, it may be said that intellectuals in politics were not a common commodity and had not established a firm tradition. We can see gradual changes, but they were more of degree than of kind. The real breakthrough was still to come.

It came with Franklin D. Roosevelt in the 1930s. The story is familiar to students of Rooseveltiana, but it is worth repeating for what we can learn or relearn from it.

The intellectual breakthrough was a by-product of Roosevelt's first presidential campaign before he was elected president. According to the most circumstantial version, candidate Roosevelt and his faithful factotum, Samuel I. Rosenman, were sitting around in March 1932 talking about how to organize the campaign. Roosevelt was a quick learner, but he had much to learn about national problems and policies. As Rosenman later recalled, he told Roosevelt that they ought to get some people together "and see whether we can come up with some answers or at least some good new intelligent thinking, pro and con, and some new ideas. . . ." Whom did Rosenman have in mind? Rosenman's answer suggests something important about the whole phenomenon:

Usually in a situation like this, a candidate gathers around him a group composed of some successful industrialists, some big financiers, and some national political leaders. I think we ought to steer clear of all those. They all seem to have failed to produce anything constructive to solve the mess we're in today. Now my idea is this: why not go to the universities of the country? You have been having some good experiences with college professors. I think they wouldn't be afraid to strike out on new paths just because the paths are new. They would get away from all the old fuzzy thinking on many subjects, and that seems to be the most important thing.[7]

Rosenman's version lends itself to a broad generalization about the necessary social condition for such an intellectual breakthrough. "The mess we're in today" was, of course, the greatest economic crisis in American history.

A different kind of crisis had brought the Wilsonian intellectuals into politics. The Rooseveltian crisis was far deeper, implying the bankruptcy of the whole social system, and the successful industrialists, big financiers, and national political leaders who dominated it. Roosevelt as governor of New York had already used professorial experts for specific problems and projects. Rosenman wanted to use professors to fill a general political vacuum—that was what was new about it. The way into politics was opened for the early Rooseveltian intellectuals not so much because Roosevelt was so different at that stage from previous American politicians but because the period in which he wanted to become President was so different. The economic crisis was the midwife of the Rooseveltian breakthrough for the intellectuals.

The first intellectual to be recruited into the Brain Trust, Professor Raymond Moley of Columbia University, did not like Rosenman's version because it gave Rosenman too much credit for the historic innovation. Moley's account also lends itself to a larger consideration. The real reason for the Brain Trust, according to Moley, was Roosevelt's and Rosenman's extreme limitations in national affairs. They brought in the professors because they had found them so useful during Roosevelt's governorship and had merely expanded the practice to broaden their political education.[8] No doubt the original Brain Trust—which soon included Professor Rexford Guy Tugwell and Professor Adolf A. Berle (both of Columbia), with Professor Felix Frankfurter (of the Harvard Law School) lurking in the wings—started as a curious sort of private seminar for Franklin D. Roosevelt. Tugwell called it a "course in socio-economics."[9] It thus served an educational purpose for which professorial intellectuals were particularly well fitted. Another presidential candidate might not have been so responsive. Nevertheless, it may be doubted whether Roosevelt would have had the incentive and patience to meet with the professors in long night sessions if economic conditions had been less ominous.[10]

The learning process, however, was not a one-way affair. One of Moley's admitted reasons for accepting the invitation to teach the future President was that the teacher was also going to learn—learn about politics from the inside or, as Moley put it, "satisfy my desire for wider experience in politics." He was not the last professor who has dealt with politics in the classroom and has sought to increase his knowledge of politics in the back rooms. Max Weber said that "either one lives 'for' politics or one lives 'off' politics."[11] Many an intellectual has lived for politics before living off politics, and then managed to live both for and off politics.

The Brain Trust did not long remain an informal educational institution. Politically, its key members served three main functions—as idea men, as talent scouts, and as speech writers. These functions have continued to be typical of those intellectuals whom we might call "generalists." Roosevelt himself once defined the Brain Trust's role in these words:

> You study the problems, work out the best answers you can, and bring them to me. Don't mix in politics—it is unpleasant, sometimes a dirty business. Leave that to me.[12]

The tasks of intellectuals may also seem more glamorous from the outside than from the inside. Moley later complained that he was called to work on a speech "just as I'd be called in if I were a plumber and a pipe needed fixing."[13] Tugwell referred to himself as an "errand boy."[14]

The early Brain Trusters had grave misgivings about switching from professor to politician. Moley fervently protested that he had no intention of giving up his intellectual freedom, his aspiration to be accepted "on the basis of what I had to say, rather than because I was part of a governmental machine," and his conviction that "honest teaching and writing about public affairs precluded not only White House cup-bearing and administrative paper-shuffling, but party goose-stepping"—before being prevailed on by Roosevelt to give them up. Tugwell had a similar struggle with himself. When he first considered the prospect of an official post in Washington, he told himself that "from professor to the government is a great transformation." He also reflected: "If I am in the administration, I'll have to make endless compromises—a far different position from that of critical observer. . . ." But he soon capitulated and went to Washington. Berle held out the longest. He told a colleague that "all of us can be a good deal more useful hoeing our own row than monkeying with obscure under-secretaryships or commissionerships." Incidentally, Berle used to write letters to the President addressed to "DEAR CAESAR." Roosevelt once replied that he did not mind being called *Caesar* but hated being thought of as *Napoleon*.

The Rooseveltian Brain Trust as such was relatively short-lived. Raymond Moley, the key figure, defected from the New Deal in 1935. He disagreed on a matter of high policy, and I suppose his case might be taken to mean that intellectuals cannot be trusted to be unconditionally loyal to politicians, at least not as much as other politicians. Rex Tugwell, next in line, became the chief whipping boy of the anti-Roosevelt opposition; the attacks on him were easily as disgraceful as any later unleashed by Senator Joseph McCarthy. Not the least reason for Tugwell's vulnerability was his status as a professor and intellectual. By 1936, Tugwell had become such a political liability that Roosevelt did not try to save him. His case may illustrate another function of intellectuals in politics—as scapegoats and sacrificial lambs. A. A. Berle stayed out of Washington until he accepted an appointment as Assistant Secretary of State in 1938 but lasted only about half a year in that office. (His real political career came somewhat later, a circumstance which enabled him to last longer and go further than the other two.)

So the political careers of the most famous early Brain Trusters were not too promising. Nevertheless, much more was happening during the first Roosevelt years to intellectuals lower down on the scale. Professor Arthur Schlesinger, Jr., described the New Dealers in terms of the following occupations—"they were mostly lawyers, college professors, economists, or social workers." Lawyers had long had a virtual monopoly of the American government, but college professors in second place—that was something new. Presumably some of the economists as well as the social workers were intellectuals, too. The Brain Trust received most publicity but it was only the tip of the New Deal's intellectual iceberg. The Moleys and Tugwells played for big stakes and eventually lost; many others, less well known or less exposed, came and stayed. The larger influx had a more stable structural foundation; the New Deal brought into existence a whole series of government agencies and bureaucracies devoted to public works, social security, energy and reclamation, and reforms in many other fields. New agencies and new policies demanded new people and new capabilities. If professors did not get most of the new jobs, their students did.

The New Deal, however, was only the first stage of the Rooseveltian breakthrough for the intellectuals. As the New Deal waned, the influence of its intellectuals declined. But for the Second World War, the United States might have gone through another cyclical movement of intellectuals in and out of government favor. The war completed the process which the New Deal began. With or without the New Deal, the war would have brought in intellectuals *en masse*. The First World War had already shown the way, but it had not gone so far because it had not lasted long enough (for the United States) and had not ended with the assumption of American responsibility for the fate of the world, or at least the Western world. American intellectuals supported the Second World War with greater unity and enthusiasm. The new war agencies swallowed up thousands of older and younger intellectuals. Well over a hundred new agencies of the executive branch were formed during the course of the war. Many of the postwar intellectuals were infected with the political virus in these agencies, never to recover. The distinguished politicized intellectuals who came out of the Office of Strategic Services (or OSS, predecessor of the C.I.A.) could easily staff one or more good-sized universities.

The war and its aftermath produced a new type of American intellectual in politics. The earlier variety had almost always been brought in to advise on domestic policies, such as financial reform or criminal justice. "The Inquiry" of Wilson's day had been devoted to foreign affairs, but it had not been given an opportunity to do much beyond preparing documents and memoranda for the peace negotiations; and it had not been able to perpetuate itself.

Now a new breed of politicized intellectuals appeared—the foreign-affairs intellectuals. What had been a fairly small field became a minor industry with branches in international politics, international economics, international arms proliferation and control, foreign aid, area specialization, and the like. Exotic fields could attract hundreds of specialists virtually overnight and flourish as long as the government or foundations were willing to subsidize them. If anything more were needed to reinvigorate the wartime and postwar boom in the procreation, care, and feeding of politicized intellectuals, the Truman Doctrine of 1947 and the Marshall Plan of 1948 came just in time. They enabled large numbers of American intellectuals to fan out all over the world at government expense, scattering their largesse and advice far and wide. It was also a time for some to learn the difference between Meursault and Montrachet. All this has nothing to do with whether the War, the Doctrine, or the Plan were good or necessary; most American intellectuals thought they were. What is more to the point for our purpose is that they provided the political, structural, and material foundation for the new breed of intellectuals. A different kind of United States was needed to produce a different kind of intellectual in politics. The rise of the United States as a preeminent world power was a necessary condition for the rise of the intellectual as an eminent political force in the United States.

Nevertheless, the pendulum continued to swing. The upsurge of McCarthyism in 1950 and the defeat of Adlai Stevenson by General Eisenhower for the presidency in 1952 gave intellectuals in general and politicized intellectuals in particular a feeling of rejection if not persecution. Writing in the midst of the Eisenhower period, C. Wright Mills did not consider intellectuals to be part of "the power élite," barely bothered to discuss them at all and then only to dismiss them contemptuously as "hired men."[15]

Towards the end of Eisenhower's administration, a survey of opinion of social science professors showed that most of them were convinced that the professoriat was not "much appreciated" by businessmen and congressmen.[16] In 1959, Professor Seymour Martin Lipset was impressed by the self-pity and the self-image of low status among intellectuals, neither of which he believed was justified by the evidence. Other indications supported a more optimistic view. By 1958, of the fourteen US Senators who had taught in some college or university, nine might be classified as professors, a higher percentage than ever before. One writer claimed that the Eisenhower administration employed more professors than the New Deal had ever done. In 1959, one of the most astute observers, Professor David Riesman, held that the status of intellectuals was "good and getting better." And soon after the end of the Eisenhower years, the one and only authority on the American Establishment revealed that "the presidents and senior professors of the great Eastern universities frequently constitute themselves as *ad hoc* Establishment committees." Since he also confessed that the only thing we can apparently know about the Establishment is that it exists, it was not altogether clear just what importance should be attributed to these self-constituted committees. Still, even to be mentioned in such high and mighty company suggested that the status of some university presidents and senior professors had risen spectacularly despite all the pessimism and discontent of the Eisenhower period.[17]

An article of particular interest, owing to the future career of its author, appeared in 1959. It was called "The Policymaker and the Intellectual" and was written by Henry A. Kissinger, at the time of publication a Lecturer in Government at Harvard and already knowledgeable from personal experience about the vicissitudes of intellectuals in politics.[18]

Kissinger thought that a case could be made even then that "in some respects the intellectual has never been more in demand" by policymakers. As much autobiographical as anything else, most of the article was a cry of pain at the way policymakers mishandled and misunderstood intellectuals. Kissinger's catalogue of woes was revelatory—

> the intellectual is rarely found at the level where decisions are made. . . . It is the executive who determines in the first place whether he needs advice . . . he [the intellectual] is asked to solve problems, not to contribute to the definition of goals . . . in short, all too often what the policymaker wants from the intellectual is not ideas but endorsement.

The great problem for the intellectual, according to Kissinger, was to decide whether to participate in the political process as an intellectual or as an administrator. If he chose the role of intellectual, it was essential for him

> to retain the freedom to deal with the policymaker from a position of independence, and to reserve the right to assess the policymaker's demands in terms of his own standards.

Kissinger in 1959 had already had a good deal of experience dealing with policymakers from a position of independence, which, in practice, meant staying out of the administration and dispensing advice to those in both parties who asked for it. The Kissinger of 1959 still thought like an intellectual in politics; it took ten more years and the temptation of office to make him more like an intellectual politician. As one reads the 1959 article, one is not sure that the earlier Kissinger would have approved of the later Kissinger.

In any case, the cyclical theory as interpreted by Professor Arthur Schlesinger put the 1950s on the downward swing. It may well be, however, that the cyclical theory operated, but on a higher and higher plane. Thus the Eisenhower period was a letdown from the heady

Roosevelt and Truman years but still represented an advance over pre-Roosevelt times. Another possibility is that intellectuals in politics do not count other intellectuals who have the wrong kind of politics.

Professor David Riesman proved to be right. It did not take long for the political status of intellectuals to get better, indeed, better than ever. When John F. Kennedy was elected President in 1960, he was not the intellectuals' first choice. Most of them preferred Adlai Stevenson and distrusted Kennedy. By winning over two of Stevenson's most important intellectual backers (Arthur Schlesinger and John Kenneth Galbraith), Kennedy turned the intellectual tide in his favor. They preferred to pick a winner, an urge not conspicuously characteristic of previous generations of liberal intellectuals. In fact, the Republican presidential candidate, Richard M. Nixon, tried to stigmatize the Democrats as "the party of Galbraith and Schlesinger and Bowles"—not a bad score for the intellectuals, if only it had been more accurate. This line of attack showed that intellectuals were still functioning as political whipping boys. In Schlesinger's view, Kennedy himself was a latterday intellectual politician "as politicians go"—possibly fainter praise than was intended. Schlesinger also explained why the intellectuals had changed their attitude towards Kennedy from cold to hot—"their gradual recognition of his desire to bring the world of power and the world of ideas together in alliance."[19] A better diagnosis of the passion for politics by Kennedy's intellectuals would be hard to find; it suggests that the older faith in the power *of* ideas had given way to the newer preference for power *and* ideas. Kennedy's closest aide, Theodore C. Sorensen, claimed that Kennedy had appointed to important posts a higher proportion of academicians (including sixteen Rhodes scholars) than any other President in history and even more than any European government had ever done. Sorenson also boasted that Kennedy's appointees had written more books than the President—a fast reader at twelve hundred words a minute—could read in a four-year term.[20] One dreads to think how long it would have taken a President like Eisenhower to read the same number of books.

The White House was not the only source of political advancement for intellectuals in the transition from the 1950s to the 1960s. A former Rhodes scholar, Representative John Brademas of Indiana, has related how he was told to play down his Harvard-Oxford background when he first ran for office in 1954. Four years later, his local backers were urging citizens to "vote for Brademas because he has a fine education."[21] By the mid-1960s, almost a seventh of the members of the US Senate were former professors.[22] It may be said without exaggeration that professors, ex-professors, and would-be professors were all over Washington—in the White House, in the bureaucracy, in Congress and on congressional staffs, at almost all levels of government.

Then the cyclical theory began to work again. President Lyndon B. Johnson had inherited many of Kennedy's intellectuals, but they could never be as happy with Johnson as they had been with Kennedy, if only for stylistic reasons. It is hard to imagine Johnson concluding an informal talk with representatives of national organizations by reading to them Blanche of Castile's speech from *King John*, beginning with the words:

The sun's o'ercast with blood; fair day, adieu! . . .[23]

Johnson's intellectuals were enormously productive during his first two years of domestic reforms; the Vietnam war destroyed him politically and isolated them morally. One historian of the period asserts that the defection of "liberals and intellectuals"—it is sometimes hard to tell them apart in the literature—finished off Johnson as a party leader and forced him to abdicate.[24] For once, a President needed intellectuals more than they needed him.

Lyndon Johnson lost the intellectuals; Richard Nixon never had them. Nixon would have had trouble with intellectuals even if he had not been Nixon. He was a Republican, and intellectuals have been allergic to Republicans at least since the New Deal. Nixon even had trouble giving away jobs to well-known intellectuals. Those few who took them felt as isolated and embattled as if they had decided to sacrifice themselves in a lost but somehow necessary cause. Indeed, the best of Nixon's intellectuals accepted his call to duty because he was the President and had a right to summon them to serve the country, not because they were particularly fond of him. Professor Kissinger was notoriously dubious about Nixon's qualifications before proximity in the White House made him change his mind. After Nixon's disgrace, the intellectuals who had enjoyed his favor in better times felt that he had betrayed them—not that they had betrayed themselves. What disturbed them was Watergate, not Vietnam. In a sense, intellectuals never had so little and yet so much power as under Nixon—so little because most of them did not want it from him and so much because they could now take it or leave it.

It is too soon to say much about President Carter's intellectuals, except that they are all over Washington again. By this time, intellectuals seem to have pre-empted some key governmental positions— Assistant for National Security Affairs, Science Adviser, and Chairman of the Council of Economic Advisers among others. Academic economists have done especially well in the Carter administration. If we may trust that high authority, Professor Galbraith, a hard man to please, President Carter has appointed no fewer than four "professional economists of full academic qualifications" as Secretary of the Treasury, Secretary of Commerce, Secretary of Labor, and Chairman of the Council of Economic Advisers.[25] It may be surmised, however, that presidents have been turning to professional economists not merely for their academic qualifications but because they enable them to avoid appointing a businessman who might annoy labor or a labor official who might annoy business. The new Science Adviser, Professor Frank Press, recently declared that "Jimmy Carter doesn't have the fear of academics and intellectuals" that several previous Presidents are said to have had.[26] Presumably we will now find out whether intellectuals are better off when they are not feared.

By now, the sub-species which Dr. Ralf Dahrendorf, Director of the London School of Economics, recently called "the important group of those who 'straddle' academia and decision making" has been recognized internationally. The latest and most conspicuous straddler is Professor Zbigniew Brzezinski, Dr. Kissinger's successor in the White House. The typical straddler is most frequently found in research institutes such as the Brookings Institution of Washington, D.C., whose members must sometimes be confused about whether they are coming from or going into the government. Straddlers have become so indispensable in the modern state that we may soon have, according to Dr. Dahrendorf, a Social Science Research Council institute for policy research and a more modest "LSE Brookings" in Britain as well as a "European Brookings" and a "Third World Brookings."[27] Professor Brzezinski prepared for his present position by straddling in not one but two such organizations—his own Research Institute on International Change (originally Communist Affairs) at Columbia University and his brainchild, the "Trilateral Commission," in which he first attracted the attention of Governor Jimmy Carter and vice versa. Straddling has now been institutionalized to such an extent that it must be considered the highest form of life among intellectuals in politics.

Some deep structural changes must have taken place in American society to account for the change from the nineteenth century, when intellectuals were alienated from American politics and politicians from intellectuals, to the latter half of the twentieth century, when a kind of symbiosis has taken place between intellectuals and politics. These changes are not uniquely American but they have probably gone further in the United States than anywhere else.

One of the deepest aspects of the change is the shift in perspective from the past to the present. The native habitat of scholars used to be the past; real scholars did not go beyond 1789 or, in extreme cases, the Renaissance or even the Middle Ages. A few such purists remain but they are a vanishing breed. The cult of the present has almost replaced the cult of the past. When intellectuals go into politics they go into the world of the present, the pragmatic, the manageable. As a result, fields such as economics, political science, and sociology, which are themselves concerned almost wholly with the present or recent past, make the most fertile breeding grounds for intellectuals in politics. Such intellectuals do not have to jump from the past to the present; they jump from the study of the present to the practice of the present—and then jump back to the study of their own practice. The university has become a preparatory school for government, and government has become the ultimate in post-professorial education. Professor Moynihan is an extreme case in point. He spent thirteen of the twenty years between 1950 and 1970 in government. Reflecting on this background, he has confided that "as a teacher I find these experiences are the largest store of knowledge on which I have to draw. . . ."[28] Teachers have long taught politics; some now teach their own experiences in politics. It becomes virtually impossible to draw a line between intellectual work and political work.

The fields I have mentioned are not the only ones which have made this temporal leap. They at least were always located mainly in the present. But what shall we say of the transformation that has taken place in anthropology? When I went to school it was still thought to be the study of primitive societies. Not long ago, however, I sat next to a young woman studying at a large American university. I politely inquired what she was doing. "Anthropology," she said. "And what kind of anthropology?" I asked. She replied she was doing a dissertation on one of the "new towns" that have sprung up in the United States—so new that it is still not quite finished. The anthropologists, having exhausted or having been expelled from the society of primitives, have invaded the society of the present, thus creating an awkward situation for the sociologists, who presumably should take revenge by moving from the present to the past. We are obviously in the presence of an intellectual transmutation that goes far beyond politics but is particularly conducive to participation in politics.

Sociologists know when they have a good thing and have no intention of giving up their stranglehold on the present. An American sociological journal recently asked a group of sociologists what they expected from the Carter administration. Some replies were euphoric. Congress, one experienced practitioner jubilated, "is increasingly dependent on the products of social science research." Some Congressional committee reports are stuffed with it. The executive branch increasingly finds that it can hardly get along without sociological research.

> In learning to live with an all-volunteer army, for example, the army is calling on social scientists to study how to deal with race and sex. The Army Corps of Engineers is calling on social scientists to help it understand the impact of its projects on communities. The State Department needs sociological research not only for briefing foreign affairs officers, but also in administering Agency International Development programs. . . .

Another sociologist lamented that the government was driving out "the amateur in the social science business" by supporting large-scale research institutions which

> are geared to the major consumer—the government— . . . understand the cost guidelines . . . know how to do business in Washington.

He was, however, somewhat cynical about the outcome—"the bulk of academics will be used as window-dressing for the proposals that are written." Another professor thought that "the long latent lust for being close to power—or at least the trappings of power," which gripped academics and intellectuals during the Kennedy-Johnson years and went underground with Nixon and Ford was staging a comeback with Carter. He looked forward to the emergence of a new type of "born-again" social scientist, committed to political action with "open political values." A fourth foresaw the evanescence of "a good many of the former reservations about government funds and consultancies, expressed in academia with such fervor in the late 1960s and 1970s." Well-known scholars were worrying that the government would not lavish enough of its largesse on the academic community. "Gone, apparently, are all the qualms." Here, apparently, is a new generation of intellectuals awaiting its turn at the political trough.[29]

Thus far I have emphasized the intellectual shift from the past to the present. Intellectuals who go into politics, however, make an even greater leap in time. After all, intellectuals almost always work for politicians—and politicians live *in* the present *for* the future. I am always astonished at the kinds of questions that government officials and politicians ask. What they want are prophets, not historians. Politicians are always worried about policy—what to do to meet this-or-that problem or eventuality. They want to know what is going to happen if they take this action or adopt that strategy. Policy is the politician's game, and policy is future-oriented. Intellectuals cross an invisible line into politics whenever they get into policy. Yet it is at that point that they really begin to interest politicians, who may listen patiently to the background of a problem but wish desperately to get to the foreground.

As a result, intellectual trends and fashions have been following political needs and conditions. We now have, for example, an academic field known as "public policy" or "policy studies." In one branch of this field, a school of thought interprets the making of foreign policy largely in terms of "bargaining" among bureaucrats in the government hierarchy. Whatever we may think of this "Bureaucratic-Politics model," as it is called, it is clearly an intellectual child of the times. It reflects the preoccupation of intellectuals with policy, in part because intellectuals are increasingly called on to pronounce on policy, in part as a result of their increased experience with it.

Or consider the ups-and-downs of the field known as "Area Studies." It shot up in the 1950s when the United States was drawn in—or drew itself in—to virtually every area in the world, often without preparation, personnel, or policy. For about a decade, no self-respecting university could get along without "area specialists"—Southeast Asia, East Africa, West Africa, Middle East, Far East, Latin America, etc., or any portion thereof. By the end of the 1960s, area studies went into decline; many of its former practitioners have turned to more promising fields. One reason for the popularity of area studies had been the availability of funds from the government or wealthy foundations; as soon as these lost interest, the programs shriveled. Another reason for their decline was the growing reluctance of many areas, especially in Africa, to let Americans, particularly anthropologists, roam freely in villages, asking all sorts of suspicious or outlandish questions—from the point of view of the natives. The rise and decline of Area Studies was at least as much politically as intellectually motivated.

The same intellectual cycle of rise and decline has characterized Russian studies, Chinese studies, Latin American studies, and guerrilla-warfare studies—to name but a few. Government policy has not always been the main reason for such fluctuations. In the case of Russian studies, the New Left wave at the end of the 1960s was partially responsible for their decline by spreading the word that the Soviet Union had become conservative, unfashionable, boring. These academic trends behave like the stock market; their intellectual stocks go up and down depending on the public's interest and investment in them.

Other structural changes in society have also changed the role of intellectuals in government. In the past half century or so, three great proliferations have taken place, so familiar that I need only mention them—the proliferation of government, of the so-called knowledge industries, and of colleges and universities. Each of these proliferations produced a demand for more and more trained personnel, at least some of whom may be classified as intellectuals. By now the American government has become so pervasive that even the Carter administration, which came in committed to cutting it back, seems to be giving up in despair. The three proliferations add up to a new or at least a very different social order, for which no one has yet been able to come up with a good name. The most popular name—"the Post-Industrial society"—tells us what it followed, not what it is. A crisis in the social order brought American intellectuals into politics; a change in the social order has kept them there in larger and larger numbers.

How important are intellectuals in American politics?

The short answer is, I think, that they are generally as important as politicians want them to be. Intellectuals may have influence but they almost never have power. President Truman is supposed to have said: "I think intellectuals in government are great as long as there's an old pro to tell them what to do." Intellectuals may find this Trumanesque candor offensive or demeaning, but it comes out of long, hard experience and cannot be easily rejected. Politics demands 60–40 decisions, even 55–45, and in extreme cases 51–49. Politicians who cannot make such decisions do not get to or stay at the top. For intellectuals, such decisions may be agonizing, often impossible. If the odds are so close, it is intellectually better to reserve judgment, wait for more evidence, report results without prejudice. Thus it has become the accepted function of intellectuals in government to present the available options as fairly and fully as possible, but to let the "old pro" decide on which option to adopt. The way options are presented may influence the decision. Still, presenting is not the same thing as deciding, and responsibility goes to the political decision-maker, not the intellectual option-merchant.

On the other hand, intellectuals are not likely to do much good until they lose their awe for the "old pro."

The experience of Professor Schlesinger in the case of the ill-fated Bay of Pigs expedition in 1960 should be a warning to all intellectuals new to government. Arthur Schlesinger was officially designated a Special Assistant to President Kennedy without specific duties; he thought of himself as a "historian-participant," itself a new intellectual-political role. As a newcomer to the government, he was given the assignment of writing a White Paper to justify the attempt to overthrow Castro. It was a pretty good paper, but it had little relation to the political realities behind the enterprise: Schlesinger himself thought that the project was ill-conceived and privately expressed his opposition to President Kennedy. In the critical discussions at which the heads of the CIA, the Joint Chiefs of Staff and Departments of State and Defense were present, Schlesinger said little. Later he explained why:

> It is one thing for a Special Assistant to talk frankly in private to a President at his request and another for a college professor, fresh to government, to interpose his unassisted judgment in open meeting against that of such august figures as the Secretaries of State and Defense and the Joint Chiefs of Staff, each speaking with the full weight of his institution behind him.

The fiasco changed all that. "The Bay of Pigs gave us license for the impolite inquiry and the rude comment," Schlesinger recalled, no doubt with grim satisfaction.[30] That was probably the last time he was over-awed by anyone.

One of the things an "old pro" tells intellectuals to do is to write speeches for him. Professor Raymond Moley, the original Brain Truster, will probably be remembered most for inserting three words, "the Forgotten Man," in a campaign speech for Franklin D. Roosevelt in April

1932. The phrase was not original with him; it had first been used in a different context by the sociologist, William Graham Sumner; presumably, however, it took an intellectual to remember the words in the first place. But would they have reverberated in the same way if Moley, the intellectual, not Roosevelt the politician, had spoken them in his own name?

Then there is Professor Galbraith who wrote a draft for the inaugural address of President Kennedy in January 1961. Kennedy seems to have used little more than one sentence. Galbraith later commented ruefully on the fate of his draft:

> A ghost-writer is like an unloved dog in a poor family. He must be content with scraps.[31]

More than one intellectual has felt like an unloved dog in a politician's extended family. Still, intellectuals must get a great deal of satisfaction from ghost-writing—they do so much of it. It may well be the ultimate expression of the intellectual's role in politics—words, not actions; ideas without responsibility.

Intellectuals as idea men and as talent scouts—their two other favorite occupations—obey the same rules of the game.

Intellectuals propose; politicians dispose. To be successful, the intellectual must often propose just what the politician wants him to propose. "I've been an adviser of the President," Professor Paul A. Samuelson, the eminent economist, recently confessed:

> You sometimes have the impression that you call the shots, but as you think about it you realise that you are selected because your brand of moonshine, of snake oil, sits well on the scalp or in the stomach of the President.[32]

To say that intellectuals have become important is largely to say that they have become important to politicians. To gain real power, the intellectual must become a politician. The only independent source of power in the American system comes from having a constituency, and most intellectuals have a constituency of one—themselves. Thus Senator Moynihan, after having suffered repeated frustrations in appointive offices, sought and won an elective office. His case suggests how really powerless—if real power is understood to be the power of decision—an appointed intellectual can be and what he can do about it. One sociologist was so elated by Dr. Moynihan's election to the Senate that he celebrated it as the beginning of "a new era of seeking and winning office" by social scientists. In this latest of new eras for the intellectual in politics, "if social scientists want to, they may begin appointing the lawyers—a long overdue switch in roles."[33] One might almost imagine that the real struggle for power was between intellectuals and lawyers.

Professor-Ambassador-Senator Moynihan is one of our two most celebrated intellectuals in politics. His career merits a little closer examination because he illustrates a number of different types of the species. For years he went in and out of university and government; in this phase, he was what may be called an "in-and-outer," which is what most intellectuals in government are. In this capacity, he set something of a record by impartially serving Presidents as different as Kennedy, Johnson, and Nixon in succession. Professional politicians must envy his survival rate; no politician has ever given a better exhibition of how to survive the downfall of at least two presidential patrons and come out on top on his own. As Senator, Pat Moynihan is presumably in politics to stay, though one cannot be sure of anything in his case—he recently referred to himself, perhaps jokingly, as a "displaced professor." In effect, he illustrates two paths of the intellectual—from in-and-outer to stay-in, and from the appointive to the elective.

The question arises whether Senator Moynihan is still an intellectual in politics. This question was implicitly raised by Mr. James Reston, who holds the Chair of Political Commentary endowed by the *New York Times*. Mr. Reston recently remarked that Dr. Moynihan had markedly changed since he was elected to the United States Senate. Before putting on his senatorial toga, according to Reston, Moynihan "saw the world as a whole and was almost recklessly honest in defining America's widest possible interests." Now, as Senator from New York, Moynihan has been advocating a limitation on foreign imports on behalf of the hard-pressed garment industry in New York. As a result, Reston concluded sorrowfully, Moynihan is fighting for the interests of his particular rag-trade constituents and "defending their local, personal and political concerns," as he apparently would not have done in the old days when he could still afford to see the world as a whole and be almost recklessly honest.[34] Now, if we believe Mr. Reston, Senator Moynihan has to see the world through the eyes of his constituents and be as honest as their interests will permit. Thus Moynihan illustrates the distinction between an intellectual in politics and an intellectual politician.

Senator Moynihan figured in another recent incident which tells much about the difference between a pure-and-simple intellectual, an appointed intellectual, and an elected intellectual. The story is worth relating in some detail because it concerns two intellectuals in politics in the same field but cast in different roles.

Dr. Moynihan went to work for President Nixon in 1969 as Assistant for Urban Affairs. His job entailed responsibility for drawing up a plan for the reform of the welfare system. It took almost seven months for the Nixon administration to present Congress with a project, known as the "Family Assistance Plan," which provided for a guaranteed annual income. The plan was shot down in the United States Senate, and Dr. Moynihan published a book in 1973 (*The Politics of a Guaranteed Income*) about the politics which had killed it. In that same year, Professor Henry J. Aaron put out a staff paper entitled *Why is Welfare So Hard to Reform?* for the Brookings Institution. Moynihan's book might have had the same title.

During the 1976 presidential campaign, Dr. Moynihan as a member of the Democratic platform committee was instrumental in writing into the platform a commitment for an "income maintenance system," another form of his old guaranteed-annual-income plan. The newly elected Senator Moynihan also succeeded in getting a seat on the important Senate Finance Committee and in heading its Subcommittee on Public Assistance to consider the promised Carter reform of the welfare system. Meanwhile, Professor Aaron was appointed Assistant Secretary of the Department of Health, Education, and Welfare (HEW) in charge of welfare. Thus the two authors of 1973 found themselves in different political positions in 1977.

On April 25, 1977, Senator Moynihan learned that the administration bill would not be ready by May 1 as he had expected and that only a statement of principles would be forthcoming by that date. The delay was sorely disappointing. It meant that his subcommittee would not be able to hold early hearings on the bill as he had planned. The urgency of such hearings was not apparent inasmuch as the Majority Leader, Senator Robert Byrd, had already put off welfare reform in favor of energy legislation for at least that session of Congress. In any case, Senator Moynihan blew up at the news of the administration's delay. In his wrath, he told reporters that "you can draft that bill in the morning"

—the sort of bill which had taken him almost seven months to draft for President Nixon without getting Congress to approve it and which the Carter administration was expected to draft in only four months.

The chief culprit, according to Senator Moynihan, was Assistant Secretary of HEW Aaron. Referring to Professor Aaron's staff paper of 1973, Senator Moynihan exploded:

> This is HEW at it again. They produce wonderful books telling you why you can't do things.

Senator Moynihan seemed to have forgotten that Professor Moynihan had also produced a wonderful book in 1973 telling why he couldn't do the same things.

After Senator Moynihan's public denunciation, Assistant Secretary Aaron was clearly in trouble. So Assistant Secretary for Public Affairs Eileen Shanahan came to Assistant Secretary Aaron's assistance by announcing that the staff paper of 1973 no longer reflected the latter's views.

This cautionary tale shows how dangerous it is for intellectuals to write books before becoming government officials. But if they did not write books, how would they become intellectuals? There is no easy way out of this dilemma. We have here two former professors who, as intellectuals, were not so very far apart. As Senator and Assistant Secretary, however, they moved into positions of antagonism. The Senator forgot how embarrassing the written word had more than once been for him. The Assistant Secretary decided—or had it decided for him—that it was better to repudiate his book than endanger his job.

Three months later, the Carter administration finally produced its new welfare program. Senator Moynihan immediately called it "magnificent, superbly crafted," without waiting for any hearings on the proposed bill by his subcommittee.[35]

Senators, then, have political "muscle" and "clout." Assistant Secretaries do not. Senator Moynihan had himself been an Assistant Secretary not so long ago. It is interesting to speculate what would have happened if the roles had been reversed—if Senator Aaron had denounced Assistant Secretary Moynihan. Probably they would have acted out their respective roles in much the same way; the rules of the game put an Assistant Secretary at a disadvantage in confrontation with a Senator, especially the head of the very subcommittee that must pass on the Assistant Secretary's handiwork.

.   .   .

That less polymorphous but even more celebrated intellectual in politics, Henry A. Kissinger, suggests another side of the phenomenon. The species is apt to suffer from a rare form of psychological conflict. As Secretary of State, Dr. Kissinger lived with an acute case of this subtle affliction. In an interview with James Reston, Dr. Kissinger said that he thought of himself as a historian more than as a statesman. For our present purposes, we may interpret this to mean that he thought of himself as an intellectual more than as a politician. As a historian, Secretary Kissinger explained, one had to be a pessimist or, to use his exact words, "one has to live with a sense of the inevitability of tragedy." But as a statesman, he said, one had to be optimistic or, again in his own words, "one has to act on the assumption that problems must be solved."[36] Who was the real Kissinger, the pessimistic historian-intellectual or the optimistic statesman-politician? One suspects that the real Kissinger thought of himself as an intellectual pessimist but felt that he had to pretend to be a statesmanlike optimist. In any case, Kissinger could not lose. If he succeeded, the statesman-politician was right; if he failed, the historian-intellectual was right.

Nor was this the only evidence of an unresolved conflict in Kissinger's intellectual makeup. On the one hand, he was forever calling for "concepts" in the formation of foreign policy. On the other hand, he insistently maintained that "nuances" were what really counted. He never explained how concepts can be crucial if nuances are all-important.

It may be objected that Dr. Kissinger was an exception to the rule that appointed officials lack real power of decision. If he was an exception, however, no great generalities can be drawn from him. It is not yet possible to be sure just how exceptional he was throughout the eight years that he served under Presidents Nixon and Ford. We are most likely going to find out that he did what Nixon wanted him to do, and he did not do what Nixon did not want him to do, until the Watergate crisis of 1973. He became more and more independent of the presidency as the President came closer and closer to self-destruction. Kissinger was the product and beneficiary of an afflicted system. Yet he somehow contrived to be in and out of it at the same time. The sicker the system became, the more indispensable he appeared to be. He was its symptom far more than its cure.

In any case, it will take some time to disentangle Kissinger's publicity from his power. Favored writers paid him back to the point of inanity. For example, one virulently anti-Israel book on the Arab-Israeli conflict (based in large part on some twenty-five interviews with Kissinger and two of his closest aides as well as on secret documents secretly leaked) told readers that "Kissinger was in real measure running the world" during the Yom Kippur war in October 1973.[37] The *whole* world? Brezhnev's Russia? Mao's China? Castro's Cuba? Even Indira's India? Still, one can only regard with awe an intellectual who was voted "the greatest person in the world today" by the Miss Universe contestants in 1974.[38]

I am inclined to think that Kissinger's power over the American media was greater than his power over anything else. I doubt whether future historians will agree with a court biography which was written with his help and which flattered him in these terms: "He is a professor who had been given the unique opportunity to put his theories into practice and to shape history."[39] The pre-Nixonian Kissinger had anti-détente theories but did not put them into practice; the Nixonian Kissinger improvised one theory of détente after another to suit his practice; the post-Nixonian Kissinger warned in effect that détente in theory was Soviet expansionism in practice, as demonstrated by the Soviet-Cuban intervention in Angola. How much history was actually shaped by Kissinger has become more and more dubious as less and less of his handiwork remains. It looks as if the further we get away from Kissinger's accomplishments, the more insubstantial and ephemeral they appear to be. The more illusions a statesman inspires about himself, the more disillusionment he invites from future historians. The latter may even have trouble figuring out what all the excitement was about or what Kissinger did to earn it. As a shaper of history, Kissinger was most successful in shaping his own histrionics, not history.

Yet Kissinger's self-aggrandizement paid off in a little noted way. In the transition from the Nixon to the Ford presidency, Kissinger emerged as the critical element of continuity and stability. That President Ford should have had to announce without delay that he was keeping Kissinger in office testified to the independent role that Kissinger had achieved. Unfortunately, this feat was predicated on the degeneration and disintegration of the political régime of which he had been an integral part and to which he had lent some respectability. How he managed to save his political skin was a tribute to the political, not the intellectual, side of his personality. Whatever the reason or the means, he was thereby able to help the country through a dangerous moment. It may well come to be regarded as the time when he did the least and gave the most.

What does the future hold for intellectuals in politics? The high point for the species was probably reached during the Kennedy years and, for an individual, by Henry Kissinger during the Nixon years. The ubiquity and complexity of the modern state assure a continuing need for intellectuals —fully licensed, semi-, quasi-, and pseudo-.

But American intellectuals themselves have changed. When they first invaded the government in large numbers, they were filled with self-confidence. The economists forged into the lead, setting an example of worldly success and mathematical precision. Much that happened in the other social "sciences" was imitative of or at least inspired by them. By 1973, the economists again led the way—in retreat. That year, the new President of the American Economic Association, Professor Walter Heller, former Chairman of the Council of Economic Advisers, spoke for the profession when he said:

> Economists are distinctly in a period of re-examination. The energy crisis caught us with our parameters down. The food crisis caught us too. This was a year of infamy in inflation forecasting. There are many things we really don't know.

Such uncertainty still characterizes the intellectual mood, and not only of economists. One of our best sociological minds, Professor Daniel Bell, has recently put into words what is common knowledge—"the social-science knowledge to design a proper health system, or a housing environment, or a good educational curriculum, is inadequate."[40] If intellectuals cannot cope with these tasks, they are in much greater trouble than at any time since the great breakthrough almost half a century ago. The quantity of intellectuals in politics may not change much, but the quality of their work is being downgraded by the intellectuals themselves.

If the intellectuals do not watch out, they may bear out the low opinion of experts expressed exactly one hundred years ago by Lord Salisbury, who knew something of politics:

> No lesson seems to be so deeply inculcated by the experience of life as that you should never trust in experts. If you believe the doctors nothing is wholesome, if you believe the theologians nothing is innocent; if you believe the soldiers nothing is safe.

He might have gone on to say: if you believe the intellectuals, nothing is right.

The difficulty is that there is no good substitute for "experts" and "intellectuals." If they are not to be trusted, who should be? They may not be trusted as much as before, but society and government are likely to be just as dependent on them in the foreseeable future. The reason is that the intellectuals are but the most articulate, self-conscious repositories of the accumulated learning and experience of a society. If the intellectuals are in trouble, they are not the only ones; the society is in trouble.

Encounter, December 1977

Notes

How Not to Think about Nuclear War

1. "Peace and Deterrence," delivered at the Center for Strategic and International Studies, Georgetown University.

2. Richard Halloran, *The New York Times*, April 15 and 29, 1982.

3. *Common Security: A Blueprint for Survival* (Simon and Schuster, 202 pp., $10.95; $5.95 paper).

Secretary of Defense Weinberger's Letter of August 23, 1982—No notes.

The Western Misalliance

1. William Pfaff, *The New Yorker*, September 1, 1980, pp. 30–34.

2. *Public Papers of the Presidents of the United States: John F. Kennedy, 1961* (April 10), p. 255.

3. "The essence of a genuine alliance system is that both the commitments and aid to be expected are precisely defined" (G. F. Hudson in *Diplomatic Investigations*, ed. Herbert Butterfield and Martin Wight [London: George Allen & Unwin, 1966], p. 178).
   "An alliance adds precision, especially in the form of limitation, to an existing community of interests and to the general policies and concrete measures serving them" (Hans J. Morgenthau, *Politics Among Nations* [New York: Knopf, 1967], p. 176).

4. *Reviews of the World Situation: 1949–1950*: Hearings Held in Executive Session before the Committee on Foreign Relations, U.S. Senate, 81st Congress, 1st and 2nd sessions, Historical Series, 1974, pp. 382–83.

5. *The Atlantic Alliance*: Hearings before the Subcommittee on National Security and International Operations, U.S. Senate, 89th Congress, 2nd Session, April 27, 1966, p. 10.

6. *The Vandenberg Resolutions and the North Atlantic Treaty*: Hearings held in Executive Session before the Committee on Foreign Relations, U.S. Senate, 80th Congress, 2nd session, and 81st Congress, 1st session, May-June 1948 and June 2–6, 1949, Historical Series, August 1973, pp. 143–44.

7. Secretary of State Dean Rusk, *The Atlantic Alliance, op. cit.*, p. 231.

8. Dean Acheson, *Present at the Creation* (New York: Norton, 1969), p. 277.

8a. The Canadian Secretary of State for External Affairs, Lester B. Pearson, who fought most strenuously to implement Article 2, later admitted: "Article 2 remained virtually a dead letter for substantive action in economic matters. . . . The reality is that the spirit to implement the economic aspects of Article 2 was *never* there and that an economic basis for the realization of its larger political goal was never created" (*Mike: The Memoirs of the Right Honourable Lester B. Pearson*, New York: Quadrangle/The New York Times Co., 1973, p. 66).

8b. *Ibid.*, pp. 93–97.

9. Morgenthau, *op. cit.*, p. 178.

10. Henry Kissinger, *The Troubled Partnership* (New York: McGraw-Hill, 1965), p. 108.

11. We are going to limit ourselves to the Western alliance and exclude Japan though it is often referred to as if it were a Western ally in the East. In fact, Japan represents an even more extreme case of a unilateral American military guarantee rather than a true alliance. The most recent formal treaty with Japan consists of little more than verbiage elaborating on what the first United States–Japanese Security Treaty of 1951 stated explicitly—to permit the maintenance of U.S. armed forces in Japan "so as to deter attack upon Japan." Most recently, the new Japanese Prime Minister, Zenko Suzuki, reiterated the traditional policy of "meeting small-scale, limited aggression with Japan's own defense capability and relying upon the deterrent strength of the U.S. under Japan-U.S. security arrangements to meet situations beyond our capabilities" (*New York Times*, September 26, 1980). Whatever mutuality and reciprocity may be lacking in the relationship between the NATO allies, these are virtually nonexistent in respect to Japan. The Japanese "alliance" is either a courtesy title or a convenient fiction.

12. Walter Millis, *Arms and Men* (New York: G.P. Putnam's Sons, 1956), p. 330.

13. It has been little noted that Dulles himself formulated what later became known as "flexible response": "To deter aggression, it is important to have the flexibility and the facilities which make various responses available" (*Foreign Affairs* [April 1954], p. 358).

14. Maxwell D. Taylor, *The Uncertain Trumpet* (New York: Harper & Bros., 1959), pp. 26–27, 58.

15. Jerome Kahan, *Security in the Nuclear Age* (Washington, D.C.: Brookings Institution, 1975), p. 272.

16. Hedley Bull, "America and the World 1978," *Foreign Affairs* (1979), pp. 445–46.

17. Colin S. Gray, *Daedalus* (Fall 1980), pp. 135–54.

18. "None of this means that an actual upset of the balance of power has become any less improbable. . . . But sudden and dramatic changes in the present distribution of power have become more likely . . ." (Hedley Bull, *op. cit.*, p. 462).

19. U.S. Department of Defense Annual Report, Fiscal Year 1981, pp. 65–66.

20. Sir Hermann Bondi, "Defense and the Citizen: A European View," *Bulletin of the American Academy of Arts and Sciences,* November 1979, pp. 26–34.

21. And not only in 1979—in 1980 also. In *Fortune* of August 11, 1980, former British Defence Secretary Denis Healey wrote: "The bedrock of allied security is the commitment of America's strategic nuclear forces to retaliation against the Soviet Union if it attacks Western Europe." Without even considering the implications of *mutual* deterrence, Healey also states: "America's nuclear guarantee is at least as effective a deterrent as it was when NATO began"—that is, when the Soviet Union had not even exploded its first atomic bomb.

22. Charles de Gaulle, *Mémoires de guerre* (Paris: Plon, 1959), Vol. III, pp. 62–70.

23. Charles de Gaulle, *Discours et Messages* (Paris: Plon, 1970), Vol. III, p. 134.

24. *Ibid.*, Vol. IV, pp. 71–73 (January 14, 1963); p. 96 (April 19, 1963); p. 124 (April 19, 1963).

25. Taylor, *The Uncertain Trumpet, op. cit.*, p. 44.

26. *Ibid.*, p. 61.

27. *Nomination of Christian A. Herter*: Hearing before the Committee on Foreign Relations, U.S. Senate, 86th Congress, 1st Session, April 21, 1959, pp. 10, 44.

28. Cited by William W. Kaufmann, *The McNamara Strategy* (New York: Harper & Row, 1964), p. 165.

29. David Packard in *The New Atlantic Challenge*, ed. Richard Mayne (London: Charles Knight & Co., 1975), p. 208.

30. Gallois' view was cited with reason by Kissinger in *The Troubled Partnership, op. cit.*, p. 13.

31. Alan J. Taylor, *English History 1914–1945* (New York: Oxford University Press, 1965), p. 222.

32. Konrad Adenauer, *Erinnerungen 1945–1953* (Stuttgart: Deutsche Verlags-Anstalt, 1965), Vol. I, p. 351.

33. *Ibid., Erinnerungen 1955–1959*, Vol. III, pp. 159, 163, 166.

34. *Ibid.*, pp. 320, 334–36.

35. André Fontaine, *L'alliance atlantique à l'heure de dégel* (Paris: Calmann-Lévy, 1959), p. 73.

36. *The Atlantic Alliance, op. cit.*, Part 7 (Supplement), August 15, 1966, pp. 230–31.

37. *Discours et Messages, op. cit.*, Vol. III, pp. 247–48.

38. Theodore Sorensen, *Kennedy* (New York: Harper & Row, 1965), p. 561. Arthur M. Schlesinger, Jr., devotes two sentences to Kennedy's statement, as if he could not take it seriously (*A Thousand Days* [New York: Houghton Mifflin, 1965], p. 856).

39. *Public Papers of the Presidents of the United States: John F. Kennedy 1963* (June 25), p. 518.

40. *The Troubled Partnership, op. cit.*, pp. 246–48.

41. *Le Monde*, May 25–26, 1980.

42. *Ibid.*, April 18, 1980.

43. Maurice Couve de Murville, *Une politique étrangère 1958–1969* (Paris: Plon, 1971), p. 273.

44. *Bundeskanzler Brandt Reden und Interviews* (Hamburg: Hoffmann & Campe, 1971), pp. 203–4.

45. *Le Monde*, February 28, 1980.

46. New York: Atheneum, 1970, pp. 3, 6, 227, 230.

47. Ronald Steel, *Pax Americana* (New York: Viking, 1967), pp. 45, 315, 345.

48. Henry Brandon, *The Retreat of American Power* (New York: Doubleday, 1973), pp. 3, 5.

49. *The Troubled Partnership, op. cit.*, p. 7.

49a. Alastair Buchan, *The End of the Postwar Era* (New York: Saturday Review Press, 1974), p. 32. Buchan also saw in NATO after a quarter of a century, "the familiar characteristics of ossification." It had still not solved the problem of what kind of war it was prepared to fight or as Buchan put it, it was "not even possible to get a coherent decision on what the principal security problem in Europe now really consists of" (p. 233).

50. C.J. Bartlett, *The Rise and Fall of the Pax Americana* (London: Paul Elek, 1974), p. 183.

51. *Public Papers of the Presidents of the United States: John F. Kennedy, 1961* (November 16), p. 726.

52. *Ibid.*, 1963, p. 894 (prepared but not delivered).

53. *U.S. Foreign Policy for the 1970s: A Report to the Congress*, February 18, 1970, pp. 29, 31.

54. John F. Kennedy, *The Burden and the Glory* (New York: Harper & Row, 1964), pp. 16, 106, 111, 114.

55. *U.S. Foreign Policy for the 1970s: Building for Peace* (A Report to the Congress, February 25, 1971), pp. 28, 44.

56. *Foreign Affairs* (January 1963), p. 284.

57. July 6, 1971 (in *Department of State Bulletin*, July 26, 1971, p. 93).

58. Henry Kissinger, *White House Years* (Boston: Little, Brown & Co., 1979), p. 1386.

59. The axiom was stated by former Secretary of State Christian Herter in 1966: "I think we are the only nation today, if you want to exclude Russia and China, that feels global responsibilities. It is a question of the extent to which we can exercise our power wherever it might be required or be desirable in the world. Obviously we cannot do everything alone. We have to have partners. We have to retain them on the European scene. If possible, we ought to keep partners on the Asian scene" (*The Atlantic Alliance, op. cit.*, p. 119).

60. *Department of State Bulletin*, May 14, 1973, p. 594.

61. In *The Troubled Partnership* and "Central Issues of American Foreign Policy," *Agenda for the Nation* (Washington, D.C.: Brookings Institution, 1968).

62. *New York Times*, July 24, 1980.

63. *White House Years, op. cit.*, p. 83.

64. *Alternative to Partition* (New York: McGraw-Hill, 1965), p. 175.

65. *Department of State Bulletin*, July 3, 1967.

66. *Encounter* (January 1968), p. 25.

67. *Between Two Ages* (New York: Viking Press, 1970), pp. 305, 308.

68. Brzezinski in *The New Atlantic Challenge, op. cit.*, p. 315.

69. W.W. Rostow, *The Diffusion of Power* (New York: Macmillan, 1972), p. 214.

70. Robert Triffin, *Europe and the Money Muddle* (New Haven: Yale University Press, 1957), p. 9.

71. C.L. Sulzberger, *New York Times*, December 21, 1974.

72. This paragraph is largely based on Robert Triffin's books: *Europe and the Money Muddle, op. cit.*, and *Our International Monetary System* (New York: Random House, 1968); Charles P. Kindleberger and Andrew Shonfield, eds., *North American Western European Economic Policies* (New York: St. Martin's Press, 1971), p. 68.

73. Arthur F. Burns and Paul A. Samuelson, *Full Employment: Guideposts and Economic Stability* (Washington, D.C.: American Enterprise Institute for Public Policy Research, 1967), p. 8.

74. Raymond Vernon, *Foreign Policy* (Winter 1971–1972), p. 56.

75. This aspect of the Vietnam war deserves far more study and publicity than it has received. It is mentioned by Arthur M. Okun, former chairman of the Council of Economic Advisers, in *The Political Economy of*

Prosperity (Washington, D.C.: Brookings Institution, 1970), p. 70, and James Tobin, *The New Economics One Decade Older* (Princeton: Princeton University Press, 1974), pp. 34–36. For some of the "dubious practices" used to doctor statistics in order to conceal the unfavorable results of Johnson's decision, see Milton Gilbert, *Quest for World Monetary Order* (New York: John Wiley & Sons, 1980), pp. 140–41.

76. Robert Gilpin, *U.S. Power and the Multinational Corporation* (New York: Basic Books, 1975), p. 163.

77. Interview with Felix G. Rohatyn (senior partner of Lazard Frères & Co.; special economic adviser to the governor of New York; chairman, Municipal Assistance Corporation, New York), *U.S. News & World Report*, September 1, 1980, p. 31.

78. Paul W. McCracken, *Wall Street Journal*, June 17, 1980.

79. ". . . we know that our former unique physical security has almost totally disappeared before the long-range bomber and the destructive power of a single bomb" (*Public Papers of the Presidents of the United States: Dwight D. Eisenhower, 1953*, p. 205) "There comes a time, possibly, when a lead [in hydrogen bombs] is not significant in the defensive arrangements of a country. If you get enough of a particular type of weapon, I doubt that it is particularly important to have a lot more of it" (*ibid.*, 1955, p. 47). To which may be added the view of former Secretary of Defense Robert S. McNamara: "You cannot make decisions simply by asking yourself whether something might be nice to have. You have to make a judgment on how much is enough" (April 20, 1963).

80. McGeorge Bundy, "The Future of Strategic Deterrence," *Survival* (November-December 1977), p. 269. Bundy also observed: "We did assert that we had strategic superiority and we did assert that having it made a difference. What we did not say was that the principal use of this numerical superiority was in its value as reassurance to the American public and as a means of warding off demands for still larger forces" (p. 270).

81. Walter Slocombe, "The Political Implications of Strategic Parity," *Adelphi Papers*, No. 77, May 1971, p. 5.

82. Deputy Secretary of State Kenneth Rush, *Department of State Bulletin*, April 23, 1973, p. 479.

83. The publicly announced Soviet military budget rose from 12.8 billion rubles in 1965 to 13.4 in 1966, to 14.5 in 1967, 16.7 in 1968, 17.7 in 1969, and 17.9 in 1970—an increase of 40 percent. The real resources, including secret and hidden allocations, devoted to the Soviet military amounted of course to much more. (Thomas W. Wolfe, *Soviet Power and Europe 1945–1970* [Baltimore: Johns Hopkins Press, 1970], p. 429).

84. *Nomination of Henry A. Kissinger: Hearings Before the Committee on Foreign Relations*, U.S. Senate, September 1973, Part I, p. 101.

85. Department of State, *United States Foreign Policy: An Overview*, January 1976, p. 16.

86. "Nato: The Next Thirty Years," in *Survival* (November-December 1979), pp. 265–66.

87. *Ibid.*, p. 271.

88. Pierre Lellouche, *Politique étrangère* (December 1979), pp. 490–93, including the substance of the following two sentences.

89. François de Rose, *Foreign Affairs* (Summer 1979), p. 1065.

90. *Le Monde*, April 18, 1980.

91. "America and the World, 1979," *Foreign Affairs*, pp. 634–35.

92. *Foreign Affairs* (Summer 1979), pp. 1062–63.

93. *Ibid.*, p. 1063.

94. The text of Schmidt's lecture appeared in *Survival* (January/February 1978), pp. 2–10.

95. Kissinger, *White House Years, op. cit.*, p. 393.

96. Albert Wohlstetter, *The New Atlantic Challenge, op. cit.*, pp. 253–54.

97. Cited by Alton Frye from an unnamed commentator, *Survival* (May/June 1980), p. 102.

98. Maurice Duverger, *Le Monde*, February 19, 1980. Duverger went on to assert that if nuclear arms that can strike the U.S.S.R. are stationed in Europe but controlled by the United States, they should count as part of the nuclear potential of the United States, which decides whether to employ them. But, if no theater nuclear arms are emplaced, only the French nuclear force is left. And the French force, unfortunately, is not strong enough to defend Europe. A reader might pardonably not know what to conclude.

99. Kissinger had used almost the same words in *White House Years*, p. 94. Someone in the Carter White House must have read the book carefully.

100. *U.S. News & World Report*, August 4, 1980, p. 26.

101. Felix G. Rohatyn, *op. cit.*, p. 32.

102. *New York Times*, August 21, 1980.

103. *New York Times*, September 18 and October 5, 1980; Marshall I. Goldman, *The Atlantic* (September 1980), p. 61.

104. *Times* (London), June 27, 1980; *New York Times*, August 31–September 2, 1980.

105. *The New Atlantic Challenge, op. cit.*, p. 37.

106. *Survival* (November-December 1979), p. 271.

107. Flora Lewis, *New York Times*, June 15, 1980.

108. Cited in the *Economist*, April 26, 1980, p. 39.

109. Uwe Nerlich, "Western Europe's Relations with the United States," *Daedalus* (Winter 1979), pp. 96, 99.

110. Peter Jay, "Europe's Ostrich and America's Eagle," *Economist*, March 8, 1980, pp. 25–26.

111. Hans J. Morgenthau, *A New Foreign Policy for the United States* (New York: Praeger, 1969), p. 7.

112. At a meeting of the Atlantic Treaty Association, Copenhagen, September 27, 1962.

113. *Foreign Affairs* (January 1963), p. 298.

114. *Ibid.* (Summer 1979), pp. 975–86.

The Dilemma of the West—No notes.
Western Insecurity—No notes.
Rolling Communism Backward—No notes.

Ghosts of Vietnam

1. In his *Kissinger: Portrait of a Mind* (New York: Norton, 1973), Stephen R. Graubard claimed that Kissinger "had nothing to say" because he still "did not know enough about the issues" until 1968 (pp. 279–80). Graubard gives no evidence of knowing about Kissinger's article in *Look*—it is not listed in his bibliography—in which Kissinger had quite a lot to say before 1968. And if two anything-and-anyone-you-want-to-see-and-hear personal tours of Vietnam, lasting altogether a month, and top-level briefings in the Pentagon, let alone mere reading of the newspapers, were not enough to give one something to say about Vietnam, very few Americans would have felt obliged to summon up the moral courage to take a stand against the war. John G. Stoessinger in his *Henry Kissinger: The Anguish of Power* (Norton, 1976) gave two different reasons—that Kissinger did not speak up until 1968 because he was interested "in a global conceptual approach" and because he was looking for an opportunity to test it in action (p. 43). Stoessinger also seems to have been ignorant of the *Look* article, which would have spoiled his time scheme, and which, in essence, already contained the Kissingerian conceptual approach, albeit not with its "global" trappings.

2. *No More Vietnams?* Richard M. Pfeffer, ed. (New York: Harper & Row, 1968), pp. 11–13.

3. The article on "The Vietnam Negotiations" in *Foreign Affairs* of January 1969, written in the late summer and early autumn of 1968, was reprinted in *American Foreign Policy* (Norton, 1969). The idea of the "subtle triangle" appeared in one of Rockefeller's speeches (Graubard, *op. cit.*, p. 252).

4. Stoessinger, *op. cit.*, pp. 60, 65, 76–77.

5. Lewy says that only a part of the "working paper" was published in *Viet-Nam Documents and Research Notes*, issued by the U.S. Embassy in Saigon in June 1968. It appeared in its entirety in the United States as an appendix to *The Vietnam War and International Law*, Richard A.

Falk, ed. (Princeton: Princeton University Press, 1969), Vol. II, pp. 1183–1206. All the paper gives is the number of prisoners and captured documents on which the data is based, but not their provenance or anything else about them. The paper is said to be based on a "compilation" of material, which, however, is not given. One cannot tell from the paper itself how "carefully researched and documented" it is, despite Lewy's touching assurance.

Détente

1. *New York Times*, October 31, 1973 and March 12, 1974.

2. George F. Kennan, "Europe's Problems, Europe's Choices," *Foreign Policy*, Spring 1974, p. 8.

3. Henry A. Kissinger, *The Troubled Partnership* (McGraw-Hill, 1965), p. 4; Richard M. Pfeffer, ed., *No More Vietnams?* (Harper & Row, 1968), p. 11; *Foreign Affairs*, January 1969, p. 101; Press conference, March 21, 1974.

4. *Foreign Affairs*, January 1963, p. 285; *The Troubled Partnership*, pp. 57, 251.

5. February 1, 1973 (in *Department of State Bulletin*, April 2, 1973, p. 394).

6. Speech before American Society of Newspaper Editors, April 16, 1954; speech of March 15, 1965 (*Congressional Record*, House of Representatives, September 2, 1965, pp. 21928–30); "Asia After Vietnam," *Foreign Affairs*, October 1967, pp. 111–25.

7. *The Troubled Partnership*, pp. 9, 232.

8. Stephen R. Graubard, *Kissinger: Portrait of a Mind* (Norton, 1973), pp. 225–26.

9. *Ibid.*, p. 243.

10. *No More Vietnams?, op. cit.*, pp. 11–13.

11. "The Vietnam Negotiations," *Foreign Affairs*, January 1969, pp. 233–34.

12. November 2, 1972 (in *Department of State Bulletin*, November 20, 1972, p. 605). One wonders whether Mr. Nixon had in mind the kind of peace that General W. C. Westmoreland, the former U.S. commander in Vietnam and Army Chief of Staff, recently described: "A full year after the cease-fire, which many thought would bring peace to Vietnam, the country is still ravaged by war, with the prospect of continued bloodshed ahead. The ceasefire did bring about an end to United States military action, cause our 588 prisoners to be released, and set the stage for a truce in Laos. But little else has been accomplished. During the last year, there have been more than 10,000 hostile contacts and over 13,000 armed attacks resulting in the deaths of more than 33,000 Communists and 6,000 South Vietnamese military men

Also there have been thousands of civilians killed, injured, or abducted in the South" (*New York Times*, April 18, 1974).

13. July 6, 1971 (in *Department of State Bulletin*, July 26, 1971, p. 93).

14. January 31, 1973 (*ibid.*, February 19, 1973, p. 195).

15. Albert Wohlstetter, statement before the Senate Armed Services Committee, April 23, 1969 (*Congressional Record*, Senate, May 1, 1969, p. 10957 note). The persistent underestimation of Soviet military capabilities is dealt with at length in Albert Wohlstetter, "Is There a Strategic Arms Race?," *Foreign Policy*, Summer 1974.

16. Deputy Secretary of State Kenneth Rush, *Department of State Bulletin*, April 23, 1973, p. 479.

17. Walter Slocombe, *The Political Implications of Strategic Parity*, Adelphi Papers, International Institute for Strategic Studies, No. 77, May 1971, p. 5.

18. Thomas W. Wolfe, *Soviet Power and Europe 1945–1970* (Johns Hopkins Press, 1970), p. 429.

19. Oriana Fallaci, "Kissinger," *New Republic*, December 16, 1972, p. 20.

20. NATO Ministerial Council Meeting, April 10, 1969.

21. *U. S. Foreign Policy for the 1970's: A New Strategy for Peace*, A Report to the Congress by Richard Nixon, President of the United States, February 18, 1970, pp. 27–31.

22. February 25, 1971 (in *Department of State Bulletin*, March 15, 1971, p. 307).

23. July 6, 1971 (*ibid.*, July 26, 1971, p. 96).

24. *Time*, January 3, 1972, p. 15.

25. Deputy Under Secretary for Economic Affairs Nathaniel Samuels, April 14, 1972 (in *Department of State Bulletin*, May 1, 1972, p. 633).

26. Deputy Secretary of State John N. Irwin II, October 18, 1972 (*ibid.*, November 20, 1972, p. 612).

27. Counselor of the Department Richard F. Pedersen, September 7, 1972 (*ibid.*, October 2, 1972, p. 371).

28. David Landau, *Kissinger, The Uses of Power* (Houghton Mifflin, 1972), p. 26.

29. Fallaci, *op. cit.*, p. 21.

30. Stanley Hoffmann, "Will the Balance Balance at Home?," *Foreign Policy*, Summer 1972, p. 80.

31. November 5, 1972 (in *Department of State Bulletin*, December 4, 1972, p. 654).

32. February 1, 1973 (*ibid.*, April 2, 1973, p. 395).

33. March 21, 1973 (*ibid.*, April 9, 1973, p. 419).

34. David Calleo, *The Atlantic Fantasy: The U.S., NATO, and Europe* (Johns Hopkins Press, 1970), p. ix.

35. *The Necessity for Choice* (1961), p. 204; *The Troubled Partnership* (1965), p. 217.

36. *Nuclear Weapons and Foreign Policy* (Harper, 1957), pp. 142–43, 350.

37. *The Necessity for Choice*, pp. 178–81, 194–95.

38. *The Troubled Partnership*, pp. 192, 197–98.

39. "Central Issues of American Foreign Policy," in *Agenda for the Nation* (The Brookings Institution, 1968), pp. 599, 608–9.

40. *The Necessity for Choice*, pp. 172–73.

41. *The Troubled Partnership*, pp. 248–49.

42. September 5, 1969 (in *Department of State Bulletin*, September 22, 1969, p. 259).

43. "The condition of the *Soviet economy* is clearly the primary determinant of present Soviet foreign policy" (Marshall D. Shulman, *Foreign Affairs*, October 1973, p. 43). "The first and most decisive reason for this change in [the direction of a more moderate and more flexible] foreign policy was the stagnation in the Soviet economy" (Wolfgang Leonhard, *ibid.*, p. 66).

44. October 6, 1970 (in *Department of State Bulletin*, November 23, 1970, pp. 642–43).

45. Charles de Gaulle, *Mémoires de guerre* (Plon, 1959), Vol. III, pp. 62–70.

46. *Ibid.*, pp. 179–80.

47. Charles de Gaulle, *Mémoires d'espoir* (Plon, 1970), Vol. I, pp. 175–76.

48. Maurice Couve de Murville, *Une politique étrangère 1958–1969* (Plon, 1971), pp. 194, 206–12. Kosygin also made some most revealing remarks about China and the United States more than six years before President Nixon's pilgrimage to Peking: "China was also disquieting [to Kosygin], but perhaps the major preoccupation from this angle was [for the Russians] to know what the game of the United States would be in the future. In fact, the most alarming [*redoutable*] unknown factor was the possible Chinese-American connection [*conjonction*]" (p. 212).

49. *Ibid.*, pp. 78–79, 218–21.

50. *Mémoires d'espoir*, Vol. I, p. 177.

51. *The Troubled Partnership*, pp. 44, 63.

52. "The Search for Stability," *Foreign Affairs*, July 1959, pp. 539–42. In all of his extant writings, Dr. Kissinger never changed his position on these questions; see *Foreign Affairs*, January 1963, pp. 263, 269, 271, and *The Troubled Partnership* (1965), pp. 216–18.

53. Couve de Murville, *op. cit.*, p. 273.

54. Marshall D. Shulman, " 'Europe' versus 'Détente,' " *Foreign Affairs*, April 1967, p. 396.

55. *Bundeskanzler Brandt Reden und Interviews* (Hamburg: Hoffmann & Campe, 1971), pp. 203–4.

56. Among the others were such notable authorities as Professor Zbigniew Brzezinski, *Alternative to Partition* (McGraw-Hill, 1965, pp. 137–40) and Professor Hans J. Morgenthau, *A New Foreign Policy for the United States* (Praeger, 1969, pp. 170, 177–81).

57. W. E. Paterson, "Foreign Policy and Stability in West Germany," *International Affairs* (London), July 1973, pp. 426–27.

58. Josef Korbel, *Détente in Europe: Real or Imaginary?* (Princeton University Press, 1972), pp. 204, 242.

59. Werner Kaltefleiter, *Orbis*, Spring 1973, pp. 91–92.

60. *Le Point* (Paris), December 10, 1973, p. 56.

61. "The great-power status which Great Britain has so tenaciously sought to sustain throughout the postwar period can now be achieved only through the closest association with the Continent. But to do this effectively Great Britain may have to adopt views similar to France's, ameliorating them with its own subtle style" ("Strains on the Alliance," *Foreign Affairs*, January 1963, p. 283).

62. Marc Ullmann, "Security Aspects in French Foreign Policy," *Survival*, International Institute for Strategic Studies, London, November-December 1973, pp. 262–67.

63. Arthur M. Schlesinger, Jr., *A Thousand Days* (Houghton Mifflin, 1965), p. 904. Theodore C. Sorensen quotes Kennedy as saying, "We are not wedded to a policy of hostility to Red China. I would hope that . . . the normalization of relations . . . between China and the West . . . would be brought about," which would suggest that Kennedy anticipated Nixon in at least the projection of a policy of rapprochement with China. But Sorensen also says that Kennedy regarded the "isolation of the Chinese" as a major gain of the Test Ban Treaty with the Soviet Union in 1963 (Theodore C. Sorensen, *Kennedy*, Harper & Row, 1965, pp. 665, 736).

64. Sorensen, p. 745.

65. Schlesinger, p. 921.

66. *New York Times*, October 9, 1963, p. 19, and October 25, 1963, p. 18. As far back as 1956, when Adlai Stevenson had called for a test ban, Nixon had denounced it as "catastrophic nonsense" and had given as one reason that the Russians "haven't kept many agreements as we well know" (*New York Times*, October 4, 1956, p. 22, and October 5, 1956, p. 16). He was at least consistent—until he had to deal with the Russians himself.

67. William F. Kaufmann, *The McNamara Strategy* (Harper & Row, 1964), pp. 152–58.

68. Speech of October 7, 1966.

69. President Nixon at least three times named the "understandings on Berlin" as the turning point which had led to the May 1972 summit meeting in Moscow (*Department of State Bulletin*, January 24, 1972, p. 81, and June 12, 1972, p. 803, and interview in *Time*, January 3, 1972, p. 14).

70. Assistant Secretary of State for Economic and Business Affairs, William C. Armstrong, *ibid.*, December 25, 1972, p. 721.

71. *Nomination of Henry A. Kissinger:* Hearings Before the Committee on Foreign Relations, U.S. Senate, September 1973, Part I, p. 122.

72. *Ibid.*, p. 111.

73. John Newhouse, *Cold Dawn* (Holt, Rinehart & Winston, 1973), p. 272.

74. *Department of State Bulletin*, June 26, 1972, pp. 886, 894.

75. The full text of the "Basic Principles" may be found in the *Department of State Bulletin*, June 26, 1972, pp. 898–99.

76. *Ibid.*, p. 896.

77. Assistant Secretary for Near Eastern and South Asian Affairs Joseph J. Sisco, *ibid.*, April 23, 1973, p. 485.

78. Press conference of March 21, 1974.

79. Address to joint session of Congress, June 1, 1972.

80. Press conference of March 21, 1974.

81. Interview in Peking, November 12, 1973 (*New York Times*, November 13, 1973).

82. *Congressional Record*, Senate, November 9, 1973, p. S-20136.

83. Marshall D. Shulman, *New York Times*, March 10, 1974.

84. John Lukacs, *A New History of the Cold War* (Anchor Books, 1966), p. 273.

85. Press conference of October 25, 1973.

86. André Fontaine, *Le Monde*, October 30, 1973.

87. *Nomination of Henry A. Kissinger, op. cit.*, pp. 10, 118.

88. Press conference of November 21, 1973.

89. *Nomination of Henry A. Kissinger, op. cit.*, p. 101.

90. This paragraph is based on Albert Wohlstetter, "Threats and Promises of Peace: Europe and America in the New Era," *Orbis*, Winter 1974, pp. 1107–44. The entire article should be compulsory reading for anyone interested in this subject.

91. *Nomination of Henry A. Kissinger, op. cit.*, p. 43.

92. June 15, 1972 (in *Department of State Bulletin*, July 10, 1972, p. 40).

93. *U S Foreign Policy for the 1970's: Shaping a Durable Peace, op. cit.*, p. 232.

94. Press conference of November 21, 1973.

95. Marshall D. Shulman, *Foreign Affairs*, October 1973, p. 45. More details of the 1970 approach are given by John Newhouse, *Cold Dawn, op. cit.*, pp. 188–89.

96. Theodore H. White, *The Making of the Presidency 1972* (Bantam edition, 1973), p. xviii.

97. Alastair Buchan, *Power and Equilibrium in the 1970s* (Praeger, 1973), p. 18 [for 1968]; *The Military Balance 1973–1974*, International Institute for Strategic Studies, 1974, p. 6 [for 1974].

98. In a press conference on November 10, 1959, de Gaulle said that Soviet Russia needed détente in the West in order "to reckon with the yellow multitude which is China" and which threatened to expand at the expense of Russia, "a white nation which has conquered part of China" (*Discours et Messages*, Plon, 1970, Vol. III, p. 130). A decade later, he wrote retrospectively of his belief in 1958 that the Russians would be attracted to détente with the West because of "the eternal alternation which dominates their history and which today makes them turn their worries toward Asia rather than toward Europe on account of the ambitions of China and provided that the West does not threaten them" (*Mémoires d'espoir*, Vol. I, p. 213). On July 29, 1963, de Gaulle remarked sardonically that the Sino-Soviet conflict could "add a note of sincerity to the poems [*couplets*] which the USSR devotes to peaceful coexistence" (*Discours et Messages*, Vol. IV, pp. 122–23).

99. John F. Kennedy, *The Burden and the Glory* (Harper & Row, 1964), pp. 16, 106, 111, 114.

100. "Strains on the Alliance," *Foreign Affairs*, January 1963, pp. 267, 284.

101. *The Troubled Partnership*, op. cit., pp. 7–8, 227, 229, 234, 248.

102. "Central Issues of American Foreign Policy," *Agenda for the Nation*, pp. 596–99, 607, 609.

103. *U.S. Foreign Policy for the 1970's: A New Strategy for Peace*, op. cit., pp. 5, 8, 29.

104. *U.S. Foreign Policy for the 1970's: Building for Peace*, A Report to the Congress by Richard Nixon, President of the United States, February 25, 1971, pp. 11, 25–26.

105. *Department of State Bulletin*, May 14, 1973, pp. 594, 598.

106. Speech in London to the Pilgrims, December 12, 1973.

107. *Nomination of Henry A. Kissinger*, op. cit., p. 8.

108. In the National Assembly, October 17, 1973 (*Le Monde*, October 19, 1973, p. 10).

109. Lawrence L. Whetten, *Germany's Ostpolitik* (Oxford, 1971), pp. 208, 212.

110. *New York Times*, March 29, 1974, p. 3.

111. *Agenda for the Nation*, op. cit., pp. 594–96.

112. *The Troubled Partnership*, op. cit., pp. 205–6.

113. *Fortune*, November 1972, p. 148.

114. *U.S. News & World Report*, May 13, 1974, p. 44.

115. According to the official custodian of Leninism in the United States, Gus Hall, General-Secretary of the Communist Party, U.S.A., détente

means, among other good things, "retreat" by and "struggle" against
the United States (*Political Affairs*, March 1974, pp. 7, 9).

Kissinger's Apologia

1. Theodore H. White, *The Making of the Presidency 1972* (New York:
   Bantam edition, 1972), p. xviii.

2. In an interview in the *Wall Street Journal*, January 21, 1980, Kissinger
   reiterated: "Well, I have always objected to the concept of the China
   card. I do not feel happy with the notion that we use China to annoy
   the Soviets as a penalty for Soviet conduct." His reasons were that the
   Soviets may not react rationally and that the Chinese may think that
   we might downgrade them if we improve our relations with the Soviet
   Union. This reasoning makes it appear that if we call our rapprochement with China something other than a "card," it will make the
   Soviets less likely to react irrationally or China less nervous about improved Soviet-American relations. As a political theorist, Kissinger
   sometimes betrays a peculiar propensity to substitute words for realities,
   as if a "China X" would be in reality so different from a "China card."

3. *Department of State Bulletin*, June 26, 1972, p. 885.

4. The second principle read in part: "The USA and the USSR attach
   major importance to preventing the development of situations capable
   of causing a dangerous exacerbation of their relations. Therefore, they
   will do their utmost to avoid military confrontations and to prevent the
   outbreak of nuclear war." It also stated: "Both sides recognize that
   efforts to obtain unilateral advantage at the expense of the other, directly or indirectly, are inconsistent with these objectives." The third
   principle committed both powers "to do everything in their power so
   that conflicts or situations will not arise which would serve to increase
   international tensions."

5. *Department of State Bulletin*, July 10, 1972, p. 40.

6. Kissinger was not always fully consistent. On the occasion of signing
   the principles, he stated: "Of course, these principles have to be implemented. If there is bad faith on either side, the aspirations expressed
   here cannot be realized. Speaking for our side, I can say we will attempt
   to implement these principles in the spirit in which they were promulgated. We have no reason to suppose that this will not be done by
   the leaders of the Soviet Union, but if events should prove these hopes
   on either side to be incorrect, then we will, of course, both of us, have
   to draw the appropriate conclusions" (*ibid.*, June 26, 1972, p. 885).
   According to the theory of marginal advantages, however, neither side
   would gain any increment of usable political strength even if it failed
   to implement the principles.

   The theory of marginal advantages was also written into the President's foreign policy report to Congress of May 3, 1973. It took the
   position that a certain balance of power was still inherent in any international system, but that it was no longer "the overriding concept"
   because continual maneuvering for marginal advantages in the nuclear

era had become "both unrealistic and dangerous." Why? Because "both sides possess such enormous power, small additional increments cannot be translated into tangible advantages or even usable political strength. And it is dangerous because attempts to seek tactical gains might lead to confrontations which could be catastrophic." But if the tactical gains were sure to be wasteful, why should they lead to catastrophic confrontations? "Unrealistic" maneuvering should be more dangerous to the interests of the maneuverer than to anyone else.

7. "I think the relationship has had a setback. It has had a period of stagnation. I have the impression that the Soviet Union is now fairly anxious to pick it up again" (interview with Pierre Salinger in *L'Express*, Paris, April 12, 1975).

8. San Francisco, February 3, 1976; Laramie, Wyoming, February 4, 1976; Boston, March 11, 1976.

9. *Wall Street Journal*, January 21, 1980.

10. Interview, *New York Times*, October 13, 1974.

11. "Statesmen must act, even when premises cannot be proved; they must decide, even when intangibles will determine the outcome" (speech before the American Society of Newspaper Editors, April 17, 1975).

12. This is something of an exaggeration. A marked aspect of the work of Frederick Jackson Turner was geopolitical. As late as 1918, long after he had developed his "sectional" theory of American history, Turner "still thought in terms of geographic determinism, and he sought explanations for political and social behavior in physiographic pressures, rather than in the many forces responsible" (Ray Allen Billington, *Frederick Jackson Turner*, New York: Oxford University Press, 1973, p. 372). A fully developed American geopolitical system appeared in 1942 with *America's Strategy in World Politics* by Professor Nicholas John Spykman of Yale University (New York: Harcourt, Brace & Co., 1942). One reason why geopolitics never came to dominate American political and historical thought is that, as Professor Hans J. Morgenthau once put it, "geopolitics is a pseudo-science," based on "the fallacy of the single factor" (*Politics Among Nations*, New York: Knopf, 2nd ed., 1955, p. 146).

13. The father of modern geopolitics, Sir Halford Mackinder, saw Eastern Europe as the key to world power and, therefore, believed that Russia was the most probable victor in the coming struggle to dominate the world. The school of pre-World War II German geopoliticians, headed by General Karl Haushofer, held that it would be possible for Germany to gain the upper hand through an alliance with Russia or outright conquest of Eastern Europe. Professor Spykman did not expect any one dominant world power to come out of World War II; he foresaw three "autonomous zones" in the Far East, North America, and Europe, with China favored in the first, the United States in the second, and a difficult balancing act between Great Britain, Russia, and Germany in the third. Geopolitics tends to regard "space" as fundamental, and the power with the greatest amount of space at its command the most likely to expand and conquer. The geopolitical tradition has emphasized war through geographical expansion rather than peace through equilibrium.

14. *Look*, August 9, 1966.

15. *No More Vietnams?* Richard M. Pfeffer, ed. (New York: Harper & Row, 1968) pp. 11–13.

16. July 6, 1971 (in *Department of State Bulletin*, July 26, 1971, p. 93).

17. Spykman, *op. cit.*, p. 469.

18. "In all my conversations with Dobrynin I had stressed that a fundamental improvement in US-Soviet relations presupposed Soviet cooperation in settling the war [p. 266]. . . . But Hanoi would not move without some pressure. Therefore Soviet participation could become crucial [p. 267]."

19. "All his life, he too had known only war; his entire career had been based on American support. A world in which the South Vietnamese would have to stand entirely on their own was full of terrors that his pride would not let him admit [p. 1320]. . . . We had no way of understanding the primeval hatred that animated the two sides [p. 1325]. . . . What was success for us—the withdrawal of American forces—was a nightmare for our allies; even with a cease-fire they simply could not imagine how they would be better off without us [p. 1372]. . . . The South Vietnamese, after eight years of American participation, simply did not feel ready to confront Hanoi without our direct participation. Their nightmare was not this or that clause but the fear of being left alone [p. 1375]. . . . We failed early enough to grasp that Thieu's real objection was not to the terms but the fact of any compromise. . . . And from his point of view Thieu was right [p. 1391]. . . . Peace involving American withdrawal was a traumatic event for the South Vietnamese. . . . That his [Thieu's] methods were obnoxiously Vietnamese, that in the process [of balking] he nearly wrecked our own internal cohesion, does not alter the reality that he fought valiantly, that he was right by his lights and the realities of what he knew of Hanoi's purposes [p. 1467]."

20. Nixon's version is characteristically disingenuous. First, he relates (as does Kissinger) that he sent a message on December 19 to Thieu about his "irrevocable intention to proceed, preferably with your cooperation, but, if necessary, alone." Because Thieu made known that he had been faced with an ultimatum, which he had rejected, Nixon says that he was "shocked" and "I felt we would now be justified in breaking with him and making a separate peace with Hanoi"—as if he had not already threatened to make a separate peace.

21. "Our constant search for some compromise formula illuminated the cultural gap between us and the Vietnamese because the very concept of compromise was alien to both Vietnamese parties. We had no way of understanding the primeval hatred that animated the two sides" (p. 1325).

22. *Foreign Affairs*, Winter 1979/80.

23. "Thus, we can anticipate no lasting peace in the wake of a consummated agreement, but merely a shift in Hanoi's modus operandi. We will probably have little chance of maintaining the agreement without

evident hair-trigger U.S. readiness, which may in fact be challenged at any time, to enforce its provisions" (p. 1435).

24. William Safire, *Before the Fall* (New York: Doubleday, 1975), pp. 666, 669–70.

25. James Reston, *New York Times*, December 30, 1972.

26. Marvin Kalb and Bernard Kalb, *Kissinger* (Boston: Little, Brown & Co., 1974), pp. 3 ("He has come to be recognized as the very portrait of American diplomacy, the way George Washington is identified with the dollar bill"), pp. 5, 544.

27. Henry Brandon, *The Retreat of American Power* (New York: Doubleday, 1973), p. 22.

28. Edward R. F. Sheehan, *The Arabs, Israelis, and Kissinger* (New York: Readers' Digest Press, 1976), p. 38.

From 1967 to 1973

1. The full text of Nasser's statements during the 1967 crisis period is given in the appendices to my book *Israel and World Politics* (New York: Viking Press, 1968). These translations, made in Washington at the time, have been checked with the Arabic original and some minor revisions have been made here. The dates in parentheses are the dates of delivery. Research for this article in Arabic sources was done by Professor Boaz Shochan.

2. Anthony Nutting, *Nasser* (New York: Dutton, 1972), pp. 397–98.

3. Badran testified on February 24, 1968, and a verbatim report appeared in the Cairo paper, *al-Ahram*, the next day. The testimony came too late for my book, *Israel and World Politics*. In the literature on the subject, only Nadav Safran seems to have used it beyond a mere reference, and he was barely able to insert four last-minute footnotes based on the testimony as his book, *From War to War*, went to press.

4. The visit to Pakistan actually took place December 5–12, 1966, and the meeting of the Arab League's Supreme Council occurred December 7–11, 1966.

5. According to a UPI report from Cairo of February 24, 1968, Badran testified that the Egyptian Chief of Staff, General Muhammad Fawzi, had been sent to Syria on May 14, 1967, to check on the Syrian and Soviet reports of Israeli forces massing on the Syrian border. Fawzi found that the reports were unfounded and said that the Soviets "must have been having hallucinations." The same version of this portion of Badran's testimony appears in Safran's book (pp. 274–75) and in the *Middle East Record, 1967* (p. 191), both of which attribute it to *al-Ahram* of February 25, 1968. A search of the paper of that date in the copy at the Library of Congress has failed to locate and verify this passage. Conceivably, it may have appeared in a different edition of the same date and was eliminated from the Library of Congress's edition. If it should be confirmed, it would show even more emphatically that

everything the Egyptians did after May 14 had nothing to do with the ostensible Israeli provocation of Syria.

6. Nutting, *op. cit.*, p. 409.

7. Sa'd Jum'ah, *al-Mu'amara wa ma'rakat al-masir* ("The Conspiracy and the Battle of Destiny"), in Arabic (Beirut), 1968, p. 176.

8. *Nasser* (New York: Knopf, 1973), p. 301.

9. *Nasser* (London: Allen Lane, 1971), p. 482.

10. Jum'ah, *op. cit.*, pp. 171–72.

11. Vick Vance and Pierre Lauer, *Hussein de Jordanie: Ma "Guerre" avec Israël*, Albin Michel (Paris), 1968; Peter Snow, *Hussein*, Barrie & Jenkins (London), 1972.

12. Sa'd Jum'ah, *Mujtama' al-Karahiyah* ("The Society of Hatred"), in Arabic (Beirut), 1972, pp. 127–28.

13. Nutting, *op. cit.*, p. 419.

14. *New York Times*, August 8, 1970.

15. "The demon which impels certain rulers always to seek a little more gain or 'profit' incited the Soviet-Egyptians, after the cease-fire of August 7, to place their missile launching sites nearer the canal. These were the famous SAM-3's, obtained by Nasser six months earlier from Moscow" (Jean Lacouture, *op. cit.*, p. 341). ". . . The Egyptians were unable to install all the missiles within the time limit and so were obliged, to the accompaniment of loud protests from the Israelis, to commit a technical breach of the cease-fire by moving the late arrivals onto appointed sites after the August 7 deadline" (Nutting, *op. cit.*, p. 450).

16. *New York Times*, October 17, 1973.

17. *Journal of Palestine Studies* (Beirut), Autumn 1971, p. 19.
    On July 14, 1972, Heykal denounced the widespread visits of Arabs to Israel—150,000 a month that summer—by arguing: "Israel wants to deprive the Arabs of their chief weapon, which is their nonacceptance of Israel . . . it is a method of disarming the Arab rejection of Israel. . . ."

18. *Ibid.*, Spring 1972, for the text of both speeches.

19. Hisham Sharabi, *Palestine and Israel*, Pegasus, 1969, pp. 125–26.

20. *New York Times Magazine*, October 21, 1973.

21. Y. Harkabi, *Arab Attitudes to Israel*, Israel Universities Press (Jerusalem), 1972, p. 390.

22. The above two paragraphs are based on: Robert A. Divine, *Roosevelt and World War II*, Johns Hopkins Press, 1969, p. 77; *F.D.R.: His Personal Letters, 1928–1945*, Duell, Sloan, and Pearce, 1950, Vol. II, pp. 961, 1204–5; *The Public Papers and Addresses of Franklin D. Roosevelt*, Macmillan, Vol. IX, p. 93; Vol. X, pp. 401–2; Vol. XII, p. 558; Sumner Welles, *Where Are We Heading?*, Harper, 1946, p. 37; Robert I. Gannon, *The Cardinal Spellman Story*, Doubleday, 1962, p. 224.

23. Henry A. Kissinger, "Reflections on Cuba," *The Reporter*, November 22, 1962, pp. 21–22.

24. *The Necessity for Choice* (New York: Harper, 1961), p. 3.

The Road to Geneva

1. "From 1967 to 1973: The Arab-Israeli Wars," *Commentary*, December 1973.

2. United Nations, Security Council Doc. S/1342 (May 24, 1967), p. 4.

3. *Ibid.*, S/1343 (May 29, 1967), p. 20.

4. El-Kony stated that "there is not a shadow of doubt as to the continued existence of the state of war between the Israelis and both the Arabs of Palestine and their brethren in the Arab countries" and that "a state of overt war has been existing." It was this state of war, he insisted, that gave the Egyptian government "the legitimate right" to restrict navigation in the Straits of Tiran "with respect to shipping to an enemy" (S/1343 [May 29, 1967], p. 8).

5. Arthur Lall, *The UN and the Middle East Crisis, 1967* (Columbia University Press, 1968), p. 51.

6. Lall, p. 65.

7. S/1351 (June 8, 1967), p. 4.

8. Lall, p. 106.

9. On September 2, 1964, *Pravda* defended the Soviet acquisition of territory in these terms: "A people which has been attacked, has defended itself, and wins the war is bound in sacred duty to establish in perpetuity a political situation which will ensure the liquidation of the sources of aggression. It is entitled to maintain this state of affairs as long as the danger of aggression does not cease. A nation which has attained security at the cost of numerous victims will never agree to the restoration of previous borders. No territories are to be returned as long as the danger of aggression prevails."

10. Al-Pachachi, United Arab Emirates, S/PV. 1724 (June 13, 1973), p. 51.

11. S/PV. 1726 (June 14, 1973), pp. 117–18.

12. Lord Caradon, interview of February 10, 1973, and Arthur J. Goldberg, speech in Washington, May 8, 1973, cited in S/PV. 1721 (June 11, 1973), pp. 43–45, 56.

13. Eugene V. Rostow, *Peace in the Balance* (Simon & Schuster, 1972), p. 270.

14. Lall, pp. 253–54.

15. S/1382 (November 22, 1967), p. 7.

16. *Parliamentary Debates* (Hansard), House of Commons, November 17, 1969, p. 846. See also George Brown, *In My Way*, Gollancz (London, 1971), p. 233.

17. S/PV. 1721 (June 11, 1973), p. 33.

18. *Department of State Bulletin*, June 11, 1973, pp. 846–47.

19. S/1382 (November 22, 1967), pp. 6–7 (Parthasarathi); 7 (Caradon); 10 (Eban); 12–13 (Kuznetsov); 14 (Tarabanov); 15 (Riad, Rifa'i); 18 (Goldberg); 19 (Eban).

20. S/PV. 1723 (June 12, 1973), p. 11, and S/PV. 1733 (July 20, 1973), p. 58.

21. S/PV. 1733, p. 32.

22. On Resolution 242, see also Eugene V. Rostow's article in *Commentary*, February 1974, especially pp. 52–53.

23. The final report on the Jarring mission, with documents, is S/10929, dated May 18, 1973.

24. *Al-Ahram*, February 2, 1968.

25. S/PV. 1717 (June 6, 1973), p. 41.

26. S/PV. 1721 (June 11, 1973), pp. 9–10.

27. *Ibid.*, p. 72.

28. S/PV. 1724 (June 13, 1973), pp. 98–100.

28a. On the "two-stage" strategy, see also Gil Carl AlRoy's article in *Commentary*, February 1974, p. 56.

29. *Al-Ahram*, December 6, 1973.

30. *Le Monde*, November 24, 25–26, 1973.

31. Edward R. F. Sheehan, *New York Times Magazine*, November 18, 1973.

32. Ze'ev Schul, *Jerusalem Post Weekly*, December 4, 1973, p. 12.

33. Interview on Israeli radio, *Jerusalem Post Weekly*, December 11, 1973, p. 11. According to the former Israeli Chief of Staff, Haim Bar-Lev, now Minister of Commerce and Industry, Israeli intelligence had no shortage of reliable information on Egyptian and Syrian preparations, but "the evaluation did not stand the test" (*ibid.*, November 6, 1973, p. 8).

33a. "Insight on the Middle East War," *Sunday Times Weekly Review* (London), December 9 and 16, 1973.

34. S/7930/Add. 2141 and S/7930/Add. 2142 (October 6, 1973).

35. John W. Finney, *New York Times*, October 31, 1973.

36. The full extent of the Soviet Union's investment in this war may be gathered from Israeli estimates, which are probably as close as we can get to it. According to Defense Minister Moshe Dayan, Syria used 450 tanks in 1967 and 2,700 in 1973, the Egyptians 1,000 tanks in 1967 and 2,600 in 1973 as well as 230 planes in 1967 and 680 in 1973 (*Jerusalem Post Weekly*, November 27, 1973, p. 5). The Syrians used about the same number of tanks against the Golan Heights as General

Sir Bernard Montgomery had at the Battle of El Alamein in World War II.

37. S/PV. 1743 (October 8, 1973), pp. 3–43.

38. Anthony Astrachan, "The October War at the UN," *Midstream*, December 1973, p. 53.

39. S/PV. 1744 (October 9, 1973), pp. 8 (Minic), 41 (Ismail), 43–45, 47 (Malik), 51 (Tekoah, Malik).

40. S/PV. 1745 (October 11, 1973), pp. 31 (Baroody), 77, 81 (Malik), 97 (Tekoah), 103–5 (Malik).

41. S/PV. 1746 (October 12, 1973).

42. *Le Monde*, November 25–26, 1973.

43. S/PV. 1747 (October 21, 1973), pp. 6 (Scali), 12–15 (Baroody), 53–55 (Sen), 67 (Huang).

44. S/PV. 1748 (October 23, 1973), p. 27–30 (Chiao).

45. *Le Monde*, November 25–26, 1973.

46. Astrachan, *op. cit.*, p. 57.

47. S/PV. 1748 (October 23, 1973), pp. 16–36 (Malik, Chiao), 42 (Khalid), 61 (Anwar Sani), 62–63 (Pérez de Cuellar), 66 (Huang).

48. S/PV. 1748 (October 23, 1973), p. 46.

49. *Ibid.*, p. 122.

50. *Jerusalem Post Weekly*, December 4, 1973, p. 10.

51. Interview in Peking, *New York Times*, November 13, 1973, p. 16.

52. Speech in Tel Aviv, *Jerusalem Post Weekly*, November 27, 1973, p. 5.

How Not to Make Peace in the Middle East

1. I dealt with these sources in detail in my article, "From 1967 to 1973: The Arab-Israeli Wars," *Commentary*, December 1973, pp. 33–35.

2. In his book, *Decade of Decisions* (University of California Press, 1977), William B. Quandt criticizes American policy-makers in 1967 for having been "ultimately insensitive to the danger that war might break out at Israel's instigation" (p. 39). The book was completed just before Quandt was chosen by National Security Adviser Zbigniew Brzezinski for the Middle East post on the National Security Council.

3. *Hussein de Jordanie: Ma "Guerre" avec Israël* by Vick Vance and Pierre Lauer (Albin Michel, Paris, 1968); *Hussein* by Peter Snow (Barrie & Jenkins, London, 1972).

4. Who misled whom still needs some clarification. A telephone conversation between Nasser and Hussein intercepted by the Israelis made it appear that Nasser may have suggested to Hussein that they should blame the United States and Great Britain for aiding Israel. But this

conversation was obviously garbled and fragmentary in transcription. Nasser later, in a speech on July 23, 1967, related that Hussein had phoned him on the evening of June 7, 1967, and had told him that Jordan had been attacked by 400 aircraft. Nasser implied that the planes could only have come from the United States.

5. Before going to Jerusalem, Sadat had merely informed Assad of his intention.

6. Brzezinski liked the term "leverage" so much that he repeated it at the Overseas Writers' Club on October 18, 1977. The term was not original with him. It had been used twice by George W. Ball in his article, "How to Save Israel in Spite of Herself," in *Foreign Affairs*, April 1977, pp. 454, 459. Ball had made clear just what "leverage" meant—that "America's continued involvement in the area depends upon acceptance by both sides of the terms it prescribes" (p. 459).

7. Brzezinski for one could not have failed to understand what this term was supposed to mean. The 1975 article had noted that the "commitment [of the Arabs] to the 'legitimate rights of the Palestinian people' would under the traditional interpretation mean the demise of Israel ..." (p. 9).

8. With varying degrees of emphasis and discretion, this premise may be found in the articles in *Foreign Affairs* by George W. Ball, April 1977, especially p. 468; Stanley Hoffmann, April 1975, especially pp. 421–22; Nahum Goldmann, October 1975, especially p. 124.

   The origin of this statement is somewhat confusing. Reporters were first told that it was a Soviet idea and that the final text was based on a Soviet draft. Then the story was changed so that Secretary Vance had conceived the idea two months earlier but the Soviets had submitted a draft which had been modified by both sides. In any case, it must have been clear to the Soviets from previous articles and statements by leading officials in the Carter administration what they could expect and how far they could go.

9. George W. Ball provides a good example of how a guarantee can be bandied about without giving the slightest hint of what it would entail (*Foreign Affairs*, April 1977, p. 461).

   Professor Stanley Hoffmann would have had foreign troops, not excluding the possibility of Soviet and American soldiers, stationed in the Sinai, at Sharm el-Sheikh, the Golan Heights, and those portions of the West Bank closest to the Mediterranean "for a long period." His "guarantee" would have virtually amounted to a foreign military occupation by an international conglomeration under the aegis of the United Nations, whose tender mercies toward Israel are so well known. Professor Hoffmann thought of guarding against "the tragic experience of UNEF in 1967" through an agreement "against the arbitrary dismissal of the peace forces by one of the countries in which they are stationed, or the arbitrary removal of a national contingent by the country of origin." Apart from the fact that all these agreements would hinge on the interpretation of the term "arbitrary," and every participating country would interpret it as it pleased, Hoffmann chose to ignore the larger problem—that such a UN force would ultimately be controllable by the Arab bloc and its allies, and a good part of it would have to be contributed by countries which do not recognize Israel, do not see fit to have diplomatic relations with Israel, or are subject to Arab oil blackmail (*Foreign Affairs*, April 1975, p. 425).

Professor Richard H. Ullman has proposed a plan for guarantees, the effect of which "would be to make it exceedingly unlikely that those forces would ever be involved in combat" (*Foreign Policy*, Summer 1975, p. 26).

10. Someone ought to remind Hussein of what happened to him in 1970. When Jordan was invaded by Syria in support of the PLO in September of that year, Hussein frantically called for U.S. help. The U.S. in turn, having no other immediate way to help Jordan, turned to Israel for assistance. Hussein himself urged Israel to engage in ground action against Syria. Then Ambassador Yitzhak Rabin and National Security Adviser Henry Kissinger worked out a plan for Israel to send 200 tanks into Syria; President Nixon finally approved an Israeli plan for an Israeli air strike and, if necessary, tank attack against Syrian forces in Jordan. As the present Middle East expert on the National Security Council tells the story: "Hussein, with the assurance that Israel and the United States were behind him, finally ordered his own small air force to attack the Syrian tanks around Irbid, which it did with satisfactory results" (William B. Quandt, *Decade of Decisions*, pp. 116–19). Faced with evidence that Hussein had recovered his nerve and with the threat of U.S.-Israeli intervention, the Syrians withdrew.

11. The responsibility of the American press and especially television for this sorry state of affairs is, I believe, considerable. The personal favoritism and political myopia exhibited by the media have been flagrant. I have seen interviewers fawn on Sadat and badger Begin or Dayan. The Egyptians could not demand too much and the Israelis give up too much to please most of them. Sadat could say, with a straight face, "We have given Israel everything," without being challenged to name anything in particular that he proposed to give Israel beyond what it already had, without his help, within the pre-June 1967 armistice lines. I can well understand that American correspondents and interviewers should find Sadat's personality more beguiling than Begin's or Dayan's. But even Israeli Defense Minister Ezer Weizman received the same prosecutorial treatment. I have watched an interview with Weizman by Barbara Walters in which she dropped the mask of interviewer midway through the program and openly announced that she was going to adopt the role of antagonist. The television bias was so flagrant that it seemed to be competitive.

12. One who should know from his personal experience as deputy in the Middle East office of the National Security Council staff from 1972 to 1974 described this view as follows: "The conventional wisdom, especially in the State Department, was that American support for Israel was an impediment to U.S.-Arab relations. By granting economic and military aid to the enemy of the Arabs, the United States was providing the Soviet Union with an opportunity to extend its influence in the Middle East. Although few questioned that Israel's existence should be defended by the United States in an extreme case, many felt that an

'even-handed' policy, whereby the United States would not always align itself with Israel and would not become her primary arms supplier, was the best guarantee of the United States interests in the region. In this view, Israel was more of an embarrassment for the United States policy than a strategic asset. Even if Israel was an impressive military power, that power could be used only to defend Israel, not to advance American interests elsewhere in the region" (William B. Quandt, *Decade of Decisions*, p. 120).

Podhoretz's Vietnam War—No notes.

Mrs. Kirkpatrick's Theories—No notes.

Prophets of the "Cold War"

1. Alexis de Tocqueville, *Democracy in America* (tr. George Lawrence, ed. J. P. Mayer and Max Lerner (New York: Harper & Row, 1966), p. 379). The older translation by George Reeve, which was alone in the field for over a century and may still be better known though much less accurate, gave the same passage as "each of them seems to be marked out by the will of Heaven to sway the destinies of half the globe." The first part of *De la Démocratie en Amérique* originally appeared in two volumes in 1835, the second part in another two volumes in 1840.

2. *Democracy in America*, p. 286. Tocqueville seems to have been little concerned with Russia in later years. A German historian found only two more references to Russia in all Tocqueville's later works. Bernhard Fabian, *Alexis de Tocquevilles Amerikabild* (Heidelberg, 1975), p. 81, n. 3.

3. *Democracy in America*, pp. 210, 212. James Bryce interpreted Tocqueville to mean: "It [America] is eminently ill-fitted to conduct foreign policy. Fortunately, it has none" *Studies in History and Jurisprudence* (1901), Vol. I, p. 395.

4. In this case, I have gone back to the original French, which strikes me as more explicit than "among the leading nations" (Lawrence) or "a most prominent place amongst the nations" (Reeve).

5. Just what term should be used for Tocqueville's conception of this division of the world can be a problem. Professor Golo Mann once referred to Tocqueville's "famous prophecy" of Russia's and America's *"Weltmacht-Zukunft"* ("Tocqueville und das Amerika von heute," in *Jahrbuch für Amerikastudien*, Vol. V, 1960, p. 23). If the term were not so misleading, *"Halb-Weltmacht Zukunft"* would be closer to Tocqueville's meaning.

6. In 1835, Tocqueville noted, the United States extended over an area half that of Europe. He was almost exactly right in his prediction of the final American boundaries: Europe covers 4,000,000 square miles, the USA 3,022,387 square miles. In 1835, however, many still expected Canada to fall into the lap of the USA; Tocqueville must have had

Canada in mind if he thought that the USA was going to extend as far north as the "polar ice." What he conceived of as the "tropics" is more uncertain. He seems to be referring to the "vast provinces extending beyond the frontiers of the Union toward Mexico," which would put it in the territory of Texas, where separatist sentiment among US settlers was already strong during Tocqueville's visit to the US.

7. Auguries of universal Russian influence go back to Leibniz in the late 17th century (Fabian, pp. 82–85). On the American side, the famous last sentence by Alexander Hamilton in *The Federalist* (No. 11, 1787) had advised the newly independent states "to aim at an ascendant in the system of American affairs."

8. *The London Review* (1836), pp. 85–129. *The Quarterly Review* (September 1836).

9. *The American Quarterly Review* (March 1836), pp. 130–131. The review as a whole was patronizingly critical.

10. *United States Magazine and Democratic Review* (October-December 1837), p. 95. This review was far more favorable.

11. *Revue des Deux Mondes* (April 1, 1835), pp. 739–741. There is an entry on Corcelle, including a statement about his friendship with Tocqueville, in *Dictionnaire de Biographie française* (1961), Vol. IX, p. 614.

12. I owe to Melvin J. Lasky my belated acquaintance with Gurowski's work. Gurowski wrote another book, *America and Europe* (New York, 1857), in which he argued for the orthodox American position that Europe should stay out of American affairs and the United States should stay out of European affairs. In questions of general policy, however, he maintained that European governments "must yield to the principles asserted by the American Republic. . . ."

13. T.V. Smith, "Hindsight on de Tocqueville's Foresight," *The University Review* (Kansas City: Autumn 1942), p. 23.

14. Charles de Gaulle, *Discours et Messages* (Paris: Plon, 1970), Vol.II, p. 15.

15. Ernst Jünger, *Strahlungen* (1949), pp. 15–16.

16. Max Lerner, *America as a Civilization* (New York: Simon & Schuster, 1957), p. 938.

17. Raymond Aron, *Paix et guerre entre les nations* (Paris, 1962), pp. 156, 527; *Peace and War* (Garden City: Doubleday, 1966), pp. 149, 536.

18. Tocqueville "predicted an eventual clash between the United States and Russia because large land-mass societies with great natural resources would inevitably expand their living space" (Daniel Bell, *The Coming of Post-Industrial Society*, New York: Basic Books, 1973, p. 318, n. 31). There is no such "because" in Tocqueville. He expected Russia and America to "expand their living space," but within their own halves of the world and without the implication of an eventual clash between them. Others may draw this implication: Tocqueville did not.

19. Alexis de Tocqueville, *Oeuvres Complètes*, ed. by J.P. Mayer (Paris, 1957), Vol. V, Part I, pp. 143, 259.

20. Francis Wharton, ed., *The Revolutionary Diplomatic Correspondence of the United States* (Washington, 1889), Vol. II, pp. 331–33.

21. John C. Miller, *Triumph of Freedom* (Boston: Little, Brown, 1940), p. 586. Miller cited only one sentence from the entire letter; it was not his fault that quite a number of writers were led astray by failing to check the entire letter. A more accurate interpretation may be found in Richard V. Van Alstyne, *Empire and Independence* (New York: John Wiley, 1965), p. 124.

22. Paul Dukes, *The Emergence of the Super-Powers* (London: Macmillan, 1970), p. 35.

23. W.P. Cresson, *Francis Dana: A Puritan Diplomat At the Court of Catherine the Great* (New York: Lincoln MacVeagh, 1930), pp. 245–46.

24. *Sbornik imperatorskago russkago istoričeskago obščestva* (St. Petersburg, 1881), Vol. 33, pp. 293–94. The correspondence was carried on in French.

25. Las Cases, *Mémorial de Ste.-Hélène* (Paris: P. Garnier, 1823), Vol. I, p. 298.

26. Abbé de Pradt, *Du système permanent de l'Europe à l'égard de la Russie et des affaires d'Orient* (Paris, 1828), p. 75.

27. From his *Lutetzia*, cited by Dieter Groh, *Russland und das Selbstverständnis Europas* (Neuwied: Luchterhand Verlag, 1961), p. 178.

28. *The Life of Cassius Marcellus Clay: Memoirs, Writings and Speeches* (Cincinnati, 1886), Vol. I, p. 445.

29. *Dictionary of American Biography*, Vol. III, p. 54.

30. John Bristed, *The Resources of the United States of America* (New York, 1818), pp. 1–2, 247–48, 476, 494. The London edition is called *America and her Resources*

31. The 1832 edition, Vol. I, pp. 341–42.

32. The French version has been cited as an anticipation of Tocqueville by René Rémond, *Les États-Unis devant l'opinion française 1815–1852* (Paris, Librairie Armand Colin, 1962), Vol. I, p. 379, n. 19. The credit belongs to the French translator rather than to Bristed.
    Rémond also cites a statement by Stendhal to the effect that *"la Russie pourrait devenir la maîtresse de l'Europe, si seulement elle le voulait, et que l'Amérique était la seule puissance à pouvoir s'y opposer."* Stendhal's actual words were: *"La Russie a toujours cru, depuis Pierre le Grand, qu'elle serait, en 1819, la maîtresse de l'Europe, et l'Amérique est désormais la seule puissance qui puisse lui résister."*
    This off-hand remark appeared in Stendhal's *Vie de Napoléon*, apparently written in 1817–1818 and published in full for the first time in 1929 (edited by Louis Royer in the *Oeuvres Complètes* published by the Librairie Ancienne Honoré Champion, p. 233). Did Stendhal mean

that America might be able to oppose, check or challenge Russia's domination of Europe? Or did he simply mean that America could possibly resist being itself dominated by Russia?

It is difficult to be sure just how far Stendhal intended to go in this reference to America's resistance to Russia's ambition. If Stendhal meant that America was from then on the only power that might be able to oppose or check Russia's westward drive, it would make him— of all people—the first true prophet of the post-World War II Cold War, though not of Tocqueville's prognosis. (I am indebted to Professor Victor del Litto of the University of Grenoble and to Professor Victor Brombert of Princeton University for tracking down this intriguing statement by Stendhal.)

A peculiar linguistic prophecy also appeared in 1818 in *The Quarterly Review*. It turned up in a review of a book by Sir Robert Wilson, *A Sketch of the Military and Political Power in Russia, in the year 1817* (published in London and in New York in 1817). Stendhal is said to have "borrowed" several phrases or sentences from a French translation of Wilson's book, also published in 1817 (*Vie de Napoléon*, p. 429). The writer in *The Quarterly Review* predicted that English and Russian were the languages which "are one day to divide the world" (April 1818, p. 177).

33. De Pradt is still without a good, full study of his life and works. There is a mediocre popular biography by Emile Dousset, *L'Abbé de Pradt* (1959). The best short sketch of his life is that of Josanne Pothier, "L'Abbé de Pradt, archevêque de Malines, d'après une correspondance inédite," *Almanach de Brioude* (1962), pp. 119–43.

34. The entire list may be found in Michaud's *Biographie Universelle*, 9th ed., Vol. 34, pp. 281–82. It fills two-and-a-half large columns of small print.

35. These figures are based on Michaud, and on Laura Bornholdt, "The Abbé de Pradt and the Monroe Doctrine," *The Hispanic American Historical Review* (May 1944), pp. 206–7.

36. *Writings of John Quincy Adams* (ed. W. C. Ford, 1916), Vol. VI, pp. 217–18. *The Writings of Thomas Jefferson* (Lipscomb-Bergh ed.), Vol. XV, p. 145. Jefferson to George Otis, July 8, 1820, cited by T. R. Schellenberg. "Jeffersonian Origins of the Monroe Doctrine," *The Hispanic American Historical Review* (February 1934), p. 7, see also pp. 3–6. Bornholdt's article is a critique of Schellenberg's thesis.

37. *The Papers of Henry Clay* (ed. J. F. Hopkins, 1961), Vol. II, p. 856.

38. M. de Pradt, *Des Colonies et de la révolution actuelle de l'Amérique* (Paris, 1817), Vol. II, pp. 350, 355, 358.

39. *L'Europe après le Congrès d'Aix-la-Chapelle* (1819), pp. 42, 266. In this book de Pradt uncannily formulated the main points of the Monroe Doctrine four years in advance, even if they were not original with him (pp. 283–84). At least he was able to recognize the lineaments of the future when he saw them.

40. *L'Europe et L'Amérique en 1821* (1822), Vol. I, pp. 16, 20–21, 116; Vol. II, p. 331. *Parallèle de la puissance anglaise et russe* (1823), pp.

158, 161, 168. *Vrai système de l'Europe relativement à l'Amérique et à la Grèce*, (1825), pp. 82–83, 158, 184, 280.

41. *Du système permanent de l'Europe à l'égard de la Russie et des affaires d'Orient* (1828), translated by Edward Everett in the *North American Review* (April 1830), p. 447.

42. Cited by Henri Peyre, "History as Prophecy: French Predictions of Russian-American Antagonism," *Laurels*, Spring 1982, p. 17 (published by The American Society of the French Legion of Honor). I am indebted to Professor Peyre for calling my attention to other French precursors.

43. Tocqueville, *Oeuvres Complètes, op. cit.*, Vol. V, Part 1, p. 95; George Wilson Pierson, *Tocqueville and Beaumont in America* (New York: Oxford University Press, 1938), p. 417.

44. *North American Review* (July 1822), p. 204. Everett did not use his name because he was still in active diplomatic service.

45. Conrad G. F. E. von Schmidt-Phiseldeck's book had as its subtitle, "or the relative state of the civilised world at a future period." It belonged to the prophetic literature of the time, but concentrated almost wholly on America with no similar consideration of Russia and, therefore, has not been included here. Schmidt-Phiseldeck contributed to the idea that the centre of gravity of world power was moving to America with such statements as that, after 1814,
> "the impulse towards a new change of events, ceased to proceed from the old continent, and it is possible, that in a short time it will emanate wholly from the new one" (pp. 3–4).

His book first appeared in German and was translated the same year into English, of which a facsimile edition was put out by the Royal Danish Ministry of Foreign Affairs in 1976. It was also translated into Danish, Dutch, and Swedish.

46. *The Letters of Ralph Waldo Emerson*, ed. by Ralph L. Rusk (New York: Columbia University Press, 1939), Vol. I, p. 107.

47. Hans Kohn, *American Nationalism* (New York: Macmillan, 1957), pp. 32–37.

48. Heinz Gollwitzer, *Geschichte des weltpolitischen Denkens* (Göttingen, 1972), Vol. I, pp. 408–25.

49. By a Citizen of the United States [Alexander Hill Everett], *Europe: or a General Survey of the Present Situation of the Principal Powers: with conjectures on their Future Prospects* (1822), pp. 348, 351, 420, 447–49. This volume was translated into French, German, and Spanish.

50. *North American Review* (July 1822), p. 187.

51. By a Citizen of the United States [Alexander Hill Everett], *America: or a General Survey of the Political Situation of the Several Powers of the Western Continent, with conjectures on their Future Prospects* (1827), pp. 18–19, 256, 347, 349.

52. *North American Review* (April 1830), pp. 399–454. Edward Everett is identified as the author of this review by William Cushing, *Index to the North American Review* (1878), pp. 38, 87.

53. Letter of Beaumont to his brother Jules, May 26, 1831, in Pierson, *Tocqueville and Beaumont in America*, p. 85; *Oeuvres Complètes*, Vol. V, Part 1, p. 95.

54. I have used a later edition, *Notices politiques et littéraires sur l'Allemagne* (Brussels, 1835), pp. xiv–xix.

55. This is the interpretation of Michel Cadot, *La Russie dans la vie intellectuelle française* (Paris: Fayard, 1967), p. 234. He seems to have borrowed it from Pierre Moreau, *Revue de Littérature Comparée* (Paris), October-December 1950, p. 603, who attributed to Saint-Marc Girardin the "perspective of a partition by which the Slav and American worlds will absorb all the vital forces of old Europe." There is a biography in English, *Saint-Marc Girardin, bourgeois*, by Laurence William Wylie (Syracuse University Press, 1947), but it does not touch on this aspect of his thought.

56. Claude Pichois, *Philarète Chasles et la vie littéraire au temps du romantisme* (Paris: Librairie José Corti, 1965), Vol. I, p. 480.

57. *Oeuvres de Claude-Henri de Saint-Simon* (Paris: Edition Anthropos, 1966, reprint of edition of 1868–1876), Vol. II, pp. 140, 149. Frank Manuel, *The New World of Henri Saint-Simon* (1956), pp. 280–81.

58. Georges Weill, *L'École Saint-Simonienne* (1896), p. 23.

59. Pierson, *Tocqueville and Beaumont*, p. 726. Michel Chevalier, *Lettres sur l'Amérique du Nord* (1936), Vol. II, p. 420, n. 1, alludes to Tocqueville's book, which he had evidently read at the end of 1835. This book was incompletely translated in a Boston edition of 1839 as *Society, Manners and Politics in the United States* (repr. 1966 and 1969).

60. "As a result, he [Chevalier] was to make an economic study and a factual survey of America as valuable and as prophetic in its way as Tocqueville's more institutional and more philosophical descriptions" (Pierson, p. 175). ". . . the *Lettres sur l'Amérique du Nord* seems to us worthy of being placed immediately beside *Démocratie en Amérique*" (Rémond, Vol. I, p. 376).

61. This letter appeared in the *Journal des Débats* of 11 June 1834. But this sentence did not. The key sentence, *"Qui peut dire . . . la domination de l'Univers,"* was cut out of the newspaper version and appeared only in Chevalier's book in 1836 (p. 141). Thus Chevalier may have written his version of the idea before Tocqueville published his; but Tocqueville was first in point of publication.

   In the next decade, however, the *Journal des Débats* came much closer to the future "Cold War" and its repercussions on Europe. In an editorial leader, expressing alarm at the US annexation of Texas at the expense of Mexico, the following comment appeared in the issue of September 24, 1845:

   "Between the Russian autocracy in the East and the democracy of the United States thus enlarged in the West, Europe could one day find itself compressed more than would comport with its independence and its dignity."

62. *Lettres sur l'Amérique du Nord*, Vol. I, pp. v, xi, 154–55, 177; Vol. II, pp. 415–17.

63. "The West has known nothing like it [expansion of American power after the Second World War] since the Roman Empire" (Raymond Aron, *Peace and War*, p. 1).

64. Waddy Thompson, *Recollections of Mexico* (New York, 1847), pp. 237–38.

65. Department of State, *Papers relating to Foreign Affairs*, 1861, p. 277.

66. Cited in Cadot, *op. cit.*, pp. 501–2 and in Denis de Rougement, *The Meaning of Europe* (London: Sidgwick and Jackson, 1965), p. 104.

67. Cited by Cadot, *op. cit.*, p. 530.

68. Ernest Renan, *Oeuvres Complètes* (Paris: Calmann-Lévy), Vol. I, pp. 364, 460.

Intellectuals in Politics

1. Richard Hofstadter, *Anti-Intellectualism in American Life* (New York: Knopf, 1963), p. 187.

2. *Ibid.*, p. 39. Hofstadter says that the term *intellectual* first came into use in France and was "soon exported—at the time of the Dreyfus case" (p. 38). This seems hardly likely in view of the fact that the *Oxford English Dictionary* has an English usage of the term as far back as 1652, and three perfectly recognizable uses in the 19th century, one by Byron in 1813.

3. *The Letters of William James*, edited by Henry James (1920), vol. II, pp. 100–101.

4. Arthur S. Link, *Wilson: The Road to the White House* (1947), pp. 149–50, 158.

5. Hofstadter, *op. cit.*, p. 211.

6. Senator Lawrence Sherman, *Congressional Record* (September 3, 1918), p. 9877.

7. Samuel I. Rosenman, *Working With Roosevelt* (1952), p. 57.

8. Raymond Moley, *After Seven Years* (1939), pp. 5–6.

9. Rexford G. Tugwell, *The Democratic Roosevelt* (1957), p. 218.

10. These meetings are vividly described by Moley, pp. 20–21, and Rosenman, pp. 63–64.

11. "Politics as a Vocation" (1918), in *From Max Weber* (ed. Gerth & Mills, 1947), p. 84.

12. These words were said by Roosevelt to Berle but intended for the entire group. See Adolf A. Berle, *New Republic*, March 7, 1964, reprinted in *Navigating the Rapids 1918–1971: From the Papers of Adolf A. Berle* (1973), p. 114.

13. Arthur M. Schlesinger, Jr., *The Coming of the New Deal* (1959), p. 549.

14. Bernard Sternsher, *Rexford Tugwell and the New Deal* (1964), p. 308.

15. C. Wright Mills, *The Power Elite* (1956), p. 351.

16. Paul F. Lazarsfeld and Wagner Thielens, Jr., *The Academic Mind* (1958), p. 12.

17. *Daedalus*, Summer 1959, p. 469. *New York Times*, November 9, 1958. John Fischer, *Harper's*, March 1958, p. 18. *Daedalus*, p. 492. Richard H. Rovere, *The American Establishment and Other Reports, Opinions and Speculations* (1962), pp. 8–9.

18. *The Reporter*, March 5, 1959, pp. 30–35.

19. Arthur M. Schlesinger, Jr., *A Thousand Days* (1965), p. 109.

20. Theodore C. Sorensen, *Kennedy* (1965), p. 246.

21. *The Intellectual in Politics* (ed. H. Malcolm Macdonald, 1966), pp. 103–4.

22. Arthur M. Schlesinger, Jr., *The Crisis of Confidence* (1969), p. 79.

23. Schlesinger, *A Thousand Days*, p. 725.

24. William L. O'Neill, *Coming Apart: An Informal History of America in the 1960s* (1970), p. 146.

25. *Esquire*, May 1977, p. 70.

26. *New York Times*, May 2, 1977.

27. *The Times* (letter), August 4, 1977.

28. Daniel P. Moynihan, *The Politics of a Guaranteed Income* (1973), p. 13.

29. Professors Jessie Bernard, George Sternlieb, Brady Tyson and William Glade, *Society*, May–June 1977, pp. 8–21.

30. Arthur Schlesinger, *A Thousand Days*, pp. 249–55, 297.

31. John Kenneth Galbraith, *Ambassador's Journal* (1969), p. 16.

32. Interview in *Challenge*, March–April 1977, p. 31.

33. Irving Louis Horowitz, *Society*, May–June 1977, p. 22.

34. *New York Times*, April 16, 1977.

35. This story can be followed in the *Washington Post*, April 26 and 27, August 8, 1977, and *The New York Times*, April 26, 1977.

36. *New York Times*, October 13, 1974.

37. Edward R. F. Sheehan, *The Arabs, Israelis, and Kissinger* (1976), p. 38.

38. Leslie H. Gelb, *New York Times Magazine*, October 31, 1976, p. 79.

39. Marvin Kalb and Bernard Kalb, *Kissinger* (1974), p. 544.

40. "The Future World Disorder: The Structural Context of Crisis," in *Foreign Policy*, Summer 1977, p. 120.

About the Author

THEODORE DRAPER is a writer and scholar who has devoted himself to political and historical work for over four decades. He was born in Brooklyn, New York, and lives in Princeton, New Jersey. He has been a five-year research fellow at the Hoover Institution on War, Revolution and Peace at Stanford, and a five-year member at the Institute for Advanced Study in Princeton. He is a member of the Council on Foreign Relations and the American Academy of Arts and Sciences. He has written ten books and has contributed to the *New York Review of Books, Encounter, Commentary, Dissent* and other publications.

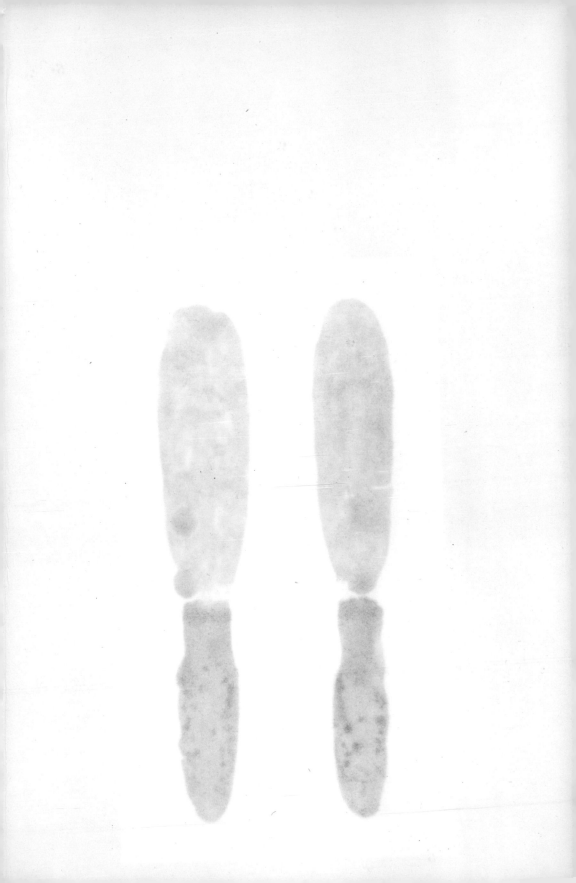

DATE DUE

GAYLORD   PRINTED IN U.S.A.